# *Smart Blonde*
# DOLLY PARTON

# *Smart Blonde*
# DOLLY PARTON

## STEPHEN MILLER

**OMNIBUS PRESS**

LONDON / NEW YORK / PARIS / SYDNEY / COPENHAGEN / BERLIN / MADRID / TOKYO

**Exclusive Distributors**
Music Sales Limited,
14/15 Berners Street,
London, W1T 3LJ

Music Sales Corporation,
257 Park Avenue South,
New York, NY 10010, USA

Macmillan Distribution Services,
53 Park West Drive,
Derrimut, Vic 3030,
Australia

Every effort has been made to trace the copyright holders of the photographs in this book but one or two were unreachable. We would be grateful if the photographers concerned would contact us.

Printed and bound in Great Britain by MPG Books Ltd, Bodmin

A catalogue record for this book is available from the British Library.

Visit Omnibus Press on the web at www.omnibuspress.com.

*For Molli*

# CONTENTS

# ACKNOWLEDGEMENTS

"I hear she's very effusive. It might be easier than you think." This was the opinion of a contact of mine in Nashville when asked about the prospects of an interview with Dolly. He was both right and wrong. Dolly *is* extremely effusive and has always been keen to do interviews in the print and broadcast media in order to generate publicity for herself and her projects. However, these tend to be fairly short exchanges (Dolly's personal assistant and lifelong friend Judy Ogle has been known to use a stopwatch) during which Dolly bowls over her interrogators with a series of well-honed, sharply delivered answers which stick firmly to a script of her choosing. A lot of information, some quite personal, is disclosed but ultimately this conspires to maintain the image of her life and career that Dolly has carefully developed over the years. This is not to say that what she says about herself is not true, rather that it represents a particular spin on events which doesn't necessarily tell the whole story. As one journalist put it, Dolly is the master of saying a lot while not saying much at all.

Needless to say I did try to secure an interview but the reception I received from Teresa Hughes at Dolly's Nashville office could not unreasonably be described as frosty. I was told that Dolly was considering a further autobiographical volume of her life story and that there was little prospect of her talking to me. Hughes has been a loyal employee for many years and so it occurred to me that she would be a good interviewee. She responded to this request as if I had made an indecent proposal. Those closest to Dolly do not talk publicly. Carl Dean, her husband of 40 years, has never spoken to the press and very few photographs of him (even fewer of him and Dolly together) are in the public domain. Their relationship is an enigma which has fascinated and frustrated journalists for years. The same could be said of Judy Ogle. I suspect if one day these two were prepared to open up to a writer or journalist, a different side of Dolly would emerge, one which thus far has only been guessed at or alluded to. I did actually get to speak by phone to Don Warden, the manager Dolly inherited from Porter Wagoner and one of her most loyal lieutenants for more than three decades. While perfectly pleasant, Warden said he had not given interviews for many years and had no intention of making an exception in my case, complaining that journalists and writers had invariably misquoted him in their follow-up articles.

Other musicians who worked with Dolly were wary of getting involved principally because they did not want to do or say anything that might jeopardise their relationship. Porter Wagoner did not reply to my request for an interview despite the fact that it was supported by a highly respected senior figure in the Nashville music fraternity. One musician who backed Dolly for a number of years could not have been more pleasant but told me that, in common with other ex-employees, there was a confidentiality clause in his contract. He did proffer that she was a great employer, "the best imaginable person to work for" but he did not want even this unequivocal compliment quoted unless it had received prior approval from Dolly or her management. He would be happy to buy me a drink, but not to give an interview. Even the tourism authorities in East Tennessee would not talk. When simply seeking confirmation that Dolly has contributed greatly to a substantial increase in visitor numbers to East Tennessee since the Eighties, I was told by a senior representative that with Dolly being one of his department's spokespeople, "We only comment on her in a limited scope."

However, this attitude was by no means universal. Dolly's sister Stella graciously consented to a full and frank interview in Nashville though there were several topics I raised which she was not prepared to discuss (her response in these cases being, "I won't touch that"). Stella spoke with candour about her sister, which took courage since she was well aware that some of her remarks would be less than flattering. At one stage in the interview she said her sisters were going to hate her for some of the things she was saying, "But what the hell, they can't divorce me." Nothing however took away from the deep love and admiration Stella clearly feels for her elder sister. Steve Buckingham, Dolly's producer and general musical facilitator since the start of the Nineties, gave a lengthy and detailed interview which particularly threw light on Dolly's creativity. For years Jack Clement has been one of the most respected producers in Nashville and though he has not worked extensively with Dolly (much to his regret) his views on her inevitably carry weight. Our conversation was an entertaining affair, enriched as it was by Jack's forthright views and fruity language. I phoned him at about three o'clock Nashville time. "You know I've just come from a three martini lunch?" he drawled, and before the interview proper, he asked if I had "anything good to smoke there". None of this impaired the incisiveness of his comments.

I must give particular mention to Michael Creed, a long-time Dolly fan who, along with Joe Skelly, runs a newsletter called *Dolly Part'ners*. It is not an overstatement to say that Michael is devoted to Dolly. Over the years he has built up a formidable collection of cuttings, books, films, recordings and other artefacts and he has provided material for television programmes about Dolly. This passion has resulted in press articles about his interest and his undying admiration for his heroine. He most generously allowed me to borrow a large quantity of items, some of them irreplaceable. We had never met prior to my visit to his house last spring, so I can only imagine what thoughts must have gone through his mind as he watched me drive off to Scotland with some of his most treasured possessions. I also wish to think Duane Gordon who runs Dollymania, one of the very best Dolly websites. Despite the fact that he has a day job and spends time nearly every evening updating the site, he responded very quickly to all of my e-mailed requests for information or clarification; his knowledge of Dolly, her life and career is gargantuan.

Regrettably, owing to copyright restrictions, I have been unable to quote extensively from Dolly's lyrics.

My thanks go to Chris Charlesworth who, in the wake of my Johnny Cash biography for Omnibus Press, broached the idea of this biography and to Andy Neill for editing the text. Thanks are also due to the following people who all helped in various invaluable ways. David Allan, Dick Barrie, Janet Beck, Bill Black, Wayne Bledsoe, Suzy Bogguss, Bobbi Boyce, Tony Byworth, Bob Cheevers, Darryl Clark, Terry Eldredge, Narvel Felts, George Hamilton IV, George Hamilton V, Patrick Humphries, Byron House, Dave Johnston, Stan Laundon, Albert Lee, Scooter Lee, Ronny Light, Tommy Loftus, Susan McCann, Ken MacDonald, Sue Marshall, Jimmy Mattingly, Murdoch Nicolson, Dawn Oberg, Beth Odle, Jackie Pratt, Ronnie Pugh, Bill Ritchie, Marty Raybon, Dave Roe, David Sinclair, Ray Stevens, Alan Stoker, Tom Travis, Alan and Sue Vere.

Finally, my love and thanks to Judy for her unwavering support.

# INTRODUCTION

"D'Y'ALL know Dolly's gonna be touring the park this afternoon?" It was the start of the build-up on a perfect, early autumn day. My wife and I were among the first to arrive at Dollywood, Dolly Parton's authentic, though idealised, rustic theme park, on the edge of the Smoky Mountains in East Tennessee. The lady taking our entrance money appeared genuinely delighted that we had come all the way from Scotland to pay homage to her boss; the warmth she exuded went well beyond the ubiquitous, automaton admonition to "Have a nice day." Though some come from further afield, the majority of the two million plus people visiting the park each year do so from within a radius of about 400 miles. Dolly herself only visits a few times a year, mostly to perform at special concerts at the beginning and end of the main six-month season. The proceeds from these concerts provide support for the Dollywood Foundation, a philanthropic institution responsible for various good works in Tennessee, notably the encouragement of literacy skills in young children.

When in residence there, Dolly undertakes a form of regal procession around the park; in keeping with her desire to make the biggest possible splash in any public situation, staff will talk up the event from early in the day thus creating a buzz of anticipation. "Everybody loves Dolly . . . y'all have a great time, and you be sure to see Dolly . . . should be here about five." The words rang in my ears as we headed towards the attractions. There was much to see but the idea had been planted; whatever else happened, we had to be sure not to miss the Dolly parade. With so much to take in, we soon realised why some people bought season tickets. We watched moccasins being made by people dressed in clothes from the early 20th century, glass being blown into shapes by men in overalls, lye soap being manufactured as it was 100 years ago and a blacksmith at work, while an original steam train thundered across a bridge a few feet above our heads. We took in the white-water rafting and the wooden roller coaster known as the Thunderhead, getting totally drenched on a hair-raising ride which crashed through water at the bottom of its descent; nobody told us it was not a good idea to sit in the front carriage without waterproof gear!

We sat and people-watched while drying off in the sun. Speaking a year or so after the park opened in 1986, Dollywood's director of marketing said visitors tended to be "traditional social families". Many come from white, working-class protestant families in the Southern states prompting some detractors to dub Dollywood "the redneck Disneyland". The advertising literature invariably portrays a utopian world where exclusively slim, healthy-looking people have the time of their lives. In reality the people who visit the park include a cross section of society, a fair number who have overindulged in American food staples such as burgers, fries and sodas, some having to move around in motorised buggies. On sale at one of the many gift shops was a T-shirt imprinted with the redneck definition of "fascinate". Underneath a picture of a smiling obese man bursting out of his top it read, "Fascinate. My shirt has nine buttons, but I can only *fascinate*." Such corny humour was in keeping with Dolly's own. Some visitors wear their religion prominently; one seriously overweight woman had on a T-shirt inscripted, "XXXL. Property Of Jesus".

In homage to Dolly's childhood surroundings, a scale replica of one of the small log cabins Dolly grew up in with her parents, five brothers and five sisters, stands next to a one-roomed school house and a plain country church. We then moved on to the museum full of artefacts covering the transition in Dolly's life from rural poverty to international stardom and wealth, a journey built on the back of a dazzling career and a shrewd business mind. When mentioning the name Dolly Parton, the first thing that comes to many people's minds is not a singer and songwriter of great distinction but an outrageous cartoon-like figure with big hair, big boobs, tight-fitting dresses, long fingernails and high-heeled shoes. It is an image she deliberately engineered, hoping and believing that her outward appearance would draw people in to listening and appreciating her all important musical talent. The strategy has been highly successful, though there have always been a considerable number who have never seen beyond the gaudy exterior.

Dolly was one of the few women to carve out a successful career in the male dominated world of country music in the Sixties. Dolly got her big break in 1967 when she was offered the chance to become a regular on a popular television show. Plenty of other singers were considered and if she had not been chosen then her eventual career path might well have been radically different. However, whereas some in her place might have been discouraged or given up completely, the eventual outcome in Dolly's case was never in doubt. Even when she had achieved a substantial level of success her burning ambition was such that her sights were set higher still.

"I don't want a tombstone. I want to live forever. They say a dreamer lives forever. I want to be more than just an ordinary star. I want to be a famous writer, a famous singer, a famous entertainer. I want to be a movie writer, I want to do music movies, do children's stories. I want to be somebody important . . . I want to be somebody that left somethin' good behind for somebody else to enjoy . . . I'm not near what I want to do, what I want to accomplish . . . I want to be somebody that extremely shines. A star shines, of course, but I want to be really radiant."

In 1987, writer Frank Gannon encountered Dolly in a room full of people. "The room feels like it will explode with all the energy this woman generates. She kids. She chats. She flatters. She flirts . . . she fluffs her wig. She checks her make-up in the mirror. She deals with the dozen interruptions by the two dozen people who need her opinion or bring her information. And all the time, without being heavy handed and without missing a beat, she's making exactly the points she wants to make."

Dolly remains a remarkably positive person who continues to busily pursue numerous projects, plans and ideas. While some succeed, others fail or never get off the ground. With the exception of a difficult spell in the early Eighties which threatened to overwhelm her, Dolly has invariably managed to take problems and failures in her stride and to move resolutely onwards. The fact that she has built up a substantial and varied business empire, largely without the involvement of her husband, is unusual too.

As the day wore on at Dollywood, and the time of her visit drew nearer, word of the route she would follow started to emerge. Stallholders and some of the older, retired folk who make up a substantial proportion of the staff were unfailingly polite and helpful in sharing their knowledge with us, though accounts conflicted. Dollywood is a large place, covering well over 100 acres, and so by four o'clock or thereabouts it was becoming a matter of some importance to be in the right place at the right time not least because Dolly's tour would neither last long nor cover much of the park. There was a sudden movement of people towards the road leading from the main entrance into the park when word spread that Dolly would pass that way. We were fortunate to be in that area, in a raised stall displaying a selection of handmade harps. As the crowds increased, in a well-rehearsed operation, a number of rangers, mainly older men wearing khaki shirts, brown trousers and cowboy hats appeared. Politely but firmly they moved the crowds back behind lengths of tape stretching out between the trees and lampposts. The road, previously teeming with people, was now deserted as the crowds obediently gathered behind the cordon.

Our situation was slightly awkward. We had been looking at the harps for some time and there was really no reason to stay longer but it provided such a prime vantage point. After a few minutes people fetched up in front of the stall and it was obvious that the main event was imminent. We exchanged understanding looks with the harp makers who seemed happy for us to stay. In the distance, just as the noise of spasmodic cheering and whooping hit us, we caught our first glimpse of Dolly. She was in a vintage car travelling at walking pace, surrounded by a posse of Dollywood rangers. Sections of the not overly rowdy crowd cheered and called out politely as she passed by, smiling at all and sundry, acknowledging the cheers and waving randomly. Though Dolly has usually avoided expressing direct support for any political party she has evidently learned a trick or two from politicians. From time to time her face suddenly lit up, wide-eyed and wide mouthed, and she waved wildly, as if she had just seen a long lost friend, but her actions were simply aimed at an indeterminate point in the middle distance. Dolly soon passed by and the crowd dispersed.

The whole experience had much in common with the atmosphere of a crowd gathering to catch sight of a member of the royal family on public duty. Dolly would doubtless appreciate the comparison with royalty. Any kind of normal discourse is impossible. Those who get close are in awe and resort to utterances of the "we love you Dolly" variety. A journalist who once met her remarked that Dolly tells you everything except the important things. Veteran British broadcaster David Allan also touched on her propensity to filter content. "She is always in total control during interviews and only lets you know what she wants to disclose. Of course she's funny, wonderful company – great to interview – but the agenda is always hers. Hence we know nothing about the strange arrangement she has with her husband – apart from what she wants us to know – and the same goes for many aspects of her life." Country music broadcaster Bill Black said, "She is very good at appearing to be open but is quite skilful at answering in the way that she wants to . . . you will see if you look at a lot of different kinds of interviews that there is a standard response."

But what of the persona Dolly has created for her public; the show business disguise assiduously developed over the years and maintained in all situations other than those involving her closest inner circle. What is she afraid of? What cataclysmic event would ensue if somebody saw her with her image down? The image, which Dolly compares to a cartoon, is one she regards as separate from her real self. "I look one way and am another. It makes for a good combination. I always think of her, the Dolly image, like a ventriloquist does his dummy. I have fun with it. I think, 'What will I do with her this year to surprise people; what will she wear; what will she say?'"

She claims to have never got caught up in the Dolly image, other than to develop and protect it. "If you start believing the public person is you, you get frustrated and mixed up." Given that she can hardly ever bring herself to be seen without her image firmly in place it must, at the very least, be quite a challenge to become the real Dolly again, whoever she is. On one occasion she joked that she would one day unveil the real Dolly to the world: "Okay, the joke's over, now here's what I was born to." The world is still waiting; the real Dolly is further away than ever.

Despite the iconic image she has nurtured so carefully over the years, one which bears no relation to her musical gifts – some would say it distracts attention from them – she is one of the most original songwriters and singers of popular music to have emerged in the last fifty years. Her music will be remembered and played long after her image has faded.

One night, while driving around Nashville, we were listening to radio station WSIX 97.9 when a woman phoned in to request a particular song. The disc jockey, probably in his late twenties, asked for the caller's name. "It's Jolene." Mr DJ was ecstatic as speech turned to song. "Jolene? Jolene, Jolene Jo-leeeene." His parents probably didn't even know each other when Dolly wrote the song.

Stephen Miller
Edinburgh, July 2006

# ACT I

## 1946–1964:
## My Tennessee Mountain Home

# Chapter 1

IN 1967, when Dolly Parton had been in Nashville for about three years and was on the verge of making her name in the music business, she gave an interview to a young journalist called Everett Corbin in which she talked about her early life. In subsequent years Dolly became adept at dazzling and charming interviewers with her earthy, quick-fire delivery and down-home common sense but at the age of 21, she came over as hesitant and a little awkward, evidently not yet used to dealing confidently with personal questions.

Asked where she was born and raised and whether it was a community or a town Dolly said, "It was really – I guess you'd call it a community but it was just, it was called Pittman Center Road, but the town, the little community was called Pittman Center but, where I lived, you might say most, you know, up until I moved out – I lived on Birds Creek; now, my folks do. But it was called Locust Ridge." When asked what town she claimed as home, she replied, "Well, it's Sevierville, Sevier (pronounced 'severe') County, but it's called Birds Creek." Corbin then asked, "And all the communities are in the county?" to which Dolly responded, "Yeah, Caton's Chapel community and all that . . . just a few miles between each one, yeah."

These were the places where Dolly Parton grew up; all within a fairly small area of the foothills of the Smoky Mountains of East Tennessee, which separate Tennessee from North Carolina, about 200 miles east of Nashville. The family moved several times but stayed within the same general area of Sevier County, sometimes in remote spots well off the beaten track, "over in the holler" as the family put it.

As the crow flies they were only a few miles from the towns of Pigeon Forge and Gatlinburg, which even then were becoming established as destinations for tourists seeking a base from which to explore the beautiful Smoky Mountains, before unwinding at the town's many tourist attractions. However, in terms of the norms and comforts of modern life it was as if they were from a different epoch. Young Dolly's family had no indoor plumbing, and until the Fifties, electricity did not reach the valleys up in the furthest reaches of the mountains.

Such luxuries were unheard of when Dolly's distant ancestors came to America in the 17th and 18th centuries; from far-off lands in Europe like Scotland, Ireland, Wales, England, Holland and Germany. The name "Parton" comes from a medieval English place name derived from the old English *peretun* meaning a pear orchard, which came from *pere* meaning pear and *tun* meaning enclosure. The pronunciation of -er changed to -ar during the Middle Ages. There are towns called Parton in Dumfries and Galloway in Scotland, and Cumbria in northern England.

Many sought to escape from desperate situations. Some of the impoverished and unemployed Scots had been sent from their own country to Dublin to help subjugate the Irish. Disgruntled and desperate for a better life in the New World, they migrated to America and trickled down to the Carolinas along with other settlers. Some came over as indentured servants and when their period of service ended they moved further into the Appalachian Mountains where land was cheap. In 1772, not far from Dolly's homelands, some settlers founded the frontier community of Watauga, one of the first truly independent settlements in America beyond the reach of British colonial rule. One of its members, John Sevier, who later became Governor of Tennessee on two occasions, took a leading role at the decisive battle of King's Mountain in which the Patriots defeated the Loyalists (Americans whose allegiance was to the British). One historian described this overwhelming military victory as the turning point of the American Revolution.

The European pioneers followed old Indian trails into the Smoky Mountains and built their log cabins down in the hollers, little hollows or valleys among the hills and ridges out of the way of the winds and storms that regularly swept across the hills. The settlers were largely cut off from the outside world which meant that their way of life changed little over the years. They brought with them the early foundations of the music which Dolly grew up with and which, in forms evolved over generations in the mountains, would inspire her towards a life in music from a remarkably early age. Their instruments were bagpipes and lutes, and though these were gradually replaced by guitars, banjos and fiddles the essential elements in their songs, of love and lament and of storytelling, remained; what evolved over generations was a mountain music which encompassed folk, country and bluegrass (though this term was not coined until well into the 20th century). These historical pioneers from Europe were not, however, the first people to inhabit this part of the world.

The Smoky Mountains were part of an area of land first settled around AD 1000 possibly by a breakaway group of Iroquois who migrated south from lands in New England. They were later known as Cherokee and the name "Tennessee" derives from the Cherokee word "tanasi", the name of one of their villages on what is now the Little Tennessee River. The Cherokee enjoyed a settled life based on agriculture. They raised crops of corn, beans, melons and tobacco, hunted wild game and gathered plants for food and trade. Their towns, of up to 50 log-and-mud huts, were grouped around the town square and the "Council House", a large, seven-sided (representing each of the seven Cherokee clans) dome-shaped building. Public meetings and religious ceremonies were held here. They worshipped one benevolent god and ruled their villages democratically, with men and women sharing power as well as household duties. By the time they first encountered Europeans in 1540, when Spanish explorer Hernando de Soto led an expedition through Cherokee territory, the Smoky Mountains were already sacred ancestral homelands.

When settlers from Ireland, Scotland, Wales, England and Germany arrived in significant numbers the Cherokee were friendly at first but there were inevitable territorial tensions with the new, more powerful settlers, which spilled over into physical confrontations. The Cherokee nation attempted to make treaties and to adapt to European customs. They adopted a written legal code in 1808 and instituted a supreme court two years later. Sequoyah, a Cherokee silversmith, created an 86-character alphabet for the Cherokee language and in the space of two years nearly all of his people could read and write the language. Not long afterwards, they published a newspaper, *The Cherokee Phoenix*, and created their own constitution based on that of the United States itself.

However, like their fellow Native Americans in this vast land, theirs was a lost cause. In the wake of the Revolutionary War of Independence white settlers continued to occupy Cherokee lands in large numbers, and by 1819 the Cherokee were forced to cede a portion of their territory, which included the Great Smoky Mountains, to the United States. The discovery of gold in northern Georgia in 1828 sounded the death knell for the Cherokee nation. In 1830, President Andrew Jackson signed the Removal Act, calling for the relocation of all native peoples east of the Mississippi River westwards to Indian Territory, now Oklahoma. The Cherokee appealed their case to the Supreme Court, and Chief Justice Marshall ruled in their favour. President Andrew Jackson, however, disregarded the Supreme Court decree and in 1838 and 1839 the US government compelled some 13,000 Cherokee to march to Oklahoma along what has become known as the Trail of Tears. Altogether about 100,000 Native Americans, including Cherokee, Seminole, Chickasaw, and Choctaw, survived the march to Oklahoma, but thousands died from malnutrition and disease including about a third of the Cherokee. A small number of Cherokee disobeyed the government edict, hiding out in the hills between Clingman's Dome and Mount Guyot, and somehow managed to survive by using native skills handed down over generations. Eventually, in 1889, the 56,000-acre Qualla Boundary Reservation was officially chartered by the government; it had a population of about 1,000 people. More than 10,000 of their descendants now live on the reservation.

Like the Cherokee, 18th-century pioneers who settled in the Smokies also coveted the fertile lowland valleys. The arrival of more settlers throughout the 19th century meant an ever-increasing scarcity of land and as the century progressed, recent immigrants found the going harder. They had to establish their homesteads along steep slopes and infertile valleys. Two hundred million years of erosion turned the Appalachians from high, Alp-like peaks into rounded hills, but ridges of hard quartz sandstone survived, forming long valleys of softer shale. This produced a long range of accordion-like steep ridges, full of foliage entanglements like mountain laurel alongside valleys and hollers full of barren soil. The Appalachians therefore tended to attract poorer folk looking for cheap or unwanted land. They became known as hardscrabble farmers simply because they had to scrabble hard in order to extract a living from the land, which was rocky and low in quality.

Their basic cabins contrasted dramatically with the larger homes in more prosperous locations such as Cades Cove and Cataloochee Valley, where the dark soil was rich and fertile. Even into the early 20th century, farmers in the poorer areas lived almost entirely self-sufficiently. They grew their own food, raised their own livestock, ground corn (the main staple), wove cloth, and made their own clothes. They even made their own door hinges, carved from branches. By the late Twenties, when a cash economy was finally established, about 7,300 people lived on 1,200 farms. Wider economic problems had their effect as well. It is said that the Great Depression started long before 1929 in East Tennessee and lasted long after the rest of the country had "recovered".

The plentiful supply of timber in the Smokies was exploited for commercial gain. Logging began slowly, but by the time it had run its course, the small industry had radically changed the land and the life of the people. Timber, of course, was vital to the early pioneers. They used it for homes, furniture, fences and fuel, and only began cutting it down for cash in the mid-19th century. There was little noticeable effect on the forest, though, thanks to the minimal quantities that men and animals could carry. At the turn of the century technological advances and the eastern United States' need for lumber almost eliminated all of the southern Appalachian forests. Lumber companies had turned to the southern Appalachians after exhausting timber supplies in the north-east and around the Great Lakes.

Railroads were the key to the companies' large-scale logging operations and once they were extended deep into the mountains much of the previously inaccessible timber could be harvested. Steam-powered equipment, such as skidders and log loaders, also contributed to the cost-effective removal of large numbers of trees. By the Twenties, some 15 company towns were constructed along with a like number of sawmills. Mountain people who had once ploughed fields and farmed hogs began to cut trees and saw logs for a living, abandoning their farms in favour of the company towns. They were attracted to logging by the promise of a steady pay cheque, but their security was short-lived. By the Thirties, the lumber companies had logged all but the most inaccessible areas and were casting their sights to richer pickings out west. Some of the mountain people returned to farming, while others left the area to seek jobs in mines, textile mills and automobile factories.

In 1904, a librarian from St Louis named Horace Kephart came to the Smokies for the good of his health. He found that large-scale logging was decimating the land and disrupting the lives of the people. As the years progressed, he promoted the idea of preserving the Smokies as a national park. In the Twenties, prominent residents from the nearby town of Knoxville joined his efforts, forming the NPS (National Park Service). Along with other concerned private benefactors, the NPS promoted the idea of a national park. The states of Tennessee and North Carolina as well as countless citizens responded enthusiastically and donated millions of dollars to purchase parkland. The federal government was reluctant to buy land for parks, since national parks which had previously been created in the west were formed from land it already owned, but eventually it did contribute $2 million.

With a donation of $5 million from John D. Rockefeller Jr the NPS reached its goal. Lumber companies were bought out in agreements that phased out operations over several years. Less creditably, hundreds of people living within the proposed park boundaries were forcibly relocated, though after protests some were allowed lifetime occupancy rights. Finally, on June 15, 1934, The Great Smoky Mountains National Park was officially established. Under NPS management, the land has gradually been allowed to revert to its natural state, and the Smokies are being preserved for generations to come. Although the area has now become a major tourist attraction, exuding a positive image associated with family-friendly activity holidays, the reality is that to the present day, further back in the valleys, away from the tourist hot spots, many residents get by on low-level wages earned in the service industry associated with tourism. Educational attainments are below the national average and the drop-out rate from school is high. In subsequent years, these issues would come to be of great concern to Dolly Parton.

Dolly's closer ancestors hailed from a fairly small area of East Tennessee on the edge of the Smoky Mountains, near the Little Pigeon River, and the place names she haltingly provided in her 1967 interview made up a large part of her early formative years. There are few detailed records of Dolly's ancestors and much of what is known today has been passed down anecdotally from one generation to the next. This knowledge often consists of people's childhood memories of older relatives who loomed large in their lives not least because up until the Forties and Fifties families did not stray far from their home territory. A child growing up at that time would be surrounded by an assorted group of close and distant relatives, from very young to very old. It was an unquestioned part of life in those times, and in Dolly Parton's case virtually all of her traceable family members hailed from East Tennessee. The distinction between friends and relatives was sometimes blurred. Family ties might go back five or more generations so that the precise relationship of two people in the present might be hard to define.

Some might not be real kin at all. Much information about Dolly's relatives and neighbours that does survive has been gathered and recorded by her eldest sister Willadeene Parton, whose writings have brought to life some of the colourful characters that populated those bygone times. She tells of a man in his late sixties who attended a family reunion. When asked, "Now, how are you a'kinned?" he said, "Oh we're not . . . but your granddaddy took my father in when his daddy died, 'cause his mama couldn't feed them all . . . I'll never forget it." Going back to her great grandparents' generation, Dolly's family ranged in size from eight to 13 (not one of whom failed to get married), a phenomenon which helped to make women old before their time.

Her paternal great grandfather, Houston Parton (born 1865), was a handsome man with thick dark hair and blue eyes. He enjoyed teasing his wife Tennessee (born 1872), known as Tenny, because of the way she invariably rose to the bait. On one occasion she was "doctoring" a sick heifer with whisky and was infuriated when her husband helped himself to some of the medicine on the basis that there was plenty for him and the heifer to share. Whisky, of the bootleg variety, was a subject he was familiar with. He had a wagon with a secret compartment in which he stored his moonshine. As Willadeene puts it, "He took the respectable wagonload of vegetables to sell to the respectable ladies; and then the real produce in the false bottom of the wagon was distributed to the regular customers, the husbands of the respectable ladies." Though disapproved of by church folk and other upstanding members of the community, whisky making provided a vital means of support for poorer families, though of course some did it just because it was a cheap way of acquiring a little of what they fancied.

Grandma Cass (born 1860), Dolly's paternal great grandmother, made clothes for her children and wove blankets from wool yarn and made quilts from scraps of cloth sewn together. Mattresses were made from fresh pine needles, leaves, corn shucks or straw. Pillows for the beds were made from the feathers she picked from the breasts of their geese and ducks. There was little room for sentimentality when it came to animals – feathers were sometimes plucked when the birds were still alive. Women had to be collectors of anything that might be of use – boxes of buttons for mending clothes, human hair for funeral wreaths, bits of string. Grandma Cass was a midwife for the area and used many traditional herbal remedies: Jerusalem tea helped to increase the flow of mother's milk and relieve pain associated with birth. For fever there was snakeroot, wild ginger and pennyroyal and for burns, burdock.

Dolly's maternal great grandmother Lindy (born 1880) regularly sang to her children and grandchildren and it was from her that Dolly's mother learned old time folksy songs such as 'Two Little Babes', 'Little Bessie' and 'Letter To Heaven' as well as sad, mournful old ballads such as 'Barbry Allen' and 'The Letter Edged In Black'. Lindy was carrying on a tradition going back to the first European settlers. Appalachian music is based in part on Anglo-Celtic folk ballads and instrumental dance tunes. The former were almost always sung unaccompanied, usually by women fulfilling roles as keepers of the families' cultural heritage; singing helped them rise above their dreary and monotonous work, especially during the long winter months, through fantasies of escape and revenge. Many ballads were from the British tradition of personal narrative and spoke of loss, heartbreak and suicide; less common were songs of happiness and romance.

Lindy also helped to instil in all the children an appreciation of nature by telling them about wild herbs and their medicinal and culinary qualities. In the springtime she took them into the woods and showed them the secret places where the wild flowers grew. It is striking just how self-sufficient people had to be in the harsh economic climate that prevailed and yet how ingenious they were at coming up with simple ways of enhancing their quality of life. Lindy brightened up the children's winter clothes by dyeing them in large black kettles of boiling water: rich brown from walnut shells and blue from indigo root. Easter eggs were also brought to life with the aid of natural dyes: onion skins for yellow, oak bark for orange with some of the eggs being left natural white.

The poverty which affected so many in rural East Tennessee was no guard against the less salubrious aspects of communal life – perhaps it was a contributing factor. Gambling, drinking, brawling, theft and prostitution all caused serious concern to law-abiding citizens and there were times when it seemed that the law was powerless in curbing them. It was against this background that a notorious vigilante group known as the White Caps began to enforce its own kind of justice in the late 19th century, at a time when Dolly's maternal great grandfather Lloyd Henry Valentine (born 1874) served as a deputy sheriff. It was believed that the White Caps were made up of community leaders who were determined to clean up their domain, keeping their identities secret by wearing white cloth hoods. In addition, they wore their overcoats turned inside out to avoid the possibility of recognition and all members were strictly sworn to secrecy.

When they became aware of someone whose activities offended them they would ride out to the miscreant's house and nail a note to their front door warning them to leave the area by a certain time or face the consequences. The notes were signed "White Caps". If the warning was ignored a group of men would appear at night, batter down the front door and drag whoever it was into the yard; a severe whipping would then be administered in a circle of lantern light. Many otherwise law-abiding citizens were prepared to turn a blind eye to such practices since it often achieved the desired result. However, as time went on a more moralistic element, emboldened by earlier successes, administered whippings to women living alone with their children and those who indulged in pre-marital sex; the general level of violence against offenders increased and eventually there were murders. Sometimes the victims were people who breached the White Caps' oath of secrecy. Instances of whippings, beatings or barn burnings became increasingly frequent but the law seemed strangely impotent.

It seems that the White Caps and their silent supporters and benefactors occupied positions of power and importance in the area and helped out fellow members when they fell foul of the law. Of course no one other than themselves knew who they were. Eventually another band of citizens, called the Blue Bills, was formed in opposition to the White Caps. They required neither masks nor secret oaths and made it their business to thwart the activities of the vigilantes. Their eventual success was due in part to the loss of public support for the White Caps whose activities had gone far beyond what many people had been prepared to accept at the outset.

Dolly's paternal grandparents were Walter (born 1888) and Bessie Parton (born 1898). One unhappy incident occurred when Dolly's father Robert Lee Parton, usually just known as Lee, was a boy. Walter and Bessie's daughter, Margie, died at a mere 18 months after succumbing to pneumonia in the wake of a bout of measles. Today she could have been cured with everyday drugs but back then the country's health care was underdeveloped. On the other hand it was a given that relatives and neighbours would rally around in any way that was required and help out with practical tasks such as sewing the infant's burial dress and preparing the padding to line the tiny coffin. Grandma's Cass and Tenny bathed Margie's body with camphor and dressed her in her burial gown. On the day of the funeral the chores still had to be done and it was only after wood had been chopped, the animals fed and the cows milked that the grave could be dug and the funeral could take place.

While a young boy, Lee Parton witnessed one particularly traumatic incident. Walter Parton was gambling with some neighbours when a man who had earlier lost all his money as well as a prized watch, returned to demand his watch back. His request was declined on the basis that it had been won fair and square. The response was dramatic. The man produced a gun and shot Walter's two companions and would have done the same to him but though he pulled the trigger, the gun was by now empty. Lee Parton had been sitting beside his father throughout the drama.

Dolly's maternal grandfather Jake Owens (born 1899) was a schoolteacher who also taught and wrote music. One of his songs, 'Singing His Praise', was later recorded by country singer Kitty Wells. From an early age Jake had a powerful religious calling and went on to become a preacher of the hellfire variety as part of his perceived mission to lead souls to Christ. He married Rena Valentine in 1919 and in the Twenties the couple moved from Sevierville to Lockhart, South Carolina, Rena's home town, where they found jobs in a cotton mill. They lived in a house built on a strip of land close to a river not far from a dam. There was panic one night when, without warning, cracks started to appear in the dam. Along with their neighbours, Jake and Rena and their children hurriedly evacuated their house taking with them only their most treasured possessions, including the family Bible and a violin which was a valuable heirloom. According to family lore it had belonged to Jake's great grandfather Solomon Grooms, who had it with him when, walking in the mountains with his two grandsons, he was confronted by a group of vigilantes hostile to union men like him. They forced him to play a tune on the violin and as he did they shot him dead before riding away. Solomon's grandsons retrieved the violin, which was then passed down through various members of the family before being sold to Jake by one of his uncles and is still in the family to the present day.

The dam gave way not long after Jake and Rena had managed to scramble to higher ground from where they watched in horror as a roaring flood raced by, destroying virtually everything in its path. They were transfixed by the sight of a wooden house floating by, an oil lamp still burning in the kitchen, with the woman of the house sitting on the roof singing 'Nearer My God To Thee'. One of Jake and Rena's eight children, Avie Lee Caroline Owens (known as Avie Lee), Dolly's mother, was a young girl at the time but she always remembered the awesome roar of the floodwater, which reverberated throughout her entire body. Soon after this incident Jake and Rena returned to Sevierville.

Lee Parton first saw Avie Lee Owens through a church window. A group had gathered for a revival meeting at which the Reverend Jake Owens was passionately launching forth against the evils of sin, in the robust style which was his trademark. Avie Lee had accompanied him and was sitting in the congregation. Lee happened to be outside with some friends and it seems he was immediately smitten by her brown eyes, long black hair and high cheekbones. A number of sources have pointed to Avie Lee being one quarter Cherokee (making Dolly one eighth) and such claims have often been repeated. However, recent detailed research by one of Dolly's relatives has cast doubt on this. Apparently many people living in East Tennessee have family legends of Native American ancestry. Avie Lee was barely five feet tall and weighed about 100 pounds; her skin, smooth and unblemished had, according to Willadeene, "never known make-up". She was shy and modest, the product of a fairly strict Southern Christian upbringing.

Though still only in his late teens Lee already had a reputation as a heavy drinker and had no qualms about helping friends move moonshine liquor around the countryside at night to avoid detection. His feelings for Avie Lee were evidently reciprocated and soon Lee became a regular visitor to the Owens house, ingratiating himself with the family by doing various chores around the homestead. He would regularly accompany Avie Lee to church on Sunday and their contrasting appearances must have been striking; he tall and blond, she petite with long black hair down to her waist. Love grew despite the fact that Avie Lee's efforts to get Lee to give his soul to Jesus Christ, as she herself had done, proved unsuccessful.

They were married by Jake Owens on August 17, 1939, not long after they had tried, unsuccessfully, to elope. Lee was 17 and Avie Lee a mere 15, young even by the standards of the time though in 1948 another girl from the country, Loretta Lynn, who would grow up to be one of the most important female country singers of all time, got married at the age of 13. While Lee's new father-in-law might have had misgivings about his lack of religious conviction he nonetheless admired the fact that he was a hard worker. Lee made sure they would have peace and privacy on their wedding night. Without telling anyone his plan he hustled his new bride away from the house, where a collection of family members were staying, and took her to the loft of the barn where they shared a feast of corn bread, ham and sweet cakes before bedding down for the night on some new mown hay in the company of mules and cows.

For the start of their married life, the young couple rented a small log cabin (originally built as a garage) consisting of one room and a washroom, in a hollow deep in the forest far from any neighbours. To get water Avie Lee had to walk through the forest to a springhouse. At night the stillness of the country was broken by whippoorwills calling to each other near and far, while unknown and unseen wild animals scurried about around the house. Wild cats were known to inhabit the area and according to one story a panther had snatched a baby from an open window and carried it off.

The marriage was soon in difficulties. Although his wife was pregnant Lee resumed drinking with his male companions and would regularly leave Avie Lee on her own at weekends despite her protestations that she was frightened and lonely. After only three months she went back to her parents – a blow to her pride and a breach of the convention that women should stick it out whatever the difficulties. The marriage was almost over before it had started. Lee did appear after a few months expecting that his wife would obediently trail home after him but Avie Lee was not prepared to comply unless she was sure that Lee had changed his ways and she knew perfectly well that he had not. It was a year after the baby (Willadeene) was born before they got back together to try and make a go of the marriage after the initial false start. Lee was never afraid of hard work but without any educational qualifications (he never learned to read or write and may have been dyslexic) he was limited to working the land and taking labouring jobs. He worked as a sharecropper, that is to say a tenant farmer who was provided with equipment but who had to give a substantial proportion of the value of crops produced to the landlord. As Rachel Parton later said he "started from scratch".

He grew what crops he could, partly to generate income, partly to provide food. The family moved in response to the vagaries of economic circumstances and the availability of properties – wooden shacks with tin roofs – but they never moved far. Lee sometimes took labouring work as a logger on construction sites or dug ditches, and there were occasions when he might have to travel up to 300 miles from home for a couple of months at a time. He also tried his luck in the automobile industry in Detroit but soon gave it up as a bad idea, preferring to stay closer to familiar home territory. The world Dolly Parton grew up in had extremely limited physical, geographical and cultural horizons. The income from Lee's various jobs merely supplemented the money he was able to make from growing tobacco as a sharecropper, the main source of income for the family. As well as tobacco he grew beans, potatoes and turnips to feed the family. Being tenant sharecroppers the Partons sometimes worked for another farmer and lived on his land, although they were eventually able to scrape together the money to buy their own house.

While Lee provided material support for the family, Avie Lee used the domestic skills she had absorbed throughout her brief country upbringing to build a home fit to raise a family. Family planning did not exist and according to Dolly her mother "didn't know how to prevent a pregnancy occurring". According to writers Mary A. Bufwack and Robert K. Oermann the kind of advice which mothers might have given to their daughters would not have changed much since the 19th century and might be along the lines of, "If you don't want butter, pull the dasher out in time." In the machismo culture of the day the idea of men resisting sexual urges or exercising abstinence would have been given short shrift. Before long the Parton family increased in size with the arrival of first David and then Denver. On January 19, 1946, the year in which Hank Williams cut his first songs and Nashville was starting to make a name for itself in the recording industry, a fourth child was delivered. Dolly Rebecca Parton was the last of the Parton children to be born at home, which at the time was a one-room cabin close to the banks of the Little Pigeon River.

Dolly was named after two aunts, maternal and paternal, though one spelt her name "Dollie". Research carried out by writer Steve Eng at the

Vital Records department in Tennessee some years ago revealed the existence of a birth certificate in name of "Dollie Rebecca Parton born January 9, 1946". Subsequent investigations at the Vital Records department produced the standard, long accepted version but apparently birth certificates can be amended by affidavit so a whiff of mystery remains.* However, the world would come to know her as Dolly Parton.

Dolly was delivered by Dr Robert F. Thomas, a well-known and much respected figure in the area. It was a snowy winter's night – so cold that when the kitchen was mopped the water froze leaving a thin film of ice on the floor – bringing a clear blue sky the next day. Dr Thomas originally came from New York and arrived at Pittman Center in 1929 as a medical missionary; he had spent time in Malaya prior to gaining his medical degree. A certain missionary zeal was a necessary attribute for a doctor whose patients inhabited valleys in the far-flung reaches of the foothills of the Smoky Mountains. Regardless of the weather, when he made house calls he did so on foot, horseback (as when he delivered Dolly), wagon and sled, and only much later by jeep. He served the rural and mountain areas of Sevier County for over 50 years and records show that he was often out 300 nights of the year treating the sick and injured as well as delivering babies.

Like other professions he had to use his initiative and imagination in combination with his medical skills to deal with a wide range of problems with the limited resources at his disposal, and he lived to the grand old age of 91. Lacking a state funded health service, Dr Thomas had to be paid for bringing Dolly into the world but since money was scarce at the time, he was paid in kind, with a bag of meal ground from corn Lee had grown himself. The younger Parton children had spent the night with a neighbour so that they might be spared the sights and sounds of their mother giving birth. The next day each of them got to hold the new arrival for a few exciting moments. Willadeene's glee was all the greater because she was told that Dolly was to be "her" baby – a family custom followed with subsequent babies who were "given" to the next child in line. As Lee said a baby was better than a doll: "It walks and talks and pees and everything."

Dolly's birth date of January 19 falls on the cusp between Capricorn and Aquarius, the 10th and 11th signs of the Zodiac. For those who attach significance to such things, people born on that date are said to be

---

* Early school records alternate between "Dolly" and "Dollie". A song contract was witnessed as "Dollie Parton" in 1961 and in one letter from a publishing company around this time she was referred to as "Dollie".

humanitarians and philanthropists, the visionaries of the Zodiac and have many acquaintances in addition to close friends. They are also ambitious and disciplined, dedicated to achieving goals. Capricorns are said to be independent and individualistic, within the world but detached from it. The astrological symbol of Aquarius is the water bearer. Like the bearer bringing water to his people, people born under this sign are said to bring new ideas to the world. Those born on the cusp, like Dolly, are both unpredictable and unconventional, while at the same time happy to uphold tradition and conservative belief systems. Original, offbeat, even eccentric, they are also rather bored by detail. Sometimes overly critical, even bossy, this is because of a strong desire to achieve goals, not because of rudeness. In fact, they are generally polite because of an understanding that making enemies will not help to achieve anything in life. Freedom is important and they are often driven to help others become free as well. Thanks to an inexhaustible ambition, they are not easily deterred when their goals are in sight.

The new arrival attracted special interest and favourable comment because of her beautiful ivory skin, her father's blond hair, and her mother's high cheekbones. Dolly later said that she inherited her father's pride and determination and her mother's no-nonsense attitude to life. Now she had arrived in the world she would waste no time in using these and other qualities to make her own distinctive mark on it.

# Chapter 2

DOLLY Parton was born into a rural world where the mere act of day-to-day survival was both a challenge and an achievement. One of the houses she lived in as a young child was remote, two miles from the nearest neighbour, and was reached by a rope bridge slung across a river. There were no radios, televisions or newspapers. Births and deaths were announced by church bells ringing on the mountain. The nearest mail box was miles away. The children were always excited when another baby was due but sometimes the doctor was far off in the mountains and it might take two days to track him down. It was a world of hardship, conflict and deprivation but it was also a world out of which grew the communal support systems associated with large extended families and close neighbours in difficult circumstances who, like their pioneering ancestors before them, had to rely on wit and initiative. They also had to co-operate with each other in order to face up to and overcome the demands of everyday life.

As Dolly said, "It was very much like what you see in old movies. Our homes were scattered around, and everyone walked to church and school. We banded together as a community to help each other. If someone needed help, they would ring the bell at the church and everybody would meet at the church to see how they could help. People were glad to help . . . there was this old woman named Evie Barnes who would sometimes have extra milk and butter, and she'd say to my mama, 'If you want some of that milk and butter, send them young guns over to get it.' There were people that would give us extra vegetables out of their gardens."

Dolly has drawn comfort from her upbringing over the years. "The people are so sweet and kind and so deep and gentle. It's kept me sane through the years, staying in touch with my home." It was a world which also introduced Dolly to music and religion (she was baptised at the age of six in the Pigeon River by the Reverend L. B. Smith) and helped form her character.

For years Avie Lee either had a new baby or was pregnant with the next one ("One in her and one on her" as Dolly would put it). Lee and Avie Lee went on to have 12 children, Willadeene, David, Denver, Dolly,

Bobby, Stella, Cassie, Randall (Randy), Floyd and Frieda (twins) and Rachel. One baby, Larry, died soon after birth and there were miscarriages. The size of the family later gave Dolly an opportunity to crack one of the lame jokes she has always favoured. "My mama named her last four children, Eeny, Meeny, Miny and Henry, 'cause she didn't want no Mo."

Since Avie Lee was invariably snowed under with domestic and maternal chores, children had to take on caring roles. Once, when Dolly was a baby, Willadeene, herself very young, was given the job of looking after Dolly as she lay in her crib while her mother cleaned clothes at a nearby washhouse. Willadeene took Dolly out of the crib and threw her up and down in the air as she had seen her parents do. Unfortunately she dropped the baby and Dolly landed on her head before rolling down a steep hill. Dolly was unharmed and she later joked that her sister, "gave me a head start in life and I've been on a roll ever since".

The Second World War had brought about major societal changes in many parts of America. With so many men at the battlefront, large numbers of women were required to leave their domestic routines, often moving from the country to the city, in order to carry out a wide variety of jobs to support the war effort. When the war was over many were no longer content to stay at home raising children and sought to develop their own careers providing independent income. Such aspirations were greatly aided by the arrival of new labour-saving devices which did away with time-consuming domestic tasks. Rising economic prosperity meant that such luxurious items fell within the grasp of many households. However, such progress was still a far-off dream for many people living in East Tennessee. Lee Parton continued to coax a meagre living off the land and Avie Lee did what she could to clothe and feed their children.

When Dolly was about four the Partons managed to buy a farm of several hundred acres on Locust Ridge, for around $5,000, where the family stayed for about six years. It was cheap because the land was poor and the farm was "way back up in the holler". When writer Alanna Nash tried to locate the house in the late Seventies she found that even some of the locals could not find it. The Parton children never starved but there was little variety when it came to food. Breakfast when Dolly was younger was usually just biscuits and gravy. Despite limitations on the degree of choice, Avie Lee used her imagination to brighten up whatever food there was.

To make the meagre food supply go further, she thinned ketchup with a little water and when making bread she would grease the cooking pans with the fat in meat skins so as to save lard. Avie Lee combined this "waste not, want not" approach with her imaginative storytelling skills. When ingredients for soup were sparse she would tell the children a story about a man who conjured up a pan of tasty soup with water, a few scraps of food and a magical stone. The children would be despatched to the yard to find the smoothest possible stone so that they could bring the story to life in their own kitchen. Avie Lee picked the best one and would add it to the pan along with water and whatever ingredients she had to make 'stone soup'.

The shelves were filled with home-canned fruit, vegetables and pickles. On the floor were crocks of pickled beans, kraut, corn on the cob and chow-chow (a kind of pickled relish) all made when the produce was available and stored for later use. Lee made his own contribution by buying reject tins of hominy (ground maize cooked with water or milk) or green beans from a canning factory at greatly reduced prices. A thrifty approach was also necessary for clothing and bedding. Avie Lee had an old treadle Singer sewing machine with which she made new clothes, patched up old ones and altered hand-me-downs to fit the next wearer. Pillowcases and sheets were made out of the coarse cloth of hundred pound feed and fertiliser sacks which were bleached by being boiled in lye water. They lasted indefinitely but as Willadeene said, "The seams felt like-two-by-fours when you had to sleep on them."

The kitchen was the centre of family life in the house. Lee built the basic table, covered with a red-and-white-chequered oilcloth, where meals were eaten; at each end was a cane-bottomed chair and on either side were long benches for all the children to sit on. The cooking stove burned wood and had a reservoir for heating water and a warmer to keep leftovers warm. The basic ingredients for most meals were beans, potatoes, meal, lard and eggs, plus a few valued mainstays such as chicken and sausage, to introduce a degree of wholesome variety. Herbs were widely used to enhance the natural flavours. In the winter months Avie Lee devised a treat called "snow cream" in which a large wooden spoon was used to mix a concoction made up of snow (gathered by Lee), milk, sugar and vanilla flavouring which was then poured on top of home-made treats such as blackberry cobbler. Willadeene recalls that Dolly always seemed to be the one carrying out the coveted job of stirring while other family members were reduced to the more menial job of pouring in the other ingredients to produce the chilly treat. Of course not all of Avie Lee's ideas and recipes were original since many were handed down from one generation to the next.

In marked contrast to the present day, children were not overfed, depending on the foods that their families grew or gathered wild from the fields and hills around the home. Lee fished, grew sugar cane for molasses and kept bees for honey. In the vegetable patch he cultivated such staples as beans, corn, potatoes and turnips. He also hunted animals in the mountains so that the children ate bear, turtle, rabbit, squirrel and groundhog. Lee did, however, draw the line at possum, which he regarded as no better than rats. Dolly said that in the mountains you grew up, "eating whatever's running around". Once a year Lee killed hogs; the hearty appetite of the family for fresh meat meant they didn't last long. Just about the only things they bought from the grocery store on a regular basis were coffee and sugar.

Necessity was the mother of invention when it came to medicine. Tonics were made from camomile, liquorice or dandelions. Colic was treated with catnip, ginger or sassafras tea; headaches and other pains with valerian, comfrey and gentia. In the summer months the children took off their heavy winter shoes (known as brogans) and went around barefoot. On one occasion, when she was collecting up bits of broken glass and other debris, Dolly injured her foot badly while jumping over a fence. She had failed to notice a piece of metal that had come from an old piece of farm equipment and landed on it heavily. In her 1994 autobiography Dolly wrote, "My foot was severely cut. My toes were dangling, barely hanging on." While the men held her down her mother put kerosene on the cut to fight infection, packed it with cornmeal to stop the bleeding and used the same needle she used to make quilts to stitch the wound. With the benefit of such skills and knowledge acquired and passed down over generations, Dolly's foot soon healed.

There were also more conventional medicaments such as carbolic salve and red liniment supplied by travelling salesmen from the Watkins and Raleigh companies as well as locally bought items which filled the children with dread. Once a year they were lined up and, despite vigorous protests, given large doses of spring tonic followed by castor oil as a general prophylactic. Lee stood by, ready to hold the nose of any child who didn't swallow, though afterwards he would soften the blow by giving them grapefruit juice to take away the taste.

Lee was adept at producing various crude alcoholic beverages: wine, brandy, beer and moonshine, or "shine" as it was known, a drink that burned the throat as it went down. Avie Lee viewed alcohol as a sin and sometimes warned that "papa was going straight to hell." As Stella Parton puts it, Lee "let off his own steam" in town, while at home he hid his whisky in various places around the house. Though the children knew where some of these places were, they also knew they would be in trouble if they let on. Their natural curiosity drew them into finding out more about the mysteries of hooch. One Sunday Dolly, Willadeene, David and Denver misappropriated some of their father's whisky and poured it into snuff cans from which they sipped all the way to church. The service was something of a blur but their misdemeanour went undetected.

Once, when Bobby was young, the girls became aware that David and Denver, just into their teens, were up to something when a number of Avie Lee's fruit jars had mysteriously gone missing. They followed the boys into the woods one day and found that they had set up an illicit still along with some other local lads, which they were tending enthusiastically much as the older menfolk did. The scheme had been concocted with the older brother of a friend who could see its commercial possibilities and was happy to provide technical advice and assistance in constructing the still. The girls were also struck by the fact that the boys were carrying on some of the coarser country customs just like the men, chewing tobacco, spitting and cursing.* Production continued over the summer until Lee got wind of the project and put a swift end to it.

Mealtimes were when the family came together to talk about the day's events and to address any problems that might be troubling people. Community events were also centred on church suppers, family gatherings and funerals. There were few funeral homes; if an elderly grandmother died, it was most probable that she would be laid out in the living room. Meanwhile, a feast provided by family, friends and neighbours was spread out in the dining room or kitchen. When Dolly was young a neighbour called Martha Williams, who owned the land her father farmed, died and her body was duly displayed in her house. Dolly had been very close to her and songs she sang to Dolly, which she changed round to include Dolly's name, were among the first she remembers hearing. With devilish glee her brothers described in graphic detail the embalming process. They also dragged Dolly to the side of the coffin and forced her to look at the corpse and touch it. In her 1994 autobiography Dolly claimed this had a "spirit-shattering effect" on her which she has never quite outgrown. She still cannot view a dead body, and has an aversion to funerals.

Community gatherings, sometimes referred to as all-day singing and dinner on the ground, either took the form of a one-day revival or what used to be called a camp meeting, which might be the culmination of a

---

* Apparently Dolly herself was taught how to chew and spit tobacco at an early age by one Jackson Taylor, her inspiration for the song 'Applejack'. She later said, "We could knock a chicken's eye out." Taylor died when Dolly was about 12.

week-long revival. Revival meetings generally aimed to consolidate or reawaken religious fervour in the members of a particular church or community and would sometimes include preaching or personal testimony. Talking about such gatherings Dolly said, "The practice of religion in the south was almost invariably connected with good food and plenty of it, and family, and plenty of it, and celebrating all three things, religion, food and family in a very special way."

Another popular communal gathering was Decoration Day, which before the Second World War had strong Civil War connotations. The commemoration was held on Confederate Memorial Day and families would go to the local cemetery to decorate the graves of family members killed during what was sometimes referred to as the "War of Northern Aggression". Nowadays it is observed on Memorial Day at the end of May when those killed in all wars are decorated. Decoration Day is also an occasion for families to gather together, to eat, and remember those who have passed on and bring together families who no longer live in one valley, town or even state.

In keeping with their religious nature such gatherings featured lots of music – mainly hymn singing, in which Dolly required little encouragement. As her grandfather Jake Owens put it, "She started singing as soon as she quit crying." Dolly said that music was particularly important on her mother's side of the family which she affectionately claims included vagabonds and dreamers. Dolly claimed that being a dreamer helped her to be less aware of her family's poverty. Avie Lee noticed that from a very early age Dolly hummed recognisable melodies. "When the radio would be on or I would sing, Dolly would carry the tune along with me. Before she was a year and a half old, Dolly could sing a little rhyme or a little song." She would pick up on the most unlikely rhythms in the house, tapping her feet in time to, for instance, her mother shelling peas. Avie Lee said the first time Dolly sang to an audience other than the family was in church. Although Dolly never had formal music lessons there were influences close at hand as she was growing up.

Avie Lee regularly sang to the children, who especially loved her rendition of Christmas carols such as 'Silent Night' and 'Oh Little Town Of Bethlehem' with what Willadeene describes as "her haunting pure mountain voice". She also sang the old-time songs she had learned from her mother, such as 'Little Rosewood Casket', which Dolly came to love. Some of the songs Avie Lee sang had been written by Dolly's great grandmother, known as Mammy, who smoked a cob pipe, played the dulcimer, made up stories from things that were happening in the family and turned them into songs. As Dolly said, "My family says I'm a lot like her in the way that I use the old mountain melodies – even a song that's brand new sounds like it's old. Mammy created a lot of her own music. She would take her feelings, her own heartbreak, and write it up, and I'm able to do that, too. I've always been grateful for that gift."

Sundays were usually set aside for family visits, often to Dolly's grandparents, who would have the radio on for religious singing and preaching. The grandchildren would sing for them and Dolly liked to sing solo while snuggled up to her Grandma Bessie, for whom she had particular affection. Many people in Dolly's large family circle, particularly on her mother's side, could sing or pick a little. As she put it, her people, "Always played every type of instrument and every kid in every family was used to somebody's banjo laying around, somebody's fiddle being around, somebody's mandolin . . . so I just love the sound of every instrument." All the Parton children were influenced by the music around them and more than half went on to have musical careers of one sort or another. From a very early age Dolly displayed an ability to compose music. It seems she was able to do this before she had learned to write proficiently and so she would sing some of the songs that were floating around in her head and ask her mother to write them down so that they would not be forgotten.

According to oft repeated legend, the first song she composed, around the age of five, was called 'Little Tiny Tassel-Top', inspired by a doll her father made out of a corncob, marking the eyes with a hot poker and a wig made out of corn silk. As well as illustrating the loneliness of a child growing up in a large family, especially one who wanted lots of attention, the song displayed Dolly's instinctive aptitude for alliteration. Avie Lee was also struck by the gift for rhyme in some of the other songs and poetry her daughter wrote. However, the truth about the very first song Dolly ever wrote is probably lost in the mists of time. In a Seventies interview with Joshua Castle Dolly said, "I wrote my first song when I was five years old[*] and had my mother write it down for me. It was a song called 'Life Doesn't Mean Much To Me'. A pretty deep song for a kid but I always did look and act older than I was and still do." From an early age Dolly used every opportunity to sing, usually in front of an audience made up of family members and friends. She had a particular liking for sad songs, especially the tragic Appalachian ballads her mother used to sing.

Dolly also had early experience of singing hymns at church. The family

---

[*] In her 1967 interview with Everett Corbin she said she wrote her first "real song" when she was eight.

regularly attended Grandpa Jake Owens' House of Prayer and Church of God in Sevierville to which the faithful would bring a variety of musical instruments, banjos, mandolins, tambourines and guitars, and sing gospel hymns and old time spirituals. Her own family were major contributors. People were encouraged to sing out, or shout out, strong emotions they felt and Dolly said, "I came to know what freedom is so I could know God, and come to know freedom within myself." Singing with religious fervour was acceptable but this licence did not extend to the pleasures of the flesh. As Grandpa Jake said, "A dancing foot and praying knee don't fit on the same leg." When Elvis Presley burst onto the scene the more conservative elements regarded him as Satan incarnate. Dolly, fidgety and restless, did not like the fact that she had to sit still in church; she did, however, appreciate the fact that she got a break from her chores on Sundays.

Sometimes church attendance involved less pure motives. On occasion Dolly would sit in the last pew of the church, and the boys would come and scratch on the window to get her to go outside. As she said in a *Rolling Stone* interview, "Sometimes I would go to church just to see who would walk me home." Bearing in mind the way Lee first courted Avie Lee she was carrying on a family tradition.

When she was seven a local holy woman laid her hands on Dolly and declared, "This child is very anointed." Her mother said, "You have a mission . . . God has placed his hand on you to do some special things in this world, praise Him and maybe help people." On another occasion Avie Lee apparently told Dolly that it would be part of her mission in life to lead people to the Lord. However, the influence of religion was not always unequivocally positive. Dolly has said that the hellfire sermons scared her and that they "inspired me or depressed me into writin' all these sad, mournful songs. You kind of grew up in a horrid atmosphere about fear of religion. We thought God was a monster in the sky."

As a child Dolly developed her own opinions and did not understand fundamentalist preachers who instilled fear in people when they portrayed God as a "scary thing" that might strike down sinners. She wondered where "judge not lest you be judged" fitted in. There are many churches in Tennessee that appear to be similar in their core beliefs but with key differences. Dolly's sister Stella attempted an explanation. "They said that my Grandad's (the Reverend Jake Owens) church that we grew up in was the House of Prayer, which was kind of affiliated with the Church of God in Cleveland, Tennessee . . . So we believe in the gifts of the church . . . that Paul sets out in the scripture, interpretation, discernment, speaking in tongues, healing and all those five gifts, so to be Pentecostal or to be holiness is to be Church of God and the Assembly of God is like that.

"The Baptists is Daddy's people. Pentecostal Church of God holiness people were Mama's people and we mostly associated with them but my dad's brother was a missionary Baptist pastor and that entire side of the family were missionary Baptists and Southern Baptists which is several different sects, I guess, of the Baptist faith and they believe a lot like the Pentecostal holiness Church of God people do."

Religion was an integral part of life for the Parton family as Stella says, "It was everything. That's all we had and that's still all we have." Willadeene Parton: "God and church were as much a part of our daily lives as breathing. It wasn't 'religion' to be practised at church, but a natural faith that was and is part of our everyday living and thinking. Mother saw to it that we knew just who God was and what He could do. Mother believed it was her duty to teach us, and she did her duty, not only for her children but for her grandchildren as well . . . we grew up never separating God from any aspect of our lives."

Avie Lee told them the story of Noah's Ark and how God resolved to destroy all the world's inhabitants save a small band of people and animals who would be protected during 40 days and nights before returning to the land to make a fresh start. This offered little comfort when spring floods in the mountains caused the streams to overflow their banks. Willadeene gave this dramatic description: "The friendly, lazy little branches and creeks, some only a few feet wide, became monstrous torrents of death and destruction. With the sound came horrible, helpless fear." However, it did stop the children, fearful for their own safety and that of their father who went out to check on the safety of neighbouring families, from bickering.

As Willadeene put it, "Mother controlled us with religion, fear and love. When none of these worked, she told papa on us." Dolly told Melvyn Bragg in 1999 that corporal punishment was part of her life when growing up and her father whipped them, "a bit too hard" but that it did not amount to "dangerous abuse", joking that she should have been whipped more.

Avie Lee also enlisted the power of song in her attempts to maintain order. "When you've got 12 kids you've got to do something to keep them out of meanness . . . I'd sing till they'd cry. If I kept them sad enough, they'd quit fighting."

Dolly has clearly stated in a number of interviews over the years that she is not a Christian though she does have a Christian outlook in the way she treats people. She feels she and God have always been ". . . good friends. I talk to Him just like I talk to anyone . . . I feel He helps me even though I am a sinner . . . to be a Christian, I would have to devote as much time to the church as I do to my music. Until I do that, I could never be a hypocrite."

Stella Parton: "I think Dolly's very spiritual but as she would say herself, she was always so mean she'd have to repent every revival; she would always say she was so naughty that every spring she'd have to go back down to the altar and repent again." Stella also confirms that her elder sister is "not a big church-goer as such but she prays and she reads the Bible and she believes that everything good comes from God . . . I read my scripture every day, I pray all the time and I know she does but then the next minute we might be cussin' like a trucker, that's just the way we are."

Despite the advantages of a supportive family upbringing, hardship and conflict were the ever-present realities of life. Avie Lee was continually pregnant and in view of the limited nature of local health care and the sheer physical demands placed on her body, on occasion her life was put at risk. She once had a miscarriage on a weekday, when only Bobby and Stella, too young for school, were at home. She was bleeding heavily and told Bobby, who was about three years old at the time, to walk to the school where the older children were. It was a long and frightening journey for a young boy, which took him through a field with bulls in it. He got to the school and the older children, including Dolly, then six, immediately headed back to the house with him.

They found Avie Lee lying on her bed clutching a Bible with Stella beside her crying. The bed was soaked in blood which was dripping through the mattress onto the floor. The means of getting help was protracted and archaic to say the least. According to Willadeene, David and Denver went by horse to Grandma Rena's and then on to find Lee.* It was only much later that serious help arrived in the form of a hearse, serving as an ambulance, from a local funeral home. Even then the closest it could get to the Parton home was the schoolhouse, a mile or so away, so that Avie Lee had to be placed on a stretcher and carried about half a mile through a sedge field before she could be placed in the back of the vehicle. Dolly recalls running alongside the stretcher and crying because she was frightened she would never see her mother again. Avie Lee spent a lengthy period of recuperation in hospital so the family was looked after by a

---

* Dolly said in a 1978 *Playboy* interview that they went to neighbours and in another interview that they had to go into town.

combination of Lee, the older children and family and friends. As Dolly said, if her mother wasn't pregnant, "She was just really rundown, sick, and back then you didn't have doctors that much."

Pregnancy for women in rural America in the Fifties was still fraught with dangers despite some improvement over the years: at the turn of the century one in every 30 mothers died during their childbearing years but in the mid-19th century the number was twice that. Avie Lee also nearly died from spinal meningitis contracted when she was again pregnant. At one point she slipped into a coma and the doctor said there was little prospect of recovery and that even if she did survive she would be, as Dolly put it, "crippled up" with brain damage. Avie Lee's temperature rocketed and she was packed with ice but amazingly she survived the ordeal, the only lasting effect being deafness in one ear. Dolly claimed that the doctor treating her mother said her recovery had been nothing less than miraculous, while her grandmother Rena attributed Avie Lee's recovery to divine intervention.

In line with the family custom of new babies being "given" to one of the children, Dolly asked her mother if the baby she was carrying at the time could be hers. However, the child, named Larry, was born with defective lungs and only survived a few hours. Dolly was understandably distraught especially at the funeral home where the baby was taken when she heard one of her relatives suggest that the boy's death was a blessing in disguise as the family had enough children already. Dolly says she always saw each new child as a special gift. Neighbours and family rallied round by helping to feed and support the children for a time but such aid only lasted a short time; they had their own hard lives to lead. Despite Avie Lee's traumatic experience she went on to have further pregnancies.

The dramatic recovery from illness of another member of the Parton family was also attributed to an act of God. Randy Parton was born with an open heart valve and specialists said that his prospects of survival into adulthood were poor. Willadeene says the children were taught that there was nothing God couldn't do and that if He could create people He could also heal them. Prayers were said for Randy by friends and relatives and, one night when he was nine years old, Willadeene says that he came back from church in a high state of excitement. He claimed that he had experienced a warm fiery feeling in his chest and that he had been healed; subsequent medical examination apparently confirmed this to be true. She cites this as one reason for the family's belief in God.

Sceptics could point to the prayers of others which failed to be answered. In a sense though this misses the point of a believers' church.

The people can pray and question but ultimately they accept what happens to them, good or bad. They believe, conveniently some might say, that whatever happens is for the best because in some way it is part of God's plan, however mysterious. Perhaps the religious belief system so prevalent in the mountains evolved as a necessary support and comfort for the people whose lives were at times so dreary and bleak.

Dolly brilliantly evoked her early life experiences in the ironically titled, 'In The Good Old Days (When Times Were Bad)' released in 1969. She described the song as "the way it was and the way it still is for some people back home. It's sort of like everyday living . . . every bit of it is true. It's a memory of how things were over in the holler in Sevierville, Tennessee."

True to the message of the song, Dolly knew early on that she wanted to break free from the life of drudgery she had been born into. Although she made moves in this direction sooner than most, it would be some years before she achieved her aim. As she said, "I didn't know what was beyond the mountains but I knew there was something."

# Chapter 3

ALTHOUGH there was much mutual support among East Tennessee families, this was not universal. It seems that some people in the country were just born mean. In her 1978 *Playboy* interview Dolly told the story of an unpleasant feud which blew up for no apparent reason between her family and some near neighbours. As she described it, "They would whip us every day as we walked to school, hit us with rocks." Lee Parton devised another school route for his children but once this was discovered the attacks continued and so, angry and exasperated, he went to the neighbour's house. There was a confrontation and threats were made; after that Lee and the older boys were involved in physical fights with members of the family, the situation went from bad to worse and as Dolly said, "We couldn't go by their house – they had dogs and they'd let them loose on us if we had to walk that way."

One of the children's popular pastimes in winter was to walk and slide on thin ice when the river froze over. The dangers did not seem to occur to them and sometimes they fell through into the freezing water below. Sledging was another favourite winter activity – there were heavy snowfalls in East Tennessee around Christmas time – but the Partons and their friends had to make do with sliding down hills on old bits of cardboard. According to her Aunt Estelle, Dolly joined in all such activities enthusiastically when she was younger and many described her as a tomboy. Most families could not afford to give their children lavish presents and each year the Mission Board sent boxes of used toys and clothes to all schools in the area. Every child received at least one toy and was permitted to choose items of clothing he or she needed.

Everyday tasks such as washing posed a major challenge in houses with large families and no running water. In summer the Parton family bathed in the river which also provided the setting for one of Dolly's favourite games, pretending to be baptised. One particular joke Dolly has told in numerous interviews and talk shows illustrates the kind of ribald humour that appeals to her. "We just had a pan of water and we'd wash down as far as possible, and we'd wash up as far as possible. Then, when somebody'd clear the room, we'd wash possible." The toilet was situated in an outhouse – a wooden shelf over a hole in the ground – a "one-holer" – only rich folks had "two-holers". For toilet paper they made do with old newspapers and magazines contributed by relatives. An avid reader, Dolly would gaze longingly at the pictures of expensive clothes and jewellery and the articles relating to the stars of the day, fuelling her dreams of a better life. Helping her father in the fields sometimes brought unexpected delights. If Dolly dug up an old piece of glass, after washing it in the river it would immediately set her imagination racing. Was it a precious stone, might it be worth money, could it buy her beautiful clothes?

In describing her early life Dolly dramatised, "It was a fight for survival to keep the rats from chewing fingers and noses off the little babies," but on a more credible note she said, "We were so poor, I thought anyone whose house was clean was rich. If someone came to our house who had a lipstick, I thought they was millionaires." Dolly and Loretta Lynn, who had a similarly poor country upbringing, sometimes reminisced about life in "them old cabins" and how snow and rain used to blow through the cracks in winter. Even summer brought its problems. Dolly once said to Loretta, "Remember when you had company coming, how you'd shoo the flies out the door with a towel, then slam the door real fast."

The Parton children slept fully clothed three or four to a bed and would continue to wear the same clothes, sometimes after a sibling might have wet the bed. In wintertime covers were kept securely in place to keep the generated heat in the bed. The bedclothes were recycled sacks or rough blankets which kinfolk had brought home from the army. The first time the children saw white sheets was on the stretcher used to take Avie Lee to the hospital when she suffered a miscarriage.

Lee Parton had a short temper and exploded on one occasion when he found a grey kitten belonging to Dolly on the kitchen table. He took it outside and killed it by throwing it against a tree. Bobby kept a rooster in a cage specifically for fighting. He would take it to school and during breaks forced it to fight against other so-called game roosters belonging to his friends. Such acts of cruelty were commonplace in rural East Tennessee. Though Dolly was introduced to many of the harsher aspects of nature, she was also imbued with a sense of reverence for the natural world around her which she has never lost. As she told one interviewer, "What was good about growing up here, out in the country, is that we're very close to nature, and free to grow up the way we did. We didn't have cars to get hit by, we didn't have neighbours to get raped by, we just lived way up out in the woods, close to God and close to nature. I think coming out of that gave me a real good solid foundation, a good wholesome attitude."

Talking in 2003 she related her love of nature to her spiritual feelings. "I guess the beauty that surrounded me was what I loved the most. I loved the mist on the mountains, the bluebirds on the fencepost and the pastures filled with purple ironweed and wild daisies." Such feelings were poetically illustrated in lyrics Dolly wrote and published in a 1979 book called *Just The Way I Am*. The selections in the book aimed to give, "reasons to live, reasons to love and reasons to smile". When talking about her upbringing Dolly usually pulls the same stories out from her back pages, the ones she has chosen as suitable for public consumption. While not omitting the grimmer realities of her childhood, as Dolly has said, "It's really just my true nature to be a positive person. I have no negative sides." This perhaps explains her tendency to make light of the problems in her parents' marriage. Despite their endurance over trying times, the tensions between Lee and Avie Lee affected their children. Marrying young and being launched into a life of hard graft, there was little in the way of romance. Lee rarely remembered birthdays and Avie Lee pretended not to notice. By contrast, one Christmas he swore the children to secrecy over his plan to buy a wedding ring for his wife – they had never been able to justify the cost before. According to Dolly all of the children were happy to go along with Lee's plan. Generally they were given at least one shop-bought toy at Christmas; for Dolly something made of plastic, even if it was just a cheap doll, was regarded as a luxurious treat.

Willadeene portrays her parents as contrasting in character, to put it crudely, the mother's saint to the father's sinner. Lee swore quite a lot and to try to counter this Avie Lee would teach the children an alternative lexicon but the children invariably preferred their father's vocabulary. The common and often tempestuous rows were inevitably a source of worry for the children since they lived in a house which afforded no escape. When things got really bad Avie Lee would threaten to leave. It then became an issue as to which of the children was going to stay with their father and who was going to leave the security of the established family home to go with their mother; there was never any question of Lee being the one to move. Invariably Dolly found it impossible to choose. It was in her nature to want to remain on good terms with both parents, and rather than make a choice she would run back and forth between her parents in a way that caused amusement all round and helped to break the tension. In this way she acted as a kind of emollient figure, using humour to bring peace in the family. Willadeene makes light of it but such a role can be extremely stressful for young developing children who tend to suppress their own strong emotions for the good of the family.

Regarding her parents Stella Parton said, "Well, my dad had all he could handle, working from the wee hours of the morning till late at night trying to provide for a family of 12 children and an ailing wife, so he really was not there to observe us other than to make sure that we were provided for, which was a roof over our heads and food and if, you know, we became critically ill, to make sure that there was money to get us into hospital." Interviewed in 1994 Dolly said, "Mom and Dad loved us but didn't have time for all of us. We only got picked up when we were being nursed or to have our butts whipped."

The reasons for the family conflicts were easy to attribute to Lee's desire, "to blow off his own steam", as Stella puts it. "He was quite absent basically." Blowing off steam usually meant drinking at weekends; Avie Lee was against having alcohol in the house and so, apart from his furtive domestic supply, if Lee wanted to drink openly he had to go out. Subsistence farmers like Lee had few prospects of advancement beyond daylong physical toil, and with the constant demands of a large family it's unsurprising that he sought release in this way. To a large extent life was mainly a question of survival. It seems though that the attraction of town to Lee might have gone beyond simply drinking with friends. In a place and at a time when there were few entertainments to be had, election year in Sevier County provided an excuse for revelry.

Many townsfolk stood for public office as road commissioners and district constables, and months before Election Day in August, candidates and their teams tried to garner support by offering free drinks, meals, or financial bribes. By the time evening came round many of the men were very much the worse for drink and in the mood for the company of what Willadeene refers to as "shady ladies" or "strollops" (a combination of "strumpets" and "trollops") as Avie Lee called them.

On one particular Election Day Avie Lee asked if Willadeene had seen her father anywhere – he was supposed to have taken her to vote – and Willadeene naively replied that she had seen her father and two male relatives in the company of three women near a school which was serving as a polling station. Avie Lee immediately set off in hot pursuit. Although not widely publicised or reported, it is a matter of record that Lee Parton fathered two children outside of his marriage – one of them a boy the same age as Dolly. No doubt this only added to the tension. Dolly has stated that Avie Lee subsequently proposed that the children produced by Lee's extramarital liaisons should become part of the family, though this did not happen.

One of the children bore a strong resemblance to Lee and attended the same high school as Dolly. "He had a thing for me, he had this feeling for me," she said, describing it as "awkward and strange". The boy was unaware that he was Dolly's half-brother and she did not see it as her place to tell him. The incident would inspire Dolly to write a song simply called 'Robert'. In a 1984 conversation with Mauria Moynihan and Andy Warhol for *Interview* magazine, she confirmed that her father ran around and had some children "outside of us". However, in mitigation and in probable recognition of the era's realities, she said, "He was a good father and a good husband. He always came home. He was just a little wild . . . I'm a combination of both of them. But he always loved Mamma and he always treated us good."

Dolly later conceded that life did gradually get easier when her parents were able to afford a larger home. One bright spot came when Dolly saw television for the first time when the whole family drove to Knoxville, to her Aunt Estelle's house, to watch a film on the life of Dr Robert F. Thomas.

Once she achieved fame, Dolly did her best to encourage children to stay in school and to get the most out of education. Her own schooling, however, was largely an unpleasant experience. Living way back in the holler the Partons had a walk of around two miles over mixed terrain to get to the schoolhouse. In the summer they usually went barefoot (which to this day conjures up a sense of liberation for Dolly) and in winter their footwear was often insufficient to protect them against the elements. The children received only one new pair of shoes each year that soon wore out and once they arrived at the schoolhouse they had to warm themselves beside the stove before they were ready for lessons.

One of the first schools Dolly attended was Locust Ridge, located in the foothills of Webb Mountain in a spot also known as Mountain View. Dolly has said she doubted if the one lady teacher there had much more than a high school education. The schoolhouse comprised as few as 15 pupils who sat in rows according to which grade they were in. (Locust Ridge covered grades one to eight. Dolly left in grade five when the family moved house.) The teacher would sit and work with one row while the others got on with their studies.

"I hated it," Dolly told *Playboy* in 1978. "Even to this day, when I see a school bus, it's just depressing to me. I think, those poor little kids having to sit in there in the summer days, staring out the window . . . It reminds me of every feelin' and every emotion that I had in school . . . but it was better than stayin' home every day. Momma was sick a lot; we had some real hard times . . . The first four or five members of the family had it real bad, you know, rougher than the rest."

Dolly claimed in *Rolling Stone* that by about the age of 10, after Willadeene had got married and left home, she sometimes found herself running the family when her mother was ill. As with many rural families, the need for help on the land ensured school attendance took a back seat as Dolly confirmed, "My daddy didn't particularly want me to go to school, my momma didn't care. In the mountains schoolin' is not that important . . . if you make it through the 8th grade (approximately age 13) you're highly educated . . . I had a lot of ambition and needed school because I needed to be with people." According to some reports when Locust Ridge burned down Dolly did not attend school for some time afterwards.

There were a number of reasons why the local children did not go on to high school – one of them being the simple fact that to catch a school bus involved such a long walk. In later years, after the roads were improved, buses were able to get closer to where the children lived and the numbers going to secondary school increased.

When Dolly moved to a larger and newer public school at Caton's Chapel, she found that many of the pupils came from better-off back-grounds and she and her siblings were often singled out. One of Dolly's teachers, Tillman Robertson, recalled that the Parton family "were not paupers, just good poor people". When the family budget could not accommodate Dolly's new school coat, Avie Lee sewed together a collection of odd scraps from coloured material that were intended for a quilt. Perhaps with the intention of making the garment appear more attractive to Dolly she told the biblical story of Joseph and his coat of many colours, even though this risked drawing attention to the fact that the coat had been a cause of family jealousy because Avie Lee had spent so much time making it.

Dolly, who was about nine at the time, hoped that her distinctive coat would attract admiring looks but when the other pupils saw the homespun garment, they teased her. "That's why it hurt me so bad when the kids laughed, because I was so proud of it. I especially liked the bright colours, and I thought I was the prettiest thing in school." Dolly could not under-stand how something her mother had built up to be special in her mind could be the cause of such cruel mockery. She was pushed and pulled by the children who shouted, "Rag top."

Dolly wore the coat for a school photograph and produced a defiant smile to match. Though she has invariably claimed to be proud of her background, it was a potential source of embarrassment and discomfort at school. During one class on the subject of health and nutrition a teacher asked each student to say what he or she had eaten for breakfast, so that the other members of the class could decide whether it was a balanced meal. When the other students talked about fruit juices, cereals, bacon, eggs and toast, Dolly knew her biscuits and gravy would be held up to ridicule so she decided to lie by saying she'd had orange juice, oatmeal and eggs and bacon and toast. Unfortunately her brother Denver was in the same class and Dolly worried that he would tell the truth. Fortunately he said, "I had the same thing Dolly had."

Though she made little effort at school, Dolly never failed a subject. Those teachers who have subsequently talked about her all claim that it never occurred to them that she would be somebody famous. Several did, however, comment on her good memory, especially for lyrics. One teacher, Mrs Archie Ray McMahan, noticed the early signs of determination on Dolly's part. "Sometimes if she thought she ought to have her say, she said it . . ." she told writer Alanna Nash. "If she wanted to talk, or tell something, she did, or if the other children said anything to her, she always had an answer for them. I don't remember anyone ever trying to run over Dolly, so I guess she had spirit from the beginning."

Avie Lee also recalled Dolly's singing getting her into trouble at school. "She'd just be sitting there singing when she should have been paying attention to the teachers." On other occasions she disrupted classes with her exuberance by suddenly bursting into song. She also talked a lot in class and used to have to write out hundreds of times, "I will not talk in class." Dolly had an aversion to physical education and did her best to avoid it though she did do well at home economics, no doubt because of the many practical lessons absorbed at home. She became a member of the "Future Homemakers of America", a local state and national organisation whose goal was to improve the quality of individual, family and community life. Dolly was awarded high grades for music which helped boost her average marks even though all this involved was playing snare drum in the school band.

In the band with Dolly was Judy Ogle who was born on the same day.[*] It was the start of a lifelong, symbiotically close relationship as Dolly says, "She knows everything it's humanly possible to know about me. We met when we were around seven. The day I walked into the schoolroom, our eyes just kinda interlocked. We were just ugly, poor little trashy kids. But

---

[*] As with many of the people close to Dolly, Ogle is an entirely private figure about whom very little is known beyond the snippets Dolly chooses to reveal.

that thing within me said, 'This will be your lifelong friend. This is the one.' She felt it too."

Writer Steve Eng described Ogle as Dolly's "surrogate sister"; Dolly herself calls Judy "sissy" and has said that she is as close to her as any of her real sisters. Judy recalled band rehearsal with Dolly: "We both played drums. We were assigned a kind of practice period in the band room before regular band practice. We were supposed to use the time to learn how to read music and all that, but we never did. Dolly always went to the piano and wrote songs . . ." Judy would write down the songs as Dolly wrote them, a pattern that became an established part of Dolly's creative process in later years. To the present day she still cannot read music, preferring to sing her songs into a tape recorder to be professionally transcribed.

Looking back, Avie Lee never thought of the Parton family as particularly destitute, rather they simply did the best under their circumstances. As she said, "Some people may look at it as if we were real poor, but I can't see it that way. We were just ordinary Americans, and I was always real proud of what we had." Dolly thought her father was stingy with money but soon came to realise that he had to be careful as there was little to spare. Indeed she attributes her own skill with money to lessons learned from her father.

Knowingly or otherwise, Dolly's parents taught her many other import-ant lessons in self-sufficiency. Dolly also acquired the assertiveness and toughness that came from having to compete with a large number of sib-lings. Stella confirms that her sister had big dreams which her parents actively encouraged. "I used to feel bashful and shy," Dolly recalled, "but I quickly learned something – you are just as important as anyone else. We all put on our shoes and britches the same way."

# Chapter 4

OVER the years Dolly Parton has been asked what she would have done if she had not turned to music. On one occasion she claimed she was so determined to escape the monotony of life in the mountains that the idea of being a stripper briefly crossed her mind; another time she mentioned the possibility of becoming a beautician. Her desire to get away was such that as a child it was said she once started digging a hole after learning that it would lead her to China; she knew nothing of that far-off land but in her mind it symbolised an exotic place of escape. "I suppose the only other desire I ever had was to become a missionary. I was brought up in a religious family."

Dolly could have been forgiven for seeking to escape from her roots. Apart from her parents' privations and lack of prospects, she was a girl. In those days, that meant overt discrimination in the South simply on the basis that girls would grow up into women and would therefore be expected to keep the home fires burning while raising children, in other words following in the footsteps of their mothers. It was a lesson learned the hard way at school by Frieda Parton. Being twins, it was natural for Frieda and her brother Floyd to sit together. However, after a short time it was decided that Floyd should be moved to a different classroom. Frieda protested with bitter tears to no avail. According to Willadeene, the teacher explained that Floyd was cleverer than Frieda was and so should be in a class for brighter children and that, "Because Floyd was a boy, he had to know so much more than a girl, since he would have to support a wife someday and [Frieda] would just be a wife."

The idea of a woman escaping her place in life through a career in music was virtually unimaginable. However, the crucial underlying factor was Dolly's rare musical gift. It was noted by members of the family and some of her teachers that she had a voice of exceptional individual quality though there were some dissenters who felt Dolly was not a good enough singer to be performing in front of the whole school. Where her vocal ability came from was not obvious. There was music in the genes but no individual vocal gift which stood out in a distinctive way. One possible source, doubtfully proposed by Dolly's mother, was a childhood illness which caused her tonsils to swell up; a pustule formed on one of her tonsils which later burst. In reality Dolly's striking singing voice came about by chance. However, its headlong development towards that special timbre mixing childlike tenderness with adult passion and emotion – a fitting combination to emanate from her particular upbringing – was almost certainly attributable in part to more circumstantial reasons.

Dolly grew up without the influence of singers on television or films as the Parton's budget would not stretch to such luxuries and the church disapproved. Accordingly Dolly's voice developed through the various stages of childhood. Family and church provided much of Dolly's early musical experiences; once, when asked about influences, she said she was more impressed by the singing of her uncles, aunts and her mother than by any singing stars. "I think what soul I have in my voice, the feeling that's there, is strictly from my church-singing days. I get a feeling from singing gospel songs that I never get from singing anything else. But that same soul and feeling and sincerity leaks over into anything I sing . . ."

When talking about her own style of music Dolly claims she was more akin to authentic folk than traditional country. This is logical in view of the nature of the music she was exposed to as a child. Firstly there were the Elizabethan ballads, based on Anglo-Celtic folk songs, preserved for centuries by Appalachian mountain people and handed down through generations. The songs were often written from the standpoint of women struggling against the odds – whether against the rigours of life or their menfolk. The vocal improvisation found in many Celtic ballads seems to have led to that particular tonal, nasal quality preferred by many traditional Appalachian singers. Even as the content was changed to reflect American locations, contexts, and occupations, many 19th-century versions of the child ballads still referred to lords and ladies, castles and ghosts, and retained as their central theme, love affairs and personal relationships. Under the puritanical influence of the church, many explicit lyrics were softened and cleaned up. British paganism was frowned upon, and religious censorship resulted in ballads where repentance supplanted sinful behaviour. American tastes meant that male-dominated occupational experiences, such as logging, ranching and mining were showcased, as were disasters and tragedies.

Then there was the powerfully emotional religious music of the fundamentalist churches which took the form of ballads, hymns and revival spiritual songs. One of Dolly's all-time favourite gospel songs was (and is) 'If We Never Meet Again'. Services in East Tennessee were sometimes accompanied by shouting, rolling on the floor and even snake handling, a particularly hardcore exercise of religious faith. It was based on a literal interpretation of Mark 16:18. "They shall take up serpents . . . and it shall not hurt them." In the early 20th century former bootlegger George Went Hensley, aka Little George, took a rattlesnake box into the pulpit. He reached in and lifted out the venomous viper, showing his faith by taking God at his word. He then challenged his congregation to do the same. The practice continued for years among small groups of devotees despite deaths and injuries. Church, emotion and singing were inextricably linked and formed a lasting impression on Dolly's musical development.

It was only later, when there was a radio in the house, that Dolly got to hear the country music of the early Fifties on a regular basis. Lee Parton acquired a battery operated radio when Dolly was still quite young but the reception was poor. Dolly heard the cream of country music from its spiritual home, Nashville's Grand Ole Opry, but the singers' voices were often muffled. Of the non country people she professed a liking for bright and peppy singers such as Connie Francis and Brenda Lee. When it came to generating her own music she said, "It was natural, when I wrote, to reflect back to the old songs we used to sing, and part of my melodies kind of carried that old-timey flavour without me realising it until after they were done. And I still do that, those folky type melodies are the best of all." It could of course be said that many children experienced similar influences, but unlike other children Dolly had an uncommon need to make music, storing her lyrics and poems in an old battered wooden box. She craved an audience, taking every opportunity to sing for relatives, at school concerts, talent shows and church halls. Speaking in 1993 she said, "I thought I was singin' to a lot of people when I was singin' to my brothers and sisters and the chickens and the dogs with a tin can as a make-believe microphone."

Her elementary school teacher Tillman Robertson arranged for some of the pupils to visit Cas Walker's radio show in Knoxville, a city which represented a radically different world from the one Dolly was accustomed to. The children got to see the midday *Merry Go Round* show and, as a group, sing a song. Dolly was instantly smitten by the scene in the recording studio and a photograph of the children's appearance has Dolly, wearing a simple smock and a pair of sports shoes, right at the front of a nervous-looking group of girls next to Walker himself. Dolly was also drawn to the idea of playing an instrument and around the age of six or seven she rigged up a guitar from an old mandolin and a couple of bass guitar strings; it was crude but she could pick out a few sounds.

There is a certain perception that people with exceptional creative gifts are aware of their ability. In a 1970 interview John Lennon said he believed he was a genius from an early age and could not understand why it took so long for others to recognise the fact. Dolly also made it clear that she felt she was destined to be famous. "I tried to be different, 'cause I knew I was different in every other way. My voice was different, I looked different, even the reaction in school when I grew up – I was just different. I don't know why I felt like a misfit. It bothered me for a long time. I just couldn't relate to the things they did, and they couldn't relate to the things I was doing, because I was somewhere out in left field writin' songs and livin' within myself, livin' in a world beyond what we were. I always wanted to look different, too, I didn't want to look ordinary."

Of her singing style she continued, "I just never wanted to be like anyone else . . . I never tried to imitate anybody and I just let it come out like it did, and I know I have developed my own voice since I never tried to do anything different with my voice, what was really there. I just tried to strengthen it." Veteran country music disc jockey Bill Black concurs. "With Dolly you can't really hear somebody who came before her that has influenced her."

Dolly also had particular character traits which were important elements in the development of her vibrant persona. Stella describes her sister as a hyperactive child, saying "I think that if they had Ritalin (a powerful drug given to children with Attention Deficit Hyperactivity Disorder – ADHD) back when Dolly was a kid she would have definitely been put on it, because she was always into everything . . . she would have needed it. Hyperactive children can get in a lot of trouble, they can be somewhat obnoxious but you don't think about that as a child, you just think of your older sibling as being a pain in the neck. Just recently I have viewed a piece of home video, the only piece of home video that we have . . . and you can see on that Dolly was so hyperactive that she was just a misbehaving child actually. I thought that she misbehaved badly and I wonder if she saw it herself as an adult and thought, 'Lord I was a real pain in the butt.'

"She knocks a cigarette out of a guy's mouth onstage, she butts in and gets in the camera when it's not really about her; she was a needy child. I guess she needed attention so [singing] was a perfect career for her . . . on the home video she's like, 'Where's the camera? If it's not on me I'll make sure it is.'"

In an interview with disc jockey Barbara Barri Dolly confirmed that she always needed a lot of attention. "I guess I was a little spastic jerk. Probably a pain in the butt." Asked if she was thought of as the class clown, Dolly replied, "Yeah, pretty much. I was always in trouble; not meanin' to be. I got a whippin' every day I was in school 'cause I couldn't sit still. I'd sit and not even knowin', I'd be bangin' my heels against the desk, makin' noise or I'd get up to sharpen my pencil a thousand times. Didn't know it. I was always in some kind of trouble. I was so fidgety, spastic is the word."

Dolly's desire for attention was simply not able to be accommodated in a large family whose parents were so unavoidably preoccupied with day-to-day living. This in itself may have acted as a spur towards her burning ambitions. Stella Parton: "I think my mother was one of the most insightful people of all and she knew that Dolly needed that attention and she knew that she was not going to be able to give that to her and so she tried to make each of us special in our own way."

Avie Lee was encouraging when it came to her children's dreams. "Give them a free mind and they'll go places," as she said in a television interview.

Dolly's own description of her place in the family revealed a deep sensitivity, insecurity even, on her part. As she saw it older sister Willadeene got more attention being the responsible one, her older brothers were stronger and bigger, and then there was her. "I was born in an odd spot. My feelings could get hurt so easily because I always wanted to be loved, I wanted to be touched, I wanted to touch somebody. I wanted everybody to love me, so I think I was louder than I should have been. I was just trying to get attention. Always felt like I was somebody special, maybe it's because I needed to be somebody special. I just always knew I was going to be a star. I was always going to be rich so I could buy things for Mommy and Daddy . . . buy them a big house.

"I knew before I was 10 that I was going to be a star and be famous and that I was going to make money. I did truly." Her mother remembered one occasion when Dolly saw a magazine with a picture of Marilyn Monroe and said, "I wanna be like her and be a movie star." Such an ambition was as likely to attract ridicule as encouragement – folk in the mountains of East Tennessee were too busy wondering where the next few dollars were coming from than to entertain such fantasies – but for Dolly it was for real. "I believed it would come true because I put legs on my dreams the way people ought to put legs on their prayers." Dolly wrote down all the goals she wanted to achieve out of life and what she had to do in order to realise them.

In the old days Avie Lee had a catalogue, which she called "the wish book" because it "made you wish you had things you never did have". In compiling her own wish list Dolly may well have been taking a leaf out of her mother's book the difference being that she truly believed she could attain all she had written down. "I think I'd make it at anything I did. If I had to work in a factory, I'd be the best worker there. If I was in a restaurant, I'd end up headwaiter. I can be happy anywhere. People have got to learn the difference between success and being successful and failing and being a failure." Such a go-getting attitude was all the more remarkable since Dolly is on record as saying that self-pity and depression was a trait of her family.

As a child Dolly was curious to the point of being nosy. "I was creative and real impressionable, but I always had a sparklin' personality, and I was always just real happy when people came to see us. I was always real curious and I was afraid somebody would say somethin' and I'd miss it, so I'd just play around the porch or sit under the porch and listen. The women would be talkin' about all their personal problems and all the pains they had with the time of the month and their pregnancies. I didn't know what to make of all that, but I knew there was a great mission there that I was gonna find out about. There was no way that they could have a secret from me." Dolly saw herself as an observer, something of an outsider, mature before her time. "I don't even remember thinkin' like a child. I remember always being curious about things, out in the woods by myself, or in the fields taking flowers apart, or something, to see how they got that way. I'm just a curious person. I guess that explains why I write a lot of the deep songs that I do."

Dolly had an uncle, one of her mother's brothers, called Bill Owens whose musical outlook went further than having folk appreciate his contribution to an informal sing-along session at a relation's house. He had been writing songs since before Dolly was born and hoped that he might achieve some kind of musical career for himself as a writer and performer, though he did not think in terms of stardom as his young niece did. Bill recognised Dolly's talent; seeing a spark of something in her he hadn't seen in any of the other children. As he said, "Dolly was singing around home all the time. She'd sing whilst she washed dishes; she'd sing when she put her younger brothers and sisters to bed. And she sang good."

When about eight a delighted Dolly was given an old guitar by one of her uncles. After Bill showed her the basic chords, in no time she was creating licks and building tunes. As Bill said, "All of a sudden the thought came to me that I should take her to the Cas Walker broadcasts." Caswell (invariably known as Cas) Orton Walker, a former Kentucky coal miner, was a swaggering entrepreneur of the old school, a self-made supermarket tycoon who had started off with a wheelbarrow of groceries which he took door to door before opening his own small grocery store. He was also a local politician, first elected to Knoxville City Council in 1941, and was once described as the best-known institution in Knoxville. The city was only about 40 miles from the Parton's house but for 10-year-old Dolly it might as well have been on the other side of the world. Of her visits to Knoxville she said, "I really thought it was the whole world right in one town."

Walker had an ebullient personality and was always looking for ways to promote his business. He purchased blocks of airtime on television and radio from early morning until late at night, every day of the week. The shows he sponsored were broadcast to the East Tennessee, Virginia and Carolina areas and provided a springboard for many country and bluegrass artists. He talked a lot about politics on the radio and his views were often more liberal than many of his audience even though he openly dis-approved of rock'n'roll. Bill Owens, who had previously played on Walker's show, arranged for Dolly to attend an audition at the same studios Tillman Robertson had taken her class to. There are differing accounts of the outfit she wore for her first audition but it was definitely something special. According to one report, she was dolled up in a blue silk dress, bought specially for the occasion; another had it that she was wearing a gingham dress and her hair was tied in pigtails. It seems likely that she asked to be able to sing a religious song as part of her audition.

Dolly acknowledges her debt to Owens in getting her early career off the ground, "When I was 10 years old, Bill worked with me and rehearsed songs with me, and he got me ready to audition for the Cas Walker show in Knoxville. So really he was the start of it all . . . he had the confidence in me; he believed in me. Everything I did in the early part of my career he was responsible for. Of course it might have happened anyway, but there's a chance it might not have happened if it had not been for him." Although Dolly has said that Owens was more like a brother than a manager or an uncle, the writer Steve Eng has suggested that he and Avie Lee signed a contractual document giving him the right to manage Dolly until she was 18.

Lee Parton was doubtful about the merits of Dolly going to Knoxville. As Dolly said, "He was real dyed-in-the-wool country. When I was growing up, he didn't believe in women cutting their hair, or wearing trousers or anything like that – and he sure didn't like the idea of me becoming a singer. He had never heard tell of someone from our poor, unknown background making it in music." However, Lee was too busy making ends meet to be able to pay close attention to what one of his daughters was doing or to put any obstacle in the way of her progress. The audition duly took place and caused quite a stir. As Owens recalled, "When Dolly started to sing, announcers and other people from all over the building came in, announcers from upstairs and everywhere, just to hear this new kind of talent. She was an instant hit, and Cas hired her on the spot."

Walker said that he offered Dolly a job because unlike most other people, she said she wanted to *work* for him. Though Dolly had something of the tomboy about her as a young girl and was reasonably self-confident, she was, unsurprisingly, scared and extremely nervous before making her first appearance. However, she soon overcame her nerves and received a rapturous response from the small studio audience, stating in her 1994 autobiography it was as if they were saying, "Yes, yes we love you." It was the start of a lifelong love affair with her public.

Dolly started making regular appearances on Cas Walker's *Farm And Home Hour* on station WIVK, Knoxville in 1956. Some early broadcasts on radio station WSEV took place at the Paris Theater, Sevierville; Walker sponsored a live country and gospel radio show there on Saturday afternoons. Dolly included the occasional gospel song in her repertoire which was particularly well appreciated by the local audience. Soon she included a few spiritual and country songs she had written herself. Interviewed in 1977 she described some of her material as "just real dreadful, plain, sorrowful country songs". To begin with she had no idea what all the equipment was for; she just stood where she was told to and sang into the microphone on cue. Initially she felt the acclaim she received came not because she was especially good but rather because she was a cute little girl who had the nerve to get up there and do it.

Her love of singing and her desire to perform in public helped to overcome her initial nerves. Quite apart from the learning experience such performances afforded Dolly, the Cas Walker shows were beamed over a wide geographic expanse and thus introduced her to thousands of households. Dolly was soon appearing on television as well as radio for Walker and during the following eight years, she worked at various Tennessee venues. In surviving cine film taken when Dolly was about 11, it's striking just how young and small yet equally feisty and determined she looks, as she sings her heart out. A fast-talking Walker made the introductions while plugging his business. He would walk behind the singers or banjo pickers holding a sign saying something like, "Fresh greens, 19 cents a mess." Interviewed in old age Walker recalled that Dolly's voice was "always unusual . . . most young people's voices changed, but hers never did. She was always great fun." He also claimed that he had the biggest radio show of anybody at that time and that Dolly was the biggest draw.

She performed all through the Easter vacation, on holidays such as Thanksgiving, and all summer long, sometimes missing school. This was hardly a source of regret not least because her local celebrity status attracted unwelcome attention from some of the other children at school. On one occasion she was dragged into the school cloakroom and locked in. There was no light and she was terrified; she also hated the dank and sweaty smell. The incident left her with a fear of the dark and she has always slept with a night light on. On another occasion some kids tried to rip her top off at a time when her breasts were starting to develop.

Long aware of Dolly's passion for music, in contrast to her husband, Avie Lee took a more indulgent view of Dolly's forays into the world of entertainment. "Dolly didn't go for sports and things . . . she was thinking of her music every moment she had off . . . she was afraid she would miss out on getting to go somewhere to sing. If she had a date . . . if her Uncle Bill came by and said, 'Dolly we are going to so and so to do a show,' why she'd break that date. She played hooky but the teachers knew Dolly had this special feeling towards music. I imagine any teacher could see that Dolly was better off laying out one day and doing what she had in her heart to do, because then she could come back and be a good student the rest of the week."

Dolly's mother apparently had no qualms about her daughter entering the world of show business so young. "I turned them loose with free wings. They went wherever they wanted to go, because you don't hold nobody back in life. I've always been free-spirited and I wanted my family to be free-spirited. I didn't ever know she would be a successful singer or movie star, but why on earth would I tell her that she wouldn't be?" Avie Lee may have "turned them loose" because the realities of everyday life meant she had little option to do otherwise.

Dolly later professed disappointment at her parents' laxness when they allowed her to go and see a 1958 Robert Mitchum film, *Thunder Road*, which was particularly popular in the rural south. Dolly's parents originally deemed the movie – about moonshiners and bootleg liquor – unsuitable but then relented. She felt that having made a rule they should have stuck to it. However, when Dolly was impatient to get ahead, as she had previously illustrated with biblical allusions, Avie Lee used metaphors from nature to make her point, saying that tadpoles had to go through a lot of changes which took time to achieve and that butterflies did not appear straight away from the cocoon, but this was necessary for them to acquire their strength.

Cas Walker was known for his colourful promotions and on one occasion he laid down a challenge that only somebody with Dolly's grit and determination would be equal to. He advertised a show in Sevierville at a place called The Pines Theater, featuring a 50-foot greased pole erected in the centre of the hall on show nights. It was carefully oiled with petroleum jelly and waiting at the top for some brave soul was a $50 bill. Many tried but most failed to get off the ground. When Dolly was about 11, she was present when Walker put on one of these Saturday night promotions. During a recess she disappeared from the auditorium and went to a nearby mill where she sometimes played, waded out in the water and then rolled around in the sand, which gave her the right type of grip. When Dolly returned to the auditorium she skittered right to the top of the pole and claimed the $50. It was the sort of challenge she could not resist, and showed she had the wit and ingenuity to succeed.

# Chapter 5

DOLLY Parton was a mere 10 years old when her career in music properly began. She still had some growing to do but already her attention was firmly focused on singing, though of course this had to be fitted around school attendance during term time. School itself afforded opportunities, for instance Dolly sang at her college's variety shows, one of which was called 'Gay Times'. Holidays were largely taken up by showcases and attempting to interest people in the music business. In view of her age Dolly was dependent on family members to facilitate her appearances, some of which started as early as 5.30 a.m., which meant rising at four in the morning. For these shows Dolly was driven to Knoxville and then back to school. Bill Owens usually took on the necessary chauffeuring duties while another family member who helped out was Dolly's aunt Estelle Watson, who lived in Vestal, near Knoxville. Dolly stayed with Estelle during holidays to cut down on travelling and her aunt acted as something of a chaperone.

Like Owens, Estelle recognised Dolly's talent and was happy to take her niece to and from the studio. When Dolly started working for Cas Walker she was paid around $20 per week. His shows were "how it all started". Dolly was at the beginning of an apprenticeship which would give her an invaluable grounding, rubbing shoulders with Walker's other weekly guests including The Everly Brothers and Carl and Pearl Butler. One particularly useful piece of advice Walker gave her was to be friends with the camera. "Think of it as somebody you are looking at and like." Remarkably, Dolly appeared on television before her family actually owned a TV set.[*]

With the help of Owens in particular, Dolly was soon on the trail of other outlets for her musical talents. George Hamilton IV first met Dolly when she performed at an annual festival called the Hillbilly Homecoming near Knoxville. Bill took her to the festival as George recalls. "I believe her uncle brought her because she was still a schoolgirl. I remember everybody was so impressed with her and her voice and she was very

[*] She eventually bought them their first TV.

precocious, very young and very confident, in control of everything. The Dolly Parton that we all think of today is completely unlike the way I remember her as a child. She didn't have the platinum blonde hair." Bill told Dolly he was going to make her a star and as he remarked, "She sure did like to hear that." Apart from gospel songs such as 'How Great Thou Art', her growing repertoire included popular songs of the day such as 'Tall Man' by Rose Maddox and 'Everybody's Somebody's Fool' by Connie Francis. However, it did not stretch to the new phenomenon which was exploding out of Sun Studios in Memphis a few hundred miles to the west, courtesy of Elvis Presley, Carl Perkins and Jerry Lee Lewis.

Some evenings Bill and his brother Louis, another family supporter, would drive Dolly back to the studio so that she could record demo tapes which were then sent off to record publishers, companies and the Grand Ole Opry. In one interview legendary Nashville producer Chet Atkins said he first received a tape of Dolly from the Grand Ole Opry announcer Grant Turner, who had been impressed by her appearance on a talent show. Chet turned it down simply because of her age and as he said at the time, "She needs to go to school." Atkins said that he remembered her voice as being quite low when she was young, and that when he heard her again later it was much higher. He reportedly quipped, "I've got to ask her about that some time and see if she's had a sex change operation since then."

In 1957 Dolly travelled to a small recording studio, home to the Goldband label, in Lake Charles, Louisiana where she recorded two songs 'Puppy Love' written by Dolly and Bill Owens and 'Girl Left Alone', a "weepy", which she wrote with Bill and her aunt Dorothy Jo Hope (nee Owens). Another of Dolly's uncles, Robert Henry Owens, generally known as John Henry, was stationed near the studio at the time and he befriended the owner, the late Eddie Shuler, who had the honour of being Dolly's first producer. In a career that lasted well over 50 years he recorded many artists but none would be more famous than the young girl from East Tennessee. John Henry thought the connection with Goldband was a perfect opportunity for Dolly to record her first single. "I was going on 12 when I cut my first record. It was nerve-wracking. I had an uncle who was in the army, stationed in Louisiana. He sent the money for my grandmother and me to buy tickets out there. We didn't have enough money ourselves to buy any food. We cut the record and then he brought us back." Once more Dolly's extended family were involved in helping her budding career though Grandma Rena took a lot of persuading before she would undertake the trip, as she had rarely travelled far from home. Apart from getting to record, for Dolly the trip was a cause for excitement simply because she was in a different part of the country with new surroundings.

Shuler recalled that the tallest stool in the studio was used, "so the microphone could fit and we could get the fullest capabilities of the song she was recording." His son, Johnny, was also present for some of the session and Dolly has said that he was her "first true love", with the pair heading off to sit under an oak tree during breaks in recording. She loved his Cajun-French accent and experienced "bedroom eyes" for the first time. Goldband produced Dolly's first publicity photograph; with short tousled hair brushed back behind her ears and her arms awkwardly folded in front of her, she did not look the part of a recording star in the making; rather a plucky little girl with an endearing, if slightly mischievous grin. The single was not released until 1959 and despite good local promotion it duly disappeared but is now immortalised in the Dolly Parton museum at Dollywood where visitors can listen to the record on a set of headphones and hear a brief burst of its scratchy sound while viewing the original disc.

Shortly after making her first recording, Dolly debuted on the most hallowed stage in country music, the Grand Ole Opry. The Opry was a radio show dating from 1925 and featured many of the top country artists of the day who had to contractually bind themselves to appear there on a regular basis. The Opry only paid union rates but for many the kudos and the publicity were invaluable. The show went out live every weekend on radio station WSM ("We Shield Millions", the catchphrase of the sponsoring insurance company) for many years from the Ryman auditorium in Nashville. From here, the station's 50,000 watts of output meant it could be heard in almost 30 states from Canada to the Rockies and from the Rockies to the Atlantic Ocean. In the days before television it brought music and a sense of community into isolated rural homes.

According to one version of what followed, on a trip to Nashville, Cas Walker discussed the possibility of Dolly appearing, with Jim Denny of the Grand Ole Opry. Though no definite arrangement appears to have been made, Walker obviously received some encouragement because a few weeks later Bill Owens, his brother Louis and wife Colleen drove the 200 miles to Nashville. Initially they were told that Dolly could not appear on the prestigious Saturday night show because union rules dictated that performers had to be at least 18 years old and union members. Dolly listened to all of this naively uncomprehendingly, thinking a union was perhaps some special kind of costume. However, the Friday night show (*Friday Night Opry*) was a possibility.* Having made their way backstage and joined in the general melee of artists, managers and hangers-on in the rather cramped quarters, efforts were made to persuade one of the artists to give up part of his or her slot, each of which consisted of two songs. According to legend, Cajun country singer Jimmy C. Newman was the one who succumbed to the earnest representations made on Dolly's behalf. When interviewed some time later he only had a vague recollection of events. However, there is no doubt that Dolly did get to appear and was introduced by Johnny Cash, then "hotter than a two dollar pistol" in the wake of his massive success with 'I Walk The Line'.

Dolly had met Cash during a previous trip to Nashville when she and Owens had been on a mission to pitch songs. They waited for him in the parking lot outside a venue where he had just played a show. Dolly was tired but she recognised star quality. As she wrote in her 1994 autobiography, "I have never seen a man with such a presence, tall, lanky and sexy with that trademark voice that cut through me like butter . . . I was blown away . . ." According to a number of accounts, including Dolly herself, she sang just one song, the George Jones hit 'You Gotta Be My Baby' and earned thunderous applause from a highly enthusiastic audience which demanded and got around four encores. On a recent radio interview, however, Dolly claimed that she also sang 'Tall Man'. Her last minute inclusion wreaked havoc with the show's time schedule. Despite the evening's great success the group was low on money and so while Dolly and Colleen shared a cheap room in Nashville's YWCA, Bill and Louis slept in the car.

When it came to early efforts to make records and secure appearances such as that on the Grand Ole Opry, song selection tended to focus on popular music or country songs of the day. However, in school and to some extent on Cas Walker's shows, Dolly sang religious and gospel songs of the kind she had been brought up on. Some of her early experiences of attending church had left her with doubts about the merits of religion as practised in her part of East Tennessee, and unconvinced that everybody who got histrionically caught up in expressing their religious conviction on Sunday was genuine; she was left with the feeling that some of them were putting on a show to gain peer approval. It seems she could not quite reconcile the dichotomy between the earthly sins she saw all around her,

---

* In her 1994 autobiography, Dolly said she appeared on the Saturday night show.

such as drinking, cursing, gossiping, womanising, and so on, with the pious platitudes and holy aspirations emanating from the minister and the congregation on the Sabbath day. "So there I sat, trying to be holy, praying for forgiveness for sins I couldn't put my finger on," she wrote in her 1994 autobiography.

For many of her early childhood years Dolly did not make a connection with God in the way that many of her friends and relatives professed to do. However, she desired to have some religious experience, not least because she wanted to develop the same spiritual feelings as others around her. Her parents had bought a farm with about 40 acres of land in Caton's Chapel where Dolly lived until she left home for good in 1964. Dolly was drawn to a derelict church which, over the years, had become the scene of a range of activities not normally carried on inside God's house, namely fighting, drinking and sexual liaisons – Dolly found the empty condom wrappers particularly intriguing.

There was an ancient old piano in the church and this crude instrument provided a kind of musical backing for Dolly as she sang hymns and prayed to God.

As she wrote in her 1994 autobiography, "One day as I prayed in earnest, I broke through some sort of spirit wall and found God." She said she felt sanctified. It was important for her to have done it on her own and not as part of some organised process with surrender to God as the pre-ordained outcome. She discovered God "as a friend I could talk to on a one-to-one basis". She also said the process made it acceptable for her to be a "sexual being".

In keeping with comments made both by Willadeene and Stella, Dolly acknowledged how God came to occupy a pre-eminent position in her life. As she said in one interview, "Us kids, we grew up knowing that God was a better friend to us than either of them, Mamma and Daddy I mean. I'm not a Christian, and I can sin just as big as you or anybody else, and I often do because I'm human, but God is the strongest point in my life. I talk to Him every day." As she came to a greater awareness of the role of God in her life she was able to move beyond some of those childhood fears and uncertainties which grew out of the sometimes febrile atmosphere in church. "You fear God, but He's not a monster in the sky. God fearing to me means a great respect for God, and not fearing that He's going to come crashing down on you for something."

According to various accounts, by about the age of 12, Dolly was physically developed and had attained her fully grown height of about five foot one. However, in an interview with Richard and Judy in the late Nineties she suggested her physical maturity came much earlier. "They (her breasts) come in when I was eight. Yes. I've had titties since I was eight. Got my period when I was nine. I just grew up real quick . . . I looked grown up when I was 11." What eventually emerged was an overstated but unforgettable mixture of childhood innocence and pumped-up sexiness. It was part of the paradox that though Dolly looked brazen and erotic on the outside she also conveyed an impression of being sweet and down to earth underneath. However, her appearance was hardly a straightforward business. Lee (or the church) did not approve of teenage girls painting their faces and some of Dolly's early attempts were adjudged too extreme by her father, leading to a "whippin'" despite her attempt to persuade him that it really was her natural colour. Although she was physically chastised by her father Dolly was not easily deterred. Her efforts to make up her face made use of those ingredients which came most easily to hand. She painted her fingernails with the juice of the wild poke-berry, which yielded a red dye, and for gloss and shine on her lips, she used petroleum jelly. She powdered her face with flour and for eyeliner she used burnt wooden matches which also provided a means of creating beauty marks. Later, she applied two chemical substances, merthiolate* and mercurochrome† to her lips to give a striking rouge appearance. She particularly liked them because they kept their colour for some time.

Dolly has said that the ideas for her appearance came from "a country girl's idea of what glamour is". One of her main objectives was to look different from other girls, to make herself stand out and to thus gain attention. In one interview on the subject Dolly said she felt she was unattractive as a child and such feelings would go some way to explaining a desire to cover up her natural features. Such feelings were clearly not just teenage angst. Some years on she said, "I always thought I was ugly and I still do if I ain't got my make-up and powder on." Willadeene points to another possible reason for Dolly's growing fixation with her appearance. When the various crops that Lee Parton grew – tobacco, potatoes, beans and corn – were ready to be harvested all of the children joined in the effort to gather them in, assisted by neighbours and friends. The boys persistently

---

* The US proprietary name for Thiomersal – a bacteriostatic and fungistatic organomercury compound used as medical disinfectant and as a preservative for biological products – Dolly refers to it as "medicine".
† Proprietary name for the drug Merbromin – a fluorescein, the derivative containing bromine and mercury, obtained as greenish iridescent scales which dissolve in water to give a red solution used as antiseptic.

teased the girls, comparing them to speckled hens if they had freckles or palomino ponies if they had straight square teeth. In response to being told they were skinny or fat the girls would try to get their own back by saying the boys looked like girls. The boys would respond to the less well-endowed ones by saying, "Too bad you'uns don't."

In an interview with Robert K. Oermann, Dolly talked about the "macho redneck attitudes" of her father, brothers and other males in her extended family. While much of this amounted to no more than coarse but essentially good-natured banter, Willadeene hints that the effects of their male dominated world might have been more serious. "We girls have complexes to this day over the way the boys treated us then." Dolly has also said that there were very few "fine gentlemen" where she grew up. In an interview with *Redbook* she said, "I grew up in a house with five sisters, giving my love and bearing my soul to them and knowing that there was a kindness, a sweetness and a depth to them that I didn't get from my brothers." Could such experiences go some way to explaining Dolly's increasingly obsessive desire to disguise her appearance and con-sciously or subconsciously fit in with other people's ideas of what was attractive and what was not? Photographs of Dolly from the various stages of her childhood certainly do not support the view that she was in any way unattractive; quite the contrary – she displayed impish charm and while perhaps not stunningly beautiful she was certainly appealingly pretty. However, teenagers are often highly sensitive about their appearance and it seems that Dolly was more sensitive than most, although she did have her admirers. A display in Dollywood contains a letter (dated January 11, 1960, when she was 13), from a boy which starts, "Just a few lines to answer your letter. I am sorry you got jealous. But you're so pretty that I can't help it."

Dolly had few sartorial models to follow beyond the dowdy fashions available to the women she came into contact with, so she really didn't have much to go on. Dolly was fascinated by the exaggerated make-up and blonde hair of the local hookers in Sevierville as well as the tight-fitting, gaudy clothes they wore. As she put it, "I patterned how I look on the trash in my home town." As a naive girl in her early teens she may not have realised what they did for a living but this did not diminish her appre-ciation of their eye-catching, artificial image. "I always liked the looks of our hookers back home. Their big hair-dos and make-up made them look *more*. When people say that less is *more*, I say *more* is more. Less is *less*; I go for more."

As with the local hookers, Dolly welcomed the opportunity to see something out of the ordinary. She loved county fairs – which usually meant a day off school – and was especially fascinated by the freak shows. "We'd crawl under the fence and look until somebody would kick us in the face to get us out. There was the spider-woman, who was supposed to have been found in the Amazon. And things like the fat lady. I patterned myself after her." Her favourite characters from the stories she came across at school invariably had striking appearances: Mother Goose, Cinderella (after her transformation) and the French aristocratic hauteur of Marie Antoinette.

Around the age of 14, Dolly's baby fine hair started to turn what she referred to as "dishwater blonde" and to complement this she added peroxide to her armoury. Dolly's hair soon became one of her main preoccupations and she responded enthusiastically to the arrival of one particular fashion. "When teasing came out, I just thought I had died and gone to heaven. Being creative with my hands, I started teasing. I fixed everybody's hair. I had the biggest hair in school." Family members were enlisted to help. Stella well recalls how concerned her sister became about the appearance of her hair from the age of about 14 (when Stella was 11). "Well yeah, tell me, she used to make me get up early in the mornings when she was in high school because you know, she's always liked her hair big, fat on top . . . I was good at fixing hair and so she'd make me get up and tease her hair to make sure it was just right at the back even for school so she's always been like that; to me that's exhausting. She had her hair up high, she had a pageboy. It was a showgirl hair-do. Dolly's always wanted to look like a showgirl, a Vegas showgirl."

Stella makes the point that Dolly always wanted to be noticed and that meant having a striking look, with lashings of make-up enhanced by wigs. Speaking in 1994 Dolly related her passion for make-up and golden curly wigs to her poor upbringing. "We really did have nothing when I was a kid. So as soon as I had some money, I went way over the top." Dolly made it clear that her appearance was very much out of preference. "I don't look this way out of ignorance . . . I look this way because I like it. Anybody can look like a common Joe. I look like I came out of a fairy tale." It also made her hard to ignore. Dolly herself has said that by the time she was about 13, people thought she was 18 or 20. This was due to a combination of her well-developed physique, not least her bosom (all the more geometrically protrusive given her lack of height), glitzy make-up, candy floss hair and a penchant for tight-fitting clothes. "I wore my skirts so tight I could hardly wiggle in them."

Dolly has also claimed that when she was young she had a "real pretty body", (it seems her feelings of ugliness related mainly to her facial appearance). Unlike some girls, she did not hide her physical assets, in particular her large chest, a feature which ran in the family. Lee's sisters had large breasts as did Avie Lee because she was pregnant so much. Dolly modelled the squashed together and pushed up look on the hookers she saw in Sevierville. To add to the effect Dolly used to steal the shoulder pads out of her grandmother's coat to boost her bosom size because she realised that it not only attracted attention but was what boys liked.

In contrast to her husband, Avie Lee willingly assisted Dolly's attempts at beautification, perhaps because she herself had been prohibited from wearing make-up and fancy hairstyles as a child. She would make sure that Dolly's jeans were really tight, though "not where they cut your wind off". Dolly's appearance inevitably attracted attention, not all of it favourable. "I had lots of teachers that had a hard time dealing with me because I felt sexy . . . I was the most popular girl in the school for all the wrong reasons . . . I had a foxy personality." Some parents thought she was a bad influence on their children because she told dirty stories and was "always laughin' and jokin' . . ." However, in her defence she says, "I was not a trashy person, I was just fun-lovin'." Dolly claims it was her friends who were in the back of cars doing the very things that their parents assumed *she* did.

Dolly was not particularly popular at school, especially with the girls who assumed she was "whoring around" as she put it. Dolly also claims not to have had many boyfriends in high school partly due to her own physical maturity and social experience, which made her more like a mother than a girlfriend. One of her former suitors, Hollis Hurst, said, "Dolly wasn't ashamed of being poor, she just hated it. She didn't have a lot of confidence in herself as a person but she knew she could sing and she was secure about that. She was so convinced of her talent that she would frequently sing to me when we were out on our dates and that ain't easy for a self-conscious teenage girl to do." One school photograph of Dolly aged about 15 shows her at the centre of a group of seven boys. She always had a knack of being at the centre of photographs – in an older shot from the early Fifties of her Mountain View school group, in the middle of 28 unorganised children stands Dolly wearing a highly visible striped top. A blown-up shot of Dolly's senior trip to Washington DC* shows her symmetrically positioned at the middle of a much larger group, her bouffant hair-do irresistibly drawing attention. Was it always important for her to

* On display at Dollywood.

be the focal point of a group of people? Or did she just naturally gravitate there? There is little doubt that she instinctively knew how to make people look at her. Apparently the bus driver who transported the group around the capital constantly referred to her as "Marilyn".

Dolly's desire for attractive clothes was fuelled by shopping catalogues, an important method of acquiring goods for people living in the country. As a youngster Dolly had an invalid grandmother on her father's side, Bessie, who was largely bedridden and though Dolly undertook less pleasing chores such as cleaning out Bessie's bedpan and brushing her false teeth (a rare commodity – some sets were usually available from the local funeral home), Bessie always had the latest Sears Roebuck catalogue and enjoyed ordering things for herself and her granddaughter, even though Dolly wanted just about everything on display.

Although Dolly often talked knowingly about the opposite sex in reality she was quite shy around boys, apparently telling one friend that she, "felt like getting into a giant bag and zipping it up all the way over her head", before going out on a date. In other interviews over the years Dolly revealed that she and her contemporaries started experimenting with sexual matters at an early age, in barns and quieter parts of the forest. "You're bored, there's little to do in the mountains. You don't have toys and discos so you're going to play doctors and nurses sometimes. But I always knew the harder they tried to keep things a deep dark secret, in all truth, the more fun it must be. I wasn't afraid . . . to explore. So I don't have hang-ups about sex today. If you trust and know who you are dealing with, there should be no controls on love."

In Dolly's 1978 *Playboy* interview, when directly asked the age she lost her virginity she replied, "Now I can't tell you that, because that would probably be real perverted. As little kids we were *always* experimenting." This was an example of Dolly's professional skill of skirting around an awkward question by giving a reply which provided some insight but left specific questions unanswered. In another interview Dolly said, "When I was a girl and fooling around I was scared to death I'd get pregnant." The implication is that her first sexual experiences occurred at a comparatively young age though exactly how young remains a secret known only to Dolly and few others.*

When talking about this time in her life Dolly paints a picture of an

---

* In later years, no doubt conscious of her public image, she suggested that her loss of virginity occurred when she was older.

isolated figure. She said that she felt like a "misfit" – the girl nobody took home to their mother. It seems she did not naturally ally herself with particular groups of people, feeling close to only her family and one special friend in Judy Ogle.

Though talk of making it as a successful singer was as likely to produce sarcasm and ridicule as encouragement and support, Dolly had cultivated a single-minded streak.

# Chapter 6

BY her mid-teens Dolly had become an experienced if as yet un-polished veteran of the East Tennessee music scene, having appeared in concert at Johnson City before an audience of more than 10,000 people on a show headlined by Carl and Pearl Butler. Dolly's style was largely her own because she had not encountered or been influenced by many other artists; she was later able to make the claim that, "I was pretty much established on the radio before I paid that much attention to other people."

Dolly was making progress along her chosen course but some felt she was growing up too fast. Stella Parton: "When I think back on it . . . she left home at 10 and lived with an aunt, 30–35 miles away, and they lived a lot better than we did and it was very difficult for her to have to come back into our reality on weekdays." Dolly first used a flush toilet at her aunt's house though it took a bit of getting used to. "I just thought it was going to suck me right down." Stella recalls that Dolly's time away from her family inevitably drove a wedge between them. "All through the holidays she was never there, all through the weekends she was always gone so she really never felt like she fitted into that reality and at times she resented it and because she resented it I think she felt guilty because she loved us but she didn't want to have to be back in that reality. Can you imagine making $20 a week when you're 10 years old, when you come from such a poor family? That's like making hundreds of dollars a week now so that was like being rich and then she has to come back and share a bedroom with me or help take care of the younger children. That was not fun, so that propelled her to say, 'I think I'm getting out of here and this is what I know how to do, this is what I love to do,' and I think that's where her ambition was born in that desperation to never have to be like our mother."

Late in his life, Cas Walker, resident in a comfortable nursing home on the outskirts of Maryville, Tennessee, recalled finishing a late night show in Somerset, Kentucky not long after he gave Dolly a job on Knoxville Radio WROL. As Walker recalled, "Dolly was such a little thing . . . so very tired, that she slept on my lap the whole trip back to Knoxville." What a contrast this provides to the experiences of countless young aspiring artists of the time who travelled long journeys in cars or Greyhound buses, with friends of their own age. It could of course be argued that the end justified the means and Dolly was being presented with a rare opportunity to make something of her life. However, it was a highly questionable state of affairs to have a young girl of school age travelling to venues far from her home, singing in front of mainly adult audiences and travelling with a much older man who had a vested interest in her. Should her parents not have taken more of an active role in placing strict limits on how much time Dolly was able to spend singing and travelling?

Stella Parton: "She was 10 years old. A 10-year-old child should not be put in that situation and be shuttled back and forth. Daddy wanted his kids near him. As he put it, 'I want my damn young'uns at home,' so that meant, 'Where's Dolly?' When he was there, there was a head count and Mama had to make dozens and dozens and dozens of excuses why Dolly wasn't there for the head count. But for school and through the week she had to be home unless there was a good reason." While both of Dolly's parents had misgivings about their daughter's activities, their time was taken up with the demands of everyday living.

Stella points out that while the children all "grew up in a poor situation", Dolly had it better, from a material view, than her siblings. "She was living in a house where they had indoor plumbing and a telephone and a television and you know they lived in town and she was the only kid there and she had carte blanche to my aunt's closet, make-up, all the stuff that girls do . . . no one else in the house, so you can imagine that's got to be a contrast for her and that's got to be a conflict in her mind of like, 'How can you hide us from your mind?' You can't really, but you'd like to because it's too depressing."

Inevitably Dolly's more comfortable set-up at her aunt's bred some resentment on the part of Dolly's younger siblings. Willadeene recalls a time when Cassie had been told to hang a pile of clothes out to dry but Cassie reckoned it was Dolly's turn to help with the chores – but yet again she was in Knoxville appearing on Walker's show.

Although Stella understands how her sister was drawn to singing and performing she strongly feels that Dolly should not have become a professional entertainer so young. "It's unnatural for children to be put onstage at that young age and to be expected to gain approval of strangers; it's a form of prostitution of the mind . . . What little kid that's hyper in the first place wouldn't think it was fun to learn a song and have people applaud for them?" Stella compares Dolly's early apprenticeship with those parents who invest considerable time and effort into turning their young children into star athletes. By the time they turn 18 they have done little other than train hard to achieve a specific goal. Despite Dolly's obvious artistic gifts and the fact that her ambition came from within Stella claims that her sister's interests, specifically her enjoyment of childhood, were not safeguarded. "It's unnatural for children to be put out onstage and to become child stars. I don't want to compare her to Michael Jackson because she's not that, you know, that strange, but how unnatural is that? It's just not healthy . . . Johnny Cash was not a child star. He had already developed his persona and his personality. He knew himself as an individual. Dolly never knew herself as anything but a star. That's the difference because she was a star in our home town, in our family and our region because of that TV show and that radio show . . . like in a 500-mile radius, which was her world at that time, she was a star . . . now think about how that brands your psyche at that age."

Stella claims that much of the time Dolly has had to battle against her natural self. "Dolly's an introvert; she's not an extrovert by nature . . . she never had any other opportunity because she had to do that from such an early age, to bluff her way through the world to make something of herself and to make people love her; that's not healthy, you can't end up being what I consider an average person when you're put in that position . . . Everyone else was like adults on that TV and radio show. She was the only kid, and to be a little girl and to be this unique, almost like a little wind-up monkey, you kind of grow up with those antics of being this kid that's just kinda all over the place because it's kind of expected of you."

Stella believes the drive to exploit Dolly's talents came more from Bill Owens than her immediate family. "My mother was not a stage mother but my mother's brother *was* a stage parent. He was the one with the ambition to be a star and he could get in doorways with a cute blonde-headed impish little girl that could sing and so he pushed her and Mama allowed that and Daddy felt that she was safe as long as she was with relatives."

One of Stella's main concerns appears to be that Dolly became less and less a part of the family circle as her singing commitments increased. "Daddy was too busy working. He knew she was living with my mom's sister and he knew she was singing on the radio and television 'cos we could see her and hear her and so we knew where she was but she was not part of our household, no she was not . . . I don't think she had the time and if she had of had the time, her focus and her mission was so strong that she didn't have time to stop and pick you up along the way in the stampede of life, let's say. In the stampede of life I'm the kind of person who would've stopped and picked her up if she was falling but she would have said, 'It's every man for himself, get up if you can. I'll see you at the end of the line.' She would have stepped over me.

"Our relationship almost went, you know, became void, and you know the void was very strong, but as the years have gone by, I began to understand that she just could not bear to share the spotlight. It was very much a rejection. How would you feel if you had a sibling that was almost three and a half years older and they pushed you to the side, made you sit in the front of the bus on the way home from school and you know, pushed you away as far as possible?

"I think her need to be special in such a huge family was so strong that she couldn't help it, she really couldn't. I don't want people to think that I'm trashing my sister, I think in a way that it's a sad thing. For me I've come to see it as a sad thing for her, not for me so much. I've lived through 35 years of that hurt and I'm over it because now I'm at peace with why that was that way. It's hard when you grow up in such a huge family and there's a lot of need and there's a lot of neglect."

Stella felt excluded by Dolly at a time when she too was expressing an interest in becoming a singer. It would have been natural for them to team up, for Dolly to offer encouragement and give her younger sister the benefit of her experience. However, this did not happen though Stella recognises why. "I think she was emotionally needy of that attention and I don't know why, maybe it was just her personality. I think she certainly channelled it in a good way. Her healthy normal relationship with all of us has been thwarted and that is very sad to see . . . but she wouldn't have been happy without her career. I think it was worth the sacrifice to her because she really hasn't lost us because we will always be there for her. We will always love her."

Throughout her teenage years Dolly paid regular visits to Nashville with the help of family members to pitch songs and make recordings. Conditions were spartan to say the least and Dolly often had to wash in cold water in petrol station restrooms. The effort paid off in 1962 when 15-year-old Dolly (and Owens) were given songwriting contracts with the publishing company Tree Music, one of whose luminaries, publisher Buddy Killen, recognised her potential. Tree was formed in the Fifties, striking pay dirt in 1956 with Elvis Presley's 'Heartbreak Hotel'. According to some reports Dolly received a regular advance from Tree but she has said that Killen merely loaned her money from time to time. For about three years, she wrote for Tree but none of her offerings were successful and they eventually parted company by mutual agreement.

Killen said, "One of the things that really always impressed me about Dolly was, right from the beginning, she had a special kind of drive and determination and understood a whole lot more about the business than she even realised. She didn't quite understand it all but she had that innate sense of timing, the thing that kept her pushing to get where she wanted to go."

Killen described Bill Owens as, "sort of a driver, really wanting to get something done . . . he pushed all the time, trying to achieve", while Dolly was "very country and very raw, not pretentious at all". On occasion he had some difficulty following her high-speed East Tennessee twang.

Through the Buddy Killen connection Dolly and Bill also secured a recording deal with Mercury Records. In 1962 Dolly recorded her first major Nashville recording: the teen themed song, 'It's Sure Gonna Hurt' B/W 'The Love You Gave'. The record was credited to Dolly Parton and the Merry Melody Singers who were, in reality, a collection of singers which included members of vocal backing group the Jordanaires, most famously associated at that time with Elvis Presley. Suffering from a lack of promotion the record failed to make any impact on the charts (only gaining airplay in Dolly's home town) and Dolly was soon dropped by Mercury.*

The following year Dolly earned $240 for her recording of six songs on the album *Hits Made Famous By Country Queens – Patsy Cline And Kitty Wells* for the low budget Somerset label.† Dolly contributed one side consisting of six songs supposedly made famous by Kitty Wells; in fact only three of the songs, including the hugely successful 'It Wasn't God Who Made Honky Tonk Angels', were recorded by her. 'Letter To Heaven', written by Dolly, was an Appalachian style ballad which told the story of a girl whose mother has died; the girl goes to post a letter to her mother in heaven but is run down by a car and thus gets her wish to be reunited with her mother. Such morbid lyrics would become a Parton trademark and demonstrated the influence of the mournful story songs she heard as a child. On the other side of the album were six Patsy Cline songs recorded by an obscure and forgotten singer called Faye Tucker.

---

* Prior to this first major label outing, Dolly sang harmonies on a single cut by Bill Owens, 'Forbidden Love' B/W 'So Little I Wanted, So Little I Got' for the obscure independent label Circle B in 1960; it too sank without trace.

† Over the years the album has been repackaged and released as a "supermarket record" by various labels and would have vanished completely but for Dolly's involvement.

Kitty Wells and Patsy Cline were the two most successful female country singers of the late Fifties and early Sixties whose styles and personal qualities Dolly absorbed as she was growing up. Cline's first incarnation in the Fifties was as a cowgirl, an image that had dominated female country singers' styles during the post-war years, one particularly successful exponent being Rose Maddox who sang along with her similarly attired brothers. This general look was adaptable and allowed for a variety of styles with some artists preferring shorter skirts and tighter blouses while others chose to dress like cowboys; plain dressed, plain speaking. Cowgirls and cowboys had exemplified the qualities of spirit and resilience necessary to withstand the hardships of the early American settlers; it was a romantic and dignified image widely disseminated in films as well as via country music. Wells looked like a Thirties' country sweetheart and yet her groundbreaking 1952 song, 'It Wasn't God Who Made Honky Tonk Angels', was a controversial statement reflecting growing tensions between men and women in a world where divorce was becoming increasingly common. With a tough barroom, honky tonk sound, the song was a hard hitting riposte to 'The Wild Side Of Life', an earlier hit for Hank Thompson which portrayed women as fickle home breakers.

In a bold piece of social commentary it dared to defend women and suggested that relationships often broke down because of the irresponsible behaviour of the husband. In socially conservative Fifties America '. . . Honky Tonk Angels' was regarded as so controversial that the song was banned from being sung at the Grand Ole Opry. Ironically it was in some respects reminiscent of old moral broadsides such as 'She Is More To Be Pitied Than Censored' by The Carter Family. Cline's music had a smoother, more sophisticated sound than Wells' honky tonk style, married to bland love lyrics generally painting women as helpless victims of their men-folk's whims. This was due in large part to the Nashville Sound developed by influential producers such as Chet Atkins, Don Law and Anita Kerr, combining acoustic guitars with echoes, sophisticated string sections, rippling pianos and smooth back-up singers. The sound helped to make Cline's catchy, uncontroversial songs commercially successful. According to one school of thought, the massive impact of rock'n'roll in the Fifties robbed country of the best of its young talent as well as most of its audience. In accordance with this theory country degenerated into schmaltzy, middle-of-the-road music expounding conservative views of intense patriotism and insincere sentimentality. Some would certainly level this latter accusation at some of Cline's material, yet in real life she was a spirited hard talking, hard drinking woman well capable of standing up for herself in a man's world. She was also a dyed in the wool country music traditionalist who was always interested in her appearance, and in the course of her short career (brought to a premature end in 1963 by a plane crash) affected a variety of styles from fringed cowboy jackets and gingham dresses to formal evening gowns, furs and jewellery for which she had a particular penchant.

Though there were others, such as Molly O'Day with her soulful and passionate performances, who influenced Dolly, Wells and Cline were the role models upon which she based aspects of her own distinctive image and style. It seems that, in the early Sixties at least, Dolly was a country girl at heart when it came to her musical preferences so she was not much taken with the revolution in popular culture started by the Beatles when they reached American shores in 1964. In a 1984 interview she declared, "Coming from the backwoods there was no other way for me to start out except in country and folk music. I was very, very country."

This is not to say that the British Invasion had no impact at all in Tennessee. When still young the Parton twins Frieda and Floyd with their sister Rachel delivered an updated version of 'Jesus Loves Me' at the local church, causing amusement, and no doubt some consternation, when singing "Jesus loves me, yeah, yeah, yeah" in perfect harmony. While recording songs deemed by various producers as appealing to current tastes, Dolly continued to build up a substantial repertoire of her own often highly personal songs. She explained the influence of family and upbringing on her songwriting and how it enabled her to remain connected to ordinary people. "If I see a working man, I think of my daddy. If I see a woman struggling to bring up a bunch of kids on nothing, I think of my mama. All this is the experience and feeling I put into my songs. If I see kids, I think of my brothers or sisters or myself. I don't think I'll ever change. I know what it is to be without, and now I've got something, not to share it or to be humble about it, I'd be a fool."

In another interview she provided further confirmation of her creative processes. "The ideas come from life in general, from my own experience, from the people I know and love and from things that happen to them. A lot of the involved songs are just stories that I've created in my own mind because I have a wild imagination. I've all my life been a real curious kid; it just carried on through the years. I love to write songs with maybe tricky endings, surprise endings and this sort of thing, but I can write about my own experience a lot and I write an awful lot about my growing-up days in the East Tennessee mountains and my childhood. They are very precious to me because I come from a large family. There were 12 of us kids and we were all very happy; we were very poor people but we were very proud at the same time."

Willadeene summed up East Tennessee in 1964 as a combination of "computers and cornfields, atomic plants and outside toilets, tourism and tent revivals, breeder reactors and barnyards". Dolly was still only 18 and her earnings from Cas Walker gradually increased so that by the time she left Caton's Chapel, she was receiving $60 a week – large earnings for a schoolgirl from the Smokies. Despite her lack of interest in academia Dolly "wanted to finish high school first, just to show that I could, just to prove to myself that I could".

Dolly duly graduated "by the skin of her teeth" from Sevier County High School on Friday June 1, 1964 and the baccalaureate ceremony at which she received her diploma was held at the First Baptist Church in Sevierville. As part of the graduation proceedings each student tradition-ally addressed the assembled group of parents, family members, teachers and other students and gave details of what they intended to do next in their lives. When it came to Dolly she stated she was going to Nashville to build a career as a singer and songwriter and to be a star. The initial reac-tion was complete silence. This was soon followed by the not unfamiliar response of giggles and sniggers from some of her fellow students. Such behaviour merely stiffened her resolve.

Dolly's move to Music City was no spur of the moment decision. "I had prepared to come to Nashville as a child, and was packed and ready to go months before I graduated from High School, because I knew I was gonna become a recording star. I don't know why. It was just as if it was born in me, I guess . . . ever since I was in grade school and found out about Nashville, that was the place I wanted to be . . . we listened to the Grand Ole Opry . . . went to bed with the radio still on." She experienced pangs of apprehension at the prospect of leaving home. However, her move was the fulfilment of a dream which she resolved to see through; and for Dolly, "a dream is a terrible thing to waste", or "a peacock who rests on his tail feathers is just another damn turkey".

She was as well equipped for the particular challenges she would face as any 18-year-old girl from the Smokies could ever be thanks to her family roots, her spiritual and religious life and plenty of down home country wisdom honed over years of humble living. In a remark that was both self-deprecating and shrewd Dolly said, "I've got enough good common-sense to know what I don't know . . . just having good ole horse sense, you can make more money, and get more done than all the people who have to fumble through the books to try to find an answer."

The morning after Dolly graduated the family gathered for an at times emotional farewell party at the house. Wearing a brown dress with long sleeves and a white collar, and carrying several paper bags into which she "just threw everything" including some dirty washing and a bag of biscuits, Dolly left for Nashville on a Greyhound bus.

# ACT II

## 1964–1980:
## Dreams Do Come True

# Chapter 7

SEVIERVILLE to Nashville is only about 200 miles, but given the backward nature of life in the foothills of the Smokies in 1964, for Dolly, it was like a move from the 19th to the 20th century. The move was a major shift for a young woman of 18, even one who had a clear idea of the direction she wanted her life to take. Dolly reportedly told friends at her graduation ceremony, "I'm going to Nashville tomorrow and not coming back until I make it." It was only some time later, in a letter to her parents, that she revealed just how nerve-wracking the journey had been. "I cried almost all the way to Nashville. I wanted to turn around a few times and come back. But you know how bad I've always wanted to go to Nashville and be a singer and songwriter."

Bill Owens and his wife Cathy had gone to Nashville with their baby shortly before Dolly's graduation ceremony and rented an apartment with a spare room. In return for her board Dolly would look after Bill and Cathy's boy from time to time while Cathy worked at a Shoney's restaurant and Bill was on the road. Dolly claimed that she did not sleep alone in a bed until she moved to Nashville (though this surely ignores the many times she stayed with her aunt in Knoxville).

On her first day in Nashville, Dolly met Carl Dean, the man who would become her husband, after a visit to the Wishy-Washy Laundromat. "I didn't even know what a Laundromat was. Back home we just had a regular old washing machine. Anyway, I put my things in and . . . I will never forget that night, I remember every detail. I had on a pair of red slacks, skin tight and a little red midriff blouse that came right under the breast and showed my stomach. It was sleeveless and it had little ruffles all in the front and it was just kinda low. But there again that was the kind of stuff I liked to wear. So while my clothes were washin' I was walkin' around the street, drinkin' a Coke, lookin' around at everything and this guy came by in a white '62 or '63 Chevrolet. He looked at me and he was *real* good lookin' and of course I was kinda flirtin', too, because I didn't know no better than to speak to strangers, 'cause in Sevierville everybody knew everybody else, and if you *didn't* speak to people, you were real rude. I didn't know that you don't speak to strangers in a big city . . . but it wouldn'ta mattered; I would have done it anyway. Well he waved and hollered at me and I hollered back."

In an interview Dolly said Dean's opening line was, "You're gonna get sunburnt out here little lady." There was an instant mutual attraction. "We got talkin' and I just fell in love with him right away. He had on a pale blue shirt like golfers wear, and he always worked outside – he and his father had an asphalt paving company – so he was real brown. He's about six foot two."* Much as it had been with Judy Ogle, Dolly's realisation that Carl would be somebody special in her life appears to have been immediate. "Somehow I knew the minute I met him that there was no point in looking for somebody else." They "took up with each other" even though this was not part of her plan for Nashville, let alone on the day of her arrival. As she said in 1984, "I had just left two boyfriends back home, and I wasn't looking to get involved because I had gone to Nashville to really get started in the music business." One of her previous boyfriends had even bought a ring and was talking about making the down payment on a house. Since Carl Dean shuns publicity to the same degree that Dolly courts it, little information about him is available. However, some of his friends have spoken up and a picture emerges of a straightforward, unpretentious Southern man whose interests lie in manual work (Dolly has sometimes described him as an "outdoorsman") and domestic tasks such as cooking. A man with no creative aspirations, in essence the kind who stood for the ideals that Dolly had been trying to escape from. Dolly has said that Dean reminded her of her father; independent, honest and unselfish. Carl was born in the middle-class Nashville suburb of Radnor. His nickname in childhood was 'Deano', and boyhood friends describe him as a loner who kept to himself, while some said he resembled the actor Anthony (*Psycho*) Perkins. One school friend, Ronnie Shacklett said, "Carl was always a quiet guy and as a student just average. We went through school without studying. We were there to have a good time, but Carl was considered a pretty sharp guy. He was the witty one of the group. He was always kidding around." After leaving high school Carl went into his father's asphalt and paving business, The Dean and Dean Asphalt Paving Company, where another pal Leroy Hollis described him as a hard worker.

Dolly may have been smitten but she refused to get into Dean's car on their first meeting. As she said, country folk were friendly, "but not that friendly . . . you gotta know somebody or they may take you on a back road and kill you." She did, however, suggest that he visited her at Bill and

---

* She was evidently not put off by their difference in height of 14 inches.

Chapter 7

Cathy's house next day when she would be babysitting. He came every day that week and they sat outside the apartment as Dolly would not allow him inside the house. Not long afterwards, when her aunt had a day off, Dolly had her first chance to go out properly with Carl. He drove her straight to his house and introduced her to his parents because, "he said he knew right from the minute he saw me that that's the one he wanted." Dolly was invited to stay for dinner. "I was *real* bashful. Bein' from the country I wasn't used to eatin' with strangers or going to people's houses and you know how you're funny about your table manners and feel self-conscious? So when people ask you to eat you say, 'No, I've just had something,' and you'll be *starved* to death and wishing they'd gone so you could eat like a dog."

Dolly and Carl's relationship quickly blossomed but after a few months Carl entered the army and was away for the best part of two years, though Dolly occasionally visited him at his camp in Savannah. At the same time Dolly was struggling to face up to the reality of life in Nashville. "The beginning was tough. Walking around with demo tapes to play to a million A&R men, listening to all kinds of conflicting advice about who to sign with and who not to, months, and many times years, getting to know the business and waiting for the business to know you, while working at meaningless jobs outside the business for a scanty living in draughty garrets." The "meaningless" jobs included filing and typing in the office of a music publisher, working as a waitress in Dobb's House Restaurant and answering the phone for a neon sign company. The notion amuses Stella Parton, "I can imagine her picking her fingers and thinking, 'How do I get out of here?' writing songs while she's trying to answer the phone."

Not long after arriving in Nashville Dolly capitalised on her experience gained with Cas Walker by securing a job on *The Eddie Hill Show*, an early morning television slot which involved being in a fit condition to sing at five in the morning. Dolly sent money back to her mother when she could though this became more difficult once she rented a cheap apartment. For someone used to having a large family around her much of the time, time spent on her own provided a real test of character. "I thought I'd *die* from homesickness. I missed them kids so bad, I missed Mamma and Daddy so bad, but I couldn't go home." She felt particularly vulnerable at night; she missed the familiar sounds of home and worried about unfamiliar city noises, in the street and in the hallway.

Christmas 1964, her first away from home, was especially hard for Dolly and left her with a lifelong sympathy for those who are separated from their families at this sentimental time of year. There were occasions when

77

she did not have money to feed herself properly; at one stage she resorted to making a kind of soup from ketchup, mustard and water. If she was invited out and had a hamburger, she would get two and take one home for later. She later admitted to stealing the odd item from supermarkets when times were really hard. On visits home her parents were taken aback at how much weight she had lost.

During this time Dolly's musical inclination was still mainly towards country. "I think that what makes country music so popular is the same thing that we loved about cowboy movies, western movies. It's like the natural heroes of the earth. There's just somethin' about the dirt, somethin' about horses, somethin' about the land, somethin' about honesty."

Dolly's efforts continued less as a result of any unshakeable belief in her ability but rather her burning desire to make it in the music business. "Talent isn't going to get me where I'm going. It's my faith and determination that will do it. I'm really not all that talented. I'm not a great singer – a lot of people can't stand the sound of my voice – and I don't know music technically . . . I'm more of a stylist than I am great at anything."

The contacts Bill Owens made helped open doors for Dolly. Apart from approaching record companies, pitching songs around town, and, as one journalist put it, "eating breakfast with someone different every day", Dolly also did her best to play some occasional "bookin's", sometimes supported by a house band, sometimes by a guitarist and other musicians who actually knew her songs. Such a group usually featured Owens, who was a reasonably good picker, with or without other relatives. Dolly enthusiastically told people that she was planning to form her own musical backing group with the working name of the Kinfolk, which would feature various family members on her mother's side. Of her family's musical qualities Dolly said that though some of them sang, none "really had the ambition to make it, to really make it in the music business". She also said that she would not encourage them, "because it's a hard life". Asked if she played any instruments she responded, "I play, yes, straight guitar, and I play other instruments . . . I'm gonna try to work up a little routine and play, you know, I play piano and, you know I can do tambourine and play banjo a little, very little, but I've always played guitar. That's the only thing that I can really do a good job at. So that's about it. We've covered that part."

Even at this stage Dolly's ambition was infectious; she talked of her plans to write poetry and children's stories saying that she did not intend to go into movies despite having already received offers. Life on the road was not glamorous. She and Bill travelled to venues in an old station wagon, something Dolly particularly disliked. "That part I didn't like at all because it's real hard on a woman especially." She gave a graphic account of the kind of places she sometimes found herself in. "I was always a little scared in honky-tonks and dives and chicken wire barricade places when I played them, but I always could take care of myself . . . one time a girl in a honky-tonk got real mad that her drunk husband was paying more attention to my show than he was to her . . . she yelled out, 'Let me at that bitch. I'll get that wig offa her.' All the band was gatherin' around to protect me, but bein' a country girl I'd have taken her on if she'd-a got to me. We'd've had a brawl right there, I'll tell you." Despite Dolly's ability to handle herself in such situations she claimed not to have drunk alcohol until she was 19. "If you were a woman who had a beer you were a tramp and a drunk." Such a comment betrayed a moralistic component in Dolly's nature supplied in part no doubt by her mother's influence; it also overlooked Dolly's early experiments with moonshine. Like the subject of her virginity it was another early example of an awareness of portraying the right image to her public.

Dolly's persistence paid off when in 1966 she was offered a contract by Fred Foster, boss of Monument Records, the largest independent label in Nashville at the time, which included on its roster Roy Orbison.* Foster recognised that Dolly had talent but was not quite sure how best to exploit it. His people felt that her voice sounded very young, like that of a 12-year-old, and that she would probably only be able to sell pop songs. There were also those who thought her voice strange and that the country folk wouldn't go for it. Talking about this Dolly revealed a certain lack of confidence in the acceptability of her voice. "It irritates some people 'cos it's piercing and it's unusual."

The prevailing company view was in favour of Dolly attempting pop or possibly even rock'n'roll. Her own strong wish was to sing country but she was not in a position of strength and had little option but to go along with the label's wishes though she was concerned that they would try to drown her voice with excessive instrumentation. "They felt it wouldn't be commercial for me to try and sell a song with hard lyrics, that it would sound funny for someone who sounded like she was 12 to be singing about a marriage that went bad. So I started cutting rockabilly, a blend of country and rock, but I soon learned that when you ride the fence you just kind of

* Dolly has said that her song 'Everything's Beautiful (In Its Own Way)' helped to secure the deal.

sit there. I wasn't writing much or choosing any of my own material. I needed to do both."

One of Dolly's first producers at Monument was Ray Stevens, a multi-talented musician who went on to enjoy a successful career with novelty songs such as 'The Streak' and 'Bridget The Midget' as well as middle-of-the-road pop hits including a cover version of 'Misty'. Stevens was thrilled to be working with someone he regarded as having great potential ("she was great . . . easy-going and nice, personable. I was just dealing with a talented girl") and who was already attracting favourable comment on the Nashville scene. Though Dolly was recorded as a pop artist he recalls that song choice was a democratic process. "We all chipped in, it wasn't up to one person to do it, she had songs that she had written and I wrote a couple of songs for her and suggested some other songs and we just kinda got in there and did what we thought was best . . . That was back in the days when the girl groups were really dominant on the charts and I was shooting for that genre. I wrote a song for her called 'Busy Signal' . . . she's calling her boyfriend and the phone's going 'uh uh' and the background voices were doing that and then she would sing on top of that and I thought it was kinda sharp but of course it didn't do anything. She was *supposed* to be country just simply because she was from Sevierville Tennessee and liked country music, and so did I. I thought we'd not only do some of that but we'd throw in a few R&B type songs as well."

Stevens remembers Dolly's distinctive voice for its high nasality. "It would cut through anything, cut through the thickest fog, it was really a great sound; it was sharp, it was perfect for recording, you know you didn't have to add any highs to her, she could cut like a knife . . ." Though a married man, Stevens was well aware of Dolly's attractiveness. "She was drop-dead beautiful . . . I remember she came out to my house one day when we were going to rehearse for a session and I had a little room off the other side of the garage and I went in there to rehearse and of course my wife was in the house and she was just fuming. She took one look at Dolly and said, 'Boy, what are y'all doing in there?' I said we were just rehearsing . . . of course I was thinking 'I wish we were doing something else!'" Stevens' recollection is that Dolly did not wear wigs at this time, his theory being that she only ever took to wearing wigs, "so she wouldn't have to fix her hair. She had great hair as far as I can remember." Stevens was not the first to be aware of Dolly's voluptuousness; apparently the jokes about her figure embarrassed her to begin with but she soon came to the conclusion that it was all in fun and in subsequent years she made more jokes on the subject than anyone else.

Dolly recorded many songs for Monument including country standards such as 'Release Me' and 'Making Believe' and some of her own including 'Letter To Heaven'. However, the songs which were released as singles were pop – the first to be promoted being 'I Wasted My Tears' B/W 'What Do You Think About Lovin'' – and apart from a minor hit with 'Happy, Happy Birthday Baby', which reached 108 on the pop charts in 1965, she achieved negligible commercial success. Most of these Monument tracks have resurfaced on various compilations over the years and as part of the deal with the company, Dolly (with Bill Owens) was signed to their publishing arm, Combine Music, run by Bob Beckham whose hits had included Willie Nelson's 'Crazy'.

Writing new material was the least of Dolly's concerns as she told one interviewer, "It's just so easy. I've got hundreds of songs . . . most people will sit down and smoke a pipe, but I just sit down and pick up a piece of paper." Her skills as a songwriter allied to a desire to air her views on a wide range of topics, meant that she was never going to be satisfied with writing empty love songs. Over the years the subjects of Dolly's songs have included abortion, religion, children's issues, fear and insecurity, faith, birth and motherhood, mental illness, death, joy and country life, in addition to love and relationships. Over the course of three years with Combine Music Dolly composed well over 100 songs, some co-written with Owens, and this figure does not include the countless ideas she jotted down on scraps of paper for later use.

Owens took Dolly's demos to producers and artists – an arrangement which suited her on a practical level because as she said, "I didn't have a car at the time. In fact I couldn't drive anyway, so I spent my time writing." Despite the inevitable stresses and strains in 15 years of working together they never exchanged a harsh word. "She believes in co-operation and in sharing the workload," Owens said. Ronny Light, who was working for RCA at the time, also recalls Dolly as someone who went out of her way to get on well with people. "At Combine they had a writer's demo studio, using reel-to-reel tape machines primarily. I used to write lead sheets for the publishing companies. I was often there on business. I walked in; here sits Dolly. First time I'd ever met her. I'd heard about her. Didn't have the big bosom, didn't have the look at all that she has now. She had blue jeans and a T-shirt on. She said, 'Well hello, how are you?' all bright and cheerful. I looked over my shoulder to see who she was talking to and in fact she was talking to me, like I was a long lost friend she was so happy to see again. It took me off guard."

At this stage Dolly's songwriting was more successful than her recording career. She and Bill would try to make themselves aware of who was recording and try to pitch them some of their songs. Combine were naturally eager to push the work of their writers and they too would check to see who was in town and then select songs they felt were right for particular artists. Skeeter Davis had been a "teen sensation" in the early Sixties with 'The End Of The World', but when the pop hits stopped she returned to country with a 1966 version of Dolly's song 'Fuel To The Flame' and subsequently became the first singer to devote an entire LP to Dolly's songs. Hank Williams Jr recorded 'I'm In No Condition' and Dolly's idol Kitty Wells recorded 'More Love Than Sense'.

Demonstrating insightful business acumen she made it part of the deal with Combine Music that she could claim back any unrecorded songs when she left. She also made it her business to learn about contracts, licences and copyrights. The time since she signed a contract with Monument had undoubtedly had its frustrations but Dolly was accumulating invaluable experience which would stand her in good stead.

Now that Dolly was in Nashville, "putting legs on her dreams", her feelings of homesickness started to recede and she soon felt a sense of belonging in her chosen home. Some of the older hands showed her kindness, including one of the most revered figures in country music as she recalled: "Roy Acuff was like a daddy to me. He was to so many people. When I first came to Nashville, many times he would hand me money out of his pocket and say, 'Here, young 'un, you probably haven't eaten good today.'"

An important breakthrough came from a song Dolly and Bill had written called 'Put It Off Until Tomorrow'. As Dolly recalled, "Bill took the song to a friend of his, a country singer called Bill Phillips, who then took the song to his producer at Decca, Owen Bradley. Owen flipped over it, but he asked if he could get me to sing harmony on the record like I did on the demo. Of course I was signed up with Monument, but they were just good enough to let me do it . . . I couldn't let anyone use my name . . . but my voice was in there. Everybody got to callin' and askin' who that other singer was . . . I was more noticeable than they had intended, because my voice is so odd. You can tell who I am even when I'm singing in a group."

In effect she sang a duet with Phillips rather than simply providing backing vocals. Legendary Nashville producer Jack Clement remembers Dolly and the recording well. "The first time I met her she was about 19 years old . . . a friend of mine had rented a recording studio and was doing some demos. She really didn't look a lot like she did later, she was just this very cool looking girl, nice looking, kind of college looking girl, and she didn't have on anything that showed off her body or anything, it was very laid back but I remember her voice and I really liked it. You just couldn't ignore it, it was wonderful . . .

"There was this guy named Bill Phillips, kind of a very obscure country singer and he recorded a record, and he got Dolly to sing harmony on it, nobody had heard of her at the time. Everybody heard that harmony part and said, 'Who is that?' She'd do this little 'Hey hey' and then no one cared about Bill Phillips.* She stole the show, she's a natural born show stealer . . . and then I didn't hear any more about her for a while but the point is she made a very lasting impression on me right from the start."

Dolly also made a lasting impression on veteran country singer Narvel Felts who recalled a time when she supported Sandy Posey, who enjoyed US pop success in the mid Sixties with songs such as 'Born A Woman' and 'Single Girl', at a watermelon festival in Hornersville, Missouri. Apparently Dolly stole the show. As Felts put it, "Dolly had star quality before she was a star."

'Put It Off Until Tomorrow' made number six in the charts and went on to win a BMI (Broadcast Music, Inc) award. DJs wanted to know who owned the 'mystery voice' after receiving numerous calls from listeners asking that very question. The song's success, as well as the growing awareness around Nashville that Dolly was something special, convinced Fred Foster that she should be allowed to have her head and make country records. In truth she had reached the stage where if Monument had not agreed to her wishes she would probably have sought a contract with a different label.

When Carl returned from military service he and Dolly decided to get married. Dolly complained that his method of proposal was not exactly romantic. "When we were hanging out he was working late nights on an asphalt paving job. I was living in Madison [Tennessee] and he was living in South Nashville and this relationship was wearing him down. He said, 'You're gonna have to move closer into town or we're gonna have to get married.'" Dolly was aware that marriage might not be a good career move since the music business generally wished to present their young stars as desirably single. Fred Foster, who had wanted Dolly to wait a year

---

* Dolly and Bill Owens did write a follow-up song for Phillips called 'You're Known By The Company You Keep'.

because of Monument's expenditure in promoting her, was initially unaware of her plans. He happened to say to her, "Well ain't you glad you waited to get married?" to which she replied, "Yeah, I waited till I got out of your office."

It seems clear that Carl agreed to marriage on the explicit understanding that their union would not interfere with her career. The idea that a woman's place was in the home did not apply and there was never any suggestion that Dolly would become domesticated. "I never fell into that . . . I guess since I was a little bitty child, I was just making a bee line for what I wanted and people just accepted this as being part of my personality."

Dolly was married to 23-year-old Carl Thomas Dean on Memorial Day, May 30, 1966, in a church in Ringgold in Catoosa County, Georgia, by the Reverend Don Duvall. They had been in the town a few days before but returned still single because it was not possible for them to get married in a church, something which mattered to Dolly. Ringgold was known as the "no waiting Southern marriage capital" and at this time hundreds of couples crossed over the Tennessee state line to get married. The only requirements were that parties were 21 (17 with parental consent) if male, and 18 (14 with parental consent) if female. The fact that the wedding took place in the state of Georgia ensured that it would not be reported in the Tennessee press.

Earlier in the year, a party described by Willadeene as a "bridal shower" was held at the family home for a few of Dolly's girlfriends and some family members. The kitchen and living room were decorated in pink and white and the centre piece of the proceedings was a display of carnations. In addition there was a pink and white parasol surrounded by gifts. According to some reports the pair eloped but while very few were aware of the couple's plans, close family and friends were informed and Dolly's mother was present as a witness. After the basic ceremony the trio drove back to Nashville. Unfortunately Avie Lee left her purse in the church (she had put it down to take a photograph of the bride and groom) and so Dolly and Carl had to spend the first few hours of their married life driving back to Ringgold and then back again to Nashville.

Their wedding night lasted only a few hours because Dolly had agreed to appear on Ralph Emery's morning show. Dolly told Emery that she had woken at three in the morning in order to get suitably made up and had roused her new spouse to take her photograph. Emery had showcased countless stars and rising artists over the years so an appearance on his programme could be extremely advantageous. Dolly soon became one of

*Dolly Parton, pictured in the mid-Seventies, as her solo star was in the ascendant. "I tried to be different, 'cause I knew I was different in every other way… I always wanted to look different, too, I didn't want to look ordinary."* (CSU ARCHIVE/EVERETT/REX FEATURES)

*A logging camp in the Smoky Mountains, close to the environment in which Dolly was raised, within a fairly small area of the foothills of East Tennessee, about 200 miles east of Nashville.* (GETTY IMAGES)

*A wooden shack of the type in which the Parton family once lived. Dolly's father Lee worked as a sharecropper – a tenant farmer who gave a substantial proportion of the value of all crops produced to the landlord.* (DAVID MUENCH/CORBIS)

*As a schoolgirl. "I hated [school]," Dolly told* Playboy *magazine in 1978. "Even to this day, when I see a school bus, it's just depressing to me... but it was better than stayin' home every day. Momma was sick a lot; we had some real hard times..."* (MICHAEL OCHS ARCHIVE/REDFERNS)

*Dolly onstage with her early mentor Cas Walker. She made numerous appearances on Walker's radio show from Knoxville, Tennessee. Of her visits to Knoxville Dolly said, "I really thought it was the whole world right in one town."*

*Dolly marries Carl Dean on May 30, 1966. The couple met in a laundromat on the same day that Dolly moved to Nashville. Their marriage has since provided an endless source of fascination and speculation for the tabloid press.*

*Dolly around the time of her first Nashville recordings. She was, in her own words, "putting legs on her dreams."* (EVERETT COLLECTION/REX FEATURES)

Dolly was hired by Porter Wagoner as his girl singer in 1967. By that year Wagoner was, in his own words, "pretty much at the top of the heap in Nashville."
(MICHAEL OCHS ARCHIVES/REDFERNS)

Dolly with Sixties beehive B-52. It was when she joined up with Porter that her lifelong love affair with wigs started. "I don't look this way out of ignorance… I look this way because I like it. Anybody can look like a common Joe. I look like I came out of a fairy tale."
(MICHAEL OCHS ARCHIVES/REDFERNS)

Porter helped to establish Dolly's reputation thanks to the popularity of his television show and touring roadshows. However, the pupil's star was soon outshining the master's. (MICHAEL OCHS ARCHIVES/REDFERNS)

*Dolly with Porter Wagoner and The Wagonmasters, resplendent in trademark Nudie suits, with double bass player/comedian Speck Rhodes (far left) in yellow-checked suit and teeth blacked out.*

*Dolly and Porter with band member/manager Don Warden (standing left) and Tandy Rice, president of Top Billing, Wagoner's booking agency (standing right). Porter's presentation made Tennessee Governor Winfield Dunn (seated left) an "honorary Wagonmaster".* (MICHAEL OCHS ARCHIVES/REDFERNS)

*At the annual CMA Awards, October 1970, with Roy Clark (left) and Merle Haggard. Dolly and Porter won the Vocal Duo Of The Year award.* (BETTMANN/CORBIS)

*A publicity shot of Dolly, 1969. Much of her songwriting concerned death and other maudlin subjects. "I wrote my first song when I was five years old and had my mother write it down for me. It was a song called 'Life Doesn't Mean Much To Me'. A pretty deep song for a kid but I always did look and act older than I was and still do."* (COURTESY OF NASHVILLE PUBLIC LIBRARY)

Emery's favourites partly because of her bubbly personality, punctuality (unlike some guests), and because she was not afraid to stand up to him. It was Emery's custom to smoke a cigar during the show; if he had a male guest on he just lit up regardless, if a female, he had the courtesy to enquire if she minded. When asked, Dolly said, "Well, I been a dreadin' it." Emery was taken aback. "What do you mean?" Dolly did not mince her words. "Well, I knew I was comin' over here today and knew that you was goin' to light that stinkin' thing, but go ahead if you want to." As Emery observed, "No woman before ever complained about the smoking habits of the host of a national show that could be beneficial to her career . . . She wasn't hypocritical. She wasn't evasive. She was Dolly. She has the brains of a computer, the heart of an artist and the spirit of a minister." And yes, Emery stopped smoking cigars in the studio.

Dolly and Carl deferred honeymoon plans to an unspecified time in the future as there was simply too much happening for Dolly to feel relaxed about holidaying for a couple of weeks. She was determined not to miss an opportunity, particularly since Monument were now giving her a full promotional build-up including gushing features in fan magazines. She remained cagey about discussing her marriage – initially at least. When asked by Everett Corbin in their 1967 interview, "Do you care to mention it?" she replied, "No, I don't care. They don't usually like me to, you know, Fred [Foster] and them don't really like for me, you know, to emphasise it real big but I got married a year ago . . . we don't have any children as yet and don't have any on the way, but we're plannin' to have some children. We'll probably start our family or start tryin' to have a family next summer. I'd like to have at least four children, or I'd like to have six, if we can afford it providin' everybody is healthy and I got the energy to take care of 'em. I'll know after the first one."

When getting to record her own country song in 1967, Monument chose a hard-hitting number called 'Dumb Blonde' by Curly Putman, who had written the country classic 'The Green, Green, Grass Of Home'. The line " 'Cos this dumb blonde ain't nobody's fool" not only referenced the superficial image which would come to be associated with Dolly but also the reality of her informed mind. The song became her first hit, reaching number 24 in the country charts.

Around this time Dolly wrote to Willadeene and her family. Despite the success she was starting to achieve she characteristically spent the first part of the letter discussing routine family matters. "My 'Dumb Blonde' made Top 10 nationwide [*sic*]. I'm cutting an album this week. It will be called *Hello, I'm Dolly* so it will look like 'Hello Dolly'. That's cute don't you think? It will be out in about a month . . . my new record will be out next week. It's called 'Something Fishy' . . . I have been working my tail off. I stay gone on the road all the time now. I did *The Bill Anderson Show* two weeks ago. Do you get it up there? It will be shown in a week or two." In addition Dolly was doing some live bookings and, "tryin' to keep up with my writin' and tryin' to keep the house decent, you know, the apartment, I really don't have that much time to do it."

By 1967 there were few prominent female stars in country music. Patsy Cline had been killed in a plane crash in 1963 leaving Loretta Lynn and Tammy Wynette, as well as several less high profile singers such as Jean Shepard, a Nashville stalwart, who scored a fair number of hits without ever becoming a major force. Of the Nashville scene in the Sixties Dolly said, "There were just very few of us, and we were all under the direction of men." However, Dolly was able to survive in the male-dominated world in Nashville despite the obstacles. As she said in a 1991 interview in *Modern Screen's Country Music*, "I love men; I understand them so I have no problems. A lot of things some women would see as sexual harassment I've taken as compliments because I've always felt like one of the boys and known how men think. Being a woman always worked to my advantage. It's strength, not a weakness, but if someone crossed the line, I always said, 'That's bullshit, and you know it's bullshit. I can think like a man too, so get off of it. That's not business, and if you want my songs, fine, just give me a call later.'"

As in the lyrics to her song 'Dumb Blonde', the people who mistook Dolly for a witless country girl with little idea of how to look out for herself were misjudging the sharp and ambitious mind driving her forward. "I could outtalk or outjoke what I couldn't outsmart," she said. "I have a sense of people, a good heart, and I knew the difference between right and wrong."

In Alanna Nash's 1978 biography, Dolly denied ever having to use the casting couch route to move forward. "I didn't date anybody in the music business much because I didn't want to get a reputation. Not that I would have done anything to get one, but you don't have to really . . . You'd be amazed at the people here who've had to do that kind of thing to get started . . . I had the talent and I made it on that. I didn't have to sell my body. When I got to that point I'd already started and I didn't have to make that decision. I truthfully don't know what I would have done if I'd been faced with it. I love music more than anything . . . when you tell the folks at home you're going out to make it in the music industry, you can't go back. You can't go home and say you failed. You can get so far down you grab at anything."

Dolly was garnering rave notices where they mattered. *Billboard* said of 'Something Fishy', "More clever material penned by Miss Parton and performed to perfection. This one should fast top her 'Dumb Blonde' hit and establish her as one of the [Monument] label's consistent top sellers." It was at about this time that a phone call changed everything.

# Chapter 8

"IMPRESSIVELY ugly, tall, skinny, with hollow cadaverous cheeks and large sunken eyes; the lips of a fat man, the jaw of a stevedore", "a composite of everything that was ridiculed in country music", "the ultimate hillbilly" with "a long-jowelled companionable face" were just a few of the descriptions and comments writers attached to Porter Wagoner over the years. To the millions partaking in 1967's Summer of Love he was a complete unknown. However, by that halcyon year he was, in his own words, "pretty much at the top of the heap in Nashville". Country music was Porter's life – as he said, "When I leave this business, it will be with my hands folded, lying in a box" – and he had his own television show, *The Porter Wagoner Show*. As Bill C. Malone put it, the show, "became part of Americana, deeply beloved by those who cherished the rustic imagery it conveyed, and ridiculed by those who recoiled from its hayseed trappings". It was sponsored by the Chattanooga Medicine Company, which had a chequered history of supplying a variety of medicaments to people in the South for many years.

In return Porter had to sing jingles on his show praising the efficacy of the products that were aimed at the average working person. As Wagoner said, "I have products to sell that you can't sell to the upper class . . . I don't try to do anything for the uptown people." The show's country credentials were made clear right from the opening titles which showed a close-up of a pointed cowboy boot from which the camera panned up to reveal Porter striding into view. At its peak the show was seen in around 100 American and Canadian markets and was watched by over four million people a week.

Born in 1927, Porter grew up on a farm near West Plains, Missouri and his earliest professional work on early morning radio stations involved singing jingles, one of which promoted special offers at the butcher's shop where he worked. His earliest recordings were available only on 78 rpm discs but in 1955 Porter had a major hit with the philosophical 'A Satisfied Mind', which paved the way for membership of the Grand Ole Opry in 1957 and his television show in 1960. Being resistant to any compromise of his traditional values, even in the face of pressure from his record company, RCA, Porter produced a string of major country hits including 'The Carroll County Accident', a part-spoken morality tale about marital infidelity, emblematic of his style. Porter toured extensively and virtually every aspiring and established country artist appeared on his show at some time or other in the course of its near 20-year run; it gave many new-comers, such as Waylon Jennings, one of their earliest breaks. Though there were other programmes aiming for the same market, Wagoner's show lead by its popularity. In addition to the regulation fiddle and steel guitar players his band, The Wagonmasters, featured the humour of double bass player Speck Rhodes, who appeared in a garish yellow-checked suit with some of his teeth blacked out. Rhodes was a throwback to the days of vaudeville, described by writer Steve Eng as, "A professional leprechaun, with the playful mouth and wistful eyes of a born funnyman."

Porter Wagoner and the Wagonmasters all wore suits of bright pastel colours but the boss lived up to one journalist's description of him as "a peacock in a parade of penguins" thanks to his penchant for dressing in the most eye-catching suits produced from the colourful imagination of Nudie Cohen. Cohen was a Russian-born tailor from Brooklyn who designed extremely flashy and ostentatious outfits for the country stars as well as customising cars by adding horns to their bonnets and gleaming silver dollars to the dashboards. He actually approached Wagoner before he was popular by suggesting he could brighten up his stage appearance with one of his suits. The cost ($350) was too high at the time so Cohen took the shrewd gamble of giving him the first suit free. (Within not too many years the cost would be nearer $5,000). Porter said, "It was the darndest-looking thing I'd ever seen. It was a peach-coloured suit with rhinestones, wagon wheels, cactus, all kinds of different embroidery. When the lights hit 'em it would be really exciting. People would just go aaah!" Country music singers had often gone in for striking stage outfits but the Nudie suit took things to a different level. For Wagoner, they were the right fit in every sense and he continued to wear them long after they had ceased to be fashionable.

Since the start of Wagoner's television show the role of girl singer had belonged almost exclusively to Norma Jean Beasler, known simply as Norma Jean, who one writer described as looking "wholesome, like a beautiful housewife". Like Dolly, Norma Jean had a poor upbringing (in rural Oklahoma) and had also appeared on a local radio show at the age of 12. Her appearance on a country television show, *The Ozark Jubilee*, pro-vided the springboard for her teaming up with Wagoner on his television show and as part of his touring troupe. This in turn led to Norma Jean's contract with RCA and a series of modest country hits including 'I Wouldn't Buy A Used Car From Him' and 'Let's Go All The Way', which in the latter instance referred to getting hitched. Around the mid Sixties, she became romantically involved with Wagoner, who was then legally separated from his wife, and wanted to marry him. Porter felt that Norma Jean was prioritising their personal relationship. "With me, business always comes first; any kind of love affair is much farther down the line." By 1967, the writing was on the wall and as he said, "My affair got so intense, Norma Jean and I both decided it would best if she left my show."

A girl singer was integral both to the television show and concerts so somebody new would have to be found. For Porter it was important that Norma Jean's replacement should be entirely different ("the whole situation changes") because the audience, who had become attached to Norma Jean over the course of seven years, might not accept her replacement. In view of the high profile the show enjoyed the choice of a new girl singer was a matter of considerable interest to the industry – producers, talent buyers, booking agencies, record company officials, as well as trade and fan publications all over the world.

Porter considered well over 20 women applicants including outstanding singers such as Tammy Wynette, Connie Smith and Dottie West, but he did not regard any as being sufficiently different from Norma Jean. He may well have feared that they might steal the show. Although he had never met Dolly Parton, Wagoner was aware that "she was creating a sound that people around town really liked." How their first meeting came about is not clear. Porter has stated that his secretary got a call from Dolly asking to audition while Dolly says that she received a call from Porter's secretary asking her to go to his office, assuming that he was merely interested in one of her songs. (Ironically one of the many artists Dolly had tried to pitch songs to in the past was Norma Jean.) Physical appearance was important to Porter and he liked what he saw. She was prettier than in the publicity photographs he'd seen and he also approvingly noted that she was more "petite" than Norma Jean, and blonde as opposed to brunette.

He described Dolly's hair as being "really subdued" and how beautiful she looked in "a solid white dress". Although taken with Dolly's "down-home authenticity" he was apparently concerned that musically she might not be country oriented enough. "Dolly had brought along a demo tape to play me some of her original songs. Her voice was clear and pure, but it was real skinny, real wiry, real kind of irritating actually; listening to it almost hurt your head. Even so, I felt in time I'd be able to get her to tone her voice down a little, make it sound more pleasant without sacrificing her unique style." Ironically, Wagoner epitomised the old style country star Dolly would eventually usurp.

Like Fred Foster, Porter was particularly taken with 'Everything's Beautiful (In Its Own Way)'. Porter had a strong spiritual side and an appreciation of nature and the song was imbued with both of these qualities. Apparently Dolly wrote the song during a fishing trip with Carl in Tennessee, when she was about 20. "It could be a pop record, you know, but still it's country lyrics . . . it's a clean idea. It's somethin' people need, you know, people seem to forget about God and everything with all the stuff goin' on in the world, and they don't really think to look around to, you know, the things that really mean anything . . . There'll always be a real country song on one side and no farther out than maybe a Sandy Posey type thing on the other."

Porter has said his mind was made up at the end of that first meeting with Dolly. "The deciding factor was her bein' the type of person she is. It wasn't necessarily because she's a beautiful girl, which she is or because she sings good, which she does. It was because she had the type of personality I could sell to people on television and in person." He did, however, act coolly by telling her he would think about it and give her a call, but even this was enough for her to squeal with delight and give him a hug. "This is everything I've worked for," she told him. He asked her to come back in a couple of days with her husband. Porter took to him right away. "Carl turned out to be a quiet, very simple country person – a very fine man." Porter said he warned the couple that there would inevitably be speculation that he and Dolly's relationship was more than professional. "We all agreed we didn't want that to happen." With Dolly and Carl having been married only a year there was little chance of her embarking on an extramarital relationship with a man almost 20 years her senior.

Dolly sang 'Dumb Blonde' and 'Something Fishy' during her first appearance on Porter's show. Skirting over the fact that Norma Jean was no longer around, Porter gave her a fulsome introduction, patronisingly referring to her as a "fine little gal". Dolly wore a simple high-necked gingham dress and her general appearance was demure by later standards. She wore a wig but with some of her own hair brushed up through the front of it. As she joked at the time, "My hair is blonde and it's about the same length as my wig, not as bulky, but I always wear my own hair around the front of my face, so I'm actually not bald as some people might believe."

Dolly was noticeably nervous but she got through the songs in a competent fashion though her movements were forced and awkward. Less than halfway through her second spot, the show was unceremoniously brought to an end when Porter ambled out to say that time was up. The Wagonmasters drifted into camera shot and Dolly was left to aimlessly wander about. While indicative of the show's lack of slickness it also reinforced Dolly's lowly status. She was, after all, merely the girl singer. Dolly was prepared to go along with this at first because there was no alternative. She had not gone to Nashville with the aim of being some-body else's sidekick. However, the opportunity was far too good to pass up. As one writer put it, "She sang pretty, she spoke softly and she sat under her big blonde wigs awaiting the turn she knew would come."

One area that Dolly found embarrassing was advertising the products of the show's long-time sponsor, the Chattanooga Medicine Company (for which she had to read her lines from a teleprompter) particularly Cardui, tablets for the relief of period pains. Amazing claims were made for the earliest incarnations of this product, such as firming up breasts and treating venereal disease. Another was Syrup of Black Draught, a laxative which had its origins in a senna-based product which could be traced back to the British Navy in the 18th century. Porter sang a Black Draught jingle which, as he was required to say, made you "smile from the inside out". "I didn't think that was well suited to a pretty girl like Dolly," he said, "even though she does, you never like to think of her going to the bathroom." Porter encouraged her to make each message personal by saying, "Now, this product here is the best there is in the country. I've *tried* it, and I *know* it is!"

Dolly's spots on Porter's show were seen by her large extended family in the Smokies. Her appearances caused some concern at first, especially among the more conservative elements, but in general they were happy that one of their own had landed her big chance.

Dolly soon found herself on the road fulfilling dates arranged when Norma Jean was still performing with Porter. While adhering to tradi-tional values, Wagoner endeavoured to achieve a blend which cleverly mixed distinctive folk and country styles with popular music and even the occasional rock influence. RCA released two live albums in the mid Sixties which captured some of the energy and spontaneity of Porter's shows. Performing live with the Wagonmasters presented a challenge for Dolly as she now faced large numbers of Norma Jean fans who might well resent a newcomer. She was also conscious of the fact that some people did not particularly care for her voice. These concerns proved to be well founded.

Dolly's first appearance took place in September 1967 in Lebanon, Virginia, about 100 miles from Norma Jean's home town. Unfortunately publicity had been arranged well in advance with posters proclaiming, "The Porter Wagoner Show featuring Norma Jean". Before the first afternoon performance Porter announced to the crowd through the public address system that Norma Jean would no longer be on the show and that he had a new girl and would they please make her feel welcome. Dolly was already very nervous and sang even higher than usual. She tried to ingratiate herself with the audience with some between-song chatter but her nervousness made her talk so fast that it was hard for people to make out what she was saying. Soon cries of "Where's Norma Jean? We want Norma Jean!" reached the stage. Porter strode back onstage to make it clear that Norma Jean would not be returning. "Give this girl a chance! For crying out loud, this isn't the end of the world. This is a new person. She's not tryin' to take Norma Jean's place . . . she's tryin' to make a place for herself."

Dolly was understandably upset by the experience and cried for hours afterwards on the tour bus. Porter was capable of making tough decisions and had got rid of singers before if he felt they were not right. However, he admired Dolly's pluck as well as her natural talents and resolved to stick by her. Porter reasoned that some people didn't like change, "but that don't mean you don't make changes, or take chances. It just means that some won't like it."

According to Don Warden, Porter's steel guitar player, the negative crowd reaction continued for about six months and there were occasions when Dolly left the stage in tears. "Oh, I can never make it plain to anyone what torture it was the first few times on that show," she said, "knowin' that everybody was wanting to see and hear someone else. It was like murder."

If the hostile audiences constituted a cloud in Dolly's world it was one with a silver lining. As Porter explained, "Every time she went onstage, I wished I could do it for her. But you can't do that, and I knew it. But I also knew that she had the backbone to stand up under all this. It was hard on her, but it was just as hard on me . . . I think the duet idea arose from these rough months. You see, I wanted to make this transition period as easy on Dolly as I could. So I sang with her on the bus, to try to add to her confidence . . . and then I found that she thought like I did, along the lines of singing songs the way they should be sung, and this gave me the idea of recording a duet." Porter did not intentionally take Dolly on as a recording partner; indeed he had misgivings about the idea. His view was that

93

duos tended to bring a lot of extra problems, such as the Louvin Brothers, Charlie and Ira, whose sharply contrasting lifestyles led to tensions. Though he sang with Norma Jean many times, they had not recorded together.

At this stage Dolly was a relative unknown who needed Porter more than he needed her and there was little question of her opposing the plan, though Porter has subsequently claimed that the duet idea was a joint decision. On the bus between shows they stayed up into the small hours working out two duets, 'Put It Off Until Tomorrow' and 'Blue Eyes Cryin' In The Rain'. Initially Dolly sang lead with Porter taking harmony though they eventually switched roles depending on whose vocals were better suited to a particular part. Porter felt their voices contrasted but at the same time, sounded uncannily similar, almost like blood kin. The duets made a tremendous difference when featured at a subsequent show in Roanoke, Virginia. Porter did all the announcements in order to disguise Dolly's nervousness, resulting in the audience being far more prepared to give her a fair hearing. The coupling of Porter and Dolly as a duet team gave rise to one of country music's most memorable pairings. As one writer described, "They were one of those mismatched pairs made in heaven, a surly beanpole and a plump angel, who made beautiful music together." Porter himself spoke of "blood harmony" which may have been an allusion to the years when he sang duets with his sister Lorraine.

Porter started taking more of an interest in the development of Dolly's career. He wanted her to switch from Monument, where her contract was on the verge of expiring, to his label, RCA Victor, with the idea of recording duets to promote on the road and on Wagoner's television show. "I wanted to get her on Victor so that I would be in a position to give her more help. Then she'd be with a company that I carried 20 years' prestige with and where I knew the operation completely. But at that time Dolly certainly wasn't known to RCA. And RCA at that time wasn't interested in signing *anybody*. The roster was filled with girl singers. But I knew if they'd record Dolly, she'd be a big artist for them."

Porter respected and acknowledged that Fred Foster had worked hard on Dolly's behalf but the fact remained that in nearly three years, apart from her two most recent singles, Monument had not succeeded in shifting many of Dolly's records. The blame could partly be laid at Foster's door for making Dolly sing pop over her clearly stated preference for country. Porter exhorted Dolly to persuade Foster to release her early and despite feelings of loyalty, she agreed. The matter was broached over a fairly tense lunch at a Nashville diner at which Bill Owens was also present. Even though Foster felt that Porter had put pressure on Dolly, he was, according to Porter, "100 per cent a gentleman." Foster was extremely disappointed, not least because he had been negotiating a new contract with Dolly, on substantially better terms, which was close to being agreed. He later claimed that Porter had spoken to him about how they could best promote Dolly, the clear implication being that her future recording career lay with Monument. He was delighted at the prospect because appearances on Porter's show could only mean more sales.

There were other good reasons for Foster to be disappointed. He had taken Dolly on when every other record company (including RCA) had turned her down flat. In addition he had invested a lot of time, effort and reportedly $50,000 in cultivating various aspects of Dolly's profile in order to help her career. As well as advising her on her dress sense he hired a member of the Nashville Children's Theater, Carol Doughty, to help Dolly with stage moves, make-up and simple elocution, being conscious that her quick-fire dialect was not readily comprehensible to all. On top of this he worked hard with Dolly in trying to eliminate or at least significantly reduce the pronounced vibrato in her voice; giving her advice on phrasing. He even suggested that she might have a future in movies, which she had scoffed at. Despite feelings of bitterness Foster remained on good terms with Dolly, which was worth more to him than lost profits.

Despite Porter's position of strength at RCA it was not a foregone conclusion that the label would be prepared to take Dolly on. The head of the company's Nashville operation was Chet Atkins whom Porter described as conservative. "If Chet says, 'That's pretty good,' that means you've got a monster on your hands, a damn knock-out!" Called "Mister Nashville" by some, Atkins had the power to launch careers. "If Chet likes it," it was often said, "it'll sell." Porter took a tape of Dolly's songs to Atkins who, "frowned a little and said, 'The songs are well written . . . but her voice is just so high, so sharp, so shrill.' " Dolly was not wholly confident that she would make the grade. "Porter took a tape of my singin' to RCA, but they said they couldn't sign me 'cause they were all filled up." Another factor which might have counted against Dolly was the fact that Atkins was an integral part of the development of the so-called Nashville Sound associated with smooth orchestral arrangements and backing singers, so Dolly's voice would not have sat easily in this category. In the end Atkins signed her because he respected Porter's opinions. There may have been a more mercenary factor involved in Atkins' decision. What was said during Porter's meeting with Atkins was not recorded, giving rise to differing accounts, but a story that has been repeated many times since has it that

Porter talked Atkins into signing Dolly on the strength of their duets and, crucially, Porter's promise that if she lost RCA money, it could be taken out of his own royalties. Dolly herself has often repeated this story.

When asked, Atkins was ambivalent about the deal's terms though he did not categorically deny it. "Well, the truth about how Dolly was signed is very simple. Porter had a girl singer named Norma Jean, who got married and left, and I said, 'Who are you going to get to replace Norma Jean?' He said, 'Well, I'm thinkin' 'bout Dolly Parton.' I said, 'Who's that?'* and he said, 'She records for Monument, and she writes songs and she's great,' and I said, 'Well good.'" Atkins maintained that Dolly was essentially signed on the strength of the Porter duets and his television show. After all it was hard to resist the allure of an attractive singer who was watched by millions of people every week. Atkins later felt embarrassed when Dolly kept saying things like, "Chet didn't used to like my singin', but now he does." Dolly claimed RCA "never lost a dime . . . I started drawing royalty cheques right from the very first, which they said no artist had ever done. I was proud, but, of course I knew I hadn't done it by myself. It was because of the way Porter had handled it."

Dolly's contract ran for an initial period of three years commencing October 10, 1967. RCA agreed to record a minimum of six sides during each year of the initial period of three years, though Dolly had to agree to record such additional material as the company might request. It was also stated that in the event of RCA failing to record the agreed number of sides their only obligation would be to pay Dolly an amount not exceeding the applicable union scale remuneration to which she would have become entitled if she had recorded the tracks. The first release on RCA in late '67 was a Porter Dolly duet, 'The Last Thing On My Mind' (written by Tom Paxton), a catchy uptempo folksy song that entered the Top 10. It was a successful vindication of Wagoner's decision to record duets and captured the infectious musical and personal rapport the pair had now developed onstage. One writer went so far as to say the record, "marked the beginning of a new dimension to the industry's duet concept spawning an unprecedented number of other duet partnerships attempting to duplicate the success of Porter and Dolly". With there being quite a few other famous couplings in country music already, the comment seemed over generous but it was nonetheless an indication of the fresh impetus Porter and Dolly gave to the genre.

Country comedienne Minnie Pearl pointed out that apart from their

---

* Atkins evidently did not remember the tape sent to him when Dolly was younger.

music Dolly and Porter made a striking pair: a tall, handsome man with a petite but voluptuous blonde wearing a dazzling array of garments. For Porter it was the start of a major phase in an already successful career. For 21-year-old Dolly, it was merely the springboard to her own ambition.

# Chapter 9

THANKS to her being the new girl singer on *The Porter Wagoner Show*, overnight Dolly became one of Sevierville's most famous daughters. To celebrate her success in Nashville, Judge Ray Reagan declared October 7, 1967 to be Dolly Parton Day. The day before, Cas Walker ran an ad that read: "Welcome, Dolly! Sing some gospel songs while you are here, for Sevier County is truly God's country!" An emotional Dolly paraded through the streets in an open top car as part of a police escorted cavalcade, waving and smiling to the many locals who turned out, some of whom had sneered a mere three years before when she said she was going to Nashville to be a star. Earlier in the day she had given brief performances in the nearby towns of Pigeon Forge and Gatlinburg – no doubt the latter venue was particularly satisfying for Dolly who recalled people there looking down on her and her siblings because of the clothes they wore.

A crowd of around 7,000 people assembled in front of Sevierville courthouse to hear Dolly sing and see her presented with the key to the town by the mayor. It was originally anticipated that the event would be on a fairly small scale but the presence of Porter and his band and fellow country singer Mel Tillis (whose eldest daughter Pam began her career in the Seventies) ensured that attendance figures dramatically increased. Ironically, as a result of the large turnout and Dolly's busy schedule, some of those who had helped her in the pre Nashville days were unable to see her. Even Avie Lee found it was not easy to get an audience with her own daughter now that she was a celebrity. Though proud of his daughter's achievements, getting dressed in a smart suit and standing next to local dignitaries including the mayor was an uncomfortable experience for Lee. An RCA executive was also on hand to confirm to the townsfolk that their heroine had been given a contract with the label.

For her first RCA single Dolly could have played safe with any number of non-controversial catchy tunes. Instead she chose one of her own songs inspired by a private episode in her life. When after about eight months of marriage Carl asked Dolly if he had been her first lover she told him that he wasn't. Dolly said in a *Rolling Stone* interview that she had been Carl's first true love and for this reason her answer was all the harder for him to accept. She claimed her revelation put a strain on their marriage for some time. His response inspired 'Just Because I'm A Woman', which challenged society's notion that it was somehow acceptable for a man to be sexually experienced before marriage whereas for women, it was frowned upon. Some referred to the slow paced country song as one of the first Women's Lib anthems. However, even in a time of "free love", Dolly felt duty bound to allow that sex before marriage was a "mistake", despite the fact that in various interviews over the years she has made it clear that she was unashamed of her own dalliances before marriage. In a 1984 interview with Maura Moynihan and Andy Warhol Dolly let slip, "When I went to Nashville they liked my personality and I never sold myself out. I never went to bed with anybody unless I wanted to, never for business reasons."

In 1992, Dolly told Terry Wogan she had "fooled around" before Carl but that, "a little bit never hurt nobody". Her use of the word "mistake" in the song no doubt reflected her recognition of the prevailing conservative views in the Southern states of America. Even at this stage in her career Dolly was wary of alienating her potential audience and in one early interview she had even said that a man should rule his household, "As it said in the Bible." Still, there was no doubting the hard-hitting message of the song; the reference to a "good girl" echoing the same message in Kitty Wells' anthem 'It Wasn't God Who Made Honky Tonk Angels.' The record was too controversial for some American radio stations that refused to play it fearing their more conservative listeners might switch off in disgust. Despite this, or perhaps as a result of the publicity it engendered, the single made the lower reaches of the Top 20 (and number one in South Africa as Dolly proudly pointed out). 'Just Because I'm A Woman' was the first notable example of Dolly using personal events from her own life as part of the creative process. "She can imagine these experiences in such great detail that she can write songs about them, great songs," says Porter Wagoner. "This capacity to understand or feel, I think, is something that God gives to very, very few people."

"I like to describe my writing as being simply complicated," she told the *New York Post*. "It's got enough depth to be appreciated and enough simplicity to be understood . . . It's part of me as long as I remember, a way to describe my feelings . . . my memories . . . some of them bother me. It's almost like going to a psychiatrist if I can write a song about my problem, then I can share it with the world then it never bothers me any more."

The message in 'Just Because I'm A Woman' was of course offset by

Dolly's ultra-feminine image and personality but she, along with Loretta Lynn* – in songs such as 'The Pill' and 'Don't Come Home A Drinkin' (With Lovin' On Your Mind)' – put themselves on the line by daring to complain about the inequality between the sexes. One of today's country stars, Trisha Yearwood acknowledges the debt. In response to those who say that nowadays women are singing songs with more assertive lyrics she points out, "Well, you must not have listened to Dolly Parton and Tammy Wynette and Loretta Lynn." These crucial three competed with men as headline acts and, as writer Robert K. Oermann puts it, "Redefined what it means to be a woman in country music."

Dolly received a BMI award for being co-writer of 'Put It Off Until Tomorrow', one of the most played songs of the year. The prospect of a black tie awards ceremony was extremely unappealing to Carl but being his wife's first major award, he decided to attend. Dolly was nervous about her first ceremony of this kind but for Carl it was his last, as she confirmed, "He didn't know anybody or anything about the business, and he's a loner anyway, not a socialiser at all. He really felt out of place that night. So after we had got home he said, 'Now I know this is what you want for your life and I'm proud for you because I want you to have it if it makes you happy. But it don't make me happy and I don't want to be part of it. I'm just too uncomfortable, and it's not *me*, and I can't get involved in it.'"

On the strength of Dolly's improving financial situation, she and Carl bought a substantial two-storey house in Antioch, a residential district to the south of Nashville. Having completed four years in the Air Force, Judy Ogle was now in the area and it appears likely that she moved in with Dolly and Carl. Dolly also took some pressure off her parents by letting five of her younger siblings stay with them. She has suggested that she effectively took personal responsibility for their upbringing but given her intense involvement in the music business it's hard to see how this could have been. Stella Parton discreetly says the matter has been "overstated . . . actually I was the one overseeing their care, she was financing their care." Dolly inevitably became a larger than life figure for her younger nephews and nieces who took to calling her, "Aunt Granny".

With Fred Foster keen to make as much capital as possible from his former artist, Monument released *Hello, I'm Dolly Parton* in November 1967. The album featured 12 tracks including the hits, 'Dumb Blonde'

---

* Interestingly Loretta's breakthrough was also partly facilitated by a duet partnership with an older, well-established Nashville stalwart, Ernest Tubb.

and 'Something Fishy' as well as Dolly's own versions of songs which had achieved success for others such as 'Put It Off Until Tomorrow' and 'Fuel To The Flame'. 'I Don't Wanna Throw Rice' was a warning against competing rivals while the feisty 'You're Ole Handy Man', followed in the footsteps of 'Just Because I'm A Woman' by admonishing her fellow sisterhood not to put up with bad treatment from their men. The album reached a respectable number 11 on the country charts thus ensuring that Foster received a reasonable payback on his investment.

Not long after, in February 1968, Dolly and Porter's first duets album *Just Between You And Me* was released in a sleeve showing Dolly snuggling up to Porter, the pair smiling broadly in matching red woollen pullovers. The release established a pattern of albums with one or two of the duo's current hits (in this case, 'The Last Thing On My Mind') beefed up by a song selection of varying quality, sometimes clocking in at a paltry playing time of 25 minutes. The songs were pure old style country – weepy ballads mixed with light-hearted uptempo numbers.

Dolly managed a healthy five writing contributions to the album and the title track was written by Jack Clement who had first met Dolly when she was working at Combine Music. "I would see her hanging around there a lot and then one day I was over visiting and Bob [Beckham] said that she's going to be on Porter Wagoner's show and she's gonna be an instant star. He was right, soon as she got on Porter's TV show she was off and running, but it was his show, it wasn't like she could walk away with the show, it was purely his show but she was a big, big thing on it and it was instant."

Porter had wisely realised the commercial potential of a duets album and sure enough it made the country charts Top 10. Many buyers assumed that the pair were an item – no doubt assisted by songs such as 'If You Go I'll Follow You', 'Please Don't Stop Loving Me', 'Home Is Where The Hurt Is', 'Two Sides To Every Story' and 'Sorrow's Tearing Down The House' which seemed to be episodes in an unfolding soap opera.

At about the same time as Dolly's contract with Monument came to an end so too did her agreement with Combine Music. Instead of renewing it she took the opportunity to set up her own publishing company with Bill Owens using parts of their respective surnames to create Owepar. Her holding was 51% to Bill's 49%. This was an important move since it gave her (and Bill) control of the copyright of the material she wrote from 1967 onwards. In deciding to set up Owepar Dolly would almost certainly have been influenced by Porter and Don Warden's company, Warden Music, which had helped to secure Wagoner's financial position. Dolly arranged for Judy Ogle to work for a while as a secretary/administrator at Owepar.

Two years later Owens transferred his share in Owepar to Dolly in exchange for royalties on a list of approximately 40 songs which he hoped she would record. To a considerable extent this was a speculative move on his part because Dolly was not in a position to guarantee the recording of any particular songs. Owens wanted to make his mark in record production and tried to attract business by claiming to be able to record and ship a single for $500.* In spite of the fact that there were already indications of professional disagreements between them, Dolly subsequently transferred Owens' share of Owepar to Porter – describing it as a Christmas present – on the basis that the majority of the songs were written by them either individually or together.

The writer Colin Escott makes the point that Porter taught Dolly how to be unafraid of making an impact with her appearance. As time went on her costumes and wigs (blonde became platinum on occasion) became noticeably flashier in concert and on television. However, her hairstyle, though outlandish, was nonetheless in keeping with Loretta Lynn, Tammy Wynette and Dottie West; Dolly just took things a bit further and began to make a particular feature of her bust which would become one of the most distinctive and talked about parts of her iconic image. People who worked with Dolly during her early days in Nashville suggest that while undoubtedly prominent her bosom was not the gargantuan phenomenon it subsequently became; the source of endless jokes, speculation, double entendres, not to mention concerns over health-related issues.

Dolly also learned from Porter the importance of always looking good for your public and acting in a professional manner while onstage. Another aspect that made an impression on Dolly was his generous dealings with his musicians. He was one of the first country stars to offer shares to musicians as opposed to just paying them a fixed fee.

Once she joined forces with Porter the commitment required from Dolly increased to an extreme level. The television shows were videotaped in rapid succession in front of a live audience and if somebody made a mistake the cameras kept rolling while the offender had to cover up as best he or she could. This was due to financial constraints and because, as Wagoner put it, "I don't like it to look too rehearsed." The team recorded about 80 shows each year (aiming to have about a dozen recorded at any one time) and reached the stage where they could tape two shows in little over an hour. It was high pressure work; apart from trying to not make

* He later returned to Owepar to work as a writer.

mistakes, all concerned had to smile and look relaxed for the audience and cameras. Dolly admired the fact that Porter included religious songs and sentiments on his television show. On one show he prefaced the song 'I Believe' by saying, "Religion has always been a big part of my life and like most people, I didn't always do my very best but I try. And in my heart I can say that I do believe."

Alongside the show, a series of joint and solo recording sessions were slotted between a heavy touring schedule. Dolly and Porter were booked to do over 100 one-night stands in cities and small towns all over the country each year, which meant around the same number of days on the road. On top of all this Dolly was still writing constantly.

Porter's bus, which had cost $67,000, was better than the beaten-up old station wagon Dolly was used to, but touring could be punishing nonetheless. Dolly was in an almost totally male environment as she told *Rolling Stone* in a 1977 interview, "It was hell . . . but in the early days when I was travelling in the bus, Porter saw to it that I had my own little bathroom . . . I didn't have to pee in the same room with the guys." Porter felt the strain when he was hospitalised several times as a result of total exhaustion. Though Dolly too felt the stress, she had the satisfaction of seeing her popularity with the audiences increase as her onstage confidence grew.

In such a high pressure environment, Porter inevitably got to know Dolly over their first year together and he was surprised at what he discovered. "I soon found out that she was actually an insecure person – in the way she looked, in the way she was brought up, in every direction. Believe it or not, Dolly never used to think she was a beautiful woman, though of course she was. I feel sure that's a main reason she wears the big hair-dos." He recalled one particular incident on the bus when they were messing around. "I just accidentally knocked Dolly's wig off. Her hair was matted down real tight to her head, and she did look pretty bad. Well, that just damn near killed her. It was just such a terrible, terrible thing; she cried about it. And of course, I felt awful because I didn't mean to knock her wig off. But I learned then how sensitive she was. Insecurity also made her talk so fast. I worked with her, though, and eventually she learned to talk slower – like she talks at home with her family."

He apparently directed his pupil, "Don't try to flower it up and talk like you're so well educated that you wouldn't use 'ain't' in a sentence. ''Cause, hell, you use 'ain't' every other word up in them mountains of East Tennessee, same as we do in Missouri. People want you to be honest with 'em . . ." Porter said Dolly listened to him carefully, "because she realised I knew how to do things, and she knew I wouldn't tell her wrong." He wouldn't hold back when something was good or bad, which she appreciated because her family, like most, tended to lavish praise on one of their own regardless. Porter said that as a duet they really wanted to sing duets better than anybody else and were prepared to put in the necessary hard work to achieve this. "Dolly and I both had that hungry feeling in our souls."

The duo attracted increasingly large crowds to their shows and when appearing at the Bluegrass Fair in Lexington, Kentucky they attracted a crowd of more than 50,000 people. On occasion they found time to support good causes and during a visit to San Antonio in 1970, Porter, Dolly and Speck visited Brooke General Hospital, a temporary home to many Vietnam veterans. Naturally they could not spend time with each patient and one wheelchair-confined inmate was heard to remark, "Well if we can't get all their autographs, we'll settle for Dolly's." In addition to the endless television, recording and touring, Dolly was in demand for in-person appearances, awards banquets, industry functions, interviews and press conferences as well as meetings with producers and songwriters (though at this stage she said she had no interest in films).

Meanwhile her husband was busy fulfilling contracts with his paving and asphalting business. From the outside, Dolly and Carl's marriage looked to be in trouble from the moment she started becoming successful and few would have been surprised if their sharply contrasting aspirations in life led to a parting of the ways. A pattern soon emerged of Carl spending a lot of time at home with Dolly being absent for long spells. Dolly enigmatically remarked, "He's happy to let me be married and single at the same time."

In some ways his low profile was an advantage. In 1967, especially in the world of country music, the assumption was that if a young woman was going to take a job as an entertainer, then she couldn't possibly be married. One member of Porter's troupe said to Dolly when she first started touring with them, "Aren't you glad you're not married, or you couldn't go?" to which she tartly replied, "Well I am married and I am going." Knowledge of Carl's existence only seeped out gradually but by the time it was general knowledge Dolly was well enough established for it to be accepted.

However, the more successful Dolly became the more the relationship became the subject of speculation in the media, particularly supermarket tabloids such as *The National Enquirer*. The situation has not much changed almost 40 years on and at the time of writing there is, yet again, speculation in the tabloid press that the marriage is in trouble. Dolly and Carl's relationship is an enigma which inevitably arouses curiosity among her fans but all media comment inevitably revolves around speculation and subjective opinion.

Dolly was certainly working extremely hard but in contrast to those early struggling years in Nashville she was now receiving a significant financial reward of about $60,000 a year. Dolly's income represented an aggregate of the revenue from live concerts, about $300 per show, plus union scale for television appearances with royalties from the songs she wrote (a steadily increasing source of income). Unlike Porter's band members, however, she did not get a percentage of the take, instead receiving a fixed fee. To her family and friends back home it was fantasy money.

Swift to capitalise on the success of the first Porter and Dolly album a second, *Just The Two Of Us* collection was released in October 1968. Once more the photograph on the sleeve showed the smiling pair in matching tops, this time in pale yellow jackets, as if to project a togetherness which belied or at least tried to gloss over the 19-year age gap between the two. The album of love or love-gone-wrong songs contained the mid paced 'Holding On To Nothin'' in which a couple admit trying to keep a relationship going when it was clearly over. The song featured guitar picking, fiddle and steel guitar, which was typical of the album's overall sound, although producer Bob Ferguson often filled out the arrangements with conventional violin backing as well. Ferguson made sure that the instrumentation was there to complement the singing. Though Dolly had only been with Porter for a short time her vocals were assured; sounding very much at home. What's more, the vibrato which Fred Foster had tried to train her to lose was still in evidence, one of Dolly's distinctive trademarks.

Earlier in the year Dolly's first RCA solo album, *Just Because I'm A Woman*, was released, making a respectable showing in the country charts, just outside the Top 20. The cover has Dolly dressed in a neat fitting white dress* with prominent wig and bosom. Dolly's arms held open in a welcoming stance, allied to her glamorous appearance, lulled the listener into a false sense of security for the challenging message of the title track. Another song, 'Baby Sister', contained a strong moral element, warning young women of the dangers of being led astray by older men. The album featured some straightforward love and heartache songs, not to mention a piece of comedy hokum, 'I'll Oil Wells Love You', though it bore no relation to Dolly's subsequent classic, 'I Will Always Love You'. Her

---

* The same dress she wore when auditioning for Porter; he liked it so much he asked her to wear it for the sleeve shot.

penchant for the tragic ballads she learned as a child found expression in one of her own eerily haunting compositions, 'The Bridge'. The tale, similar in theme to Bobbie Gentry's 1967 US hit, 'Ode To Billie Joe', concerned a girl who meets her lover on the bridge. Passion overtakes them in a nearby field and unwanted pregnancy follows. The final denouement comes when the girl jumps off the bridge to her death in the river below.

Having caused a speculative buzz among Nashville insiders, in the space of a few months Dolly had exploded onto the country music scene and was now the focus of much press interest and comment. One writer said of her voice, "It has a special sound that combines childlike tenderness with adult passion and emotion." Another said of her singing, "There is a tiny sliver of frill one second, a desperate full-throttle quaver the next. Loretta Lynn's voice may echo the mountains. But at its best, Dolly Parton's voice recalls the heavens."

# Chapter 10

THE energy required for Dolly to maintain her countless commitments throughout the late Sixties and early Seventies verged on the superhuman so it was fortunate that she was able to function on only a few hours sleep a night. Dolly denied being a workaholic – more a "playaholic" – although she said she would wait till the last minute to fall asleep because of her fear that she "might miss something". Sometimes she didn't bother to take her make-up off since presumably putting it back on would be too laborious, as Stella Parton recalls, "She's spent the night with me before and never taken her make-up off and her eyelashes or her wig and just sleeps propped up on the pillows in the bed with me . . . me I wash my face and put my head under the pillow . . . I wake up and I'm like, 'Did you go to sleep?' She says, 'Well yeah and now I'm ready to go home.'" As Dolly was fond of saying, her dreams started when she woke up.

In 1969 Dolly released two solo albums. For the cover shot of *In The Good Old Days* she looked demure in a red dress, her more voluptuous image being held in check on this occasion. Wearing a conservative whitish wig, it was hard to believe the woman in the picture was a mere 23 years old. With the Woodstock Festival happening that summer Dolly looked incredibly square although the album made number 15 in the country charts. Despite Dolly's prolific song output RCA ensured that they were not putting all their eggs into one basket by selecting material from other writers. On *In The Good Old Days* covers of proven country hits, Jeanie C. Riley's 'Harper Valley PTA' and Tammy Wynette's 'D-I-V-O-R-C-E' were included as well as Porter Wagoner's small town morality tale 'The Carroll County Accident'. The album also featured 'Fresh Out Of Forgiveness' on which Dolly had a stab at sounding soulful, though Porter later described her version in disparaging terms. The memorable title track was Dolly's bittersweet chronicle of her life growing up in the Smokies. The lyrics served to continue the oral poetic tradition of the historic music of the mountains but writer Bill C. Malone made the general point that unlike a lot of her contemporaries Dolly avoided the temptation to romanticise the past: "She speaks with gentle affection about her childhood memories but pulls no punches about the hardships people endured and made it clear from early on that she would have no desire to revisit the old days."

Dolly succeeded in taking inspiration from personal experiences while at the same time giving them universal significance which others could identify with. Dolly, along with other contemporaries such as Loretta Lynn, Buck Owens, George Jones, Narvel Felts and Willie Nelson, constituted virtually the last group of American country artists who could recall and draw inspiration from genuine rural roots – for instance Willie Nelson's 'Family Bible' and Loretta Lynn's 'Coalminer's Daughter'.

The second release *My Blue Ridge Mountain Boy* was remarkable for the fact that the publicity-shy Carl allowed himself to be featured on the cover, appearing to take the part of Dolly's Blue Ridge mountain boy. Dolly lies back as if in a reverie with Carl, her pensive-looking dream object, some distance off behind her (the perspective cleverly has them deceptively close when they're not) while in the background is a wooden shack of the type Dolly grew up in as a child. The title song tells of an 18-year-old girl who breaks the heart of the country boy who loves her when she moves to the big city. Economic hardship bears down on her and she ends up a prostitute. To add to her woes, she finds out that her sweetheart has given up on the idea of waiting for her to return and has married someone else. 'Daddy' was a daughter pleading with her father not to break up the family home by continuing a relationship with a new love who was younger than her. 'Till Death Do Us Part' was a real tearjerker; a woman reminding her husband of their wedding vows following his involvement with another woman. She can't live without him and so takes her own life, wondering if he will come and place flowers on her grave. 'Evening Shade' told of the plight of children suffering under a tyrannical official at an orphanage, demonstrating Dolly's remarkable ability to empathise with the suffering of young children. Once more the album featured covers of current hits, Joe South's 'Games People Play' and 'In The Ghetto', written by Mac Davis and most famously associated with Elvis Presley. When released as a single, Dolly's version of the latter song was only a minor hit, just grazing the Top 50. The album made number six in the country charts and was the first of her solo albums to make any impression in the pop charts – albeit number 194.

The image of Dolly promoted by RCA in the early days was essentially conservative country; attractive femininity to appeal to men without alienating their women. Dolly looked glamorous in an old-fashioned way – her clothes were modest and conventional and the wigs appeared less overblown than those she wore for her television and stage appearances. It would not be long, however, before Dolly gave free rein to her preferred excessive image.

Another duets album with Porter, *Always, Always* also appeared in 1969, following the same formula created by their earlier albums: a mixture of ballads and uptempo numbers, with the occasional 'battle of the sexes' song thrown in for light relief. The tender love ballad, 'Yours Love', was a Top 10 hit. Dolly and Porter divided up the singing equitably, sometimes delivering alternate lines or stanzas with each harmonising or the other delivering a recitation. At the end of some of the "fight" songs they would trade a few jibes on the fade. There were times, especially on the earlier albums, when the childlike quality in Dolly's voice generated an air of innocence and vulnerability while Porter's was the complete opposite: at times he seemed to deliver lines with a knowing leer producing overtones of a rather unsettling seediness.

Around this time, the idea for 'Coat Of Many Colors' hit Dolly and she started scribbling down words on the nearest available object, namely the back of a cleaning tag attached to one of Porter's colourful jackets (the tag is now on display in Dollywood). Dolly was also capable of storing ideas in her head when there was no opportunity to write anything down; she even admitted to writing songs in this way in church on occasion though she doubted if this was "proper". She also mentioned in one interview that she liked to write songs in cemeteries. Ideas often came to her at night ("I guess that's 'cause it's so quiet.") She might get up and start writing or just note a few ideas down and then continue in the morning ("Depends on how knocked out I am.") Dolly has said that when inspiration strikes and she is unable for whatever reason to write something down immediately she "can't even carry on a halfway decent conversation". She also claimed to get "looking headaches" in her quest to gain ideas from observing people and situations. As she said, "I don't want to miss a thing."

She would appear at the Owepar office with 10 or more songs that she had written the previous evening and was invariably impatient to get the lyrics typed as quickly as possible so she could get into the studio to record demos. Her songs were constructed to be accessible and melodic as one writer put it, "She showed a striking ability to write songs that flowed up and down rather than just coasting along on the crest of a riff." For all her cheery effervescence, a significant number of her songs touched on unhappy topics. "Me and Porter liked to sing those old sad songs. He liked to do recitations, and I liked to sing those pitiful songs so the more pitiful I could make them the better we liked them."

Evidently the public shared their attraction to misery. 'Jeannie's Afraid Of The Dark' – originally released as the flip side of 'We'll Get Ahead Someday' and included on the 1968 album *Just The Two Of Us* – became one of the pair's most requested numbers. The song was about a child, afraid of the dark, who dies of a mysterious ailment. After her death, the child's grief-stricken parents place an eternal flame over her grave to ensure that she never has to sleep in the dark again. This resonated with Dolly's terrifying experience of having been locked in her school cloak-room though whether that incident directly inspired the song is not clear. 'The Party', also on *Just The Two Of Us*, concerned a couple spending an evening drinking, socialising and telling blue jokes, having left their young children at home alone. At the party the father has a strange feeling that he should be at home and he and his wife leave the party early, to find their children have died in a blaze at their home. Apart from the tragedy of the situation the lyrics suggest a particular kind of moral dimension to Dolly's character which seeks to mete out severe punishment to those who fail to follow God's rule. The presence of failure, unhappiness and random death in Dolly's songs may have had its origins in natural events such as floods or hurricanes which were part of life for many people from her part of the world. Writer Steve Eng goes so far as to speculate, albeit tentatively, that Dolly's preoccupation with the darker side of the human experience may signify something more sinister. "Dolly's fear of the dark, along with her many songs about oppressed children and degraded women, at least raises the spectre of child abuse, though whether experienced, witnessed, suspected, feared or merely understood, is conjectural."

Whether there is any truth in Eng's comments, Dolly, along with a few other highly original country writers such as Johnny Cash, Merle Haggard and Tom T. Hall, brought personal insight into the general parameters of the established style of country songs – as writer Stephanie Zacharek put it, "Appalachia retooled for the late 20th century." This tradition had partly disappeared in the Fifties and Sixties because a new breed of commercial writer emerged in Nashville that was hired to churn out formulaic songs to suit the styles of particular singers. (Of course Dolly had a foot in both camps since she too wrote for other artists).

Early in 1970 another solo album, *The Fairest Of Them All*, was released, the sleeve showing Dolly looking into a mirror with her reflection tanta-lisingly obscured by a purple, fan-like attachment on her dress and a bunch of white flowers. Like Porter Dolly was not afraid to address the subject of mental health and 'Daddy Come And Get Me' told of a "crazy" woman committed to a mental institution from a broken heart because her husband is involved with another. The woman implores her father to come and take her away. A mournful folk song, 'Down From Dover' was about a young couple, seemingly in love, but when the girl becomes pregnant, the boy does not come back for her from Dover as he was supposed to. The baby is born dead, a way of telling the girl that her lover will not be coming back. The song was released as a single and reached number 40* while the album made the Top 20. Dolly's singing attracted much praise. One journalist said ". . . her voice is crystal clear soprano. She has a distinctive delivery, placing her emphasis on surprising syllables, cutting off short on one word and allowing her voice to drop off gradually on another. In the finest country tradition she conveys intense emotion without using her voice as an emotional gimmick."

Maintaining the frenetic rate of production, a duet album *Porter Wayne and Dolly Rebecca* appeared later in the year, the sleeve showing Porter and Dolly as children. In the album's joke song, 'Run That By Me One More Time', a husband and wife accuse each other of squandering the family income with both providing unconvincing alibis and excuses in their attempts to refute the charges. Dolly managed to include a couple of morbid songs about children, including 'Silver Sandals', where a crippled young girl exchanges her crutches for silver sandals to climb up the golden stairway to heaven. 'Down In The Alley', written by Dolly for Porter's 1970 album *Skid Row Joe*, was about those whose lives had been ruined by alcohol.

Resplendent in a garish, lime green dress and matching hat, Dolly again returned to Sevierville in 1970 for Dolly Parton Day. For the concert, held at the school gym in aid of the Sevier County High School Band in which Dolly had been a drummer, she changed into a white dress with shiny metal studs. RCA engineers were present to record her first live album, *A Real Live Dolly*. Cas Walker introduced Dolly with Porter and Speck Rhodes appearing as surprise guests. Porter made up a story about getting lost en route to the venue which provided him with an opportunity to mention small mountain towns; Possum Holler, Frog Alley, Booger Town, a section of the crowd roaring approval at each namecheck. His description of Dolly as "the finest lady in every respect I've ever known" also went down well. It was interesting to note the

---

* It was also covered by contemporary female artist Nancy Sinatra and was featured on an album of Dolly's songs recorded by Skeeter Davis.

shift of emphasis; Dolly being the main attraction with Porter in a special guest role.*

Dolly had gained in confidence and a local paper reported that, "Her Shirley Temple dimples played effortlessly as the Dresden-like Dolly sang number after number in her slightly tremulous soprano voice." Apart from chatting easily in between songs, she told stories of Rawhead Bloody Bones and Scratch Eyes, characters Avie Lee brought to life to scare her brood into going to bed. Speck's saucy comedy routines included a phone call to his mythical girlfriend Sadie, where he learned that a bikini was now in favour over a one-piece swim suit to which he said, "Which piece do you think you ought to wear, the top or the bottom?" The evening raised approximately $2,000 and from the money raised, scholarships worth $400 were given to four senior students to assist them with college costs. The school brass band was kitted out with new uniforms and instruments for their marching display.

The Country Music Association was founded in 1958, the first organisation of its kind to promote a specific genre of music. It steadily grew in size and, in 1967, inaugurated the annual CMA awards, which were first transmitted two years later. The live broadcast quickly became the principal showcase for country music on mainstream television and today it is watched by many millions each year, by no means all specifically country fans.

In 1968 Dolly and Porter won the Vocal Group Of The Year award, presented by Chet Atkins. For the occasion Dolly wore a flowing pink chiffon top with a band of silver sequins. The pair were nominated again the following year but lost out to Johnny Cash and June Carter. A newspaper report the following day described Dolly and Porter as "RCA's favourite duet couple dressed in high fashion, Porter Wagoner in his pink ruffled shirt and Dolly Parton in her white crepe smock and rhinestone full-length gown." The pair won the renamed Vocal Duo Of The Year award in 1970 and 1971 when they found themselves in the company of such other winners as Charlie Pride and Ray Price.†

---

* Dolly later returned the compliment by appearing at a Porter Wagoner day in his home town of White Plains, Missouri. The crowd was so effusive in its appreciation of their favourite son that, at times, Porter had to leave the stage and retire to the tour bus to regain his composure.

† Dolly was a nominee for Female Vocalist Of The Year each year from 1968 to 1974 with the exception of 1973. She won in both 1975 and 1976 with either Loretta Lynn or Tammy Wynette taking the honour in the remaining years.

In 1970 Dolly enjoyed her first Top 10 hit from a fairly unlikely source. Porter was eager to find something different for Dolly, but at the same time "keep her in an area where I knew what was going on". Porter came up with the idea of a girl singing Jimmie Rodgers' 'Muleskinner Blues'. Dolly evidently did not think a great deal of the song and even asked that it not be released but Porter was confident it would "generate excitement". Bob Ferguson arranged for Porter to crack a whip on the record to add atmosphere, though whether either of them saw any symbolism can only be guessed at. The song made number three in the country charts, achieved airplay on some rock stations and received a Grammy nomination, which proved beyond any doubt that she could fare capably as a solo artist.

Yet another duets album came out in May, appropriately entitled *Once More*. For the cover shot Porter wrapped his arm around Dolly who leant in towards him. They were both smiling the obligatory smiles but there seemed to be little in the way of romantic warmth and the impression was more of a father and daughter. With Porter wearing a pink shirt and Dolly a pink dress as Steve Eng put it, "The whole effect is strawberry ice cream all a-slosh with honey." The album featured Dolly's Top 10 single, 'Daddy Was An Old Time Preacher Man', which paid lip service to the type of sermons preached in her grandfather Jake Owens' church, and 'Ragged Angel', a Dolly special about a little girl called Cindy whose only friend is a paper doll. Cindy's parents show no interest in her and she dies of neglect. 'Fight And Scratch', one of the album's more memorable songs, was another episode in the partnership's staged volatile relationship.

Dolly's drawing power had grown to the extent that, following an appearance on the television show *Hee Haw* in 1970, she was offered a permanent spot but declined. This was undoubtedly a wise move. Whilst *Hee Haw* certainly had a substantial following, the programme was a caricature of hayseed country with the performers sitting on hay bales wearing dungarees and checked shirts.

By comparison Porter's show was the height of urbane sophistication. The sets were basic and rural in theme; farm gates and pictures of houses and trees acting as bucolic symbols. Dolly relaxed more in front of the camera, introducing some of the commercial breaks and singing the jingles which Porter had initially taken care of. She also managed to sing notes way up the register without any apparent strain on her face though her stage moves remained basic, limited and stiff. Dolly sometimes imagined she was singing to her family and not to a television camera, saying this helped to achieve her aim of wanting people to look at her and think, "She means what she's saying." Porter also encouraged Dolly to have a good rapport with the audience. "One time we were doing a concert in the north-east," he said in 1985. "For the lack of anything else to say, Dolly asked the audience, 'How many of you like our new costumes?' and some of 'em applauded. Then she said, 'How many of you don't like 'em?' and a few of 'em applauded. And I said, 'Now ask how many of 'em don't give a damn,' and then they *all* applauded!" Dolly took this as a rebuff but Porter pointed out the importance of the exercise, saying, "Then it got to where she could turn lines back around on me all the time, making our shows a lot funnier."

For their concerts Dolly introduced her preferred image of big hair, big bosom, and loud outfits. However, at this stage, the way her wigs sat clumsily on her head, with the hairline far too obvious, bore more than a passing resemblance to the dress wigs worn by the 18th-century British and French aristocracy. She wore so much make-up that "you could carve your initials in her face and not draw blood," as one unkind journalist wrote.

Dolly's femininity was seen as an advantage. If she had come on in an aggressive feminist way she would have undoubtedly riled many of the men she needed to work with. "I like to think that women are the equal of men in most things, especially here in America where equality is important. When I started out in my career I was much plainer-looking than I am now. I soon realised that I had to play by men's rules to win. My way of fighting back was to wear frilly clothes and put on the big, blonde wigs. It helped that I had a small voice and that enabled me to sing songs of pain and loneliness and gentle things like butterflies and children. And I found that both men and women liked me."

In 1969, at the age of 23, Dolly became the 54th member of the Grand Ole Opry, appearing at the Opry's 44th anniversary show, singing 'My Blue Ridge Mountain Boy'. Porter appeared immediately before her but Dolly's reception was the more enthusiastic, which only exacerbated the tensions that had arisen between them. Since she was gaining so much exposure as a result of his TV show and because of the hands-on role he played in all of her musical output Porter felt responsible for making Dolly a success. In one sense he saw her as an investment that would pay dividends by helping to draw more people in at the box office.* Nevertheless

---

* There was a certain irony in this as Porter was often slow to agree to put up the prices he charged for his own concerts, a source of frustration for his manager.

he saw this as no more than he was entitled to in view of the substantial amount of time he'd invested in co-producing her records*, working out routines for the television show and generally guiding Dolly's career. Some in Porter's circle complained that he was devoting too much of his energy to Dolly, and were worried what might happen to them if Dolly decided to leave the troupe to pursue a solo career. Porter envisioned a lengthy partnership, but according to Dolly, she had made it clear from the outset that she would only guarantee to remain his duet partner for several years.

On the other side of the coin it's interesting to speculate whether Porter would have found himself on the winner's podium at the CMA Awards as often as he did were it not for Dolly. The fact is, despite his extremely high profile in Nashville's country music scene, he never won a Male Vocalist Of The Year, let alone the Entertainer Of The Year award. Porter did not recognise the partnership in terms of equality although it was obvious he was not dealing with his previous girl singers. However, Porter's band didn't refer to him as "the chief" for nothing and Wagoner felt it necessary to be strong-willed as he later said, if he had not kept a firm hand on proceedings, "Dolly would have led me off on a dark dingy road."

"I think he was a very hard driving man about their career," said Ralph Emery, "I think there were no committees." Both Wagoner and Owens could be dictatorial in their dealings with Dolly. Despite the former's prominent role in Dolly's professional life, as late as 1971, she still referred to Owens as her manager even though his role had greatly diminished. This may have been a simple tip of the hat out of family loyalty as Owens is on record as saying it was Porter who called the shots once he and Dolly became a team. Regardless Owens continued to receive a small salary for management services until the early Seventies. After Owens disposed of his share in Owepar subsequent views on his role and importance in Dolly's professional life vary. Cas Walker maintained Owens hadn't helped Dolly that much and Fred Foster has also made negative comments about his role. In some interviews Dolly simply referred to Owens as an "uncle" without mentioning him by name and there have been inevitable implications that after Dolly achieved success he rode on her gravy train. Such observations overlook the hard work Owens put in during the early days when he believed in her.

---

* A right he had been given by RCA in 1969, though he did not receive a credit on the sleeves of her albums for some years; it was Bob Ferguson's name which appeared.

Though it's not possible to point to a specific incident there is no doubt that Porter and Dolly's relationship became fractious from an early stage. Porter has said that Dolly initially agreed to his ideas on how to project her, yet Dolly claims they fought "like cats and dogs" and that their stubborn natures brought out the worst in each other. By the early Seventies she was dropping the odd hint that the idyllic partnership presented in the television studio and onstage was not reality. Their arguments mainly revolved around musical matters, what songs to record, how they should sound, what instruments to use and even what kind of between-song patter Dolly should deliver onstage. While Porter remained conservatively country Dolly was now listening to other kinds of popular music in the late Sixties and early Seventies. Being commercially ambitious she was well aware that songs which only made the country charts sold fewer copies, thus earning less money than those which crossed over to the more lucrative world of pop music.

Shrewdly realising that if Dolly did strike out on her own he could receive a share of her future earnings Porter sought to ensure a return in his investment by having Dolly sign a contract, something the pair had not previously done. Dolly later said that though she voluntarily signed the contract with Porter some time during 1970, she was inexperienced and did not take legal advice beforehand.

The contract was not particularly long. The main points were:

Confirmation of Dolly's transfer to Porter of 49% of Owepar.

If Dolly were to leave Porter's show, he would be allowed to manage her for five years with a second five-year option which either could choose not to exercise.

Porter was to receive 15% of Dolly's net income excluding income from her songwriting.

Porter would act as Dolly's personal and business adviser and act in her best interests at all times. Dolly would need Porter's written approval before entering any new music contracts of any kind.

Porter would collect fees under her contracts on her behalf.

Dolly would have first option to buy Porter's 49% in Owepar should he wish to sell.

Though she had not taken legal advice Dolly luckily realised the importance of retaining the copyrights to her songs. "I just had to protect my songs. If something happened to Porter they were always up for grabs. Everybody always wanted my songs . . . I tried to protect them for myself, from the world, as you would your children."

The contract was clumsily worded, specifically the reference to Porter "acting in Dolly's best interests at all times" which would have been difficult to define let alone enforce. It made no allowance for wider outlets for Dolly's creativity such as books, films or indeed theme parks. Any professionally drawn up contract should have covered such eventualities particularly since Dolly had, in various interviews, alluded to the possibility of moves into other areas.

It was perhaps naive of Porter to put his faith in such a limited document but of course he came from a world where a gentleman's agreement by way of a handshake was all that was needed to secure a binding agreement. The contract was duly signed and filed but while it was meant to settle future matters between Dolly and Porter it would be the inevitable cause of their falling out a few years later.

# Chapter 11

LOOKING back over Dolly's career in the late Sixties and early Seventies, the sheer number of albums and singles that were released is particularly striking. In 1971 not only was her first compilation album released (reaching number 12 in the country charts) but a best of album with Porter made number seven. Early that year 'Joshua' made it to number one on the country listings and 108 in the pop charts. 'Joshua' was a typically evocative narrative about a man who lived on his own in a ramshackle house guarded by a menacing black dog, who did not like anybody getting too close to him – physically or emotionally. Into his life comes an orphan girl who penetrates Joshua's guardedness and eventually moves into his house and his heart thus bringing together two people with a burning desire to be loved. The song's uptempo arrangement adopted a rocking country feel utilising harmonica, steel guitar and some exuberant yodelling from Dolly. Having made an inroad into the pop world, Dolly was already known by a number of artistes who had picked up on her writing skills and some specifically requested songs written by her.

'Joshua' represented a gradual shift in Dolly's songwriting away from maudlin vignettes about human suffering. Porter had persuaded her that audiences were more attuned to songs about love and relationships than the realities and hardships of country life although she still included old style folk songs. 'Coat Of Many Colors' became an established audience favourite at this time even though Dolly had yet to record it. Porter recorded two versions of the song in 1969 and there was concern that another artist might pick up on it and have a hit. Dolly eventually recorded it although for some reason RCA delayed its release. The song, which eventually reached number four in the country charts, was covered by Emmylou Harris (on her 1974 album *Pieces Of The Sky*) and, ironically, by Norma Jean.

Dolly has often said 'Coat Of Many Colors' means more to her than any other song she has written and the first time she performed it on television an image of the actual coat was superimposed on the screen. Lee Parton cried when he saw it. Dolly's uncle Louis Owens said the song reinforces his view that she wrote some of her best material when reflecting on her upbringing after moving to Nashville. Although Dolly was now well established on the country charts 'Coat Of Many Colors' failed to reach the top spot.

The *Coat Of Many Colors* album which followed included 'My Blue Tears' on which Dolly sang melody and harmony and 'Early Morning Breeze' that featured a prominent electric bass; in traditional country the bass guitar was usually 'felt' rather than heard. 'Here I Am' featured steel guitar and prominent rock style drums, while 'Travelling Man' had an unexpected lyrical twist; Emmylou Harris referred to such Dolly tricks as "O Henry songs", a reference to the American short-story writer who was the master of surprise endings.

Although there were tensions in Dolly and Porter's professional rela-tionship, Dolly would seek his advice on how best to improve a song. She also provided invaluable help to Porter. Before their meeting he had lost confidence in his ability to write songs and had effectively stopped for some time. As he said, "She encouraged me to write and made me believe in myself." Once Porter got back into writing, he would take one of his songs to Dolly for her thoughts and ideas and as he put it, "She shared in my happiness at creating it." Later they would disagree about the extent and nature of such work. Sometimes when they did write together there was a genuine sharing of ideas, one good example being the winsome 'A Lot Of You Left In Me'.

Porter was gracious enough to acknowledge Dolly's creative contribu-tion. Over the years he gave her enough diamond rings to cover her fingers and in 1971 he presented her with a Cadillac Eldorado. He also gave her a pair of glasses, said to have cost around $1,000, with 20-carat gold plated frames, decked with 14-carat gold butterflies and a diamond-studded guitar.

What her husband made of all this can only be imagined, especially now that Dolly generally spent more time away with Porter. But as he had made clear from the start Carl had no desire to be involved in the glitz and the glamour. As Dolly said, "He don't give a damn for show business or this Dolly Parton business . . . he's got tremendous pride and integrity. Carl and I are very independent people. We don't want to own each other and change things that made us fall in love in the first place." Such behaviour only helped to create a mystique around Carl, ironic for a man who simply wanted to lead an ordinary life out of the public gaze. It was later claimed that he did not attend Dolly's shows in the early stages of her career because he was afraid she would "mess up". After a while Carl did drop in on some of Dolly's shows though he kept such a low profile that not many people backstage actually knew who he was.

Under Porter's influence, Dolly's country calico and frilly dresses gave way to more sophisticated outfits such as custom-made, tight-fitting trouser suits with jewelled patterns down the legs. To some extent the garments she came up with were a mirror image of Porter's effulgent outfits. Some commentators have given him some of the credit for creating Dolly's image, described by writer Joan Dew as, "The Marilyn Monroe of Country Music – a fantasy figure of blonde curls and giggles, bosoms and bangles, earthiness and vulnerability."

Loretta Lynn empathised with Dolly's dramatic appearance. "I understand why she wears all that fancy jewellery and make-up and piles her hair up the way she does . . . she was poor when she was a kid and now she can afford pretty things. 'I'm gonna pile it all over me,' is what she said." Dolly's flamboyant image made her, as she joked to *Playgirl* magazine, "a poor candidate for espionage".

Such was Porter and Dolly's popularity in 1971 that they were the indirect cause of a disturbance at a prison in Atlanta. One of the inmates switched over from Porter's show to watch the news and a fight ensued which involved a stabbing. Wagoner had a strong following among jail-birds because, like Johnny Cash, many of his songs identified with and expressed sympathy for those of whom Hank Williams wrote, "With shoulders stooped and heads bowed low and eyes that stare in defeat." Yet even when appearing on some of his album sleeves in the role of a down-and-out, barely a hair of Porter's swept back pompadour was out of place – there was only so far he would go in straying from his public image. Porter's sympathy for those who did not comply with society's norms extended to anti-Vietnam war protestors. Fellow country singer Merle Haggard attacked them as unpatriotic in his song, 'The Fightin' Side Of Me' but Porter empathised with "the young people", many of whom came from socially disadvantaged groups, who were not able to find ways of avoiding the draft.

In March '71, another duets album, *Two Of A Kind*, was released. 'Curse Of The Wild Weed Flower', written by Dolly and her uncle Louis Owens, appeared to be a response to the burgeoning drug culture embraced by many young people in the West. However, it was no simple anti-drug diatribe. While bitterly denouncing the effects of drug use, the song showed genuine compassion for those who had succumbed. The album also featured a good example of Dolly and Porter's writing in 'The Pain Of Loving You', with its direct, heartfelt message, well complemented by a simple attractive melody. Elsewhere, 'All I Need Is You' typified the idealised view of romance so prevalent on Dolly and Porter's albums, while 'There'll Be Love' reflected Porter's solidarity with those behind bars.

The same month that *Two Of A Kind* appeared, RCA released *Golden Streets Of Glory*. It was a sign of Dolly's growing popularity that an album purely comprising religious material reached number 22 in the charts. The record featured 'How Great Thou Art', 'Wings Of A Dove' (written by producer Bob Ferguson) as well as Dolly-penned songs such as 'Lord Hold My Hand'. A mere two months later the album *Joshua* was released with Dolly writing seven out of the 10 cuts. The song selection ranged from the down-home, childhood inspired 'Daddy's Moonshine Still' to romantic numbers 'The Last One To Touch Me' and 'The Fire's Still Burning'. The album earned Dolly a BMI award and a Grammy nomination for Best Female Country Vocal Performance. Dolly was also honoured when her name, along with those of Barbara Mandrell and Lynn Anderson, was placed in the Country Music Hall of Fame's Walkway of Stars, although in return she was expected to make a donation of $1,000 to the Hall of Fame.

In 1972 RCA released no less than two more formulaic duets albums, *The Right Combination/Burning The Midnight Oil* and *Together Always*. On the soap opera-style sleeve of the former, a disconsolate Porter sits, head in hand, an anguished look on his face. Nearby is a full ashtray, a box of tissues and what may be a farewell note from his lover. In the opposing picture Dolly stares wistfully at an obscured picture she is holding. While summing up RCA's method of projecting the Porter-Dolly relationship to the public, *The Right Combination* also neatly reflected their successful musical blend. "To have a close harmony you have to be close in different ways . . ." said Porter. "The songs mean the same things to Dolly and I. It's sorta like a family can always sing close harmony."

The title of *Together Always* once more stressed the theme of united love which worked so well as a selling point. The album was released with alternate sleeves: one had the pair cheek to cheek in matching red tops and ubiquitous blonde hair, the other found them sitting together in a forest. It's significant that Dolly looked sexier in these pictures than on the earlier sleeves; not only had her voice matured with age and experience, but her bosom was more prominent. The iconic image which would soon become so familiar beyond the country scene in America was just a wig adjustment away.

Apart from turning out prodigious numbers of records, the Porter Wagoner roadshow continued to roll across the country. Porter invested in a new $100,000 customised bus decorated by road manager Don Warden's wife Anne. Dolly had her own room with oyster white curtains and a coverlet of deep pink. The mirror above her tiny washbasin and vanity shelf were kitted out with theatrical make-up lights and a small closet held her glitzy stage outfits. A book of Bible stories lay next to her bed. A tiny built-in commode was accessed via a panel at the end of the bed which saved her having to manoeuvre her way to the lavatory at the back of the bus. Warden had an office with typewriter and intercom while the Wagonmasters had to make do with snug fitting bunks with virtually no spare room; as one journalist who was given access to the bus said, "There's no space for pot bellies." The glamour of the stage belied the lack of glamour on the road, and not just on the bus; many venues were low rent and the dressing rooms were often sparse.

The troupe participated in a country package show in New York produced by Show-Biz, Inc the parent company of Porter's television show and booking agency Top Billing. As part of the visit they appeared on *The David Frost Show* and subsequently appeared before 11,000 people at Madison Square Gardens. There were many famous country stars on the bill including Faron Young and another popular duo Conway Twitty and Loretta Lynn (who also went in for "fight songs" – some of their lyrics had a nasty edge to them as in the unforgettably titled 'You're The Reason Our Kids Are Ugly'). Package shows were not a common type of engagement for Porter and he announced that he would not be involved in any such ventures in the future. Porter was an artist of traditional values and it pained him to be associated with other performers who did not adhere to his own high standards. In what was probably a sideswipe at artists like George Jones (who had earned the nickname 'No Show Jones') he said, "I can't see why anyone would take a business that has been good to them and abuse it . . . by doing bad shows, going out on the road and getting drunk . . . fans spend their hard-earned dollars to see them and they see nothing but a drunk onstage."

He also complained of artists who were slovenly and "got themselves involved in problems in clubs or alleys". His views were very much in tune with older artists such as Carl and Pearl Butler who said, "While you're thanking God for personal blessings, you might thank Him too for our great country and our freedom as individuals and things like the privilege of being able to buy and enjoy good country recordings like Porter and Dolly's."

While Dolly was sometimes hurt by comments made about her in the media, she was more upset by the flak her family received as a result of her fame. As Stella Parton stated, referring to the Parton family in general: "We've been treated like crap . . . by the public, especially people in my home town, other poor people who are jealous and think that we have it made so they make our lives harder." Dolly's parents received a variety of threats and anonymous phone calls saying, for instance, that Dolly or one of their other children had been killed or seriously injured and was in hospital. There were break-ins at their house and expensive goods ordered in Dolly's name and billed to her. Members of the family became suspicious and alarmed if cars with unfamiliar registration plates appeared near their houses; schools were instructed that children should never be collected by unfamiliar persons unless by prior arrangement. In addition, one of Porter's daughters was teased at school about rumours of a relationship between her father and Dolly.

It was almost inevitable that rumours about a non musical relationship between the two should emerge despite the obvious age gap and the fact that Dolly appeared happily married to Carl. The glamour of an apparently romantic duo only served to pique their audience's interest further. Whether the duo was an item was not the point – they looked like a couple when they were in the public eye, staring into each others' eyes singing songs of love, longing and loss and impressionable fans bought into this fantasy world.

The issue surfaced at Dolly Parton Day (the event continued in Sevierville for a few years but petered out once Dolly's career took off). Porter took the opportunity to issue a florid rebuttal of the rumours. "There's been lots of stories about a love affair between Dolly and me, and I'd be lying to say that I don't love her in many, many ways. But not in the ways the gossiping tongues will lead you to believe. To me she's like a sister or daughter I love so well. When they say things about *me* I don't mind. But when they speak of *her* I get hot and feel the fires of hell." It was ironic that in making a public statement Wagoner was unravelling the image RCA had worked to foster. Cas Walker was in the audience and commented that in his many years' experience he had generally found it better to avoid public denials if possible.

Though Dolly tried to take the media interest in her stride, there were times when stories in the gutter press upset her. She welcomed publicity in order to advance her career, but disliked the fact that things were said in tabloids that caused people to gossip about her. She learned that country fans will do anything for their heroes except leave them alone. Dolly accepted that her life had to some extent become public property but she felt that a lot of things that had been suggested about her were not true. "I'm no angel but if I'd done half the things I'd been accused of, I wouldn't be sitting here, I'd be wore out somewhere. I'd be dead."

Dolly made sure that her family were among the first to benefit from her new-found fame. Lee quipped you had to be careful if you needed anything, "because Dolly's so generous she'll just get it for you". She transformed her parents' standard of living at a stroke by buying them a new house and covered the cost of standard accessories such as curtains and carpets. Dolly also bought Avie Lee her first car, though her early efforts at driving were said to strike terror into the hearts of those brave enough to be passengers. These did not include Dolly because, as Willadeene drily pointed out, she was absent in Nashville.

Early in 1972 the solo album *Touch Your Woman* was released with a cover shot showing Dolly sitting amongst an array of colourful cushions, wearing a rich blue dress, head tilted to one side looking directly at the camera and, unusually, with no trace of a smile. The serious look on her face lent an air of confidence to her general demeanour; like someone who has arrived and knows it. The title track was Dolly's admission that during times of weakness she needed her lover to stand by her.*

The album also featured a pure country Dolly–Porter tear jerker, 'Mission Chapel Memories', about a woman abandoned so soon after her wedding that the rice thrown over her satin gown was still on the floor of the chapel. The mood was greatly enhanced by some delicate steel guitar work.

Also in 1972, Dolly released a further solo album *Dolly Parton Sings My Favorite Songwriter: Porter Wagoner*, which served to reaffirm her creative partnership with Porter in a fawning way. The sleeve features an eerie shot of Dolly, wearing a black choker with a butterfly on it, superimposed onto a large spectral picture of Porter's head so she appears to be inside it. It was the first album Dolly had recorded – either solo or with Wagoner – that featured none of her own compositions and there were some who said it was weaker for precisely this reason. 'The Bird That Never Flew' was a heartfelt recitation about a man caring for a crippled bird that cannot fly, 'When I Sing For Him' was a self-explanatory gospel song, while the chirpy, uptempo 'Washday Blues' was released as a single, just making the Top 20. One reviewer said the song made Dolly a "homemaker spokeswoman" on behalf of domesticated women. The album reached number

---

* The song's sentiment was reversed when played during the first lesbian civil partnership ceremony in 2005.

33 in the charts, a significantly poorer showing than previous entrys and a probable reflection of the fact that Dolly's material was popular with a wider audience than Porter's rather dated style.

Bob Ferguson admired the way Dolly and Porter worked in the studio. "Dolly understands everybody's job and everybody's attitude – the engineers and the producers. Her input is good, and she isn't domineering . . . that can destroy a session. The pickers can get discouraged and might shut off their ingenuity and creativity. Porter and Dolly are great professionals. With them the sessions start right on time. Generally they worked everything out on the bus, even to where the band knows what they're going to do . . . with Dolly the talent was there to begin with – great talent. It's just been a matter of helping to develop it and catch it on record." Regarding Porter and Dolly's working relationship one writer observed, "Dolly and Porter occasionally have personal opinions about songs or productions that they don't quite agree on, but they are small things and in the end Dolly accepts Porter's position as boss and experienced adviser."

On the surface Porter and Dolly's relationship appeared to be harmonious but the tensions were bubbling under. Porter had been happy with the way things went in the first year or so because Dolly accepted his pre-eminent status. Porter reminded her of her father (as Carl did) and his stubbornness "brought out the very worst and the very best in me". Dolly became increasingly vocal in her desire to try out her own ideas, stretching Porter's patience with notions of sounding, as he later described it, "like Aretha Franklin and screaming on songs". Porter was wary of working beyond the strict confines of country. On one occasion Dolly did record some pop material which she liked but Porter was scathing. "It was just a piece of shit . . . it was so far out in left field, with echo just booming in every direction." Porter generally preferred a softer sound and for Dolly's piercing voice, he used a special microphone to capture her vocal resonance. Don Warden has stated that Wagoner exerted more control over the arrangement and production of Dolly's records than he did with Norma Jean.

As Dolly's confidence grew she started openly hinting at the fractious atmosphere developing between herself and Porter. When appearing on Ralph Emery's television show she was asked whether Porter "had all the creative control", to which she curtly replied, "Well, he didn't have all the creativity; he had control, let's put it that way." In his defence Porter has stated that he did not adopt this all-or-nothing approach if he was recording with an artist who was not on his payroll. His methods were successful considering that Dolly's early solo albums broadly conformed to his vision, however, he was intent on continuing to record duets. Ferguson later recalled that Wagoner became increasingly dictatorial in the studio, making life uncomfortable for the musicians who were used to having their own arrangement ideas listened to.

Like Tammy and Loretta, Dolly was out to establish herself in a male dominated world; once when she and Porter appeared on *Tonight with Johnny Carson* Dolly had to sit silently for much of their spot while he acted as spokesman. Her cause was not helped by the fact that some of the older female country singers accepted and appeared to prefer to uphold the status quo. Jean Shepard said, ". . . the women's lib thing doesn't turn me on. I can't stand for a woman to stand up and say, 'I can do anything a man can do.' Maybe mentally she can. But I think it's still kind of a man's world and to be frank, I kind of like it that way. I'd never like to see a woman president, for instance. A woman's too high strung for that kind of job."

Against this backdrop Dolly realised that remaining with Porter indefinitely would effectively rule out the prospect of artistic growth. By 1973 she was also doubtless aware that unlike other successful female country singers she had yet to achieve a gold record. Could this be due to the fact that she was linked so closely to an artist who many outside traditional country viewed as anachronistic?

# Chapter 12

IN 1973 RCA maintained their relentless output of Dolly-related product with another four albums, all of which made the Top 20. Two duets albums, *We Found It* and *Love And Music* appeared; the sleeve for the former had the pair dressed in matching turquoise blazers lending them the appearance of staff members at an English holiday camp from the Fifties, while Dolly's unkempt wig resembled an unruly pile of blonde rope. *Love And Music* produced a number three hit, 'If Teardrops Were Pennies' and 'I Get Lonesome By Myself' in which Porter plays a man who sees a girl sitting at the window of a house. Employing her best lonely little girl voice, Dolly tells him where the house key is hidden, invites him up and tells him her story. Her mother is an alcoholic who neglects her, her father having abandoned her years before. Like all good stories, Porter turns out to be the father and is thus reunited with his daughter. Apart from recording together, Porter and Dolly also continued to make TV guest appearances, including a cameo in *Rowan and Martin's Laugh-In* that September.

Of Dolly's two solo albums released in '73 – *Bubbling Over* and *My Tennessee Mountain Home* – for the first time, all the songs on the latter album were written or co-written by her. The album was also unusual as there was no portrait on the sleeve, rather a simple photograph of Dolly's childhood home. Some of the song titles painted a fairly idealised picture of her upbringing: 'Daddy's Working Boots', 'Back Home' and 'Dr. Robert F. Thomas' (the doctor who delivered her) while 'Old Black Kettle' was a song Porter had reacted to with derision when encouraging Dolly to write more about love than her poor upbringing. For 'The Letter' Dolly recited the first letter she sent home from Nashville over a backing of 'There's No Place Like Home' played on a quivering harmonica while 'Down On Music Row' recounted Dolly's daunting early experiences in Nashville, knocking on doors and being turned away. Consistent with her sunny outlook the song ended on an optimistic note as success beckoned.

By the end of the year Dolly had decided that she had to make the break from Porter knowing it would not be a straightforward or amicable

127

process. As a duo they sold more records than as individuals, which was largely due to Dolly's greater popularity. Yet the partnership's old-fashioned image was hindering the advancement of her solo career. Ironically Porter had sent RCA a lengthy critique bemoaning the lack of support the company had given Dolly, comparing their efforts unfavourably with promotional work carried out by rival companies on behalf of artists such as Loretta Lynn and Donna Fargo. At one point he wrote, "I think it is high time that RCA gets excited about Dolly Parton and does something about it . . . Dolly is a young, vigorous talent, let's make a superstar while we have all the other things going for us. Then we can play golf, go to cocktail parties, while the harvest from our work is rolling in from a well-established record seller . . . It is hard for me to believe that RCA, the largest recording company in the world, does not have a girl singer in the top five nominees this year for the network CMA show." Porter went on to give a detailed account of the efforts he had personally expended on Dolly's behalf and specified various ways in which he believed RCA should beef up their promotional efforts.

RCA did not necessarily share Porter's concerns because of the generally good financial returns. It seems they were more concerned about Dolly's appearance. Chet Atkins said that he attended meetings where people would say, "We've got to stop Dolly Parton from wearing those terrible wigs. She looks like a hooker." Porter now realised that if he wanted to have any hope of retaining Dolly he would have to allow her more freedom, so solo spots were arranged for her on *The Mike Douglas Show*, *Midnight Special* and several others, but by this stage Dolly's momentum was unstoppable. As she bluntly summed up, "I have to dream my own dreams."

When Porter learned that Dolly was serious in her intentions there were rumours that he was upset enough to threaten to harm her in some way. For Porter it went against the established order of things he had taken for granted; for Dolly it was a bold statement of intent. In a sense it represented the dividing line between the old order and the new in country music. It was unusual for a young female country singer to be in such a dominant position, having an active solo recording and touring career (discounting her appearances with Porter) and her own song publishing company.

Each did their best to appear conciliatory when the split was made public at a joint press conference in February 1974; Dolly planting a kiss on Porter's cheek for the photographers' benefit. Clearly it was in both parties' commercial interests for public relations to remain as amicable as possible.

Porter conceded that, "Dolly is now a superstar in every way. She is well prepared to go on her own. I am very happy that I have helped Dolly in preparing for this day. I worked hard on her career to get her prepared for the day she would go out and do her own thing." Dolly, still playing the role of subservient female to the hilt, said, "He felt I was ready to go out on my own, which was a very unselfish decision on his part." In an interview with *Country Music People* Dolly said, "We're still the best of friends. Porter produces all my records, we still do the duets, we own a studio together and a publishing company – so it's really not like a split. The only difference is that I have a band of my own and work separately on the road."

However, as time went on their comments to the press ranged from rational to contemptuous. Dolly said, "I'd gone as far as I could within a group, I'd grown as far as I could grow, and I'm not one to be stale . . . that's about right . . . to be stale, you know, to grow stale within a certain situation, so I felt that I was really cramped and there was so much that I wanted to do, being inventive and creative as I like to think I am. Now see, Porter has started cutting down on his roadwork, he had been on the road for 20 years, and we were working very few shows by then, my records were still doing good, and I couldn't work outside the show, and so it made no sense to me to stay in town just because Porter did, so we talked it over and – it was not easy for me or him – but I told him that I felt a great need to go. We had discussed it many times, we didn't get along very well, we argued often." She also complained that her rewards were inadequate. "I was a big star, but I wasn't making any money."

In a television interview Porter gave the impression that he was the prime instigator of the separation. "I let her go. Dolly didn't quit me. I gave her notice in Tulsa that she needed to get her own band together because I wasn't going to travel and have a girl I'd have to fight with on the road with us. I'm not bitter because Dolly left my show in any sense . . . I was just disappointed to find out she was not maybe what I thought she was." Dolly issued this rejoinder, "We just got to where we argued and quarrelled about personal things. I'm sure he is bitter at this particular point. He is so strong-headed and bull-headed. He won't accept things the way they are. I won't either, sometimes." On another occasion Porter claimed, "Dolly was not what I would call a great melody writer, and I would create some extra little tune or some rhythm pattern that would add a lot to her songs."

This remark was all the more insensitive in view of the fact that Dolly helped Porter get back into songwriting after his confidence had failed him.

"We fought for years," Dolly said. "I tried to tell him what I was trying to do. I tried to tell him my dreams and plans, but it was too touchy a thing, I had to go, because we couldn't share it together, because he wouldn't accept it. It wasn't as if I did a bad, vicious thing . . . my dreams were so big, they were turning into nightmares, because I didn't have anyone to help me carry them out." From another interview she said: "I couldn't be creative since I was hearing live music differently than the way it was being recorded. It was affecting my creativity, and I was starting to lose the desire to write and somebody else was taking all the credit . . . if you've got to step back out of the limelight and let yourself be turned into somebody's gadget, then you're losing, and in my own case I got to thinkin' that I was a fool to let this happen . . . it's no more his fault than mine since we're both so bull-headed, but I had my life to get on with and I couldn't spend my time fighting with somebody over my music."

One imaginative journalist floridly described the pair's seven-year partnership thus: "The handsome, powerful Svengali takes the shy, starving girl and makes her a star. They are a powerful duet, so close most fans assume they are husband and wife. She grows more beautiful, more popular. He is fiercely possessive. Several times she threatens to leave him and go out on her own. Always he talks, threatens her out of it. There is a rumour he went crazy and said he'd kill her. Then one day she breaks the spell."

Fred Foster said of his former protégée, "I'm surprised she hasn't broken out and crossed all the boundaries before now. I think that Porter got her timetable all fouled up, or she would already be a superstar outside of country music. I imagine it took her longer to get out of that situation than she anticipated. But she's on her way now and she'll still get to the top."

British broadcaster/writer Stan Laundon interviewed Dolly in Nashville in 1974 when the fall-out between her and Porter was intense, but what struck Laundon was the electricity she generated in public, "a doll – chirpy, giggly and full of energy with a lovely dynamic personality". He described the buzz surrounding her entrance at the Municipal Auditorium: "It suddenly became obvious by the amount of activity taking place in the press area that someone of note was in attendance . . . the media swarmed round her . . . she happily spent ages posing for photographs, signing autographs." Laundon was also struck by her thoughtfulness. He asked if he could have a signed photograph of Dolly; she did not have one to hand but promised to send it on, which she duly did a month later, even including an extra signed 8 × 10 for his wife.

Laundon also attended one of Dolly's final appearances as part of the Porter Wagoner show at an open air concert in Nashville. He spoke to her briefly after the concert and noted that though there was some sadness she was optimistic about the future. "I am prepared for success and braced for failure. I don't expect failure at all, but I would be able to accept it because I would succeed in whatever I do. If I were a waitress, I would try to be the best one in the restaurant."

An indication of the extent to which Dolly and her physical stature had imprinted themselves on the public consciousness came on an NBC-TV show presented by Mac Davis. In one segment he wrote songs on the spot from topics yelled out at random by members of the audience. With 1974 coinciding with the height of the women's lib movement, one cried "burning bras" and Davis responded:

> *My girlfriend burnt her bra today*
> *It really was a shame,*
> *'Cos she ain't exactly Dolly Parton,*
> *That sucker hardly made a flame.**

No longer having the familiar support of the Wagonmasters behind her, Dolly turned to siblings and cousins, as she had done previously, under the name of the Travelling Family Band. By this stage quite a number of family members were involved in running her business: uncle Louis Owens had a major role in running Owepar and Dolly Parton Enterprises, an aunt made her stage clothes, while another was Dolly's personal hair-dresser – at this stage Dolly did not always wear wigs. Judy Ogle was a constant presence and Don Warden acted as managerial factotum covering everything from transport to collecting box office receipts. Apart from being Porter's steel guitar player since the Fifties Warden was an excellent tour manager. As veteran singer George Hamilton IV says, "[Don] came up through the ranks. He met Dolly in her formative stages . . . then when Dolly went on her own and became a single act, she took Don along with her because she trusted him. She had had the chance to see him operate for years as part of Porter's show. I think it's more important to her if she can trust somebody and if she feels like she knows them." It was Porter who had originally suggested he help Dolly out and Warden remains one of the people closest to her, referred to as "Mr Everything" by Dolly.

The idea of Dolly fronting a family group pushed the right buttons for many traditionalists to whom family values appeared under threat. One writer memorably described Dolly's appearance as "a triumph of nature

---

* Apparently Davis received a mountain of angry mail afterwards.

wedded to a triumph of artifice". Coupled with the voice, described by Dolly herself as, "sounding like a child with grown-up emotion", it proved a captivating spectacle. The prospect of repeatedly singing the same songs never troubled Dolly; "The fact is every audience is different . . . it's as if I have never sung it before, the reaction is going to be different and you know that some people are going to hear it for the first time so it's as though I'm singing it for the first time."

Narvel Felts toured with Dolly around this time and recalls that her fans greatly appreciated the fact that, in time-honoured country tradition, she made herself available to sign autographs at the end of a show – a "people person". Felts has favourable memories of the Travelling Family Band. "I thought it was a great package. I didn't see a thing wrong with it and I thought they all played really well. I thought they were a good backing band for her." However, others criticised their lack of experience. Stella Parton: "They were kids, they'd never been out on the road before, Randy had, he'd worked on the road with me some, and he'd worked with Jean Shepard, but Floyd and Frieda and Rachel had never been out on the road . . . it was like bringing along a bunch of kids that you know didn't know what they were doing. I mean they could sing and memorise the show but they weren't professional . . . they weren't used to being out on the grind of the road . . . they got out there and it wasn't nearly as much fun as they thought . . . they were fighting amongst themselves, you know how families do, and Dolly was, you know, probably trying to keep them from butting heads."

According to Willadeene, on one occasion Dolly performed for an Elks Lodge* in Texas when Randy Parton, having accepted a few drinks offered by the audience on an empty stomach, caused offence by referring to them as the "Moose Club". Dolly was infuriated by such unprofessional behaviour. It has also been suggested that the members' own ambitions came to the fore and there was talk of them wanting to do their own albums. The Top Billing agency booked the band so heavily that they were being overworked and the sound systems they had to rely on were so poor it meant that Dolly strained her voice to be heard. Sometimes she would be on a bill with four or five other acts playing to audiences of just a few hundred. At one show with Merle Haggard at East Burke High School, near Hickory, North Carolina, the band had to perform on a platform set down at one end of a basketball court. The basketball hoops were pulled up against the ceiling, while the wooden floor was covered with

* Part of a fraternal organisation involved in charitable works.

chairs. Bleachers had been laid out around three sides of the arena and as one report put it, "Before Dolly goes on the stage, Randy, Floyd and Frieda are hollering about how the South is gonna do it again."

In 1974 Dolly briefly involved herself in a short-lived campaign to uphold and maintain traditional standards in country music which, not for the first time, was embroiled in a debate about whether it should embrace wider popular music, in particular, "middle of the road" music (MOR). Some saw it as a case of toning down the country content in order to reclaim fans who had been lured away from country but who were turned off by full scale modern rock. Others saw any move towards the middle ground as a betrayal. Matters came to something of a head when English born, Australian reared Olivia Newton-John won Female Vocalist Of The Year at the CMA awards in 1974 ahead of the likes of Tammy Wynette, Loretta Lynn and Dolly. Newton-John did not claim to be a country singer and had only scored a few hits which could be categorised as country. To rub salt into the wound she did not turn up to receive the award after stoking outrage by her ignorant request to meet Hank Williams who had only been dead for over 20 years!

It was plain that the Nashville establishment was devoted to courting MOR artists who attracted large record sales, promoting them as symbols of "new young" country music. At the following year's presentation, when a well-oiled Charlie Rich opened the envelope and saw that John Denver had won CMA Entertainer Of The Year, the most coveted award in country music, he pulled out his cigarette lighter and burned the card in front of millions of viewers.

A midnight meeting after the 1974 awards ceremony at the residence of George Jones and Tammy Wynette led to the formation of the Association of Country Entertainers (ACE). Their stated purpose was "to preserve the identity of country music as a separate and distinct form of entertainment". Apart from Porter and Dolly, the 50 or so artists at the house included Brenda Lee, Bill Anderson, Barbara Mandrell, Billy Walker, Hank Snow and Conway Twitty. It was ironic that many of these names had recorded light pop material, and even revered members of the Country Music Hall of Fame such as Jimmie Rodgers and Bob Wills had incorporated popular elements into their music. Billy Walker declared, "Efforts to take country music to a wider audience will dilute it to the point that it no longer exists as an art form." Johnny Paycheck argued that if an artist had a crossover record played on both country and pop stations, that artist would have an unfair advantage when it came to the CMA awards. However, the likes of Dolly and Barbara Mandrell soon moved sharply in the direction of the more lucrative pop market and the organisation, lacking ongoing support, petered out after a few years.

Speaking in 1977, Dolly was eager to play down her involvement with ACE. "I only went to one meeting, and that was the first one. I didn't know what they were doing then and I don't know now. But in order not for people to think that I had betrayed country music, I kept sending in my dues and I guess you would say that I am a member, but I'm certainly not an active member. I think that anybody who is trying to preserve country music, more power to them. Whatever direction I go, I hope we still preserve the traditional country. I never ever thought that I was that traditional anyway." Stella Parton is dismissive of ACE. "Oh they just got all ticked off because none of them won that year." Stella went on to record a song called 'Ode To Olivia'. "I was trying to apologise to her . . . I thought it was embarrassing that they had got so irate that they had gone to such trouble . . . I never will forget I played that song in the studio for Dolly and she said, 'Oh Lord Stella don't let Porter hear that.' I said, 'Screw Porter, I don't care what he thinks.' "*

In the meantime Dolly had recorded enough material for a pair of albums that contained the songs which were destined to become memorable touchstones of her repertoire, as well as spreading the word about her talents as a writer. Dolly had been carrying the idea for 'Jolene' around in her head for a few years since she met a young girl with green eyes and red hair in a scout uniform after a show. The attractive girl gave her a photograph and asked her to give it to Porter; on the back it said, "To Porter, love Jolene." Dolly buried the name away at the back of her mind. Having a pretty girl with a memorable name, Dolly mixed in her negative feelings regarding her own perceived physical inadequacies – short legs, stubby hands and hair that could not be teased enough (hence the high-heeled shoes, long fingernails and wigs) – and how she looked at other women, through the eyes of boyfriends or possibly Carl, and obsessed about what they had that she didn't.† Jolene is more attractive than her and thus has the ability to take her man; hence the overpowering theme of powerlessness and jealousy. The message was quite a contrast to the punchy

* It appears that the controversy did have some effect on CMA practices. In 1977 a report about that year's forthcoming awards stated that there were no "outsiders" among the finalists, a reference, it was assumed, to artists such as Newton-John and Denver.
† Jolene is also the brand name of a women's product used to bleach unsightly hair around the lips; whether this was also a strand in the genesis of the song can only be a matter of speculation.

aggression of a song like Loretta Lynn's 'You Ain't Woman Enough To Take My Man'.

'Jolene' was a sign of Dolly's musical development; its uncommon minor key was typical of musical composition in the mountains a century before, as was the lack of a middle eight. For musical conservatives, any innovation was seen as a potential threat to the purity of the form and in a sense a song like 'Jolene' was a rebellious move though one critic dismissed it merely as "a clever hook strung together with clichés . . . the tune is highly derivative." It immediately clicked with the public and soon made number one in the country charts (the album made number six). It also reached number 60 in the pop charts and received a Grammy nomination in the category Best Country Vocal Performance By A Female and went on to sell 60,000 copies. It was later covered by, ironically, Olivia Newton-John, of which Dolly said, "It's one of the better things that's been done with my songs." When re-released in 1976 'Jolene' gave Dolly her first major hit in Britain, a market she had not been able to exploit in the past because Porter was not keen on flying. Some speculated that it was the favourable response to songs of the calibre of 'Jolene' which had emboldened Dolly finally to make the break from Porter. However, the scale of its commercial success was still small when compared to Dolly's aspirations, not to mention the costs involved in keeping a band on the road.

Apart from the title track, the album *Jolene* contained another classic, 'I Will Always Love You'. Dolly has always maintained the song concerned her trauma over leaving Porter. "I wrote it about Porter and the special, although painfully heart-wrenching time we spent together." In a recent interview Dolly threw more light on the song's genesis saying that she wrote it, "kind of like a bargaining thing when things were very difficult between us and he wouldn't listen to me . . . I played it and he cried and it bridged the problems between us and eased the way for me to be able to leave."

Later in 1974 came the album *Love Is Like A Butterfly*, the title track of which was another number one and was later used as the theme music for a British sitcom *Butterflies*. The cover had Dolly framed by a pair of enormous, brightly coloured butterfly wings – a public confirmation of her affinity to butterflies and their free spirit, something she had felt since childhood. "They just go about their business, real colourful and gaudy, don't hurt nobody." Various commentators, alluding to Dolly's strong ambition and acute business sense, have dubbed her the "iron butterfly". The butterfly subsequently became a kind of leitmotif for Dolly; once when she was singing in the Grand Ole Opry the management arranged for 3,000 paper butterflies to float down from the rafters as she started the song. The album also featured 'You're The One Who Taught Me How To Swing', reminiscent of the female perspective in the "fight songs" she and Porter had recorded. Dolly takes the part of a plain country girl whose man has introduced her to smoking, drinking and "all those worldly games". When he decides he wants her to revert to her old ways she makes it clear there can be no going back.

Hot on the heels of *Love Is Like A Butterfly* RCA released *The Bargain Store* in 1975 and once more the title track topped the country charts although it was banned by some radio stations who considered the lyrics to be suggestive. Dolly denied that she had ever intended any sexual connotation though the inferences were detectable. "That means that I have been in love before and kicked around and banged around and had my head and my heart broke, my cherry stole, but I can grow another," Dolly said in a *Rolling Stone* interview. She wasn't thinking of it as a "dirty thing", revealing the song also referred to bruised feelings after her battles with Porter. *The Bargain Store* was one of the last records on which Porter and Dolly collaborated; he was in charge of production and his musicians were featured on the album. Another song, which generated further speculation about Dolly's marriage, was 'He Would Know'. With Dolly's work commitments, despite being married, it became inevitable that she would encounter many successful and attractive men. The song addresses temptation but the message is that no matter how attractive, it's not worth giving in. In the same *Rolling Stone* interview Dolly said she had "made mistakes" and probably would again, adding cryptically, "But if I can just write it and say this is a song about our situation, I hope you can better understand how I feel about it and why it can't be." She added, "I know we will always be together. I wouldn't want to learn another man the way I've learned Carl. There is not another man in the world that can give me what I need."

Two last Porter-Dolly duets albums *Please Don't Stop Loving Me* (the title track producing another country chart topping record) and the ironically titled *Say Forever You'll Be Mine* were released in 1974 and 1975 respectively. The latter year also saw the release of *Dolly,* the first solo album to omit the Parton surname from the sleeve, often referred to as *The Seeker/We Used To*, after the titles of the songs released as singles.* Dolly's

---

* Although not enjoying the success of Dolly's recent 45s, both 'The Seeker' and 'We Used To' made two and nine respectively on the country charts.

solo albums showed a greater degree of experimentation in terms of song styles and instrumentation than the duets albums but *Dolly* sold less well than her previous albums probably because of the lack of a killer single.

Although content with her success to date Dolly felt she had what it took to be on a larger stage than that which Nashville could offer. She had been considering the idea of new management for some time and sounded out various potential candidates. Mac Davis suggested savvy West Coast operators Katz, Gallin & Cleary. Dolly was introduced to Sandy Gallin, who managed Cher and Joan Rivers and was impressed. "He's got taste and I got talent." Of the firm, she said, "I kept going back to them because they kept showing me more of what I was looking for."

Katz, Gallin & Cleary officially took over Dolly's management in autumn 1976 and Dolly also switched to a West Coast booking agency. "I was so fed up with so much, I had poor management, poor booking agency, my band was not musically qualified for all the things that I wanted to do. They were very good at what they were qualified at, and the band was mainly made up of family, but they all had their own dreams and desires to be artists, singers, and have their own little group, which they do now." Don Warden points to Dolly's favourable treatment of the band as the probable cause of her low profit margin. "She's too good to her musicians, better than I'd like her to be." For Dolly there were other problems. "I was ruining my health and my throat by working one-nighters in poor places with no lighting and no sound. We were working constantly, no one seemed to care as long as they got their 15 per cent off the top, nobody seemed to care as long as I could make it from one gig to another. Well I cared and I was a fool for too long about things like that. So I decided if I could do first quality work, why couldn't I have first quality everything else, people that could help me, so I made the move and I'm very proud." Perhaps fearing that she had gone too far Dolly qualified these remarks later in the interview. "All the people that I worked with before, the management, the band, the booking agency, they are dear friends, wonderful people, but they were only qualified to do so much; I had bigger dreams than that, but I would never want it said that I didn't like them as people because I truly did. The hardest part of all is to say goodbye."

In another conversation she remarked of her band, "It was very difficult for them and for me. I was like the mother. I felt extremely responsible. And then, of course, they were growin' and they had girlfriends and boy-friends and were gettin' married. It was hard to keep them all together . . . it's hard when it's family. You worry about them if they're sick, you worry about them if things aren't right, or whatever. But it was not the best

137

situation for any of us." Stella Parton's view is that the members were not overly concerned. "They didn't care; they knew they weren't worth a shit." One subsequent newspaper report rather patronisingly claimed, "Her kinfolk wanted to return to the land anyway."

Dolly refuted any suggestion that the change would cause changes not just in her music, but in her. "The difference will be the fact that I'm free to do my work the best way that I know how . . . I don't necessarily want to be a rock'n'roll star, but I want to be able to go into that market, into any market, and to express myself totally." She hoped her family understood and accepted the situation.

For her music to be more widely accepted Dolly's sights moved from Nashville to Los Angeles. "It is the entertainment capital in the same way as Detroit is the automobile capital and Hawaii is the pineapple capital," Sandy Gallin said in 1978. "LA is where most of the record companies are based, where the motion picture companies are based and where the majority of the TV industry is located." Gallin was clear about his firm's role. "What we do is design a programme for an artist and design a career for them." A number of Dolly's contemporaries including Waylon Jennings and Crystal Gayle (Loretta Lynn's sister), would follow the same route west, causing concern among the more traditional elements on Music Row some of whom saw it as a case of sleeping with the enemy. Don Warden remained on board and took responsibility for running the Dolly Parton Enterprises office in Nashville, road managing her tours and acting as general gatekeeper for Dolly.

Narvel Felts* spoke to Dolly around the time she was implementing the changes. "She did tell me privately that there were some decisions she had to make. She went off in the woods by herself at home in East Tennessee and wrote down what she wanted to achieve and the pros and cons of decisions . . . she said it was awful tough to get rid of her family band . . . but did she want to stay where she was or did she want to go on and be the biggest artist she could be?" Narvel was also told that RCA were less than enthusiastic about Dolly's plans at first. "She went to RCA and told them of her plans and said to them, 'Am I on the right label or do I need to go somewhere else?' Her point was that they had to fit in with her plans or else. She had the power to do that. There were a lot of dreamers but Dolly must have dreamed harder." According to another report, when Dolly first went to RCA and told them of her plans their response was outright concern; her retort was straight to the point. "As soon as you son-of-

---

* Dolly had written the sleevenotes for his album *Narvel The Marvel*.

bitches learn how to sell a female Elton John with long hair and big boobs that dresses like a freak, then we'll make some money."

A new album *All I Can Do* made the top three and received a Grammy nomination in the Best Vocal Performance By A Female category. An advertising line for the album read, "Some of the sweetest things happen on Dolly's albums."

The album was produced and arranged by Porter and Dolly to fulfil their remaining professional involvement. However, *All I Can Do* marked a further advance along the road to Dolly's full-blown musical independence, containing a cross section from folk to country to pop reflecting Dolly's eclectic musical tastes. The sleevenotes by Don Cusic aimed to get this across. "Country fans have known Dolly for years. Now, a brand new young audience is tuning in to her great talent. Did you know that Emmylou Harris and Linda Ronstadt are two of her biggest fans and personal friends as well. And did you know that three of Dolly's biggest fans on the male side are the three members of the rock group, Z Z Top." Included was Emmylou's 'Boulder To Birmingham', her response to the loss of her musical collaborator Gram Parsons. Dolly was unaware of this but the lyrics closely related to an unspecified but highly emotional situation in her own life.

In spring 1976, Dolly experienced serious problems with her voice. She had long been conscious of the need to protect her voice and sometimes she would forego encores because she was concerned about the effects of, for instance, damp air. However, things had reached a considerably more serious level when doctors told her straining her voice could result in permanent damage. Dolly had developed swellings on her vocal cords that, if they developed into nodules, could make the raspy quality her voice took on when strained permanent. If this happened, surgical intervention to remove the nodules might have been necessary, with its attendant risks. As part of her recuperation, she was told to refrain from speaking for two weeks so she communicated with pen and paper. Dolly had only recently returned from a triumphant headlining appearance at the 1976 Wembley Country Music Festival in London and had also made recent appearances in Sweden, Alaska and Hawaii as well as ongoing television and studio work. She was physically exhausted, having not taken a holiday for many months and her doctors advised complete rest.

Approximately 50 bookings, worth $350,000 in fees, were cancelled over the summer. It was reported that one promoter who had been involved in myriad negotiations planned to sue Dolly on the basis that shows had been cancelled at short notice without any proposal to reschedule them. It was during her rest period that Dolly finalised her new business arrangements and there were suggestions that this was the real reason for the cancellations which she categorically denied. "I would never have cancelled those shows unless I absolutely had to, and the rumours I just didn't want to play the typical country places are really unfair." She reinforced the point by returning to fulfil some of her obligations in October, but conditions were still well below perfect, meaning she found herself virtually screaming to be heard, causing her throat to give out again.

Nonetheless the feeling persisted among some in Nashville that for Dolly to broaden her commercial appeal, she was prepared to ditch the very people who had supported her rise to fame.

# Chapter 13

"IT sounds like something a nut would do." That was the verdict of a police spokesman asked to comment on threats made against Dolly prior to a show in Wheeling, West Virginia in 1976. As a precaution the show was cancelled even though most of the audience were already in the arena. Approximately 500 asked for a refund. George Elliot Snr was later detained by police and charged with making at least six calls to local disc jockey Buddy Ray, stating he was going to kill Dolly. Elliot served time in jail since he was unable to pay financial bonds amounting to $3,000 imposed by the court. The episode was a stark reminder to Dolly that her new-found fame came at a price.* There were fears that her domestic help may have been followed so she decided to hire the services of a top West Coast security consultant to step up protection for herself and her closest family while on the road and at home.†

Around the same time Dolly and Carl moved into a 23-room antebellum mansion built in extensive grounds of around 75 acres on Crockett Road in the then semi-rural district of Brentwood, south of Nashville. Dolly and Carl travelled around the Southern states taking pictures of a variety of old colonial and Confederate style homes to get ideas for their dream home and Carl and members of Dolly's family were closely involved in its construction.‡ The building they designed – "every inch of it is totally us" Dolly told one interviewer – had something of the look of Tara in *Gone With The Wind*; as Dolly explained, "When you grow up poor, that's what you think rich Southern folks would do."+

---

* Not long after, Dolly was offered her first TV guest star role – in *Starsky And Hutch* – as a famous singer whose life is being threatened. Dolly turned it down for obvious reasons and Lynn Anderson appeared instead.
† In her 1978 *Playboy* interview Dolly revealed that she always carried a gun, a .38 pistol, for protection.
‡ Carl worked on the land attached to the house, dabbled in real estate, restored old cars and raised cattle. It is understood that Carl's asphalting and paving business was closed down some time in the late Seventies due to rising costs.
+ Despite reports to the contrary Dolly never called the house Tara; she has always referred to it as Willow Lake Plantation.

One of the reasons Dolly liked the property's location was because it had a small stream at the entrance way with a bridge so small that no tour bus would be able to cross it. Although her earnings had increased, nonetheless the house, costing around $60,000, was a major financial commitment which stretched her resources. She and Carl saved up, partly by refraining from expensive holidays.

For help around the house Dolly, true to form, preferred to employ old friends from back home. "I don't have somebody waitin' on me hand and foot, that would bother me too, it's only I feel I owe it to my husband for him not to have to wander around in a dirty house." At one stage a residential trailer was kept in the grounds to accommodate Dolly's parents when they visited and it was only around 1978 that the last of the Parton children Carl and Dolly had been helping to bring up in their Nashville home, moved out prompting Dolly to remark, "Now we're like real parents and our kids are gone and we're retired."

Dolly had a swimming pool built, the bottom of which was adorned with a butterfly. She also bought antiques but soon realised they were not for her. "I didn't like it, it was just too drab. I like things a little more gaudy . . . something bright . . . something that stands out, that's special . . . something shining." Because she "came from the country" Dolly conceded that she had no real sense of how a house should be tastefully decorated, her aim was that the house should reflect her personality. "It kinda says hello when you come in. I always like loud colours. Lots of red, radiant colours, gold and yellow, it just kinda reflects the warmth inside." She did, however, enlist the assistance of a West Coast interior designer with a brief to create a cross section of styles including "some world religion stuff". Among the adornments he installed a number of Buddhas but, as Dolly later revealed in her 1994 autobiography, while she was away touring Avie Lee put them out in the yard because they contravened her religious views.

Despite living in a house fit for a star Dolly still found it hard to be profligate with money. She was happy buying clothes from large supermarket chains and was loathe to waste food. "I can still hear Mamma sayin', 'Ain't that something, you throwed that out, and all them kids overseas starvin' to death.'" Being Dolly, she wasn't one for keeping still for a prolonged spell. Her restless energy and hectic schedule meant that breaks were usually measured in days rather than weeks. "I don't wanna stay home, but I like to come home, and I like to be home when I'm there."

When asked if she saw Willow Lake Plantation becoming another Graceland Dolly replied, "I'm prepared for everything." There were reports in the late Seventies that Dolly wanted to sell the property because as she told Alanna Nash, "The rooms never did surround and cuddle us the way a home should." There were also rumours that she feared something in the soil or the water supply was making her unwell and for a time Dolly rented property nearer Nashville. However, Willow Lake Plantation remains her principal residence to the present day.

In 1975, Bill Graham,* president of Show Biz, Inc., the same company that produced *The Porter Wagoner Show*, had approached Dolly suggesting her own Nashville-based television variety show. Soon afterwards *Dolly* was hatched. Graham said, "The trick is to get good production without losing that warm, personal, happy feeling . . . we are shooting for prime time standards with a prime time budget . . . it takes a lot of money to do what we are talking about, but we are going to produce something Nashville can be proud of." The budget for each edition, to be shot at the Grand Ole Opry House, was said to be around $85,000 and Graham aimed to have the programme beamed into the majority of homes in America. Each show started fairy tale like with butterfly imagery overlaid (naturally) by 'Love Is Like A Butterfly' while a virginal-looking Dolly sat on a swing, vines and flowers arranged around the ropes, as she was gently lowered on to the set, and finished with her singing 'I Will Always Love You', the message that invariably preceded Dolly's signature on replies to fan mail.

The series was never anything but good clean family entertainment although Dolly complained about the poor quality of the scripts from its inception. Guests included a mixed bag of country, pop and Hollywood stars including Karen Black, Captain Kangaroo, Ronnie Milsap, Anne Murray and KC & The Sunshine Band as well as members of the Parton family. Kenny Rogers made his solo debut on the show and legend has it that Dolly approached Bob Dylan who initially agreed to appear but eventually declined due to his discomfort with the television medium at the time.

*Dolly* lasted only one season of 26 shows starting in autumn 1976. Despite the prestige of being the first female country singer to have her own TV show, Dolly asked to be let out of her contract partly due to the toll that 18-hour days were taking on her vocal cords, but mostly over her dissatisfaction with the show's content. As she said later, "A lot of the songs I sang, like 'Singin' In The Rain', were not choices of mine. They

---

* Not to be confused with the legendary rock music promoter.

were totally out of my category, and I couldn't sing 'em anyway." Other inappropriate Dolly moments included her singing 'My Funny Valentine' to a basset hound, donning a white afro wig to perform with Seventies soul band The Hues Corporation and trying to coax TV actor Anson Williams (Potsy from *Happy Days*) into singing a country song.

For one show, during the weekly location spot, Dolly walked around Nashville landmark the Parthenon, wearing what appeared to be a toga, miming to her cover of Ewan MacColl's 'The First Time Ever I Saw Your Face'. In the same episode she and actress Karen Black engaged in self-conscious, vacuous chat ("There's something about Nashville, it just reaches out and touches you") and sang 'Me And Bobby McGee', though at one stage Black messed up her lines. Dolly, the consummate professional, smiled and carried on without missing a note. On another week, for which, unusually, the host wore a black wig,* Dolly and poet Rod McKuen sat around a contrived set featuring a campfire and a group of innocuous-looking teenagers as they struggled through a feeble version of Morris Albert's 1975 MOR hit 'Feelings'. The fashions of the era, such as tight trousers and wide flares, were much in evidence, and Dolly's clothes unflatteringly emphasised her plumpness; bright primary colours, oranges, greens and yellows predominated. Dolly disliked having to read from cue cards and appeared exposed when singing solo because her backing band were not always in view, leaving her without anybody to interact with. The small studio audience's largely passive reaction didn't help either.

Dolly later commented, "I liked all of the people that were on . . . but I would have had a totally different line-up of guests myself. It was really bad for me, that TV show. It was worse for me than good, because the people who didn't know me who liked the show thought that's how I was . . . I mean, I still come through as myself, even with all the other stuff, but not really like I should. Not my real, natural way. And the people who did know me thought I was crazy. They knew that wasn't me. Including me. I didn't know that woman on TV!

"They were trying to have me being the person that I looked like . . . my magic has always been that I'm one way and look another – and I can't be the way I look 'cause that's artificial . . . it was prematurely done on my part." One critic said, "You can witness what happens when a fine entertainer finds herself in the hands of Hollywood producers who think they

---

* Interviewed by Bruce Forsyth on British television in 1978, Dolly said she had tried wearing a black wig as an unsuccessful disguise.

have the Midas touch, when in fact their only skill is muffling a truly talented performer in her prime."

The disposable nature of *Dolly* indicated that for all her sassiness and feisty ability in her dealings, Dolly found herself acceding to male television executives who had no idea how to present her. Although Sandy Gallin was now representing Dolly, the television deal was agreed prior to his appointment though he may have tried to bring some influence to bear on the material. After she was released from the programme Dolly said she would not want to do another regular weekly television show but would be happy to do specials and "guest shots". With its wider demographic appeal *Dolly* attracted roughly twice as many viewers as Porter's show and reruns were subsequently sold in nearly 100 markets throughout America. The show also achieved for Dolly her aim of not wanting to be categorised solely as a country artist.

During the time Dolly was resting her voice, she put together a new, professional backing band for the next phase of her career. With the Travelling Family Band, she had been earning around $1,500 per show but after expenses, was clearing only around $200. A more professional band would get her into bigger and better paying venues. Dolly called the new band Gypsy Fever because she felt an affinity with the gypsy spirit. "I'm a restless, blooded person . . . I like the feel of the wheels of my bus underneath me." It was also suggested that the name could tie in with some of the costumes, "gaudy gypsy things", Dolly might wear; referring to herself as a "glitter gypsy". Dolly was looking for skilled musicians with the flexibility to be able to play any kind of music in concert, in the studio and on television. Instrumentally, the emphasis moved from country to rock. "What we play I guess you could call Dolly Rock or Dolly Country or whatever name you can think up." The line-up included Randy Parton on bass and singer Richard Dennison, who was for a time married to Dolly's sister, Rachel. The troupe started touring early in 1977 on a bus ("the Coach Of Many Colors") that included sleeping accommodation for 11, colour television, a refrigerator, two bathrooms and a closet capable of holding around 20 costumes and four wigs.

A busy touring schedule took Dolly and Gypsy Fever across many areas of America well beyond the usual itinerary for country bands as well as to Western Europe. They played trendy rock venues such as the Boarding House in San Francisco, the Ivanhoe in Chicago and also received an enthusiastic reception at The Bottom Line in Greenwich Village, New York. The three-gig stint there attracted such luminaries as Mick Jagger,

Bruce Springsteen, Candice Bergen, Margo St James (the prostitutes' rights champion) and Andy Warhol of whom Dolly memorably said, "He's brilliant, but you'd think he was dyin' of leukaemia." She also said Warhol was the only person she had met who was weirder than her, "dressed worse and looked stranger, and didn't care, just like me". After one of the triumphant Bottom Line shows Dolly dazzled at a VIP party given in her honour at the World Trade Center. Dolly quickly hit it off with the urban celebrities; as one journalist noted, "It was gush at first sight."

John Rockwell of the *New York Times* was taken with Dolly's performance. "Her visual trademark is a mountainous, curlicued bleached-blonde wig, lots of make-up, and outfits that accentuate her quite astonishing hourglass figure . . . her thin little soprano and girlish way of talking suggests something childlike, but one quickly realises both that it is genuine and that she is a striking talent . . . Miss Parton stands apart for the sheer quality of her songs . . . her poetry has such a range of emotion and such a truth to it that – as always happens with the best art – the very specificity of her imagery becomes universal. Her music is often coloured by the modalities and rhythmic abnormalities of old English folk songs, and she nearly always manages to shape her best songs into something unusual without courting gimmickry. Even when she indulges in all-out sentimentality, as in 'Me And Little Andy', about a child who is abandoned by her drunken father and goes to heaven with her puppy, Miss Parton performs in a way that quiets cynicism."

One journalist who travelled with the troupe was struck by how seriously the band took their work; spending hours listening to tapes of the previous night's show. He was also impressed by their stage appearance. "Singer Anita Ball wears a peasant blouse and skirt and the six guys have beards and/or moustaches and longish hair and expensive looking three-piece suits." Dolly said she would be proud to take Gypsy Fever to the Grand Ole Opry but if it happened she would not offend any of her more traditional fans by performing any of the more out-and-out rock or soul numbers in her repertoire because, "they wouldn't be familiar with that."

Dolly also played a number of concerts in Britain in 1977. She had a loyal fan base there though RCA had not promoted much of her work in the UK. In 1976 she was named Best Female Vocalist from poll results conducted by various British country music organisations but nearly missed that year's Country Music Festival at Wembley because her passport had expired (she got it renewed just in time). This time, she caused more of a stir among mainstream entertainment journalists. Dolly told one what to expect from her show. "The new musicians are able to mix their sounds, ranging from heavier music right across to the pure country sounds. We've also rebuilt our programme by adding an old-time medley with songs like 'Wayfaring Stranger' and 'Life Is Like A Mountain Railroad'. Then we've got some of the new songs, a hits medley of some of my older songs; and I play the dulcimer, auto-harp, banjo and guitar. Really, it adds up to us having a good time, which, I hope reaches across to our audiences."

Rock newspaper *Melody Maker*, who doubtless appreciated the presence of rock guitars, electric keyboards and a drummer who, as one commentator approvingly put it, "kicks ass", described Gypsy Fever as a "massive improvement on what went before". Their view was that the Wembley country festival had been too restrictive for an exponent of so many different musical styles as Dolly. One journalist was won over by Dolly's Southern dialect noting how she said 1964 as "19 and 64". A feature in rival music paper *New Musical Express* gave an idea of the kind of pressure Dolly was under on tour when an interview could only be fitted in during the journey to Birmingham in an RCA-funded limousine. Squeezed into the car were other journalists plus a film cameraman. Having been in Germany the day before, from Birmingham Dolly flew back to London for an RCA bash where she endeared herself to the predominantly male hacks when announcing by way of farewell, "Hope y'all enjoyed having me as much as I enjoyed having you."

Dolly's visit coincided with the destructive side of punk rock. When commenting uncomprehendingly on photographs of the damage and mayhem at a venue caused by fans of The Clash she said, "My kinda show, my kinda personality is not the kind to make people wanna tear up seats. I've never had any mobs or people trying to tear my clothes, no more than trying to get my autograph." Dolly caused much hilarity when interviewed by popular television chat-show host Michael Parkinson. One of the other guests, the erudite raconteur Cyril Fletcher, told her he and his wife celebrated their wedding anniversary by revisiting St Martin-in-the-Fields, the venue of their "betrothal". Dolly leaped in with her own rejoinder: "My husband and I always celebrate our anniversary by driving out to Lovers Lane where we used to neck and make love in the back seat."

One particular treat for Dolly was performing at a Royal Variety Performance in Glasgow, in the presence of Queen Elizabeth II, to mark the monarch's Silver Jubilee. Also on the bill was Petula Clark, comedian Frankie Howerd (in a kilt), singer/actor David Soul and child singer Lena

Zavaroni. Dolly said meeting the Queen was the fulfilment of a dream. "I always wanted to build my home like a castle, with a real drawbridge and ev'rthin' . . . I love to fantasise . . . If I don't like all the realistic things around me, I can always pretend they're better than they are, which keeps me a very happy person. I mean, I know things *are* the way they *are*, but I don't have to drag myself down by thinking about it . . . I can't meet Cinderella but I am going to meet the real live Queen of England."

Her brief meeting with the Queen was not at all awkward. "She had on just as much jewellery as I did, though maybe she was a little tastier with it." Dolly looked overweight in a white trouser suit and floating cape. Wearing a large, top-heavy wig and a fistful of rings, she sang 'Jolene' and 'The Seeker' and was delighted when noticing that the Duke of Edinburgh clapped along. On an earlier visit to England her appetite for things royal had been whetted when she had been taken on a trip to Windsor Castle by PR man Tommy Loftus, who noted how she was fully made-up and bewigged at all times. Dolly was greatly impressed when Loftus arrived to pick her up in Perry Como's limousine (Como was playing a show that evening). "She'd never seen a castle before, anything like that," remembered Loftus, "and she was absolutely awestruck by it all." Dolly had asked if her personal assistant Judy Ogle could accompany them. "She was with her all the time and arranged whatever needed to be arranged." Tommy was slightly surprised when a thank you letter arrived a few weeks later because it came not from Dolly but from Porter Wagoner who thanked him for looking after Dolly.

As late as 1976, despite all the hostility and stress surrounding their separation, Porter was still battling for Dolly's commercial interests, making pitches on her behalf to RCA. He was concerned that she was still not being adequately promoted (even though he also complained that the company showed greater consideration for Dolly than they did for him!) One particular gripe was that Dolly's material was not widely available, in particular that it was not to be found in the stores of "the kids of the underground nature . . . the ones with the psychedelic windows . . . that look like someone threw buckets of paint on them". It was interesting that Porter, who outwardly appeared to be such an old guard figure, was alert to what was happening in the younger pop-oriented scene. Like Sandy Gallin he felt RCA should be making more of the fact that artists like Emmylou Harris and Maria Muldaur were Dolly fans; Muldaur said Dolly had "one of the really great voices ever issued to a human being".

Dolly made a surprise guest appearance at the Grand Ole Opry in September 1977, but in an ironic flashback to Dolly's own debut when an already established singer made way for her, Reba McEntire's debut was cut back to one song and she found herself following Dolly. Reba recalls the contrast in their appearance. "Dolly looked magnificent as always. She wore a black pants suit with chiffon transparent flowing arms. The outfit was dotted with rhinestone butterflies, Dolly's trademark. I wore a straight denim skirt with a matching shirt . . . I was totally in awe." Ironically when Reba had auditioned for RCA she chose to sing 'Jolene'. Desperately nervous she had to be physically helped on to the stage by a quartet called The Four Guys.

Dolly's physical appearance was increasingly the subject of much suggestive comment in the media. Television variety host Redd Foxx, a man with a reputation for risqué humour, joked that instead of her hands, Dolly had imprinted her breasts in the cement of the forecourt of Hollywood's legendary Grauman's Chinese Theater. He remarked that the imprints were so large that a midget who regularly appeared on his show, Billy Barty, could get lost in them. Dolly sent Foxx a wire. "Imprints of these or any other parts of my anatomy are not currently in the forecourt. I would be the first to admit that I am well endowed, but I seriously doubt that even your show's little person, Billy Barty, could be lost in such alleged imprints. I hesitate to add to your current woes, but I feel that in this case you owe me two equally ample apologies."

Of course it was all grist for the publicity mill but for Dolly it revealed only half the picture. "The whole purpose of the image was a gimmick to catch people's attention and then to let them know there was a person underneath it that did sing, and write songs, and was very serious about her music." She made the point that her country fans had always known she could sing and write songs but that new audiences had "to get over the shock of my image before they can get real serious about my music". Talking about her image, she said, "It's ridiculous, but it's fun. It's just the way I choose to enjoy the business . . . I could be very stylish if I chose to be, but I would never stoop so low as to be *fashionable* . . . show business is a big fake, anyway the biggest part of it. So I choose to do the fake part in a joyful way . . . I don't want to look like everyone else, I don't want to be like everyone else, 'cause I'm not."

She made the point to one interviewer that he would have been disappointed if she had arrived in ordinary clothes. As she put it, "It would've been a disappointment, even though you might not realise it. Because the character would have died, and characters do not die." She often talks of "Dolly" (a persona "more comic than erotic" as one writer put it) in the third person as if referring to a separate being. Country singer George

Hamilton IV is sympathetic to Dolly's approach. "I've often heard her say that she always liked to play dress-up when she was a little girl. She always dreamed of being glamorous. Some people might say that's a bit contrived to become somebody that might not be the same person that sits at the breakfast table with her husband and family. In the way most people dress up to go to a party or a ball, she just dresses up every day and becomes Dolly Parton. But when you think about it everybody does that in show business . . . like some of the guys who come onstage with holes in the knees of their jeans, always with the holes in just the right place, you know. At least Dolly is honest about it. Some of these people make out they are poverty stricken, meanwhile they are making millions and live in great mansions."

After the debacle of *Dolly* Gallin used his contacts to ensure that Dolly started appearing regularly on prime time television shows such as *The Tonight Show With Johnny Carson* and *Hollywood Squares*. Showing off her larger than life appearance and sparky personality to the full, Dolly bluntly delivered down-home common sense, becoming established as a celebrity in a great many more homes in America than Porter's show had made possible. Part of the appeal was her manipulation of those most eye-catching of assets, her breasts. For a country girl brought up in an environment where conservative values were respected, it was a daring move. It could also be seen as demeaning, amounting to nothing but smutty voyeuristic titillation of the type featured in the British *Carry On* film series. Asked about the remarks that television hosts made about her anatomy Dolly said, "I don't mind . . . just as long as nobody gets tacky." As she must have known they would, certain talk-show hosts stepped over the line.

During an appearance on the Carson show, conversation turned to Dolly's chest. Smiling in mock embarrassment she said that she had always been "pretty well blessed" and then went on to say, "People are always asking if they're real," at which point Carson denied that he would ever ask her such a thing. Egged on by the studio audience, Carson glanced sheepishly at Dolly's bosom and said, "But I would give about a year's pay to peek under there." The crowd erupted and even the indefatigable Dolly was lost for words as her face reddened and she laughed with what appeared to be genuine embarrassment. Not surprisingly Dolly became one of Carson's most popular guests for a time. Apart from anything else viewers loved Dolly's voice which had a certain novelty value outside the Southern states; as one journalist said, "You could dance to it."

Gallin was happy to maintain this kind of mainstream exposure but was reportedly opposed to Dolly being interviewed alongside Tammy Wynette and Loretta Lynn for an *Esquire* article because he did not want her to be "lumped in with those country singers". Similarly he felt that any ongoing public association with Porter would not be helpful for the plans he had for her. He was, however, happy for her to be associated with such established female artists as Linda Ronstadt and Emmylou Harris whose appeal was not so narrow and who commanded broad-based critical respect. Dolly-related articles started appearing in such high circulation magazines as *People Magazine* and *Good Housekeeping*. There was griping in Nashville about her being packaged for a larger market, but her uncompromising response, delivered in numerous interviews was, "I'm not leaving country music, I'm taking it with me. All I want is a chance to do everything I want to do in life . . . Most people don't get to do a whole lot, because they aren't brave enough to try. Well, I'm brave, and I'll try."

In amongst her media appearances Dolly found time to record two of her benchmark albums both released in '77. The first, *New Harvest . . . First Gathering* was very much Dolly's creation, with her writing all but two of the songs. The album title said much about where Dolly found herself artistically and personally and one song in particular, 'Light Of A Clear Blue Morning', captured the spirit of the record. Dolly wrote it when she decided to strike out on her own. "My creativity was beginning to die on the vine . . . I wanted to run and felt like I was being held back. And you know how it feels as a kid, when you get in a race with somebody and you start running and you start gettin' ahead and they get hold of you and pull you back. That was sort of the feeling I had, but I kept running . . ." She later said the actual moment of inspiration for the song came the day she left Porter's show for good. It was thus a song of freedom but one tinged with poignancy; it was said that many women breaking free from frustrating restrictive situations identified with the core message. The song was also an expression of Dolly finding her own niche having finally expunged her childhood feelings of not fitting in, of being different and of not belonging. The message was enhanced by the dramatic, over-wrought production, mingling soulfulness with lulls followed by crashing crescendos, speedy passages and stamping piano chords. The song was released as a single but was not a major success, because, in Dolly's view, the fans were sensitive to her problems with Porter. "It was too much of a testimonial . . . people knew what was goin' on and nobody wanted to take sides."

Dolly said that regardless of commercial success *New Harvest . . . First Gathering* would always be a special album because "it was the first time in

my whole life I got to do something totally on my own. In terms of fulfilment, it is one of the greatest things of my life." The cover shot of a
smiling Dolly sitting in the passenger seat of a car shows there is no one
sitting behind the steering wheel – she was about to slide over to drive off
wherever the mood took her. The album also featured two soul classics,
'(Your Love Keeps Lifting Me) Higher And Higher' and 'My Love' (her
reinterpretation of the Temptations' 'My Girl'), both childhood favourites, included in an attempt to secure airplay on pop stations.

Though the overall sound continued the recent trend of more pop-
oriented material, reinforced by instruments such as synthesised drums, the
album featured 'Applejack', an out-and-out country song about Jackson
Taylor, the man who helped Dolly learn the banjo as a child. As if to
reassure fans that her country credentials were still firmly in place Dolly
arranged to have some of the genre's most revered figures, including Roy
Acuff, Ernest Tubb, Hank Snow and Kitty Wells, sing backing vocals on
the song. She even peeled off her long acrylic nails to play the banjo, claw
hammer style.

*New Harvest . . . First Gathering* garnered favourable reaction in the
press but some old school critics felt that Dolly had made "too many con-
cessions to the pop idiom", bemoaning the lack of feeling which had been
the bedrock of some of her best songs such as 'Coat Of Many Colors' and
'Jolene'. One journalist found the material "disappointingly superficial . . .
her old material might have been a big bit heavy on the corn, but at least it
was the real stuff, not freeze-dried instant contemporary . . . do we really
need just another female pop singer?"

Another wrote, "There are already enough bland performers trying to
straddle pop and country while putting out twangy muzak." However,
English writer Alan Cackett adjudged that Dolly had successfully crossed
over by blending country, pop and soul, comparing the album to earlier
Linda Ronstadt recordings. On the other hand another review described
much of the music as, "hip MOR *à la* Elton John . . . with the dreadful
feel of singer/songwriter pseudo-sensitivity". For this particular reviewer
Dolly was a victim of her own ambition.

Dolly declared that her music was neither country nor pop but simply
"Dolly Parton's music." Aware of the shift in style and the effect it may have
on her existing fans, RCA took the unusual step of putting out a full page
advertisement in the music press accompanied by a quote from Dolly:

*"Any time you make a change, you gotta pay the price. A lot of country
people feel I'm leaving the country, that I'm not proud of Nashville, which is*

*the biggest lie there is. I don't want to leave the country, but to take the whole country with me wherever I go. There are really no limits now. After the first of the year my new life begins."*

*New Harvest . . . First Gathering* made number one in the country charts (for one week) and number 71 in the pop charts, but because there was no 'smash single' overall sales were disappointing, falling well short of the 500,000 required for a gold disc. Dolly later said that she may have gone overboard on the production. "I got too many hot licks in that I'd been savin' up over the years. I just wanted to hear it all at once."

Sandy Gallin believed that if he could just find the right song, then Dolly Parton could reach the wider audience she so desired.

# Chapter 14

AS a possible follow up to *New Harvest . . . First Gathering* one of the ideas mooted was an album of Bill Monroe songs, to be called *Monroe*, a weak premise to enable Dolly to replicate Marilyn Monroe's famous pose from *The Seven Year Itch* – skirt billowing up – for the sleeve. Instead, the second album from Dolly in 1977 achieved unprecedented dividends but with Dolly's duties significantly reduced. In contrast to *New Harvest . . . First Gathering*, the production role and most of the song-writing were handed over to a high-powered team with a proven track record for commercial success. *Here You Come Again* was recorded in Los Angeles at Sound Labs Inc. with top session musicians and producer Gary Klein, who had worked with Barbra Streisand. The album benefited from an instantly hooky title track written by the veteran team of Barry Mann and Cynthia Weil, writers of such classics as 'Saturday Night At The Movies' (The Drifters) and 'You've Lost That Lovin' Feeling' (The Righteous Brothers).

The idea came from the sort of real life experience which inspired so many of Dolly's songs. The songwriters had a friend who seemed unable to stop herself from going back to a lover who kept breaking her heart and that simple fact was the spark. Dolly was reportedly initially uncertain about the song, concerned that it was too pop, but Gallin pushed hard to have it released as a single and ensured that it was promoted right via coast to coast talk shows. Once it was a smash hit, Dolly's doubts were assuaged and she said, "Somebody said a monkey could have had a hit with it . . . the monkey did. You're looking at a million dollar monkey."

'Here You Come Again' made number one in the country charts for five weeks – a feat she would never repeat – and number three in the pop charts; it was her first major crossover success, earning Dolly her first gold record for a single (over a million copies sold) as well as her first Grammy nomination in the category Best Pop Performance By A Female. The album went gold and then platinum (one million sales) in 1978 – the first time a female country singer had achieved such a feat. The album stayed at the top of the country charts for nine weeks and made the Top 20 in the pop charts. The sleeve showed three shots of Dolly in blue jeans, red polka dot blouse and white high heels resembling stills from a line-dancing session. The neon strip lighting backdrop created the impression of a country girl in a high tech world. Her wig and bosom were to the fore while she held the ties of her blouse, and her playfully provocative smiles suggested more would be revealed when turning over to the back cover. The gatefold carried a soft focus shot of Dolly in a haze of pink flowers.

The album produced another number-one single – this time written by Dolly, 'It's All Wrong But It's All Right', its overt sexual overtones raising a few eyebrows. Some commentators used the lyrics as another excuse to speculate on whether Dolly and Carl had an open marriage, or whether Dolly might be upset if Carl had an extramarital relationship.

'Two Doors Down' became another popular single and a regular feature of Dolly's live concert. Although the album was predominantly pop it did include 'God's Coloring Book' which reiterated Dolly's spiritual side as she marvelled at the wonders of nature. 'Me And Little Andy' was the latest in a long line of songs about unhappy childhood situations. It was inspired by reports about child abuse and, rather questionably, Dolly had sung it to an attentive group of young children on her television show and it became a live favourite for a spell. The story featuring a young girl and her dog arriving on a stranger's doorstep on a bitterly cold night, unfolds with a surreal interplay between conventional storyline and nursery rhymes. Dolly believed children's minds switched back and forth in this way when severely upset. "Life isn't all a dance," was Dolly's flippant remark when defending this remarkable and macabre song. Of the morbid theme she tried pointing out that the main characters "go to a better place where they're real happy".

The fact that Dolly had only written four of the album's songs led some to suggest that her real strength lay in writing country rather than pop material. However, the opposite view was posited with music press head-lines such as 'So You Wanna Be A Rock 'n' Roll Star? You Are Dolly, You Are' and 'No Country Cousin Now'. Though leaning heavily towards pop and MOR Klein managed to preserve the natural charm of what some described as Dolly's "Appalachian vibrato".

Certain purists continued to carp that Dolly's "abandonment" had robbed country music of one of its more prominent figureheads. Perhaps they were harder on her because she was a woman. One Nashville music critic said, "Dolly's sound has gone slicker 'n a greased pig!" while writer John Morthland said, "Once she was free of [Porter] she wasted no time in overcompensating grotesquely in the opposite direction." Dolly defended such accusations by repeatedly claiming, "I'm not leaving country. I'm taking it with me . . . I'll be able to do more for the name of country music by going ahead and doing what I feel I should do and reaching a broader audience and as many people I can, and by having a universal appeal. I'll be able to do more for Nashville than I ever could have done had I stayed there."*

When leading British country DJ David Allan received similar complaints (though most letters were supportive) Dolly's response was, "Well, I really don't think these people can be my real fans or else they'd appreciate what I'm doing . . . Now for the first time I have the chance to expose other parts of me that people have not seen. They've seen the real me, but they ain't seen all of it . . . When I'm old I want to feel that I've accomplished all the things I could. I don't want to look back and regret not trying things." She also made the point that she had spent enough time justifying herself and would just let what she had done, "stand on its own, 'cause if it ain't good enough it won't sell anyway . . . I don't think there is a definition for country any more, you wouldn't call my music country, you wouldn't call it pop. Why should it carry any label apart from the name of the artist?" However, the issue remained touchy and in another interview she admitted, "If my music has to have a label, I will call it country, mainly because I am country. You cannot leave what you are. But I really prefer to call it Dolly Parton music."

The album won a Grammy in the Best Country Vocal Performance By A Female category but despite the prestigious nature of the award Dolly was too busy to collect it in person. Dolly's overwhelming emotion towards the record's success was relief that the dream she had pursued had come true. Narvel Felts did a three-night tour with Dolly and Gypsy Fever during this time. "She wasn't different but the way she was surrounded was." An audience with Dolly had to be arranged through Don Warden. "She was still real friendly one on one but meals for instance were specially catered in a private room, for her and me and the bands and the sound crew. Also a limousine would drive her to the stage and after the show she was back in it and she'd be gone, kinda like 'Elvis has left the building.' No autograph line. That was the way things had become. I guess it was the image her new management wanted to create. A more upmarket image, creating an aura about her probably. The move to pop never bothered me . . . more power to her. I think most people would try to be as big in the business as they could be. It's the wise thing to do and it's human nature."

---

* Dolly was sensitive enough to the charges to insist that a steel guitar be included on 'Here You Come Again'.

Despite the grumblings that she had left country music behind, in 1978, Dolly won the CMA award for Entertainer Of The Year,* the second woman to win this non gender category, Loretta Lynn having been the first. "Dolly Parton was quite the most entertaining presence . . ." wrote a journalist covering the event, "looking more than ever like a Confederate version of Barbara Windsor, in a dress so tight that she must surely have been hoisted into its confines by at least three strong men and a donkey and an intricate system of winches and pulleys and grappling hooks. She looked, as if she might have been playing hide and seek with a barrage balloon." The presentation of her award was made by Johnny Cash and Ronnie Milsap. Cash demonstrated his black humour by opening the envelope and passing the card with the winner's name to Milsap who is blind. As Dolly went up to the stage the front seams of her dress burst, which necessitated her hurriedly borrowing a mink stole from neighbour (and Kenny Rogers' then wife) Marianne Gordon which she clutched to her chest. After receiving the award Dolly said, "I guess it's like my daddy said, 'You shouldn't try to put 50 pounds of mud in a five-pound sack.'" The tabloid press had a field day; it was just the kind of Dolly story they craved, though she later insisted reports were exaggerated as to just how much the dress had split.

That same year it was reported that Dolly was in the process of agreeing a three-film deal with 20th Century Fox, which to her, was "a good number . . . if something real successful happens, I can go on and make one every so often. And if it don't work out I'll know I gave it three good shots." She also intimated that one of the films would be her life story – an idea that has yet to materialise but surely will some day. Willie Nelson tipped Dolly for a part in a film about greed and power, loyalty and love in the country song-writing business, which came to nothing. Though wading through a great many scripts, she would have to wait before the right part came along.†

In the meantime the publicity machine continued to work on making Dolly a household name with, to put it in crude commercial terms, a strong brand image and recognition. She appeared in a pin-up poster as a Daisy Mae country girl lying in a pile of hay in a pose reminiscent of Jane Russell at her steamy best. While the picture was not sexually explicit it robustly promoted the idea of Dolly as a sex symbol with no intimation

* She was also nominated for best album and best single but won in neither category.
† On the subject of films, Dolly professed an admiration for the work of Woody Allen and Neil Simon and her favourite ever movie is apparently *Dr Zhivago*.

whatsoever as to her musical qualities. It was doubly unfortunate that the poster captured Dolly looking rather like a blow-up doll and was marketed in fierce competition with other faces from the time, particularly *Charlie's Angels* actress Farrah Fawcett-Majors, which was to be found on the bedroom walls of countless adolescent males. Dolly's poster sold several thousand copies in a month at a price of $2.50 a shot. Her likeness was also marketed via the Dolly doll, about 12 inches tall, selling for around $10, which was available in various styles including the "show time" costume, a one-piece red jump suit with silver lame trim.

Also in 1978, Dolly gave an extensive interview to *Playboy* subtitled A Candid Conversation With The Curvaceous Queen Of Country Music, and appeared on the issue's front cover in full bunny girl gear. For someone who had avoided plunging necklines in the interests of modesty, a substantial eyeful of cleavage was on display. The photograph certainly consolidated the crucial role of her breasts as a key part (or parts?) of her image. The interview, expertly conducted by Lawrence Grobel, stretched to 12 pages and covered all aspects of Dolly's life from childhood hardship to multi-million record sales. Grobel pushed Dolly further than most interviewers and teased out snippets of information on subjects which went beyond the party line she usually delivered. There were limits though, as when she refused to divulge at what age she lost her virginity, though even here a clear indication was gained that it occurred when she was fairly young.

Dolly was remarkably candid about sex in particular and it was these areas that the tabloid press picked up on in salacious follow-up articles, hardly surprising considering her level of frankness. "I always loved sex. I never had a bad experience with it . . . to me sex was not dirty . . . I'm very aggressive . . . I don't mind bein' the (sexual) aggressor if it comes to somethin' I need or want . . . nothin' better than sex when you think you have to sneak it." On having an affair she said, "No matter who I met or what kind of affair I might ever have, ain't nobody in the world could take Carl's place . . . if I wanted to do it, I would; if I should do it, it should affect nobody but me and the person involved." She revealed that there had been a few people she had been attracted to "real strong" but also that there was no way she could ever leave Carl.

There was much speculation in the tabloid press about Dolly's relationships with other men, particularly singer Merle Haggard who had toured with Dolly in the early Seventies. Dolly is said to have inspired Haggard's song 'Always Wanting You' but as he later made clear in his autobiography, Merle's affection was unrequited. Haggard, married to singer Bonnie

Owens at the time, said that he once called Dolly at home at three in the morning and woke her up to sing a song he had written about her but his efforts were in vain. "Little by little I faced the fact that Dolly had meant it when she said there was no future for us." Dolly later claimed she had no idea that Haggard's feelings ran that deep. She said that if they had both been available, "Who knows how we would have ended up. Maybe like Bonnie and Clyde."

In the *Playboy* exchange, Dolly admitted that though she would be upset if Carl had an affair, "it wouldn't be like the end of the world for me . . . I would probably cry and pout for a day." She appreciated, "the way he lets me be free . . . he don't try to choke me and demand anything from me." On their enigmatic way of life she said, "If I'm home two or three weeks, I want to get to work and he wants to get back to work, so he's just as anxious to see me go as I am to leave. It probably don't make much sense but it makes sense to us." One of Dolly's Christmas presents from Carl around this time was a leather-bound tool chest which included pliers, a screwdriver and nail clippers. "He's the only thing that remains untarnished in this business," said Dolly. She gave Carl a battery charger.

The *Playboy* interview was all part of the strategy to raise Dolly's profile in the public consciousness. In realisation of this goal she was quite prepared to discuss her personal life and to flaunt herself in a magazine, albeit a "classy" one in her opinion, which contained photographs of naked women. In a clever piece of ironic doubletalk Dolly was concerned that some of her country fans might not like the interview because a lot of them were family-oriented, religious people, but, "they ain't got no business with *Playboy* anyhow!" Circulation of the magazine doubled for the Dolly issue, particularly in Nashville. One half of the last page of the interview was taken up with an advertisement for her latest album *Heartbreaker*. Dolly told Grobel that Carl really liked the album, admitting that in the past he had not always cared for her singing, but her move to a more commercial radio-friendly sound met with his approval.

*Heartbreaker* featured the uptempo disco hit 'Baby I'm Burning', replete with arresting electronic sound bursts. In keeping with current vogues, Dolly saw to it that the song was given a special disco mix, released on pink vinyl, and she became the only country artist to score a major disco hit. The disco feel to some of the album's songs coincided with the runaway success of *Saturday Night Fever*. When Dolly sang 'Baby I'm Burning' live, her more traditional fans merely gave polite applause to what they regarded as a "disco alien". 'Sure Thing' had a slow smouldering rock groove, while the power ballad 'We're Through Forever' was

MOR pop, though there was the odd number with a country feel such as 'The Man', another song with a twist in that the man in the title turns out to be Dolly's father. Sales were boosted by a massive publicity campaign including a huge billboard on Hollywood's Sunset Strip with "Dolly" blazing in neon lights. Hundreds of pairs of satin shorts with the word "Dolly" on one leg and "Heartbreaker" on the other were manufactured as giveaways for record shops and radio stations. The album topped the country charts, made the pop Top 30 and earned Dolly a gold disc. *Heartbreaker* was Dolly's only album in 1978. The pace of releases had slowed down, allowing Dolly to pursue an ever-increasing range of interests outside music.

For some time Dolly had been interested in the idea of making an album with Emmylou Harris and Linda Ronstadt. Dolly was proud of the fact that these two outstanding talents had publicly professed to be fans of her writing, as recognition from such well-respected figures only helped to broaden her appeal and enhance her credibility. However, she did feel that her music owed little in return, saying somewhat egotistically, "I'm greatly inspired by them, but not influenced. I'm so individual, so original, that I don't have to do what everybody else is doing." Emmylou had recorded Dolly's 'To Daddy' about a woman who leaves a loveless marriage to find a new life. She said, "When I first heard it, my lips were trembling . . . and I was afraid I was gonna make a scene," while Linda was responsible for one of the earliest cover versions of 'I Will Always Love You'. The three had met over the years, appearing together on an edition of the ill-fated *Dolly* series and Dolly had made contributions to some of Emmylou and Linda's albums, but what was now envisaged was an album which brought their varied talents together with the emphasis on their vocal gifts.

As well as generating considerable public interest and significant commercial opportunities, the project could introduce Dolly to a rock audience, take Linda back to her country roots and widen Emmylou's appeal in both sectors. However, given the scheduling demands placed on three major artists on three different labels with three different managers it would not be easy. Attempts were made to throw a veil of secrecy over the idea but the press got wind of it after some exploratory discussions took place at Dolly's Brentwood home and speculation about a possible release date grew. Some tracks were laid down at the studio of Brian Ahern, Emmylou's then husband, and several found their way onto albums by Emmylou and Linda, but plans for a full album were postponed indefinitely.

Dolly continued her busy touring schedule, mainly by bus since, like

Porter she was not particularly enamoured with flying. Touring in the late Seventies was a smooth business to the point where, according to Dolly, it was almost as easy and convenient as living at home. Days were set aside for laundry and a duty roster was implemented to keep the bus clean with Dolly taking her turn along with everybody else. The troupe's arrival in a small town was the cause of much excitement. Bracey, population 500, nearly came to a standstill when the Coach Of Many Colors stopped by. The troupe bought provisions and enjoyed a picnic of barbecued chicken, hot dogs and roast corn cooked up by Dolly. A procession of wide-eyed locals grabbed the opportunity for snapshots and autographs of the celebrity in their midst and Dolly obliged them with what one writer described as her 40,000-watt smile. One local was quoted, "I drove by and would have gotten out, but my wife had a gun on me." Another said, "It was the biggest thing that's happened since they flooded the lake."

If the band stayed at motels they generally chose modest chains such as Howard Johnson and group activities such as volleyball helped to relieve any stress which had built up during the day, though Dolly ducked out for fear of damaging her nails. Swimming was also popular though Dolly preferred not be seen in a bathing costume as she figured it would cause too much of a stir; she liked to be the centre of attention but she could do without being ogled. Carl joined the tour from time to time though he did not like the idea of travelling on the bus (he didn't like "all the commotion" as Dolly put it) or drawing attention to himself as "Mr Dolly Parton". Carl travelled by car and if shows were close to Nashville Dolly might accompany him back to the house. Sometimes Dolly played a series of shows at the same venue as this made it easier for Carl to visit. Dolly and Carl took a childish delight in playing pranks on each other. On one occasion he decided to appear onstage as one of her backup singers. However, she found out and decided to get her own back.* She told a policeman and said, "I've been getting death threats lately, and I don't know who that man in the red shirt is." Carl was detained and was only saved from a trip to the police station by the intervention of Don Warden.

Laura Cunningham, a journalist for *Cosmopolitan*, spent some time with Dolly on tour and was taken aback when she actually got to meet Carl. It was his birthday and Dolly had laid on a surprise party for him. Dolly entered the room and as Cunningham reported, "Behind her, a Lincolnesque man walked slowly towards us . . . 'Happy birthday!' we

---

* According to press reports Carl sometimes got onstage to do backing vocals, one occasion being at the Kentucky State Fair in 1977.

cried . . . the lanky stranger turns, enters the room backwards, as if making way for yet another person behind him. He makes mock gestures of greeting to some invisible person. 'Wal,' he laughs, 'I thank you from the bottom of mah crotch.' Tall and good-looking, rather like a young Gregory Peck, he has a way of moving his angular body so that he seems to come towards you in sections. He also makes exaggerated faces, talks to his right shoulder, hangs his head, looks under the table. His occasional speeches to our group all have the style of an impersonation."

As a boss Dolly endeavoured to be fair but she had no hesitation in dealing with a band member who displeased her. "I'm a very honest, open person. I think one of the reasons I am a good boss is because you will always know what I'm a thinkin' . . . I'll just say, 'Hey, Joe, there's somethin' that's really been buggin' the shit outa me.'" She looked for people of reliable character. *Rolling Stone* journalist Chet Flippo recalled a time when she took her band out for dinner after a show. One of the musicians started teasing Dolly's new bandleader Gregg Perry, about the fact that he was not drinking. Flippo noticed a subtle change in Dolly's expression though she said nothing at the time. When Flippo met up with the band on a subsequent tour he noticed that the musician in question had been offloaded.

A great believer in the power of positive thinking and fulfilment through hard work, Dolly used self-help books as a means to achieve these ends. "I'm willing to sacrifice to get the right group. I cannot let friendship or nothing enter into it. But it's not a matter of whether they can pick or not; it's a matter that it's not the right combination . . . if I get a negative person around me it just digs at me. Rather than let it get to me, I just replace them . . . I don't care if they smoke grass or if they drink alcohol, but not when we are working, I don't want any of that to interfere with their job. After work, I couldn't care less because I enjoy doing certain things myself." She did not object to band members bringing a "chickie" onto the bus as long as there was no one else around at the time and they used their own bunk. "Just don't let him get in mine. Don't leave something in my bed that I don't want!"

Dolly and Gypsy Fever played venues of varying size and quality. Shows were not always sell-outs and on occasion security was poor. At one show in Cuyahoga Falls a large hulk wearing a hat and cowboy boots jumped onto the stage and planted a kiss on Dolly's cheek. Ever the professional she kept performing as her two largest soundmen dragged the man away. On occasion problems arose from the choice of artist Dolly appeared with. In the early days of Gypsy Fever she supported Willie Nelson, some of whose fans lost interest in her after about the second song and started talking loudly among themselves. The problem was exacerbated by a poor sound system, which meant that fans who wanted to hear Dolly's quieter numbers had to cluster around the front of the stage. Willie Nelson called for her to join him during his set but she was already ensconced on her bus, complaining that the crowd had been drinking.

Still only in her early thirties, Dolly Parton had written a remarkable amount of songs, already more than she could ever hope to record in her career. They came from experience and her imagination but there was no set pattern to the way they appeared. As Dolly explained, "A strange feeling usually comes over me, almost like being in a trance. I know what's going on but I'm totally separated from it. When you are talented I think much of the inspiration is spiritual, from God."

Dolly claimed that anyone could get to know her through her songs. She saw them as her true legacy, allowing her to enact her whimsies. "You wouldn't want your mamma to think that you would like to go off on a wild weekend with some guy, but by writin' it in a song, you can live out that fantasy." Cover versions of her material were on the increase and hearing other people's interpretations was intriguing to her. "There have been times I've really had to adjust to hearing one of my songs. It's like taking one of your kids and doin' plastic surgery on its face . . . to me every song of mine is like a child. I don't have children of my own. But yet when I conceive an idea, I carry it in my mind until it's time to be delivered. I labour over it, then it's born. Then I watch it grow to see what it will become. Some of them are beautiful children. Some of them are not so beautiful. But each song has its individual personality." Emmylou Harris was struck by the apparent ease with which Dolly was able to write. "I've never seen anyone so spontaneously creative . . . I've watched Dolly writing one song, whilst she's singing another."

Dolly reinforced her loyalty to country music and begged her new fanbase to see it as more than some narrow genre, hidebound by rules and tradition. "Country music is music with a lot of class. And I know a lot of people who love country music, who are really sophisticated people. Especially nowadays. A lot of people used to love country music but they wouldn't confess to it because they thought it was music for people with dirt under their fingernails . . . but who's to say what country is. I don't know any more. It's really hard to define what's country, what's pop, what's rock. I don't want the old traditional sounds to die away. I love the old country. I hope it never dies, even if I don't stay there with it."

"There's a dark and solemn side to [Dolly's] music that harks back to country music's prehistory," wrote Colin Escott, "but it's offset by her bouffant sequin pantsuits, and rhinestone. She'll act like she has just ridden into town on a mule, but can look over a contract with the finesse of a lawyer. And her grown woman's songs are often sung with childlike vulnerability."

The childlike vulnerability Escott described was achieved with a range of techniques: breathy voice, quivering with emotion, coming close to crying real tears, unexpectedly speaking certain words or lines rather than singing them. Just as a comedian chuckling at key moments can generate laughter, so too Dolly was able to tug the heartstrings of her audience by emphasising the message in her songs with an outward range of feelings. An article in the *New York Times* magazine was flowery in its praise. "Dolly's work is as sheer and delicate as a butterfly's wings, she skitters over the surface of the words, barely touching them . . . sometimes she hits a high note and it breaks into pieces, and a little shower of crystally sounds come down; sometimes she hits low notes, soft and furry and filled with loneliness. Her voice can quiver, pure and tremulous, or it can twang flat out like a banjo string; it can throb, it can lift . . . it takes an octave jump with foolish ease and it is almost always true and sweet."

Dolly became a target for numerous charities and other institutions keen to gain support by associating themselves with a high profile celebrity. On one occasion she agreed to donate a personal appearance as a prize at an auction. The winners, the Dollar General Corporation, paid $3,000 for her appearance and she was photographed chasing department head Leonard Murley for a kiss because although one of her biggest fans, he was shy. As early as 1974, Dolly was named Fundraising Chairman for the Kidney Foundation of Middle Tennessee and prior to that she and Porter had agreed to be honorary co-chairmen of the State Chapters of the National Haemophilia Foundation. In the early Seventies Dolly was invited, along with legendary country songsmith Harlan Howard, to be guest instructor as part of a course on the fundamentals of songwriting at the University of Tennessee in Nashville. In 1978 it was reported that Dolly had agreed to take part in the RFK Tennis Tournament in memory of Robert F. Kennedy, assassinated 10 years previously. The aim was to raise funds for a variety of youth programmes. Other celebrities participating included Dustin Hoffman, Muhammad Ali, Jimmy Connors and Billy Jean King.

Dolly was honoured by the Nashville Area Chamber of Commerce for her involvement in an advertising campaign encouraging people to come to the city. (The campaign's strapline was, "Y'all come on down for a fun-filled Nashville music weekend!") In the course of August 1979, the Chamber received 23,500 cut out "Nashville Loves Company" coupons, requesting more information. The ultimate recognition of Dolly's achievements came when the Senate voted 95 to 0 to name a 2.6-mile stretch of US Highway 441 in Sevierville, on which Sevier County High School was situated, to be renamed Dolly Parton Parkway in recognition of the school's most famous ex-pupil's achievements. Senator Carl Koella said, "I'm just worried this may cause problems for us over in East Tennessee . . . the word is getting out that Miss Parton is how we raise all Sevier County women." State representative Clifford 'Bo' Henry quipped, "This is the straightest, most level stretch of US Highway 441. Couldn't we find a piece of road more in proportion with Ms Parton?"

In 1978 a special pinball machine – flashy blue and pink, featuring pictures emphasising Dolly's curves – was even designed in her honour. "Everybody loves Dolly" seemed to be a common refrain among fans and music business professionals alike. However, there was one who regarded her in a less favourable light. Porter Wagoner had been brooding about the terms of the agreement he and Dolly had struck in 1970 and felt he had gotten a raw deal, and as Dolly would soon find out he was not prepared to let matters rest.

# Chapter 15

DOLLY was sometimes asked about her political views and her attitudes to current, controversial issues but she usually sidestepped such questions. "I try to be careful about what I say because it's really so easy to offend people. If you made a remark, even if it's an innocent thing, and you didn't mean it to be a big deal, as a celebrity, it could easily be misconstrued . . . I think it is better to choose what you say than to say what you choose." There were times when she seemed to take this approach to extremes. During one press conference when her physique was being discussed she said, "I like to be short instead of tall," but then hurriedly added, "even though tall people are beautiful."

Dolly said that the extent of her political involvement was casting her vote. In 1973 she was one of the entertainers at an event, attended by President Richard Nixon, to mark the dedication of the Cordell Hull Dam in Tennessee. Dolly denied ever supporting Nixon, adding that she didn't vote because no politician could be trusted. Dolly said that East Tennessee was pro Republican and that her father would "kill for Nixon . . . it's like a mother and child, no matter how awful they get, how many people they kill, they still love 'em just the same," though she wondered whether the Watergate scandal might have reduced his support.

According to Mary A. Bufwack and Robert K. Oermann in their book *Finding Her Voice*, Dolly campaigned for the Democratic presidential candidate Jimmy Carter in 1976, his humanitarian views conforming to her own socially liberal outlook. "I'm for equal rights for all people. I think children and blacks and reds and all people should have an equal shot. I just think we're all God's children and should be treated with respect . . . I just think if somebody's qualified to do a job and they've got the nerve and the guts and the backbone to work and get themselves into a position, then more power to 'em." A considerably overweight Dolly sang 'My Tennessee Mountain Home' for Carter and the First Lady after his election, saying how wonderful it was that simple farm folks could grow up to be President of America. Yet a year later when asked whether Carter was an improvement on his predecessor, she was not exactly effusive in her support. "Yeah, I hope so . . . I think he's sincere, just a friendly old

Southern guy . . . I hope he'll make a good president; it's too soon to tell. But he is a character . . . the people wanted someone more like *us*, down to earth."

Stella Parton does not believe Dolly will ever feel compelled to come out strongly in favour of a political party. "I don't think she will ever do that because Dolly's on everybody's side . . . so long as they're on her side. She's very patriotic, very community- and country-minded."

Women's liberation was a hot topic in the Seventies and it might be thought that Dolly would have something to say in support of the movement; after all, she was a woman who had battled to succeed in a male dominated world. However, Dolly tended to maintain her strategy of avoidance when the subject was raised. "I really don't know what to say when people ask me about women's liberation . . . my life is a special kind of life. I mean, it's *my* life, so I don't know what it has to do with the way other women live." During the *Playboy* interview when the topic came up, she was uncharacteristically thrown:

> *Playboy*: Do you support the Equal Rights Amendment?
>
> Parton: Equal rights? I love everybody . . .
>
> *Playboy*: We mean equal rights for women.
>
> Parton: I can't keep up with it.
>
> *Playboy*: Do you read any books on the women's movement?
>
> Parton: Never have. I know so little about it they'd probably be ashamed that I was a woman. Everybody should be free: If you don't want to stay home, get out and do somethin'; if you want to stay home, stay home and be happy.

Asked about the "women's movement" in another interview she said, "To be honest with you, I don't even know what all of it involves . . . I sympathise with all people and I see both sides of any issues. I just like people."

Feminist writers might well have admired Dolly's determination in carving out a career for herself but they would surely have despaired at comments made in her 1977 *Rolling Stone* interview. "Women by nature do have it easier because they were made to be a man's helpmate, so to speak . . . but if a woman is smart enough and she has a desire and an ambition to do something else, that's fine too. I would prefer to be a woman because a man has to get out and work because that is just the law of the land . . . a woman doesn't have to unless she wants to." Similarly they would have had little time for her growing dependence on an artificial appearance. "I've become so if I wore just the right amount of make-up, a natural hair-do and simple, basic, beautiful clothes, why I'd just feel like a dishrag. I'd feel naked." Dolly subscribed to Minnie Pearl's philosophy, "Any ole barn looks better with a little red paint on it."

In Laura Cunningham's *Cosmopolitan* profile, one band member (who chose to remain anonymous) claimed to have seen Dolly's face *au naturel* and said she looked beautiful. He drew the conclusion that Dolly believed she looked less pretty without her wig and make-up. Dolly said it was all part of a ploy to make her stand out from the crowd. "I took a chance on this appearance interfering with my music because I knew that if I really had the talent I could overcome it all – the poverty, the mountain background, the bizarre artificial look. I just wanted to know myself that you can come from nothing and make something of your life. You don't have to be educated, you don't have to be stylish . . . maybe I'm setting up an even harder test for myself – like can I do it all and even overcome an image I've created?" Hollywood fashion designer, Richard Blackwell, named Dolly as the worst-dressed woman in America. "There are too many yards of Dolly poured into too few inches of fabric . . . she's like a ruffled bedspread covering king-sized pillows." Previous recipients of this dubious accolade included Elizabeth Taylor and Zsa Zsa Gabor. However, Dolly's look was memorable enough to inspire Dolly Parton lookalike competitions.

In the summer of 1978 Dolly gave a free concert in New York, drawing a huge crowd, surpassed only by that which turned out to greet a recently returned team of astronauts, which filled the City Hall Plaza and the streets leading into it. Some fans climbed trees and statues in the park to get a better vantage point. Mayor Ed Koch handed Dolly the official key to the city and blushed when Dolly planted a large kiss on his cheek. Dolly addressed the crowd, "New York is the centre of the world and I just want to personally thank the people of New York who have done so much to help me on my way." Dolly played a sell-out concert the next day at the Palladium and to promote it, hot-dog vendors were given posters to hang on their wagons. Young women dressed like Dolly roamed the downtown area during lunch hours wearing sandwich boards, and a stagecoach cruised Manhattan advertising the event. After her appearance a party was thrown for her at Studio 54, then one of the most famous disco venues in the world.

The tabloids continued to dig up dirt from people who had come into contact with Dolly no matter how peripherally. A feature in *National Enquirer*, headlined 'The Ugly Side Of Dolly Parton', carried an interview with a public relations consultant LaWayne Satterfield, who was quoted portraying Dolly as, "the Genghis Khan of country music . . . she discarded me like a used Kleenex . . . she would ride over absolutely anyone in her ruthless determination to be number one." In response Satterfield announced that she would be seeking $500,000 in damages, denying having made the remarks attributed to her saying that the reporter had asked leading questions which she tried to deal with as honestly as possible but that what got printed was fictitious and damaged Satterfield's reputation for trustworthiness as a result.

Another area of Dolly's life which fascinated the tabloids was the ongoing saga of her weight. Similarly there were various stories that her breasts were so heavy that she suffered chronic back pain. It was clear by the late Seventies that Dolly's weight had increased considerably and the tightest corset could not disguise the fact. She admitted to *Cosmopolitan* that she didn't exercise and wasn't interested in working out at gyms because she was "particular who she sweated with". During the interview Dolly had beside her a large jug of distilled water and a bottle of pre-digested liquid protein. She confided that she couldn't afford to be fat when she was renowned for her hourglass figure, that she had problems getting into her costumes and had already tried all sorts of diets. She was currently on Dr Robert Linn's *Last Chance Diet* which only allowed meat occasionally. Dolly was honest about her lack of sophistication when it came to food, describing herself as a "hog", Dolly loved to eat Southern staples such as fried chicken, roast pork, corn bread and fried okra, "the greasier the better", and was partial to Indian, Italian and Mexican food. She did not care for "pretty food", presumably a reference to nouvelle cuisine and said that while French food might be suitable for a romantic meal, "somebody else has to choose the wine".

Just one Dolly album was released in 1979, *Great Balls Of Fire*, which made the Top Five in the country charts and just scraped into the Top 40 in the pop charts. Though not performing as well as her previous two albums it went gold with the single 'You're The Only One', which spent two weeks at number one in the country charts. Her version of the title track proved Jack Clements' point that Dolly could sing rock'n'roll. The album also featured another disco excursion in 'Star Of The Show' and a cover of the Beatles' 'Help!' which was promoted, for the first time, with a specially made video. The album also included a fulsome tribute to Sandy Gallin, the man who had transformed Dolly's commercial fortunes in such a short time. 'Sandy's Song' was a delicate ballad delivered with heartfelt gratitude. The sentiments expressed indicated just how much she was putting her days with Porter Wagoner behind her. However if she thought she had finished with Porter she was mistaken. Although the pair had not performed together since 1974 and Porter was no longer involved in the production of Dolly's albums, they were still connected by Owepar and Fireside Studios. Fireside was housed in a building owned by Owepar and paid rent into Owepar for the property which also housed Dolly Parton Enterprises and Porter Wagoner Enterprises. It had been constructed, with the assistance of various members of Dolly's family, in 1972 in the former Starday Townhouse on 18th Avenue South in Nashville, when more space was needed for Porter and Dolly's various operations. The studio opened for business the following year and for a time Stella Parton was secretary. The interior design was rustic in style and featured natural rocks, wood panelling and an orange carpet. Over the years many famous names recorded there including Bobby Bare, Hank Locklin and Ernest Tubb.

As Porter watched his erstwhile protégée's continuing success, he became increasingly concerned that he was not receiving his just rewards in terms of the contract he and Dolly had signed. There had been various attempts, some instigated by RCA, to get the parties around a table with a view to settling matters between them once and for all with a neutral lawyer acting as mediator. Porter's position was that he had been instrumental in putting Dolly where she was, agreements had been signed and he wanted a fair reward for his efforts. Dolly wanted to be freed from all ties to Porter but there were rumours that his financial demands were unacceptably high in the view of Dolly and her advisers. During earlier exchanges Porter said he was happy to let a pop producer take over his production duties since this was the direction Dolly was heading in; however, by 1977 this was a *fait accompli*.

Another issue of particular importance to Porter was the release of a duets album which had been recorded some time previously but which RCA were not releasing while the legal wrangling between he and Dolly persisted. Dolly was happy for the album not to be released since she was extremely busy with other projects and it would mean bringing the pair together for promotional work at a time when there was considerable friction between them. No agreement was reached and by 1976, Porter's lawyer, John Nelley, had started writing to Los Angeles in an attempt to engage Dolly's management in the process of trying to reach a deal. However, they stonewalled him despite repeated phone calls and letters. This only served to raise the heat and reduce the chance of reaching a negotiated settlement. Matters were doubtless not helped by reports that

Gallin did not want the duets album released because the association with Porter might adversely affect the latest stage of Dolly's career he was masterminding.

"They may not be kissing any more, but they sure are telling" was how one journalist characterised the public nature of the deteriorating relationship between Porter and Dolly. There were regular stories in the local press and in 1978, not long after the CMA awards ceremony, the gloves really came off. Porter was quoted, "To me, Dolly Parton is the kind of person I would never trust with anything of mine. Regardless of what it was or who it was – I mean her family, her own blood – she would turn her back on them to help herself." Porter then claimed that Dolly had not broken away from him but that he had fired her because he did not want to be on tour while having to fight with her all the time. "Dolly's the kind of person that if you and I were sitting here with her and Johnny Cash and Huell Howser (a well-known television host) were sitting over there . . . she will turn her back on us immediately because it will help her to go over there. She would do it if it were her mother and her sister sitting here." Porter was unable to mask his contempt at some of Dolly's public activities. Referring to the *Playboy* interview and Dolly's risqué photograph on the front cover, he said, "Do you think Kitty Wells would do that . . . she's living in fairyland."

Presumably he also disapproved of the poster of Dolly lying seductively in the hay, the photograph of Dolly with a scantily clad Arnold Schwarzenegger for *Rolling Stone* – a rock publication – and was doubtless appalled by press reports that Dolly had streaked near Tom Jones' house in Los Angeles on a dare and that she and Judy Ogle had flashed their breasts at each other from separate cars. Such behaviour went against the grain of Porter's old school background. In response to the suggestions that she was ruthless in her determination to succeed Dolly told *McCall's* magazine in 1981, "It is not true that I've ever stepped on anybody to get where I am at. I've maybe had to walk over a few people because they weren't willing to budge or to walk with me. I will always step over if somebody's in the path of where I want to go but that ain't bad. It's just necessary . . . you don't get to where I am by being soft . . . you don't have to harden your heart, but you can strengthen the muscles around it." The interviewer started to feel that Dolly had "an aphorism for practically every human transaction".

Dolly was quick to publicly respond to Porter's comments about their parting, making it clear that it was she who had left him. "I mean, what are you going to do, waste your youth . . . wait until you're old and then regret never trying?" Dolly was particularly incensed because in terms of their agreement, she felt Porter was still receiving a fair amount from her earnings though it later transpired her new management had recently ceased making payments. By 1978 Dolly's legal representatives were proposing that Dolly buy Porter's share of Owepar and that as part of the deal Porter could have Fireside Studios. This appealed to Dolly because the deal would give her total control over her catalogue. The lawyers acting on Dolly's behalf valued Owepar and Fireside Studios at $306,000 and Dolly's song catalogue at $700,000. The much trickier problem was trying to reach a consensus on a figure to compensate Porter for earnings from Dolly's past and future royalties and this proved insuperable. The disagreements over the bigger picture did not stop Porter and Dolly agreeing on some areas of company housekeeping.

In June, they awarded themselves bonuses of $20,000 each in recognition of the substantial income Owepar generated for the company. This was extremely generous to Porter since it was reported the previous year that Dolly was earning over $100,000 for the company from the songs she wrote compared to the $10,000 Porter's songs were bringing in (though these figures would later be disputed). By 1979 legal action by Porter for breach of contract was looking increasingly likely in the absence of any negotiated settlement. He and Dolly had already spent large amounts of time talking to lawyers and considering legal issues for two years, all to no avail. Apart from their own difficulties, Dolly and Porter were sued by Bill Owens on the basis that the undertakings given to him when he transferred his one half share of Owepar to Dolly had been breached. The undertakings were vague and referred to the clause about Dolly recording some of Owens' songs. Owens' sought return of the 49% stock in Owepar given to Wagoner plus punitive damages against Porter for allegedly inducing Dolly to breach the agreement they had signed in 1969.

As the court action proceeded it became increasingly difficult to unravel exactly what Owens might or might not be entitled to. As per the agreement he pitched songs to Dolly, some of which were recorded, but by her own admission proper records were not kept and much of Owepar's business administration was chaotic. It transpired that Owens had not been receiving payment for songs he had written and when asking Dolly about this she told him to get a lawyer who in turn advised him to sue. This was despite the fact that Owens had received a salary of $100, rising to $200 a week, which appears to have been a kind of retainer, plus a percentage of Dolly's earnings until 1976. He had also been given several unspecified loans. Owens lawyer argued that such payments were retrospective remuneration for the years he had spent driving Dolly to Cas Walker's show, to Nashville and to countless venues in the South, though at the time it might reasonably have been thought this was done out of being family rather than in expectation of future rewards. Dolly conceded that money was due to Bill though she claimed most of the causes for him not getting "a fair shake" arose because they were country people not familiar with the ins and outs of business. For her part, all that Dolly wanted was to write and perform music – getting bogged down in legal disputes was not part of the plan.

It was hardly a coincidence that legal action was taken when Dolly was starting to prosper. Her earnings were now in the region of $15,000 to more than $30,000 per night. Porter and Dolly reached an out-of-court settlement with Porter apparently paying the lion's share. However, this was merely the prelude to the main act. Porter had grown increasingly frustrated with the tardiness of Dolly's Los Angeles advisers in dealing with requests for information and providing responses to proposals. Such negotiations as there had been had come to nothing. Porter had been advised by his attorney Tom White to resort to court action. Although reluctant to instigate formal legal proceedings against someone he had been so close to Porter felt he had little option. He announced his intentions on an evening news programme and the flippant headline in the next morning's *Tennessean* – "Porter Plans To Wrap Dolly In Flashiest Suit Yet" – eloquently summed things up. As far as Dolly and her people were concerned Porter's actions came out of left field and RCA claimed they received no forewarning. Despite the negotiations that had dragged on interminably Dolly later claimed in her 1994 autobiography that the court case came as a genuine shock.

She was described in the court document initiating the action as "Dolly Parton Dean". Porter sought 15% of her net income from June 1974 to June 1979 as well as 15% of her record royalties from 1976 to 1979. His lawyer conceded that these payments had been made from 1974 until 1976, during the period of the Travelling Family Band. As an alternative, the action sought $2 million for future loss of income and record royalties, plus $1 million for loss of producer royalties and other associated income. The action also sought to unblock the release of the final duets album and the return of 130 songs alleged to have been removed from Owepar by Judy Ogle on behalf of Dolly. It was suggested by Porter that these songs had been removed so that they might form the nucleus of the catalogues for new publishing companies set up by Dolly,

Velvet Apple and Song Yard. It was reported that Dolly claimed that she had only ever signed the contract with Porter under duress and that she had felt intimidated and mentally worn down by him, a claim Porter dismissed with scorn. Dolly also denied having anything to do with the decision not to release the last duets album, something she said was not within her control.

In addition she said that Porter had failed to tell her about potential conflicts of interest in his roles as her singing partner, record producer and business manager and that their contract was nullified because he had physically torn it up after she left his show, a claim he denied. In any event Wagoner retorted, if the agreement was not valid why had she made payments to him from 1974 to 1976 and why had she voluntarily signed a note in 1976 confirming her obligation to pay him. The note in question was as clear as the escalating claims and counter claims were opaque: "To Porter Wagoner, Now that our ties together with RCA have been cut, because of my appreciation and respect for you, for all the things you have done for me in the past, to help me become successful, I agree to continue to pay you 15% of gross income on my RCA record royalties for the duration of the contract negociated [sic] by you." Dolly appears to have signed this note of her own volition, regarding it as a personal matter between her and Porter and she did not see fit to tell Sandy Gallin about it. With regard to the songs alleged to have been taken from Owepar, Dolly admitted that they had been removed. In a court statement she said, "Those were my only copies, they were done on my tapes at my house on my machines, written on my paper with my pencils. I brought them to protect them, out of anger . . . I think there were 122, not all songs, some were work tapes and they did not belong to Owepar."

Not long after the legal proceedings commenced a rather awkward situation came about when Porter and Dolly both found themselves in the small first-class section on a flight to Nashville. Dolly had no desire to exchange small talk with her adversary and moved to the coach section of the plane, staying there until Porter disembarked. Though known for her huge reserves of energy there were reports in the press that Dolly was being worn down by the court battle, her gruelling work schedule, weight concerns and the supermarket tabloids.

Initially Dolly's legal team failed to respond to the court action and it seemed possible that Porter might win by default. With hours to spare the necessary documents were eventually lodged in court (the judge Chancellor Robert S. Brandt awarded Porter's lawyer $250 in fees for the extra work involved). Dolly's camp asserted that Fireside Studios was run for

Porter's "own pleasure and benefit" and that it did not profit Owepar. There was a suggestion that hangers-on took advantage of the studio's laid-back attitude and Dolly complained that Porter used it as his own studio and would not allow outsiders to book sessions. It was further alleged that Fireside Studios was in dire financial condition and that in order to investigate the position, Dolly intended to resign her seat on the board, commissioning her lawyer Stanley Chernau and musical director Gregg Perry, to examine the state of the studio. Tom White immediately sought to oppose this move on the basis that Dolly was planning to push through her ideas for Owepar for her own gain and without any consideration of his client's interests. The judge ruled that since Dolly was the majority shareholder she was free to rearrange the board as she pleased.

The press also reported that a public relations firm had written a 700-word biography of Dolly for release to journalists but Porter's name was not mentioned once. Rather unconvincingly a spokesman said that the omission had been a simple error and was in no way deliberate. Such incidents raised Wagoner's hackles. "I did nothing but great things for that lady . . . I don't want to be known as the person who discovered Dolly Parton. I've done many more important things in my career than just discover Dolly Parton."

On Porter's behalf White lodged a series of requests for information, "discovery questions", 21 in all, on specific points relating to Porter and Dolly's business dealings. This was a perfectly legitimate legal move but Chernau failed repeatedly to respond and eventually Chancellor Brandt, frustrated by the lack of co-operation, warned him that he must lodge answers by August 27, 1979. Brandt pointed out that he had the power to send Dolly to jail for contempt of court and that he might exercise this power as a last resort if answers were not forthcoming. This was no idle threat – Chuck Berry was then serving time in jail for his failure to comply with a court order to pay back taxes. In the event, answers were lodged with three days to spare, though Chernau objected to certain questions on the grounds that they were "frivolous". One of the more serious questions related to Dolly's net worth but the judge ruled that such information should not be made public.

Reports that Dolly had signed the original contract under duress were refuted by White who claimed that Dolly was such a strong personality it was not credible that she could be forced into doing anything against her will. If the agreement had been signed under duress in 1970, why had it taken Dolly four years to leave Porter's show? By way of a riposte the question was asked, if the contract was legally binding and enforceable, then why had Wagoner waited so long before raising a court action. Legal arguments were presented in court as to whether key terms of the document were too vague to be enforceable, indeed whether the contract was valid at all. Chernau said that Porter had failed to disclose to Dolly the extent of the financial burden being placed upon her by the agreement and that the failure amounted to "constructive fraud in the inducement" and "material misrepresentation" rendering the agreement invalid.

After further out-of-court negotiations had failed to produce a settlement, in October 1979, Dolly agreed to go to White's office to give a lengthy deposition about her business dealings with Porter. This is normal practice in America, allowing each side to gain a picture of the strength or otherwise of their opponent's claim and in turn, the prospects of success for their own case. If the prospects are poor then legal advice is far more likely to be that a party should seek to settle on the best possible terms. When Dolly arrived at White's office the press were waiting. "I would have dressed up if I'd known you were going to be here," she said. Dolly's appearance certainly was dowdy compared to what the public had come to expect. She was wearing an austere wig, a quantity of make-up most women would regard as normal and her bosom was less noticeable, leaving little doubt that its usual prominence was achieved with the assistance of artificial means.

Dolly's interrogation turned out to be quite a lengthy ordeal lasting the best part of a day and her deposition filled five cassettes. She conceded that Porter had greatly assisted her career but stressed that she had often worked tirelessly for him in ways that benefited only him. She pointed out that though the fees he could charge for his appearances rose after she joined him, her own pay did not. She revealed that by the time she left Porter in 1974 her annual income had reached around $100,000 thanks to the royalties she was earning. She acknowledged that Porter was due something but observed that the affairs of Owepar had not been well looked after and were, to say the least, in a confused state. She did not come up with any devastating facts that could have halted Porter's court action and after further discussions with her legal team it became clear that a global settlement should be sought, the financial element of which would have to be reasonably favourable to Porter.

A meeting, lasting approximately three hours, was held at which Porter and Dolly and their respective legal advisers held final, intense negotiations leading to the agreement that they were all now desperate to achieve. Tom White said, "The meeting was somewhat strained for a while, just about like any other serious business meeting . . . after the proposals were reviewed and finally signed both Porter and Dolly were obviously relieved . . . they chitchatted and wished each other well. I don't think both of them wanted to see each other again." Although they agreed not to disclose the final settlement figure Porter later revealed that it was around $1 million and since he had chosen to breach the confidentiality agreement, Dolly later confirmed the figure in her 1994 autobiography, even though her instinct in such situations was usually to talk in evocative generalities – "a very considerable sum of money" or some such.

The court action was dismissed by agreement of the parties and a joint statement was reported in the following terms, "The attorneys for Porter Wagoner and Dolly Parton announced today that their clients have agreed to dismiss the current lawsuit filed by Wagoner and to equitably divide the assets of the businesses jointly operated by the parties for the last 12 years as part of an overall settlement of all outstanding matters; Wagoner and Miss Parton may release a duet album within the next year." It was rumoured that as part of the deal White negotiated 10 of the best seats at Dolly's forthcoming concert at Las Vegas. More importantly, as part of the deal, Dolly gained control of all of her songs while Porter retained his and also gained Fireside Studios. Newspaper reports that Dolly was financially wiped out by the settlement were probably exaggerated but she did have to sell a number of assets to make good the agreed figure and there is no doubt that meeting the obligation under the deal caused her comparative hardship. Dolly later said that she had settled out of court to save Carl and the family embarrassment.

In her 1994 autobiography Dolly said the settlement affected her financial situation adversely for years, indicating that Porter's claim was largely unjustified, while making no reference to the contract she had signed. However, thanks to her ability to earn substantial amounts of money from her various professional activities, she soon recovered though, by the standards of preceding years, 1979 was less successful. She toured and recorded less and for the first time in 11 years was not nominated for any CMA awards. This may have been due to a feeling that she was becoming too pop oriented or possibly that having won so many awards in the past it was time to let others have a fair crack. She continued to receive honours from other organisations. At the Metronome Award ceremony in Nashville Mayor Richard Fulton said, "We could find no one who has meant more to country music over the past year as well as the continued vitality and growth of the entire recording industry in our city." Previous recipients of the award included Chet Atkins and Roy Acuff.

Also the prices she was now charging at the behest of her management had risen considerably and for some they were too high. The manager of the South Dakota State Fair, which drew over 300,000 people each year, complained that Dolly was asking $60,000, a figure he regarded as more than she was worth, which he simply could not afford. In the end he got the Oak Ridge Boys for a much more manageable $15,000.

It was ironic that one of her first records after the bitter court case was the duets album which Porter had been so eager to release. Simply entitled *Porter & Dolly* the sleeve gave the impression of a happy couple except the shots were taken on separate occasions by different photographers. With the wounds from the court battle still raw there was no chance that Dolly would spend an afternoon getting close to Porter for the camera's benefit. While Porter retained the same photographer, Dolly now employed the services of top style lensman Ed Caraeff, who had taken the shots for the sleeve of *Here You Come Again*. Dolly looked impressive in a shimmering white gown with a train, giving her the look of a bridesmaid at a royal wedding. Not to be outdone sartorially, Porter wore a dazzling white Nudie suit with extravagant glitzy patterns far more sophisticated than the cactuses and wagon wheels of old. As a musical pairing Porter and Dolly might have been perceived as obsolete in some quarters, but Porter was tuned in to all areas of popular music and astonished many soon afterwards by doing disco material and controversially arranging for soul legend James Brown to play at the Grand Ole Opry. With the court case generating a huge amount of publicity, the album reached number nine in the country charts while the single, 'Making Plans', reached number two. Some of the lyrics appeared prescient and could have been written to describe Porter's deepest fears at a time when Dolly was looking towards new horizons.

Shortly before the duets album came out, *Dolly Dolly Dolly* was released in May 1980. Sticking to the pop formula (the *Rolling Stone* review described Dolly as sounding like a wind-up toy) the album produced two number one hits: 'Starting Over Again', an emotional ballad written by disco sensation Donna Summer and her husband which also dented the pop charts, and the more country feeling, 'Old Flames Can't Hold A Candle To You'. Once more the production meant that her voice was hamstrung and only rarely able to shine. One critic said, ". . . every extra ingredient that's laid on top of country directness and simplicity gets in the way of the *feeling*."

While Dolly continued to churn out albums, earning a reputed $500,000 a year, she continued to look for the right movie vehicle.

## Chapter 15

Having signed the contract with 20th Century Fox she had not yet seen a script that was right for her, and was surprised by their generally poor standard. However, Jane Fonda was working on an idea and felt that Dolly might just have the right mix of qualities for one of the main characters.

*"I am prepared for success and braced for failure,"* Dolly told journalist Stan Laundon in 1974.
*"I don't expect failure at all, but I would be able to accept it because I would succeed in whatever
I do. If I were a waitress, I would try to be the best one in the restaurant."* (HARRY GOODWIN)

Dolly pictured in July 1972 at the time she started to break away from Porter Wagoner. "We're still the best of friends," Dolly later told Country Music People, "Porter produces all my records, we still do the duets, we own a studio together and a publishing company – so it's really not like a split. The only difference is that I have a band of my own and work separately on the road." (HENRY HORENSTEIN/CORBIS)

The end of a successful partnership, October 1973. "We fought for years," Dolly said. "I tried to tell [Porter] my dreams and plans, but it was too touchy a thing, I had to go, because we couldn't share it together, because he wouldn't accept it."

(COURTESY OF NASHVILLE PUBLIC LIBRARY)

Dolly goes solo. "I'm surprised she hasn't broken out and crossed all the boundaries before now," Monument Records owner Fred Foster said of his former protégée in 1974. "But she's on her way now and she'll still get to the top."

(PICTORIAL PRESS)

*Accepting the 'Female Vocalist Of The Year' award at the CMA Awards, October 13, 1975. The 'Jolene' single and album marked Dolly's commercial breakthrough.* (BETTMANN/CORBIS)

*Dolly on a US TV show. In 1976 she was given her own weekly television showcase* Dolly *which lasted for only one season. Despite the prestige of being the first female country singer to have her own series, Dolly asked to be let out of her contract, mostly due to dissatisfaction over the programme content. A repeat experiment in 1987 was similarly disappointing.* (MICHAEL OCHS ARCHIVE/REDFERNS)

*Dolly's triumphant headlining appearance at the 1976 Wembley Country Music Festival in London. The strain from constant touring took its toll on her voice and around 50 bookings, worth $350,000 in fees, were cancelled that summer.* (ARMANDO PIETRANGELI/REX FEATURES)

*Dolly in New York, rehearsing for her debut at The Bottom Line, Greenwich Village, May, 1977 (top) and (below) with mayor Ed Koch (who gave her the key to the city) at a free concert the following year. Dolly look-alikes roamed the downtown area wearing sandwich boards while a stagecoach cruised around Manhattan advertising her Palladium concert.* (BETTMANN/CORBIS AND RICHARD E AARON/REDFERNS)

Dolly and Andy Warhol dine in New York. Dolly said Warhol was the only person she'd met who was weirder than her, "dressed worse and looked stranger, and didn't care, just like me." In 2003 one of his Dolly paintings went on display in an exhibition at the Bellagio Casino in Las Vegas. (STEPHANIE CHERNIKOWSKI/REDFERNS)

In 1977, country purists complained at Dolly being packaged for a larger audience. "I'm not leaving country music," she responded, "I'm taking it with me. All I want is a chance to do everything I want to do in life… Most people aren't brave enough to try. Well, I'm brave, and I'll try." (ROGER RESSMEYER/CORBIS)

Dolly signs autographs for fans at an in-store appearance, May 1977. Her increasing popularity has never diminished Dolly's appreciation of her fans. (TOM HILL/WIREIMAGE)

*Linda Ronstadt, Emmylou Harris and Dolly pictured in the studio, February 1978. Their initial collaboration involved, in Dolly's words, "too many chiefs and not enough Indians. So we had a pow-wow between the three of us and said why don't we wait until we can do it properly." It took until 1987 for the acclaimed Trio album to become a reality.* (MPTV/LFI)

*The unresolved legal situation involving Dolly and Porter Wagoner's business affairs burst into open warfare in 1978. "To me, Dolly Parton is the kind of person I would never trust with anything of mine," Wagoner was quoted as saying. The case was settled out of court the following year.*
(MICHAEL MAUNEY/CONTRIBUTOR/GETTY IMAGES)

*"I've become so that if I wore just the right amount of makeup, a natural hairdo and simple, basic, beautiful clothes, why I'd just feel like a dishrag. I'd feel naked",* Dolly *told* Rolling Stone *in 1977.* (MPTV/LFI)

# ACT III

## 1980–1990:
## 9 To 5 And Odd Jobs

# Chapter 16

DOLLY had achieved as much if not more than she could have dreamed possible when arriving in Nashville in 1964. If any proof of her star status were required a rare appearance at Fan Fair, the annual country music bash which allowed fans to meet their heroes, provided it in spades. She was mobbed and was heavily guarded as she made her way to the RCA booth to sign autographs. A few fans fainted and one young boy was almost crushed in the flow of around a thousand people desperate to catch a glimpse of Dolly. The incident was widely reported in the press and served to reinforce the message that Dolly enjoyed a degree of fame normally reserved for a movie star.

Like most successful recording artists before her, it was inevitable that Dolly would turn to film. A young screenwriter called Patricia Resnick was interested in the notion of a film about downtrodden women in an office taking revenge on their chauvinistic boss. To test the idea Resnick went undercover in an insurance office to soak up the atmosphere. A range of office staff were asked if they had ever fantasised about getting even with their bosses. The response was overwhelming and numerous entertaining stories emerged which dictated that the film should be a comedy. Jane Fonda, whose company IPC Films were making the movie, co-starred with Lily Tomlin, who considered Dolly to have the right combination of sassy personality and brassy looks to provide what she was looking for in the third lead, an archetypal secretary. Director Colin Higgins, who had gone to see Dolly in concert and was struck by how she delivered her well-practised lines to the audience like a professional actress, said, "She's imperturbable and she trusts her instincts." There was also a feeling that Dolly would "get the south" (attract Southern audiences).

Dolly liked the initial script but her management did not commit to the film until it had undergone some re-writes and were satisfied that the part of Doralee Rhodes would be right for her. After her experiences with Porter Dolly was determined to ensure that she had creative control over her contribution and had no intention of following previous country singers who had been given token supporting roles in films.

The contrast between Dolly and Fonda was marked not least because they came from such different backgrounds; Dolly a poor country girl, Jane the daughter of a successful film star. Apart from being a renowned actress herself (she had recently won an Oscar for *Coming Home*) Fonda was a political activist, something Dolly could never be. 'Hanoi Jane' had opposed the war in Vietnam and though *9 To 5* turned out as a comedy, initial interest in the subject matter arose from her serious concern that women were regularly discriminated against in the workplace. She had met a number of organised groups (some being called "Nine To Five", hence the film's title) to hear their stories, and to get feedback on the script; at the very least it was Fonda's intention that the film should raise awareness of issues as well as making people laugh. Tomlin, too, was vocal in her support for political issues such as the fight for an equal rights amendment to US law in making it illegal to discriminate against women.* Whilst Dolly would never have taken up such causes overtly, *9 To 5* was the first of her films which featured strong roles for working class women. She was relieved that hers and Fonda's political differences did not surface during filming; there were some, such as gun control, on which the two would undoubtedly have not agreed.

Filming on a $10 million budget began towards the end of 1979 and lasted nine weeks. Perhaps it was a case of beginner's luck but for Dolly the experience was almost entirely positive. She also took comfort from the thought that if the film did flop, the blame and opprobrium would surely attach itself to her more experienced co-stars. Dolly rose to the challenge of acting without difficulty, helped no doubt by a strong belief in her own talent and a fierce ambition to succeed in an untried medium. In fact she was so determined to make a good fist of it that she arrived for the first day of filming having learned not just her own part but the whole script. Jane Fonda had never come across such a thing in 36 films. Being Dolly, she was fully wigged and made up at four in the morning so that she looked her best when arriving on the set; one of her worst fears was being caught with her image down.† Thereafter she was made up all over again for the cameras. She had lost some 20 to 30 pounds for the filming, much of which she soon put back on.

---

* Office worker Suzanne Goatz, who was a member of a national organisation representing the interests of female office workers, saw the film and though acknowledging the presence of many workplace issues of concern to her members, she felt the movie was of limited value because it was too light.
† She once proudly claimed that when staying in a hotel, she would leave some of her make-up on in case there was a fire and she had to hurriedly evacuate.

With endearing optimism she said that if she were to go on acting she would write most of the films herself. "If I write them it will be like singing a song you write. You'll be more involved in it." There were aspects of the moviemaking process that Dolly found difficult to get her head around, such as the fact that scenes were not filmed in order ("You open a door one week and you walk through it three weeks later"), and she disliked the long delays waiting to do a scene. However, during such times the theme song for the film was written, a memorable and durable piece of high energy pop which demonstrated the breadth of Dolly's writing skills. She used her fingernails to provide the rhythm, wrote the lyrics on the back of her script and used some of the extras to layer in backing vocals. (The clicking fingernail sound made it onto the song.)

Dolly had one bedroom scene with her screen husband Jeffrey Douglas Thomas, which was rather awkward since the actor was married to one of her friends. The scene might have been in a bedroom but Dolly had made it clear that she would never do a nude scene or one featuring heavy petting. "It would embarrass me, not to mention what it would do to my mom and dad." Being mildly risqué, however, was acceptable. In one scene which involved Dolly kissing Thomas, Dolly winked at him, looked up at Fonda and giggled, "I think I'm gonna lahk this business." Carl visited Dolly regularly during the making of the film. Despite press reports that the pair hardly saw each other for much of the year, he was a frequent visitor to the many professional engagements that took her away from home. Fonda met Carl and took to him though she described the marriage as "an enigma". Before she knew who he was Jane pointed him out to Dolly. Dolly beamed. "He's cute, ain't he?" "I saw him first," Fonda joked to which Dolly snapped back, "Bull . . . I saw him 20 years ago. He's my husband!"

She socialised with her co-stars on and off the set ("it was like being back at school, but with nicer girls") and one evening it was reported that they got tipsy on champagne and ate spaghetti prepared by Dolly. Fonda was taken with Dolly. "She's not the least bit phoney . . . I must say I never caught her in a false moment . . . after five minutes she has you sitting on her knee. You feel comfortable with her, love her and hug her like an old friend."

The movie's plot concerns office boss, Franklin, played by Dabney Coleman, a monstrous chauvinist, who calls the girls "cutie" and "sweet-heart" and takes them for granted while overlooking them for well deserved promotions. Doralee is Franklin's secretary (for shots of Dolly typing, the hands of a real typist were substituted though they were made up to look like Dolly's), Fonda plays the rather timid Judy, returning to work for financial reasons after years as a housewife and Tomlin was Violet, the office manager who keeps coming up with ideas which Franklin claims as his own. One evening after work the three get together to clear up a few misunderstandings including the widely held notion in the office that Doralee was having an affair with Franklin. Sharing a joint (lettuce leaves were used according to one inside report), in their mind-altered state they fantasise about the many ways they would like to exact revenge on Franklin.

Doralee, appropriately enough some might say, becomes a fringe jacketed cowgirl in a Stetson hat. Role swapping with Franklin, calling him "hot stuff", she drops things from her desk on purpose so that he has to get down on all fours allowing her to admire his backside (as he does her cleavage). Eventually she ties him up like a wild bull to complete his now-you-know-how-it-feels humiliation. In the end, order is restored when the trio take over the running of the office and are rewarded with promotions.

The film was glib and one sided in its treatment of the serious underlying subject matter it dealt with and while the female characters grow and develop, virtually all the male characters are portrayed as shallow, vain and stubborn. The storyline meandered disconcertingly at times but from the opening bars of Dolly's infectious title song, the film exuded fun which was engagingly delivered. As critic Scott Renshaw said, "The film offered the opportunity to trade on [Dolly's] va-va-voom appearance and sweet demeanour to create a beguiling screen persona . . . it's less a social statement than it is a boisterous, disorganized rally for its cause: freedom for The Woman to laugh – if sporadically – at The Man."

Dabney Coleman was also impressed. "She plays down her knowledge of technique, but the fact is she is a method actress. The method is having organically going on inside what you appear to be having going on up there on the screen." While her natural *joie de vivre* comes through, somewhere between naivety and knowing, it was largely because the part of Doralee allowed Dolly to transfer her naturally dynamic personality onto the screen. Her own verdict on her performance was mixed though she liked the overall result. "There were places I thought I was real good, but there were also places where I was real average and places where I was yuck . . . but it's real entertainin'."

After filming wrapped Dolly and Jane went on a short trip down south; Dolly felt like a country cousin introducing a city slicker to her way of life. She got together a few mountain folk to sing 'Coat Of Many Colors', an experience Fonda found very emotional and she later appeared as one of Dolly's back-up singers on 'Applejack' at the Grand Ole Opry.

The world premiere of *9 To 5* took place at the Roy Acuff Theater in Opryland, Nashville with some 1,600 VIP guests punching specially installed time clocks. In keeping with his reclusive nature Carl avoided the premiere, apparently preferring to catch it at his local cinema. As a gesture of reconciliation Dolly invited Porter to attend but he declined. At the premiere Dolly said that Nashville was still her home even though she now spent much of her time in her Los Angeles apartment when off the road. The film was a box office hit, earning upwards of $120 million. The title song topped both the country and pop charts in early 1981 making Dolly the first woman since Jeannie C. Riley (with 'Harper Valley PTA') to have a number one hit on the country and pop charts simultaneously. It was a good time for female artists; on April 26, 1980 records by women on *Billboard*'s country music chart occupied seven places in the Top 10.

The song also earned Dolly Grammy awards for Best Country Vocal Performance By A Female and Best Country Song and was named BMI's Most Performed Country Song during the past year. Although critics found Dolly entertaining on screen, they hesitated at calling her a great actress, though she was nominated for Best Supporting Actress and Best New Film Star at the Golden Globe Awards. Dolly performed the title – nominated for the Oscar for Best Song – at the ceremony.

It was Dolly's idea to turn the *9 To 5* soundtrack into a loose thematic concept of working people past and present. The album left behind much of her recent pop–disco sound and included 'Deportee: Plane Crash At Los Gatos', co-written by Woody Guthrie, about the plight of illegal Mexican immigrants, a mid-paced arrangement (by Dolly and producer Mike Post) of 'The House Of The Rising Sun', the Merle Travis song, 'Dark As A Dungeon', painting a bleak picture of a miner's working life, and 'Sing For The Common Man', written by Frieda Parton. The album was as close as Dolly got to making a political statement and the gravitas of several songs contrasted strongly with the light-hearted (and, unusually, not particularly glamorous) front cover shot of Dolly surrounded by a variety of work implements.

The album *9 To 5* was the first that Dolly had recorded in Nashville since *New Harvest . . . First Gathering* and it received a Grammy nomination in the category Best Album Of Original Score Written For A Motion Picture Or Television Special, being certified gold in February 1981. Dolly reckoned it her best offering since the hugely commercial *Here You Come Again*. The albums in between, she described as "so so . . . although they did serve their purpose". As *Rolling Stone* critic Stephen Holden summarised, "It's nice to have Dolly Parton back from the trash bin unscathed."

On the "where there's a hit there's a writ" principle, Dolly was later sued for copyright infringement to the tune of around a million dollars by Neil and Jan Goldberg who claimed that '9 To 5' was lifted from their song, 'Money World'. In court Dolly said that she had not heard the Goldbergs' song when she wrote her own ("I wouldn't know a musical motif from molasses") and entertained all present by singing '9 To 5' in support of her contention that it was not lifted. After just half an hour's deliberation, the jury found in favour of Dolly who was also awarded expenses. However, she later revealed that a cash offer had been made to the Goldbergs to drop the case, in order "to avoid the public embarrassment". The offer was rejected because it was regarded by the plaintiffs as paltry. Neil Goldberg said afterwards, "That's the power of her charisma. We were not liars, yet they ruled against us." Dolly said the whole experience had been degrading. "The lawsuit was a big pain in the ass. They claim they wrote the song four years before the movie script was ever written. The lawsuit was painful and hard because people out there still might have in their minds that I stole the song. The songwriters claim they sent Jane [Fonda] the song years ago. Anyone who knows Jane realises that she never listens to music unless she hears it on the radio while she's exercising."

As if this was not enough the musician Benny Martin filed suit complaining that '9 To 5' was substantially copied from 'Me And My Fiddle', which he composed in 1954. It was asserted that Martin had played the song on Cas Walker's television and radio programmes and that young Dolly must have picked up on his idea at the time she too was appearing on Walker's programmes. In response Dolly filed suit in the Federal Court in Los Angeles asking for a declaration that the song was an original. The matter was eventually settled out of court when it was claimed that a small payment was made to Martin, again in order to avoid unwelcome publicity. The film spawned a successful television series in which Dolly's sister Rachel played Doralee. Rachel had helped with Dolly's make-up for the film and Jane Fonda remembered Rachel, and her strong resemblance to Dolly, when casting for the show. Though there was talk of Dolly making another film with Jane and Lily (a fantasy spy film was mooted) it never materialised.*

★   ★   ★

* In 2005 it was reported that Jane Fonda was considering a sequel to be called *9 to 5.30*.

Las Vegas has a reputation for attracting millions of visitors each year with money to burn. Despite high ticket costs, top entertainers can usually be assured of near sell-out audiences at the city's most prestigious clubs. While Dolly had been interested in Las Vegas for some time she decided to wait until she was a national figure with a pulling power big enough to stand comparison with stars such as Barbra Streisand and even Frank Sinatra. By late 1979 her management had agreed a three year deal, guaranteeing record earnings, with Dolly undertaking to perform at the Riviera Hotel six weeks a year for three years commencing June 1980. Her earnings were not officially publicised but estimates varied between six and nine million dollars for the package meaning that Dolly was making at least $350,000 per week. Tickets for her shows were priced at $70 (about $160 in today's money) which included dinner and cocktails. Some fans were turned off by the idea of Dolly performing to audiences who had little knowledge or interest in her background. Dolly expressed sympathy with this view. "People come to see your show, or they go to see Wayne Newton. It doesn't matter to them."

Her debut had to be postponed for a couple of days due to a recurrence of throat and laryngeal problems, hardly surprising given the stress she continued to subject her voice to: extensive performing and recording, often in environments contaminated by cigarette smoke, travelling long distances in air-conditioned buses and planes and getting by on little sleep.

Dolly's taste for excess was given full rein when it came to the stage set, which consisted of a huge fairy-tale type castle, complete with drawbridge, through which she made her grand entrance. It was impressive but Dolly felt ill at ease, not least because for once her fancy outfits were matched if not eclipsed by her surroundings making it harder for her to stand out. Her performances, lasting around 75 minutes, went down well with the pumped up Vegas crowd who loved Dolly's suggestive dance routines and revealing costumes as well as the emotional pull of songs such as 'Me And Little Andy'. The choice of material reflected Dolly's musical journey and interwove the unadulterated pop of 'Here You Come Again' and 'Two Doors Down' with classics such as 'Coat Of Many Colors' (which several critics found ironic considering Dolly was singing to a well-heeled audience in one of America's wealthiest cities) and the obligatory 'I Will Always Love You'. Some purists might have baulked at the inclusion of 'There's No Business Like Show Business' yet Dolly had become the living embodiment of that maxim.

A few of Dolly's best known and most durable self-mocking jokes were included. "I'm just like the girl next door . . . if you happen to live next to a fairground." There were also quips about the high cost of industrial bras. By the time Dolly started her Las Vegas season her weight had become a serious issue and she was carrying around 30 to 40 pounds above what was appropriate for her frame. Her weight had built up since her mid twenties but she publicly made light of it, comparing herself to a hog tied to a banqueting table. It had got to the stage of Dolly needing a powerful corset to keep herself in, the wonder being that she was still able to breathe let alone sing with such apparent ease.

Dolly later admitted that she kept three or four sizes of clothes in her closet because she was never sure what she could fit into. "If I can get my dress on, my weight is under control . . . my fat never made me less funny." It took her about half an hour to get into her stage costumes and she demanded they be skin tight. "If I can bend down and touch the floor it means the outfit is too loose and my seamstress has to alter it."

The return of Dolly's "Las Vegas throat" ailment caused the cancellation of some of the later shows and in the end she was unable to fulfil the full quota. In her 1994 autobiography she referred to the experience as "a disaster".

Although much of Dolly's time was taken up with her professional commitments she allowed herself the occasional fun day out. In 1981 she and three friends joined the outrageous Halloween costume parade of street people gathered on Hollywood's Santa Monica Boulevard. In the crowd were several male and female Dolly Parton impersonators but none recognised the real thing prancing among them. She disguised herself to look like a pregnant hillbilly – pillow in her stomach, teeth blacked out, sores and bruises and bites painted all over her face. She told an interviewer, "I'd go up to the others and gasp, 'Are you really Dolly Parton?' and they'd holler, 'Oh, honey, of course! Who else?' I thought to myself, 'God if they only knew who I was and how ugly I can look.'"

For a while Dolly and her mother and sisters went on holiday each year. The idea was that one of them was responsible for coming up with a theme and location for the holiday which might last for several days and include a range of activities from long walks to sing-songs to girly activities like dressing up and putting on fancy make-up. In her book *In The Shadow Of A Song* Willadeene included a diary of events from one such holiday arranged by Avie Lee in the mountains: "After breakfast we went outside to a beautiful day with the sound of spring everywhere. Birds and frogs told us it was spring. I thought it was just a bit early but how can you contradict an impatient frog? And from somewhere across the hills we could hear a rooster crowing, and the hungry bawling of a new born calf. It was just cool enough for light jackets. Dolly had brought all of us a new one made in the 'Coat Of Many Colors' style. She had gotten them from fans . . . all of them were handmade and beautiful. A lady in Texas made the one I wore." She concluded, "Our vacations are times set aside for love and sharing; times when the outside world doesn't exist."

Dolly has referred to these holidays in glowing terms and while most of the Parton sisters have refrained from comment Stella, without going into detail, rather shatters the idyllic image created by her sister. "It was always a fiasco . . . always hated them, only survived two or three of them and then I decided not to go any more." When the author pointed out that Dolly always spoke warmly about these family holidays Stella is dismissive. "Oh she's full of crap . . . yeah, anybody that can write that many songs can make up a lot of stuff . . . she's got an imagination that won't quit . . . I mean I have read that we went shopping and I've seen it in *Good Housekeeping* that we shopped in New York and she's never taken me to New York shopping, ever, so I called her up and I said, 'What the heck is this? We went shopping, where's my stuff . . . I mean that's all baloney.' She said, 'I'll get it for you later. It sounds good in the press you know.'"

By the early Eighties Dolly had become a woman of property. In addition to her estate in Brentwood her portfolio included a beach-side house in Malibu and apartments in Los Angeles and New York. Over the years she would add a farm in Sevierville, a Hawaiian retreat on the island of Oahu as well as more property in LA, including offices and studios. It was a sign of Dolly's extensive involvement with activities outside music that she did not release an album at all in 1981. Her next studio outing, 1982's *Heartbreak Express*, performed only moderately after the success of *9 To 5*. While Dolly was virtually guaranteed good showings in the country charts (*Heartbreak Express* made number five) the pop audience was far more fickle and only occasionally rewarded her with a significant placing for albums with a particularly strong commercial content or those that were associated with a heavily publicised film. *Heartbreak Express* had more of a country-roots feel and some reviewers expressed relief that Dolly had taken a step away from the more overt pop material. The album mixed some of Dolly's older numbers such as 'My Blue Ridge Mountain Boy' and 'Do I Ever Cross Your Mind?' with powerful new material, notably the folksy 'Prime Of Our Love' and 'Hollywood Potters', a song evidently inspired by her recent experiences with the film industry. Though most of Dolly's public pronouncements on the making of *9 To 5* had been generally positive, she had been saddened by some of the older extras who still entertained dreams of Hollywood stardom.

Talking about 'Hollywood Potters', Dolly said, "You can be corrupted in Hollywood or Nashville. I believe in compromise and co-operation, but I don't believe in giving up your principles, your sense of what's right and wrong, to get some place. There is a price on all things and you have to give things up for success . . . but not to the point where people are doing things that they don't believe in at all." Of her Hollywood experience, "Things got twisted and changed around and watered down so much out there, that from the time a project starts to the time it's finished, it's sometimes a completely different thing. It makes a lot of people bitter and frustrated."

It wasn't long before Dolly embarked on another high profile cinema vehicle which exploited her public persona and musical skills to the full. In *The Best Little Whorehouse In Texas* Dolly played the part of Miss Mona, the madam of a brothel, co-starring with Burt Reynolds, then one of the hottest stars in Hollywood. Reynolds had a penchant for using country singers in his films, often set in the South, and in recent years he had helped to secure roles for Jerry Reed and Mel Tillis. Reynolds apparently had his eye on Dolly as a co-star since the mid Seventies when he fancied her for *W W And The Dixie Dance Kings*. As early as the start of 1980 rumours about the film surfaced in the media, one of which suggested the project was already in difficulty. In February *The Tennesseean* reported that plans to have Dolly and Burt Reynolds as co-stars had been dropped because they would only agree to do the film if the other was involved and the $6 million the pair demanded was too high. It was reported that negotiations were underway with Willie Nelson for Reynolds' part and that Barbara Mandrell and Crystal Gayle were being considered for the lead female role. The money issue was eventually resolved but Dolly had a more personal issue to face – whether it was morally acceptable to be playing the role of a madam. She sought approval from her grandfather, the Reverend Jake Owens; perhaps his views had moderated since his hellfire preaching days. As Dolly told a reporter, "He said if God could forgive me, then so could he . . . so far, I haven't heard from either."

The film was based on a play written by Larry L. King and was inspired by the true story of the closing down of a brothel, a "chicken ranch", in Texas following a crusade by an investigative journalist. The play had enjoyed successful runs on Broadway (Dolly attended one of the shows) and in London's West End. Despite initial misgivings about the subject matter and her loud and clear statement that she would not do a nude scene ("I'm not selling sex"), Dolly concluded that she was well suited to the part which once more allowed her to be an exaggerated version of herself: big hair, sexy outfits, gregarious personality and a nice line in homespun philosophy. As with *9 To 5*, *The Best Little Whorehouse . . .* was a light film about a serious subject played for laughs. Prostitution was presented in a sanitised, idealised fashion. One song was called 'There's Nothing Dirty Going On' while the girls and their customers were all portrayed as slim, attractive, happy and healthy. "Prostitutes, I will tell you, are some of the sweetest, most caring people I've known because they've been through everything," said Dolly. "I've met them at parties, and I've talked to them. Usually they're people with broken dreams who never had a chance in life or were sexually abused or ignored as children. A lot sell themselves to get some kind of feeling of being loved."

Some changes to King's original script were made. The sheriff, played by Reynolds, was past 60 and the relationship with Miss Mona was platonic. "I fixed that," explained Dolly. "If you think that I'm going to be in a movie with Burt Reynolds and not get in a little huggin' and kissin', you're crazy." King was said to be unhappy. It was rumoured that the playwright had never wanted Reynolds in the first place and suspected he was building Dolly up to influence getting the screenplay changed to suit his romantic image. Of Dolly, King reportedly said, "Too obvious. She looks as if she might run a whorehouse or work in one." Reynolds said of her, "One and only, probably a good thing because you couldn't have two or four of them in the world . . . she's human sunshine", describing Dolly as an instinctive actress, "as good as she wants to be . . . she captured all of our hearts."

Despite such warm words, the atmosphere on the set was often tense. For all his superstar status some of Reynolds' recent films had failed to live up to box office expectation. In addition two directors were fired and there were disagreements between Reynolds and King. Reynolds was moody and unpredictable, being in the midst of an acrimonious break-up from actress Sally Field. His tantrums on the set, Dolly found hard to cope with and there were rumours that she threatened to quit the film on several occasions. Though speaking favourably about the experience at the time, she later described it as a "bloodbath". During a break in filming she took off with Judy Ogle for a few days to get away from it all, explaining "Dolly didn't come along." As one film executive summed up, "The difference between Dolly and Burt is that when Dolly goes home at night and takes off her wig, she knows she's still just Dolly Parton. But when Burt goes home and takes off his, he doesn't know who he is."

Reynolds was particularly annoyed by this remark being unaware it was common knowledge that he wore a toupee. Dolly later revealed that Reynolds' grey moustache had to be blackened by the make-up people and after one screen kiss it was noticed that some of the dye had come off on Dolly's lips. Reynolds reportedly had a hernia which caused some consternation during one scene in which he had to pick Dolly up. On top of everything else the film exceeded its $20 million budget, ending up costing around $35 million.

The film was interspersed with set-piece musical numbers though despite her best efforts ("cussin' and fightin'" according to one report), Dolly did not get as many songs in the movie as she would have liked. She had locked herself away for long periods and written nearly 30 songs, more than enough for the entire musical content of the film. King felt this was inappropriate as there was already a score by Carol Hall, which he felt was suitable. In the event only four of her songs were filmed and only two, 'I Will Always Love You' and 'Sneakin' Around' made the final cut. Dolly later complained that she did not have enough control over her own contribution. "I think I'm very helpful. I think I coulda been a little more helpful if I'd been given a little more room."

Dolly was also said to be upset that the film included sequences showing bare breasts, even though they were only featured in stationary artistic tableaux, as opposed to love scenes. She advised against taking children to see the film. "I wouldn't say it's great family fun. I'm upset about it." It was later rumoured that she had tried to withdraw from the film but that her contract would not allow it. Dolly seemed to want it both ways. On the one hand she spoke about passionate scenes with Burt Reynolds and revelled in wearing sexy outfits with her breasts pushed up to the hilt but on the other she appeared prudish at the lack of decorum in a film about a brothel. "I'm not promoting bein' a whore. That's the title of the movie, but when you see the movie you don't really think about that particular thing . . ."

Despite her brazen exterior Dolly did not come over in the film as genuinely sexy, her natural conservatism only allowed her to go so far. Unlike people with a gift for character acting, Dolly essentially remained Dolly and while some bawdy humour and coquettishness were acceptable, in any scene which threatened to come close to the mark, she came over as slightly wooden. In light of this Dolly's remark, "I think I make a better whore than a secretary" simply failed to convince.* On the other hand, when singing 'I Will Always Love You', the stiffness in front of the camera evaporated because Dolly was doing what came most easily and to her. The song became the only single to reach the number one position in the country charts twice by the same artist.

Dolly was unable to attend the 1981 CMA awards because of the filming but appeared via a CCTV link. Co-host Barbara Mandrell said, "My next guest, Dolly Parton, has a problem, she's in Austin, Texas, filming a movie with Burt Reynolds. Big problem, right?" Dolly responded between giggles, "You know, it's really hard for me to be down here in Austin . . . just doing these passionate love scenes with that ugly old Burt Reynolds." Barbara responded drily, "Well nobody said show business was easy, Dolly!" Dolly did not win any CMA awards but she was voted Entertainer Of The Year and Best Female Country Star Of The Year by the American Guild of Variety Artists, previous winners including Frank Sinatra, Bob Hope and Liza Minnelli. In addition, the 1981 Tennessee Tourist Development Welcome Center visitor survey revealed that the three best-known Tennesseans were Elvis Presley, Jack Daniel and Dolly Parton. The survey also revealed that despite negative connotations in some quarters, the word 'hillbilly' was synonymous with friendly people, good food and Southern hospitality.†

*The Best Little Whorehouse . . .* gave the tabloids endless scope to specu-late about a possible relationship between its two leads, one report was boldly headlined, Dolly Agrees To Have Burt's Baby. "Carl got hysteri-cal," said Dolly. "We have this little dog. And one day I had him in my arms. Carl got the camera and said, 'Here's a picture of Dolly and Burt's baby.'" While most husbands could have been forgiven for being upset by the tabloid coverage Carl was now used to it (though according to one report he did not want Dolly to kiss Reynolds full on the mouth). Accord-ing to Dolly, Carl kept teasing her with questions like, "Well, who's baby are you having this week?" He might have been more concerned by Dolly's frankness in the press about their intimate relationship such as her comments to George Haddad-Garcia: "I never had a bad experience with sex. If I felt I wanted to share my emotion, then I did. To me, sex was not dirty. It was something very intimate and very real."

---

* Loretta Lynn once said that even in all-female changing rooms Dolly always had "a little curtain she pulls".
† In a 1978 *Melody Maker* interview, Dolly said that calling mountain people "hillbillies" was "a bit like calling black people niggers".

Carl visited the set and briefly spoke to journalist Cliff Jahr, whose attention was caught by his plaid shirt and buckskin boots. "He has big rough hands and soft brown eyes and no one can miss what Dolly must see in him. His fine features and short chestnut hair combine with about 6 ft 3 in of sinewy muscle to project, at age 38, an image of sexy boyishness." Jahr learned that Carl's favourite book was James A. Michener's *Centennial* and that he was a fan of Mick Jagger. Jahr was also taken by his laconic sense of humour. As a leggy showgirl swayed by he remarked, "That could make a person nervous."

Dolly felt that she got a gentle ride from the critics for her first two films. They were probably making allowance for her inexperience and may also have been won over by her infectious personality which brightened up several otherwise unexceptional scenes. Some politely described her performances as amusing but there were no claims to her being a great actress. She may have been called Doralee and Miss Mona but what the audience got was Dolly doing her best to be her effervescent self in different outfits and contexts. She was unable to bring to the role of Doralee any hint of the weary resignation of a long serving secretary, or to that of Miss Mona the ruthless edge and survival instinct expected of a madam who has spent years running a brothel. The predominant feeling was that for all its colourful entertainment value, aesthetically *The Best Little Whorehouse In Texas* was a disappointment. One critic found Burt Reynolds "overexposed" while another wrote "Dolly Parton and Burt Reynolds flounder through their roles like distant acquaintances who have never been properly introduced." Reynolds performance was generally poorly received not least because he appeared uncomfortable with the musical numbers.

The story itself garnered such dismissive epithets as "perfunctory" and "mediocre" and Dolly's participation attracted unfavourable comment from organisations like Citizens For Decency Through Law and the Moral Majority who charged that a self-proclaimed "religious woman" like Dolly had allowed herself to be involved in a movie that made light of sex and the exploitation of women.

The Austin premiere of *The Best Little Whorehouse In Texas* in July 1982 became a major event with around 3,000 people lining Congress Avenue to watch a parade which featured the Southwest Texas Marching Band, the Southwest Strutters Drill Team, and the Cadence Cloggers Square Dancers. The two stars rode in a convertible Texas taxi with long horns on the bonnet. Dolly wore a yellow sequined dress, chosen to sartorially chime with the yellow rose of Texas. After the premiere, the stars dined with five-hundred-dollar ticket holders in a "supper with the stars" at the

Hyatt Regency Hotel. Events to mark the launch of the film, lasting over a whole weekend, included an outdoor feast with a twilight procession of torch-bearing cowgirls heralding the arrival of the two stars, Dolly in a shiny turquoise dress and Burt in a burgundy shirt and navy suit. A celebrity party in the Chattanooga ballroom of the Opryland Hotel in Nashville that Dolly attended followed a short time later for which about 30 Dolly and Burt clones were flown in from various parts of the country.

*The Best Little Whorehouse . . .* became a box office success and was one of the top six highest grossing movies of 1982 earning around $50 million in the process.* One amusing consequence of the film was that it made the use of the word "whorehouse" more acceptable; up until then, especially in the South, it was the kind of word not to be used in respectable company. Despite this Dolly rarely used the word when interviewed about the film, preferring to substitute "chickenhouse" or "bleephouse".

The problems associated with the film only added to the significant health and personal problems Dolly had been experiencing for some time. They were to lead to a degree of personal unhappiness she had not known until then.

---

* It eventually went on to earn well over $200 million making it Dolly's most commercially successful film.

# Chapter 17

FOR some time, Dolly's bubbly public image disguised the fact that her health was suffering. In view of the degree to which she physically pushed herself this was hardly surprising. From the mid Seventies onwards Dolly's weight seesawed though she made light of it with disingenuous remarks like, "Everybody loves a fat girl," and "People are always telling me to lose weight, but being overweight has certainly never made me less money or hurt my career." That might be true but she put herself through hell with a series of severe diets including Scarsdale, Atkins and Liquid Protein to maintain the figure that fitted her ideal image of Dolly. (The right appearance was so important that she sometimes avoided wearing panties, regarding the visible line they produced as unsightly.) It was a torturous process – her propensity to put on weight and her diminutive height meant that lapses were quickly punished.

However, Dolly's problems were more serious than merely attempting to lose weight. During the making of *The Best Little Whorehouse* . . . she experienced painful and debilitating stomach cramps, describing her digestive system as "totally out of whack . . . I was getting away with murder. I wasn't watching what I ate, wasn't conscious of nutrition, wasn't taking care of myself. I was working hard and underneath I was a pile of personal and emotional problems. All at once I fell apart. It was stomach problems and female problems – all over health problems actually. It was God's way of telling me to get myself straight . . . I'm grateful to have had them when I was still young enough to bounce back." Dolly also alluded to family problems which had been brewing for some time. "I'm always the one who's up, the one who carries the ball. They came to me in time of need. But I was in need myself. It was bad timing."

To add to her woes certain confidantes had leaked stories about her to the press. Dolly was greatly distressed by the ending of a close relationship, something she referred to in non-specific terms. "I was betrayed by someone close to me . . . I won't say exactly who it was, except to say that it was an affair of the heart. Before I knew it, me, Dolly, the person, who had always been strong – lost control. So I got sick, real sick." In another interview she referred to it as a "personal business affair . . . My heart was shattered not by a romance, but by an affair of the heart. And it just about killed me." The minimal difference between a "romance" and "an affair of the heart" merely added to the enigmatic nature of her revelations. There was inevitable speculation about the person's identity and a number of names were put forward but Dolly has maintained that "I do have the right to some secret spots." Of course there were several typically lurid and no doubt, fanciful, reports in the tabloids that a suicidal Dolly might have killed herself were it not for her dog walking into the room just as she was about to pick up a gun.

Looking back on this period, Dolly claimed her spirit had been "temporarily broken". She felt able to empathise with those driven to suicide or obliteration through drink and drugs but was confident she would not have gotten to that stage herself. It was evident that dark thoughts plagued Dolly for well over a year, some of which she noted down in a diary. "Why should I commit suicide, I'm waking up dead every day." She found it hard to bear images of human suffering on the television news and went out of her way to avoid maudlin songs. Some in Nashville were taken aback at her various revelations coming out in the press; the view among certain hardliners was that Dolly was breaking yet another social taboo by broaching areas only men normally talked about publicly.

Dolly underwent a number of medical tests to investigate persistent gynaecological problems which may have been exacerbated by her use of different types of medication said to include tranquilisers and hormone pills such as Provera (taken to ease symptoms including abnormal uterine bleeding). Their side effects included weight gain and changes in the menstrual cycle and, in some cases, depression could occur. Dolly was using cortisone, an extremely powerful anti-inflammatory substance, to help reduce the swelling in her vocal cords but it also suppressed the immune system making her vulnerable to other illnesses. The drug made Dolly tenser which in turn contributed to her voice becoming hoarse thus perpetuating a vicious circle.

The delays in making the film meant that Dolly put off addressing her health problems. She went to Australia with Sandy Gallin, partly a holiday but also to look at property as she was interested in acquiring a hideaway there.* However, the trip was not a success because the press got wind of her visit and she was mobbed wherever she went. The Australian tabloids were full of rumours that Dolly's marriage was in trouble and that she was having an affair with Gallin (although, at the time, he was a closet gay). A

* She instead settled on a property in Hawaii.

13-metre cruiser was chartered to sail round some islands during which the boat got caught in a serious storm (Cyclone Abigail). Dolly really thought she might die and was half bemused by the bizarre prospect of a girl from East Tennessee drowning off the Australian coast in the company of a gay man.

When Dolly's illness returned with a vengeance the trip was cut short. Not long after her return to the States, she underwent a procedure, quite possibly the fairly routine dilation and curettage ("D & C"), in an effort to ameliorate her symptoms. While this seems to have caused a temporary improvement the underlying problems were unresolved. Dolly's major concern was that doctors would recommend a hysterectomy, which she was desperate to avoid. After the operation, following doctors' orders, Dolly returned to Willow Lake Plantation to recuperate.* She later confessed that she was not completely open with Carl because she didn't want to worry him with "the shit that I should have more control over". He was aware of her physical problems but it was only Gallin and Judy Ogle (of whom Dolly said, "She makes it possible for me not to need a psychiatrist") who really knew the full extent of her difficulties. Dolly missed out on collecting her Grammies for *9 To 5* and cancelled more concerts during the summer.

In her 1994 autobiography Dolly dwelt upon this dark period though questions still remain. Ogle had become involved with a man who became jealous of the amount of time she spent with Dolly so her contact was reduced. Gregg Perry, Dolly's bandleader, studio producer and arranger (who had received a specific namecheck on the billboards advertising the Las Vegas concerts) was also in a relationship so Dolly felt "lonely". It seems she expected those closest to her to always be on call but when their attentions were diverted elsewhere Dolly's problems worsened and in her own words, she started to "grieve". Matters improved when Ogle's affair came to an end.

Feeling her health had improved slightly Dolly decided to undertake a lengthy tour of America and Canada, 35 venues in all, beginning in late summer. The bus, her "seventh home", had a chart on the wall indicating which wigs co-ordinated with which costumes.† However, before the tour had got into full swing Dolly was once more laid low. In August 1982,

---

* Dolly was left with surgical scars from the operation and supposedly had tattoos of ribbons, bows and roses applied to conceal them.
† The wigs had to be made of durable synthetics because she wore each one only twice before it was washed and reset.

when due to perform at the Ohio State Fair, Columbus, she developed abdominal pain and doctors believed that she might be haemorrhaging internally. Despite this Dolly insisted on doing both a matinee and evening concert. Though feeling dreadful, she went on to Indianapolis a few days later, eager to please her fans who had waited throughout a driving rainstorm. Fearful that she might have to curtail the concert, she changed her set around so that her biggest crowd pleasers, such as 'Coat Of Many Colors' fell near the start. She somehow got through the show but by the time she came offstage, she was wet, cold, and in near collapse from severe abdominal pain.

Dolly's doctors insisted on admitting her to hospital right away and this time she realised that the situation required urgent attention. There was no alternative but to cancel the remaining 30 shows which ironically included dates that had been rescheduled following previous cancellations. She was flown to New York where she underwent extensive tests and examinations. While there she stayed in the 5th Avenue apartment which served as her and Gallin's office; they preferred the informal feel as being more conducive to conducting business. It was said that Gallin's favourite way of directing Dolly's career was on the telephone while lying on an expansive bed so he had numerous telephones installed and sound-absorbent fabric was fitted to the walls to allow Dolly to play music at any hour.

Dolly was reported to be sedated and drowsy much of the time in New York though she did manage at least one social engagement, attending a Southern-style supper laid on by local businessmen with Calvin Klein among the guests. However, for most of her stay she remained reclusive seeing only Sandy, Judy and Carl. Tests revealed that surgery might be necessary so Dolly flew to Los Angeles and checked into St Luke's Hospital under an assumed name. Although details of the operation Dolly underwent around the end of 1982 were not made public, there was some speculation about a partial hysterectomy or bleeding polyps. However, many newspaper reports simply referred to Dolly having minor surgery for "female problems". Dolly ascribed the various ongoing troubles she experienced to her regular use of the pill over many years; the problem was eventually resolved by a tubal ligation (sterilisation) procedure.

Carl flew out to be with Dolly and thereafter they returned to Nashville where she spent several months recovering. For someone as naturally energetic as Dolly, there were times when she felt more than low during what turned out to be a longer than expected period of recuperation. She revealed that self-pity and depression ran in her family, "and depression comes from boredom; I was bored to death because I was too ill to get out. The depression fed itself like a hungry monster." Dolly particularly disliked being seen at such a low ebb. "You've always been the rock and then you turn to sand." In a 1986 *Daily Express* interview she implied that she tried to keep much of what she was going through from her family. "I didn't want to look up and see their faces horrified that I was sick."

Over the years Dolly had made conflicting comments on the subject of starting a family. She claimed that she cried for hours because she would now be unable to bear children but in a later interview she indicated that she and Carl believed they were unable to have children before her operation. "Those parts were made to be used . . . and I mean, I used them, but it just never did take." Dolly's upbringing dictated that children were part of a woman's *raison d'être* in life and there were times when she felt guilty, particularly when her sisters managed to produce children without apparent difficulty. Her sense of injustice at this led to her having "an argument with the Lord".

After leaving hospital Dolly said that she and Carl might consider adoption although she gave the impression that he had no great desire to have children and the fact they never did was not a source of disappointment to him; it has also been reported that not having children was a conscious decision. If true this was simply a case of a woman choosing to put her career first, something which has since become commonplace.

Carl and Dolly had helped to bring up the younger Parton siblings and they were also involved with caring for nieces and nephews as they came along. Dolly spoke philosophically of the situation. "If I'd had children of my own, I would have had to save all the money for their inheritance and their education whereas now, I'm able to help everybody in the family with their kids if they need braces on their teeth or need to go to college. So I guess God, in His own wisdom, knows what He's doing. It has worked out okay. I have accepted that that's how my life was supposed to be."

Dolly suggested that if she had had children she would probably have abandoned her career because it would not have been fair to take them on the road. However, such a scenario would have been most unlikely because, "I understood, and Carl understood, that I had to do what I had come to Nashville to do. It was in my blood from the time I was a child. I would do it under any circumstances." The arrangement the couple ended up with seemed tailor-made for their needs. In her more playful moments Dolly suggested that she "was the only little girl he ever wanted. And he's the only little boy I'm ever going to have."

Despite the upheavals in her personal life, and the fact that there had been something of a slowdown in the rate of product since her days with Porter, no less than four Dolly-related albums hit the shops in 1982. *Heartbreak Express* and the soundtrack from *The Best Little Whorehouse In Texas* both reached the Top Five in the country charts though, thanks to the success of the film, only the latter album made much impact on the pop listings. RCA released another greatest hits collection in October which, although it failed to top the charts, proved to be a steady seller eventually receiving a platinum award in 1986 after a number of re-releases with the substitution of various tracks deemed likely to attract new buyers. The cover shot – a classic, though dated, glamour model pose – showed Dolly with her hands clasped behind her neck, the focus of attention being her outstretched bosom.

December saw the release of *The Winning Hand,* featuring past artists who had recorded for Monument who were permitted to take part in the venture by their current record companies. It was in effect a tribute album to Fred Foster, whose label was experiencing major financial difficulties at the time. The album used vocals Dolly had laid down during her time with the label between 1965 and 1967 while Kris Kristofferson, Willie Nelson and Brenda Lee recorded their contributions in 1982. The 20-song double album featured various permutations of the contributing artists as well as solo efforts. Dolly's vocals featured on six tracks including 'Everything's Beautiful (In It's Own Way)' with Willie Nelson (which, when released as a single, made number seven in the country charts) and 'Ping Pong' with Kris Kristofferson. Admittedly a look back to the past, the album sounded dated when set against the sophisticated pop of Dolly's recent output.

Foster was not short of goodwill thanks to his contribution to the country music scene and at the suggestion of Johnny Cash the artists featured on *The Winning Hand* joined forces at the Tennessee Performing Arts Center in Nashville to tape a two-hour television spectacular based on the album. Despite the big names on show and the release of compilation albums by the likes of Charlie McCoy and Roy Orbison, Monument's financial woes were not resolved and with nearly 700 creditors ranging from big name songwriters to suppliers of packaging and music trade magazines, Foster eventually filed for bankruptcy in 1983 with debts in excess of $7 million. Dolly was one of the creditors but she saw in the demise of Monument and Combine a business opportunity. A year later the Nashville press reported that along with two business associates, Dolly had tabled an offer in excess of $6 million to rescue and revitalise

Monument and Combine. A reorganisation plan was filed with the Bankruptcy Court which stated, among other things, that Dolly's net worth was not less than $5 million. In truth the figure was much higher.

Broadly speaking the plan was for an initial cash payment to be distributed to creditors with all remaining debts being covered through the profits of the master recordings over a period of time. Apart from Monument and Combine, Dolly was also interested in acquiring the labels' valuable premises on Music Row along with master recordings for which an additional $1 million was offered. It was a remarkable state of affairs that Dolly was now in a position to make a multi-million dollar offer to acquire and reorganise the company that 20 years before, had taken her on in return for a few desperately needed dollars each week. A number of other parties, including Mary Tyler Moore, were interested but after much speculation and behind-the-scenes negotiations Dolly's offer was withdrawn and Monument was eventually sold to Sony (Combine was sold to a separate company SBK).

Just prior to the proposed Monument/Combine deal, Dolly had renewed her business acquaintance with Tree International, another company with whom she'd had past involvement. Though Dolly now owned assets and business interests in various parts of the world, she was anxious to develop and maintain an empire based in Nashville, albeit with the assistance of her LA based management. As part of this she engaged Tree to administer and manage the catalogues of Velvet Apple and Song Yard which amounted to many hundreds of her own songs as well as other artists including her siblings Randy and Frieda, Bill Owens and singer/songwriter Frank Dycus. Dolly saw her career in terms of seven-year plans; she had just completed the first which saw her crossover from country to pop while developing a movie career and was now about to enter another seven-year phase which would not only continue in music ("her lifeblood") and films but also see the development of business interests including artist management and official merchandise.

There had already been "poseable" Dolly dolls,* suitably attired in flashy skin-tight trousers or flowing chiffon tops. Dolly also spoke of setting up companies to create specially designed lingerie and shoes as well as cosmetics and hair products for both sexes. Dolly said that the compliments which pleased her most were those in praise of her skin and the provisional name for her beauty products was "Everything's Beautiful". Dolly intended to become actively involved in directing the creative aspects of

---

* These dolls are now regularly traded on auction website eBay.

these ventures. Also proposed was a book of Dolly's poetry and the possibility of her developing, and perhaps acting in, an autobiographical television soap opera about Beulah Faye, a country girl with dreams of escaping to a more inspiring life, as well as a stage production of *Wildflower,* another semi-autobiographical idea Dolly had been working on for some time. This was to be an *Oklahoma* type musical about Dolly's experiences; life in the mountains, religion, hard times, fun times, and how she and members of her family succeeded in making their way in the music business. Dolly indicated that a considerable degree of artistic licence was envisaged. "It's not really my real story: it's just all jazzed up."

Another stage play Dolly had her eye on was *Trouble In Jerusalem*, about the relationship between an Irish girl and a Jewish boy and the difficulties they experience with her mountain relatives and his New York family. The idea might have been inspired by Dolly's connection to Sandy Gallin, who was Jewish. Reports also surfaced that Dolly was interested in playing the part of the flamboyant cosmetics queen Mary Kaye in a television movie. Though not all of these ideas ever came to fruition, Dolly's mind was sparking on all cylinders even if her health problems had temporarily slowed her down.

Throughout 1982 and '83, during periods of recuperation at home in Brentwood, Dolly gradually started the process of regaining control of her life and career. "I loved too much and left myself open . . . I knew I couldn't ride both sides of the fence any longer. So I got smart. I made changes because I didn't want to end up an old lady with health problems. I now make sure no one, not a father, mother, or husband, controls my life. I control it. That's how I eventually learnt to survive, by relying on myself more than anyone else . . . It's helped me to weed out the bullshit and take better care of myself."

Some perceived the new deal with Tree International as Dolly's way of distancing herself from certain family members who had been involved in her publishing. Though Dolly was characteristically reluctant to talk about specific instances, an interview she gave after coming through her health worries made clear that unspecified family difficulties had contributed to her malaise. "I was having some family problems, not with my husband, but you have got to understand I'm from a very large and very poor family, so there's a major burden on my back – I'm the only one who really made any money and I'm also the kind of person people come to for answers, so I look after them, not just financially but personally too."

'Family', a song she released some years later, was evidently inspired by such ruminations. The lyrics betray Dolly's acceptance of, if not enthusiasm for, what she saw as her duty of family guardian as a result of her own good fortune.

A lucrative engagement at Sun City in South Africa, during a time when the government's apartheid regime was still firmly in place, demonstrated dubious judgement on Dolly and her management's part. The huge tourist resort, located about two hours' drive from Johannesburg, was developed by hotel magnate Sol Kerzner, and officially opened in December 1979. Its tacky opulence contrasted sharply with the grinding poverty endured by much of South Africa's populace. As one travel writer said, "It quickly became a casino oasis where those with money to spend could catch a lascivious show or see an international rock star pretending that playing Sun City was no different than playing Vegas."

Steven Van Zandt, guitarist in Bruce Springsteen's E. Street Band, made Sun City the focus of his music-industry activist group, Artists United Against Apartheid, which attracted support from leading artists, including Bono, Bob Dylan, Run DMC, Joey Ramone and Jackson Browne, who collaborated on a charity single 'Sun City' condemning the resort.

In a weak effort to deflect criticism, some of the artists attracted by the high fees they could command, pointed to the fact that Bophuthatswana (the resort's location) was classified as an independent state by the South African government (although unrecognised as such by any other country), while others, including Dolly, reportedly agreed to perform on the understanding that half of their fees remained behind and that the audience should be integrated. Seemingly unaware of how deep such feelings ran, Dolly said in advance of her visit, "I'm an entertainer, not a politician . . . I can't speak to the problems of another country. I'm just looking forward to the tour, and I'm just gonna stay out of trouble." Dolly invariably expressed a lack of interest in particular political issues and there is little doubt she had no intention of actively supporting the South African regime.

Dolly was shocked when encountering the level of protest and in 1983 her name appeared on a so-called blacklist of entertainers who had performed there, compiled by the United Nations. While touring Australia with Kenny Rogers, she willingly signed the Australian Anti-Apartheid Movement pledge never to appear in South Africa again and her name was eventually removed from the UN register in 1987. Dolly quickly put the incident behind her and rarely, if ever, discussed the subject again.

The South African experience was very much the exception to the rule as Dolly's foreign forays were largely successful due to the high profile she enjoyed in the wake of hit records, two successful movies and an iconic image which was gradually being imprinted on the minds of fans all over the world. Despite the stresses and strains experienced with making *The Best Little Whorehouse In Texas* Dolly was considering the possibility of another Hollywood film. However, early in 1983, she again discovered that fame and celebrity can bring the unwelcome attention of those bearing grudges.

# Chapter 18

EARLY in 1983 the Nashville papers reported that Dolly had gone into virtual seclusion and had let go of her road band as a result of recent death threats. In January major concern was sparked off by an anonymous call to the police in Owensboro shortly before Dolly was due to appear there. The caller said she knew someone who hated Dolly and wanted to kill her. According to reports the deranged man believed he had previously been married to her and wanted revenge for the fact that she had married Carl. Apparently there had been other threats made against Dolly in the recent past, some of them in the form of notes left at her house, quite possibly from the same source, and she and her advisers, including the police, believed the threats might be credible. Two shows were cancelled and Dolly left town with a police escort.

With the murder of John Lennon in December 1980 still fresh in the collective memory Dolly's concern was not just for herself but those around her. Since her first scare in the early Seventies she had beefed up security during public engagements and was invariably surrounded by burly minders as well as a private detective. She let it be known that she carried a .38 pistol in her luggage on tour and sought professional advice from Gavin DeBecker, who served on President Reagan's Advisory Board on the Safety of Public Figures.

Dolly denied the stories that her band had been fired, preferring to keep them on retainers, while she concentrated on developing other aspects of her career. A fan club newsletter stated that Dolly was taking "a short leave of absence from the road to regroup after her illness". (Her tour bus was to be sold now that she and the band flew to most engagements.) She said that her decision had nothing to do with the death threats which she claimed had been the work of a lone crank. Local journalists, however, concluded that the cancelled concerts were a direct result of safety fears. There were times when Dolly rode in cars late at night on country roads to fulfil engagements which added to the general concern. The papers also claimed that Dolly had left Brentwood to stay with friends while security was tightened at her home. One tabloid, alluding to Dolly's ongoing weight issues said, "She went into seclusion with her refrigerator . . . the result was a big weight gain and an unhappy superstar." Though Dolly had overcome some of her more significant health problems and was able to work, she continued to experience low moods.

One bright spot was her three-night stint at London's Dominion Theatre in 1983, preceded by a media blitz which saw her plastered all over high- and low-brow British newspapers, women's magazines and television chat shows. Her presence drew all musical tastes judging by the assortment of prim housewives, business types, rockers, punks (including one with a flamboyant red Mohican) and Dolly lookalikes, who made up the enthusiastic audiences. The shows were spectacular in scale with Dolly backed by a small orchestra of around 25 musicians, including violinists and a timpanist, led by Gregg Perry. Some country instruments were in evidence but in the main Dolly's repertoire was geared up to her more commercial successes. Much had been invested in getting the shows just right, not only to give the audiences a spectacle to remember but also because one night was to be filmed for later release on video as *Dolly In Concert* (a.k.a. *Dolly In London*). When the concert was later screened on BBC television it drew an exceptionally large audience of over eight million viewers and was later shown as a special on the American Home Box Office cable channel.

For the video, a series of introductory sequences were shot – a jumbo jet arriving at Heathrow to a musical backdrop of '9 To 5' and 'Rule Britannia', a staged interview with an immigration officer during which Dolly's breasts take prominence. Dolly tells the official she is a performer and when pushed further says, "A singer." Dolly then makes her way to baggage reclaim waving to an assembly of voluble fans. After receiving a kiss from a London bobby she returns the compliment after being assured that it will get him into trouble. Following the obligatory visit to the Changing of the Guard ceremony and a limousine tour of the city (with Dolly waving to passers-by in the manner of Queen Elizabeth) she appears fascinated by traditional Cockney Pearly Kings and Queens, people after her own heart on the subject of ostentatious outfits, who engage her in a pub singalong. Next stop: a hectic press conference. When asked to compare her experiences with the stars of *9 To 5* and *The Best Little Whorehouse in Texas*, Dolly quipped that she did not dream about the women. When asked about prostitution she replied that she was not in a position to judge anyone, letting slip that she had enough problems of her own. One earnest hack put it to her that she should not forget that her fans liked her, "more as a singer, not as a sex symbol". With ironic humour she shot back, "Oh I'll try very hard not to be a sex symbol . . ." She also managed to get in one of her standard one-liners, "If I'd been a man, I'd probably have been a drag queen."

In another contrived sequence Dolly arrives at the Dominion Theatre in a London bus, escorted into the auditorium by an honour guard of Beefeaters. What the video did not reveal was that one of the performances was disrupted for a short time as a result of a bomb threat (presumably relating to the troubles in Northern Ireland, then at their height) received during the support act's set. The venue was evacuated for about half an hour while a search of the premises was carried out. The show went on without further incident though, in light of the earlier scare, Dolly recoiled with a brief flicker of shock when a pair of men's underpants was thrown onto the stage. The audience was treated to a colourful variety show illustrating Dolly's musical journey – from 'Coat Of Many Colors' and 'Applejack' to 'Here You Come Again' and '9 To 5' with nods along the way to gospel, disco and rock'n'roll. She pulled off an Elvis impersonation and joked that if she'd been performing in the Fifties, the censors would have shown her from the neck (rather than the waist) up. She even tried out a Cockney accent, evidently assuming that was how people in London spoke. Dolly also spoke between songs about her childhood, the hardship her mother endured, and, with a light but resolute touch, the importance to her of religion, her great faith in God and her belief in Jesus.

There were the ubiquitous self mocking jokes about needing to earn lots of money because of the high cost of looking cheap. Despite such gags' familiarity many would have felt cheated if they had gone to a Dolly concert and not heard the lady herself delivering them in person. References to Porter and Barbara and Louise Mandrell doubtless went over the heads of the non-country fans in the audience. All the time she spoke, the band kept up a low-level musical accompaniment adding to the sense of a non-stop extravaganza (though they were very much in the background; after concluding a number with three male vocalists she told them to get back to their cages.)

At a time when she was still struggling to keep her weight in check, Dolly's carefully sculpted, tight-fitting dress helped to hide her bulges while the combination of her platinum blonde wig and immaculate, porcelain-like skin lent her the impression of a French doll. Her overall glamour clashed with her backing band whose beards, long hair and large collared, open neck shirts gave them an unmistakably dated Seventies look. One reviewer said, "The joy of Dolly Parton is the contrast between, on the one hand, a pneumatic, gold lame-sealed myth of trash, and on the other a singer-songwriter of scope and imagination."

One album of new material *Burlap And Satin* was released in 1983, making number five in the country charts, and was nominated for a Grammy in the category Best Country Vocal Performance By A Female – Album. Dolly wrote six of the songs including 'A Gamble Either Way', a particularly winsome and empathetic tale about a young girl drawn into prostitution. Originally written for *The Best Little Whorehouse In Texas* its melancholy mood was out of keeping with the cheerful atmosphere in the chicken ranch. The concert favourite, 'Appalachian Memories', concerned poor country folk who leave their homes to travel to greener pastures. The lyrics were strong on imagery – Dolly's father Lee had unsuccessfully tried venturing north. It was an example of the type of song that prompted one reviewer to gush, "Everybody needs a secret cache of Parton records: the only known antidote to the debilitating effects of cynicism."

Producer Gregg Perry used a variety of non-country instruments such as mellotrons and flutes for even the most straightforward country style songs including 'Appalachian Memories', which bothered Dolly's old-school fans who longed for the return of fiddles and steel guitar.

Some reviewers complained that *Burlap And Satin* was overly pop oriented but English country music journalist Alan Cackett described it as "a classic album that encompasses much, much more than just simple country music, yet has much to offer a country fan". There was a cover of Hank Locklin's 'Send Me The Pillow You Dream On' as well as the punchy disco of 'Potential New Boyfriend', accompanied by a slick video directed by Steve Barron (whose CV included Michael Jackson's 'Billie Jean'). Visual effects included Dolly's image singing in a car rear-view mirror, on a ship's sail, on television screens in a store window and on a car dashboard.

Although Dolly spoke in general terms about the various factors which contributed to her depressed state it's likely that one major exacerbating factor was the unexpected departure that year of Gregg Perry. Dolly acknowledged she did not achieve large record sales until he came along. A prodigiously talented student able to play piano, organ, trombone, bassoon and drums, Gregg was elected to the American High School Soloist Hall of Fame when he was 18. The first Dolly Parton album he worked on was *New Harvest . . . First Gathering* in 1977. She not only liked the fact that he was a cultured man – being educated in art and history – but also that he was clean living. "He eats health food, doesn't eat sugar, doesn't smoke, doesn't drink, doesn't mess around with women; doctor told him even if he don't live for a hundred years it's sure gonna seem like it."

She and Gregg hit it off right away when he joined Gypsy Fever and became very close, particularly so when Judy Ogle went off to do a spell in the army. He was thoughtful and quiet whereas Dolly was loud and brash. It was a successful combination which Dolly greatly valued. She assumed their strong personal and professional bond would last as long as she wanted it to. However, Gregg found the pressures of the music business overwhelming and despite his favoured and unassailable position within Dolly's organisation he quit the music business altogether.* There was little doubt that Dolly took his move as a personal betrayal, expressing her feelings in the song 'What A Heartache' (released in 1984 on the *Rhinestone* soundtrack), which was widely assumed to have been inspired by Gregg's sudden actions. For well over a year Dolly suffered under her emotional and physical issues but she was determined to get out of the rut she found herself in. As part of her rebuilding plan, one of Hollywood's top bodybuilders gave Dolly two weeks of private classes at home, designed to decrease her weight and increase muscular firmness around her hips. Dolly generally disliked any kind of organised physical exercise so it was a surprise when she talked about the idea of setting up Dolly Parton basic training centres, designed to teach the spiritual part of fitness, including meditation. The method would involve mind, body, soul discipline and the concept would all be put into book form "along with my whole mental and spiritual attitude . . . There has to be something done to help people like me."

During the summer of 1983, Dolly spontaneously accepted the offer of a collaborative project which turned out to be one of her most successful to date. Kenny Rogers had appeared as a special guest on Dolly's television show in the Seventies and the pair had met at various awards shows and television specials. However, there were never any specific plans for them to record or tour together. Kenny had been working on a song 'Islands In The Stream', written by the Bee Gees, but when he could not achieve the desired result, it was suggested that the song might work as a duet. Barry Gibb thought that Dolly could be a suitable partner. Kenny's manager had Dolly's home number, she happened to be in town and in a spirit of *carpe diem* she and Kenny were soon in the studio. There was a great chemistry between Kenny and Dolly, and their distinctive vocal styles – his sexy rasp, her emotional soprano – gelled beautifully.

---

* It is believed that Gregg Perry went on to pursue a career in the medical profession.

When boosted by various promotional appearances the song became a major hit, making number one in the country and pop charts and performing most impressively in Canada, where it held onto the number one slot for an astonishing nine weeks. By the end of the year the single had gone platinum and received a Grammy nomination in the category. Best Pop Performance By A Duo Or Group. Kenny and Dolly's appearance performing the song at the annual CMA awards helped increase viewing figures that year and in 1984 they received CMA nominations in two categories, Vocal Duo Of The Year and Single Of The Year but failed to win either.

Also in '84 Dolly released *The Great Pretender*, an album of cover versions of some of her favourite Fifties and Sixties songs including 'Downtown', 'Save The Last Dance For Me', 'I Can't Help Myself' and Johnny Cash's 'I Walk The Line', in which she annoyed some Cash fans by changing the lyric to "I walk *that* line." The album was devoid of country content and made liberal use of rock, soul and disco production values. The trouble was that Dolly's voice was largely lost in the electronically synthesised mix. At times, it sounded as if she was making a concerted effort to be heard above the barrage, and this in turn gave her voice a high pitched vibrato quality. Reviewer Dan Herbeck saw a dilemma. "Dolly Parton, the songbird with the little girl voice and the major league measurements, appears to be caught in a career dilemma. She can't seem to decide whether she wants to try being all things to all people, or settle for being the best female country singer in the world." One critic described the musicians as "dully competent, the arrangements only memorable for their inappropriateness".

With touring unofficially on hold, Dolly had time on hand to mull over the various options for her next career move. She spent time in Hawaii, one of her favourite retreats, where she pored over film scripts. This was all the more surprising in view of the strains associated with *The Best Little Whorehouse In Texas* and the fact that she found film shoots monotonous. Dolly turned down the role of Serena, a witch, in *Supergirl* on the basis that she would not play a negative character, explaining, "Darkness is not part of who I am."* She complained about being offered "fantasy roles in fairy-tale stories". When Dolly was reportedly offered a part in a new film version of *Romeo And Juliet*, one DJ cracked, "I don't know whether Dolly can act . . . but she sure can lean over a balcony." She had also been tipped to play Marilyn Monroe and Mae West in biopics but she preferred the

---

* Faye Dunaway eventually accepted the part.

idea of living long enough to become a legend herself. In reality Dolly would have struggled to project West's constant lewdness and cynicism because her acting ability involved little more than playing herself.

Dolly was on more comfortable ground if playing comedy roles *à la* Doris Day and Mary Tyler Moore, combining the sex and wholesomeness which had constituted her first two roles. While claiming a part in a film like *The Grapes Of Wrath* or *East Of Eden* would appeal to her, or Mrs Santa Claus in a family vehicle aimed at children, Dolly eventually settled on *Rhinestone*. The idea was loosely based on the story behind the song, 'Rhinestone Cowboy', written by Larry Weiss and recorded by Glen Campbell. Weiss had for years been trying unsuccessfully to turn the song into a movie. There had been development deals and a reported six screenplays, all of which had come to nothing. Dolly shared an agent with Sylvester Stallone, who had previously rejected the film. Stallone reconsidered the film at the behest of his agent and said he was interested if Dolly was. The pair had not worked together previously but had appeared at the Oscars ceremony in 1983 where they jointly presented the award for Best Actor to Robert Duvall for his portrayal of a country singer in *Tender Mercies*.*

The original working title for the film was *Rhinestone Cowboy*, but Dolly preferred *Rhinestone* because she didn't want people thinking that the film was solely about Stallone's character; there were rumours that her people had to resist attempts to downgrade her equal billing. One of the lessons she claimed to have learned from her previous celluloid outings was the importance of retaining a large degree of control and so it was all the more surprising that *Rhinestone* was essentially Stallone's baby. While he had a hand in writing the screenplay, Dolly ensured that she had a large degree of control over the musical content, revealing to interviewer Terry Wogan in 1992 that she had a clause in her movie contracts giving her the right to record the theme song.

The highly improbable storyline revolves around a wager that popular club singer, Jake (played by Dolly), makes with her lascivious boss that she can turn any ordinary guy into a country and western singer in two weeks. If she wins she gets to leave the club. If she loses she has to stay working at the club for another five years and spend a "night to remember" with her boss. Unfortunately the candidate she selects turns out to be sullen New York cab driver Nick Martinelli (played by Stallone) who has no interest

---

* Apparently Michael Caine, one of the other nominees remarked, "When I saw a country and western star come out [to make the presentation], I knew I wasn't going to win."

in country music. Why such a script should appeal to Stallone, whose fame was built on such macho roles as *Rocky* and *Rambo*, was not clear. He had never acted in comedy and was no singer. The omens were not good but in view of Stallone's box office clout, 20th Century Fox were prepared to provide a sizeable budget, around $25 million, in the hope of achieving another blockbuster. Dolly had little self-doubt when it came to the negotiating table. "Hollywood ain't gonna give me no trouble. If they come to me and offer me big money, it's because they know who I am. They're not fools. But what's even better, I ain't either." (Her fee was said to be between $3 million and $4 million.)

To allow her time to write the film's soundtrack Dolly cancelled several television appearances and a summer tour to promote the *Burlap And Satin* album. Again some of the dates were at venues where shows had been cancelled as a result of her health problems the year before. Dolly was protected from financial loss because of a clause she had started having inserted into her contracts allowing her to cancel concerts if they clashed with unforeseen film commitments. However, in 1984 she was ordered to pay $15,105.25 to a promoter for improperly cancelling a show six years before in Tulsa, Oklahoma. It had apparently been rescheduled but Dolly claimed she had not been informed of the new date.

Dolly and Judy Ogle headed off in a camper van into the Smokies and beyond. Sometimes they would pull up next to a river, set up camp and Dolly would brainstorm ideas while taking in her childhood scenery. When checking into cheap motels Dolly waited in the van while Judy booked the room. In a matter of about three weeks, she had written more than an album's worth of material from which the film's musical content and soundtrack would be drawn. There were also writing contributions from Randy, Floyd and Stella and various friends and relatives, including Don Warden and Bill Owens, featured in the bands – The Wild Possums and the The Cut-And-Slice Band – who backed Dolly and Sly in the film. Del Wood, an old school country singer and fellow member of the Grand Ole Opry, also appeared.

The filming ran into difficulties when the original director left the film a month into shooting, so approximately three weeks of footage was forfeited. It was proposed that some scenes would be shot in Williamson County, Tennessee. Governor Lamar Alexander believed Dolly to be a "tremendous booster for the State" and in a blaze of publicity, she went to the airport to meet Stallone. Unfortunately the weather was inclement for virtually the entire time the production was in Tennessee and none of the footage could be used. Filming resumed in the Mojave Desert, California at a farm then owned by Walt Disney Productions. While in Tennessee Dolly took Sly horse riding in the rolling hills near Nashville as a way of demonstrating country living, but being a city boy Sly did not care much for peace and quiet.

By all accounts Dolly had a happier time on the set with Stallone than she did with Burt Reynolds, though she said dealing with both was, at times, like dealing with the record company executives on Music Row. "Sly has the perfect balance of total ego and total insecurity. I see how his mind works. If you were in love with him, he'd pick out all your weaknesses and either use them to help you or use them against you. I told him right up front, 'Sly, please, please, please don't get on me like you do other people. I know what I am, who I am, and I happen to be happy with me.' So he never bothered me." Like Dolly, Stallone was security conscious and was often accompanied by bodyguards. She found him to be, "full of life, crazy . . . that moved me, got me back on track." It was rumoured that originally the film was to have a sequence featuring Dolly dancing cheek to cheek with Sly but this was ruled out on the grounds that it was "a physical impossibility".

One interest Sly and Dolly shared in common was their physiques. Stallone was said to have lost 40 pounds for the film while Dolly was still trying (and failing) to get her weight nearer to her ideal level of around 100 pounds. Before *Rhinestone* she was probably 30 to 40 pounds overweight. Stallone took it upon himself to provide encouragement and reportedly talked Dolly into doing weight training and to try out his low carbohydrate, high protein plan which limited her to about 1,000 calories per day. She reportedly lost about 25 pounds. The health conscious Stallone was said to be horrified at the diet of this "junk food junky" which included Velveeta ("a delicious cheese food") and Wonder Bread, saying there were, "things in there that had no connection with life as we know it. And she'd eat these things!"

Sly and Dolly might have worked well together as weight watchers but they were doomed in front of the cameras. Stallone was never at ease with his role and Dolly's abundant vivacity was not enough to breathe life into the project. The denouement of Sly receiving a wildly enthusiastic reception at Dolly's club was farcical considering his near inaudible singing was dreadful. Perhaps another leading man might have made a difference but the film had too many flaws to be viable as a quality product. Dolly later said that though she had fun making the film, she learned nothing from Sly on the acting front.

The star-spangled Nashville premiere, attended by 1,500 paying guests, raised over $40,000 for the Grand Ole Opry Trust Fund which aided musicians fallen on hard times and Dolly and Sly became the latest actors to have their stars implanted in the grey concrete walkway in front of the legendary Egyptian Theater on Hollywood Boulevard.*

The critics were merciless. Bob Longino said, ". . . they rarely are in step as an acting duo . . . even more alarming is that Nick and Jake are sickeningly immature adults who make it desperately hard to like them." *Country Music Roundup* described the film as, "an overwrought silly affair that does nothing to show country music in an attractive light . . . entertainers are shown as hicks and its fans as stereotypical obnoxious bores. Dolly herself appears to play the part of a backward hillbilly with other characters being shown as bumpkins." Dolly was sensitive to the accusation that the film portrayed country folk as ignorant though it was hard to refute the charge. "It pisses you off because that's not who we are – that's certainly not what I am. That's not how we act or how we feel." However, she added, "The fact that they even notice us at all is something." Critic Rex Reid described *Rhinestone* as "a profoundly stupid vehicle made by greedy and untalented filmmakers . . . the moronic screenplay must have been written by somebody with something up his nose besides nasal spray."

Some resorted to sarcasm as they speculated as to who might star in *Rhinestone II*; would it be Bette Midler and Sir Lawrence Olivier or possibly Vanessa Redgrave and Liberace? When Dolly met a journalist in a restaurant, a German writer walked over asking for a few words. Before he could say anything, she asked if he had liked *Rhinestone*. The writer boldly declared he did not know anyone in the world whom he would want to subject to such a film. As the journalist witnessing this exchange said, "Most stars would have called for, in order, their bodyguard, their manager, their publicity agents and their limousine. Dolly . . . got up, hugged him and whispered in his ear, 'I'll convert you yet!'"

Despite the harsh assessments, the film attracted a few positive comments. One reviewer thought it would help promote country music because it was not overly serious and contained elements sure to appeal to a wider audience. *People* magazine described it as "a charming movie, spunky and full of surprising fun". Though they did not rate the film they admired Dolly and her attitude. The *New York Times* said, "The best thing in *Rhinestone* is Dolly Parton, who seems able to survive just about any movie unscathed . . . she is no actress, but she is fast becoming a real movie

---

* Dolly's star is located between those of Raymond Massey and Douglas Fairbanks Jnr.

star. The camera likes her, while it only tolerates [Stallone]. Better, it seems to enjoy her." Sly clearly came to admire his co-star even if they were not destined to work together again. "She is the most career-oriented person I have ever seen. Our egos never came close to clashing. And that's a very unusual thing. I believe that sort of respect for each other has transferred onto the screen." For her own part Dolly remained resolutely upbeat in the wake of all the negative press comment. "We had so much fun on this movie; we just went crazy after a bit, leaping all over the place, dancing and singing. We kept each other hysterical the whole time. It was more like play than work . . . I'm real proud of it."

*Rhinestone* took around $3 million in its first six weeks of release, a figure that compared poorly with *9 To 5* and *The Best Little Whorehouse In Texas* grossing $10 million and $9 million respectively during the equivalent period. There had been talk of 20th Century Fox making a television pilot based on *Rhinestone* but such plans soon faded. Released in July the soundtrack was a mixed bag with contributions from Dolly and various Parton family members including Stella and Randy. Dolly's 'Tennessee Homesick Blues', an uptempo country number with rowdy audience sound effects made number one in the country charts, while the tear-jerking ballad 'God Won't Get You' made number 10. Stallone's conspicuous lack of vocal ability meant that his contributions were mainly restricted to duets with Dolly although he did get one solo. A critic wrote, "His interpretation of a country accent mixed with his own unique approach to enunciation has a jaw-dropping effect. He sounds like Bob Dylan after coming in from the dentist." Despite extensive publicity surrounding the launch of the film and some good individual songs, the album failed to reach the country Top 30.

By the time *Rhinestone* was completed the experience helped to restore Dolly's self-confidence and "haul her ass" out of the negative mindset that had plagued her over the past 18 months. She took decisive steps to address her family problems, writing in her 1994 autobiography, "I got up early that morning and went straight to a list of names I'd made. I wrote letters to four people, some family, some business, who I had let mess with my head. They're people who'd had the upper hand on me for years. When I saw them comin' I'd cringe. When they called I wasn't in. The letters were very blunt. They said, 'I'm not going to put up with your BS any more. You have no control over me and little control over yourself so you should examine things very carefully.'"

It was an important turning point on Dolly's road to recovery.

# Chapter 19

IN 1984 Dolly was singled out for an illustrious honour when an exhibition devoted to her life and work was staged at Nashville's Country Music Hall of Fame. Others to have received this rare accolade included Johnny Cash and Willie Nelson. Dolly was closely involved in the selection of items to be featured, aided by Judy Ogle. The display was split into five areas: Dolly's childhood and upbringing; songwriting (included were original manuscripts of hits including 'Two Doors Down'); performing (featuring a costume she wore during the London concerts in 1983); movies (the scripts from her three hit films) and awards. The exhibit opened to the public in June and remained in place for a year. Also on display was a re-creation of the school coat of many colours Avie Lee made and a large cross section of Dolly's wigs. That same year a wax effigy was put on display at Madame Tussauds museum in London (where it remained until 1988 before being melted down to make way for new exhibits).

During the Eighties there were around 30 models of Dolly on display in various locations around the world including the Hollywood Wax Museum but by the following decade, most had been withdrawn. The figures, made up from past photographs and videos, were often rendered unrealistic once Dolly started to get her weight under control. Her fame received further recognition when top British photographer Norman Parkinson, staging a one-man show in Manhattan, asked each of his models, including Iman and Jerry Hall, to write the name of one other woman they would like to be. All wrote the same answer: Dolly Parton.

Around the same time Cher and Tina Turner lent their faces to a *McCall's* magazine advertising blitz aimed at waking up media buyers to the monthly's appeal. There was a series of giant close-ups, each with a catchy strapline, such as "One of the Plain Jane's that Reads *McCall's*." Dolly was considered for the campaign but wanted $2 million to be dubbed a "boring housewife".

Dolly's visibility resulted in countless requests for her to support various causes, most of which time demands made impracticable. However, a nationwide organisation called A Child's Wish Comes True arranged for

Vicky Perales, a terminally ill 11-year-old girl to fly to Hollywood to meet Dolly, who sang a few songs to her and then gave Vicky a miniature guitar and a director's seat with Dolly's name on it. According to press reports the request for Dolly's intervention came about because her music had a calming effect on the child. Dolly would have found it hard to resist such a story, which might have been lifted from one of her own songs. Dolly also associated herself with a campaign entitled Read America, Win America run by Project Literacy US. She was well aware of the benefits of literacy to young people and it was a theme she would return to in years to come. Dolly also made a point of supporting fellow artists in times of need. In 1984 Barbara Mandrell was seriously injured in a car crash and was unable to work for well over a year while she recovered. Dolly appeared as star guest when Mandrell returned to the concert stage in Los Angeles in 1986.

After the spectacular success of 'Islands In The Stream' the respective managements for Dolly and Kenny Rogers saw 1984's Christmas season as a golden marketing opportunity. *Once Upon A Christmas* featured a mixture of standards such as 'White Christmas' and 'Silent Night' along with five new songs written by Dolly including 'A Christmas To Remember' and 'I Believe In Santa Claus' on which Dolly and Kenny were backed by a full children's choir. The album went platinum in 1984 and subsequent seasonal re-releases helped to maintain interest with the record eventually attaining double platinum status in 1989. Initial sales were helped by a CBS television special *A Christmas To Remember* ironically recorded in scorching summer heat on location in Palm Springs and a town called Piru in California's San Fernando Valley, where many of the residents took on roles as extras.

Production crews arrived in advance to dress up the grounds of the local United Methodist Church with blankets of fake snow, complete with frosted windows and rosebushes, while Christmas ornaments were unpacked and arranged on a giant tree. To get in the right spirit, after arriving in Palm Springs, Dolly and her friends went out and bought Christmas gifts for each other, which were wrapped and placed under the tree. Judy Ogle wrote on her present for Dolly, "Do not open until all the songs are written." The special, directed by Bob Giraldi who had been responsible for the stunning video for Michael Jackson's 'Beat It', was the top rated television programme the week it was aired.

The 90-minute programme comprised a series of vague set pieces and songs interspersed with behind-the-scenes segments featuring Dolly and Kenny indulging in vacuous banter. The whole overproduced exercise lacked coherence. For no apparent reason one sequence was set in an Air Force base in England during the Second World War; another in a crowded hospital ward with an array of nurses and sickly patients. There appeared to be no thematic link to the season of goodwill apart from the two stars, having made a grand entrance, somewhat incongruously bursting into festive song. Elsewhere there were cartoons with a winter's theme and frenetic dance routines; in one visually jarring scene, dancers dressed in white robes gyrated around a church in a way that owed more to pagan rituals while the congregation uneasily looked on. Dolly, who was still struggling to control her weight, said, "Every time I see myself in it, I say, 'Look at the Christmas tree.'"

During a joint press conference to promote the special Dolly, professing herself to be a fan of Kenny's singing style, tried to explain its appeal. "I love Kenny Rogers' voice 'cause I can feel it. It's very emotional. It comes from a very deep place. Plus it has a jarring kind of vibrating sound that touches women. I know. I don't know how men feel, but it *stirs* me. I think it's sexy." The pair's contrasting ambitions were revealed when Kenny said, "I've been lucky. I've accomplished everything I set out to do. My goal is just to continue. I don't wanna be any hotter." Dolly immediately broke in, "I want to be hotter. I want to do something on Broadway. I want to publish my book on self-improvement . . ."

A subsequent tour, to promote Dolly's 1985 album *Real Love* took in over 40 venues, drawing capacity crowds. One of the biggest concerts took place on New Year's Eve at the prestigious Los Angeles Forum with tickets priced from $30 to $50. The shows were notable for their increasing use of technology with large video screens and a spectacular laser show. Some critics felt there was too much emphasis on technical wizardry and that Kenny and Dolly spent too much time exploiting their celebrity at the expense of each other's artistry. This was Dolly's first tour since her various health troubles but she did have to cancel a few concerts due to a nagging virus and the kind of voice strain which had plagued her on and off for years. She explained she could work three to five days per week without any problems but more than that and her voice tended to give out.[*]

Throughout the tour Dolly kept up the wisecracks about her prodigious bosom. At one concert, when given a bunch of bouquets, she said, "Where am I goin' to put all of them? My bus ain't big enough." When some of the crowd laughed, she responded, "I said my *bus*," which drew even more mirth. During another show she quipped, "You miss a lot

---

[*] Frankie Valli and the Four Seasons replaced Dolly and Kenny for one concert.

being built like me . . . like what's going on in the first six rows, when I'm onstage." Comedian Henny Youngman cracked, "I had a nightmare. I dreamt that my mother was Dolly Parton and I was a bottle baby."

Joel Selvin, reviewing a show for the *New York Times*, was unconvinced by the Kenny and Dolly spectacle. "This is one of the most soulful queens of country music who has been reduced to a national joke about her abundant bosom, jokes in which she is fully willing to participate. This is one of the most sensitive and gifted songwriters ever to come out of the Great Smoky Mountains, who walked away from the colourful mountain sounds she used to make in favour of the homogenised white bread kind of pop music that lacks any distinct character or depth." He described Rogers as "a modest talent with a serviceable but unspectacular voice, almost no charisma whatsoever and an irritating, self-important manner that is totally out of place on such an unremarkable entertainer. As he made his way to the stage floor, before he even said 'Good evening', he felt compelled to explain why he refused to shake hands with anyone as he worked his way through the crowd – 'Shake one, and you gotta shake them all' – setting a pompous, supercilious tone to which he stayed close throughout his set."

Ironically Selvin's comments about Dolly chimed with Rogers' own view. "Dolly could have been an even bigger star if they promoted her talent rather than her breasts . . . She is absolutely awesome . . . in her musical ability, her skill in conceptualising, her creativity."

Following the commercial success of the US tour Dolly and Kenny subsequently performed a series of concerts in Australia and New Zealand together.

Dolly's 1985 album *Real Love* mainly featured romantic pop with a bit of routine rock'n'roll thrown in, catchy but largely lightweight and unmemorable. The woman on the sleeve was a million miles from the plucky country girl who appeared on her early albums. Rhinestones and gaud were out, soft focus and chiffon, combined with pale understated colours, was in. Dolly's vocals came over as forced, high pitched and childlike, bearing more than a passing resemblance to Cyndi Lauper who had exploded onto the pop scene in 1983 with 'Girls Just Want To Have Fun' from her multi-million selling album *She's So Unusual*. The title track – a duet with Rogers – made number one on the country chart as did the follow-up single, 'Think About Love', but it was hard to escape the conclusion that Dolly and her advisers were unimaginatively trying to capitalise on current trends.

222

## Chapter 19

It seemed shameful that Dolly was releasing such inconsequential material when so much of her reputation as a musical heavyweight was built on the perceptive and dramatic stories she wrote about real lives that were capable of moving people. Despite such general criticism from reviewers, *Real Love* inexplicably received a Grammy nomination in the category, 'Best Country Vocal Performance By A Female, Album'.

Dolly had been considering plans for a theme park since the early Eighties and had discussed the idea with business associates as well as her family. She claimed the original idea for Dollywood came when she saw the world-famous sign in the Hollywood Hills and thought about surreptitiously swapping the H for a D. As a child Dolly looked forward to the country fair arriving in town, creating a magical world of rides, shows, candy and twinkling lights, so this image was very much in her mind when conceiving Dollywood. "I'm always talking about how proud I am of the Smoky Mountains, so this is just something that I felt real compelled to do. As Mamma would say, 'I felt led to do it.'"

The idea of a visitor attraction inspired by and based on a country singer was not new. Conway Twitty's Twitty City was already well established, as was Johnny Cash's museum, the House Of Cash, but what Dolly envisaged was on a different scale altogether. She foresaw a theme park covering hundreds of acres which would grow in size with the addition of new features, attracting millions of visitors, not just country music fans, to East Tennessee every year. Her intentions extended much further than a quick trawl through her life story followed by the opportunity to buy tacky souvenirs. There would be a large selection of exciting fairground rides, a log flume ride, white-water rafting, a roller coaster, a train journey through various areas of the park, as well as merry-go-rounds and bumper cars for children.* In addition down-home food, ice cream and (exclusively non-alcoholic) drinks would be available from stalls all over the site. Most importantly, visitors would be given the chance to see what mountain life was about in a beautiful setting, and have the opportunity to observe local people practising rural crafts and skills including, quilting, basket weaving, dulcimer making, blacksmithing, loom-weaving, glass-blowing, leather working, woodcarving, sewing moccasins, steam-powered saw-milling and wagon building. Dolly referred to the many talented craftsmen and women whose work would be on display as "skillbillies".

Dollywood has subsequently pursued a policy of research, sometimes with the use of scouts, to find people who still possess these traditional

---

* Dolly's motion sickness prevented her from going on many of the rides.

skills and to find a place for them. In this way the park has helped to maintain and preserve crafts which might otherwise have died out. As one commentator said, "Dollywood provides just about any version of the old days that anyone might care to sample. We all know that Dolly has her naughty side but her amusement park traces wholesome living all through the American centuries and it comes out the other side as clean and pure and delicate as a butterfly's wings." It was, as the advertising literature put it, "the Smoky Mountain Family Adventure".

Live concerts were planned in various venues at regular intervals throughout the day alongside piped music. Despite Dolly's current musical preoccupations, Dollywood mainly featured folk and roots with bluegrass also prominent. Various members of the Parton family including Stella, Randy and Bill Owens were lined up to make musical contributions at the Back Porch Theatre. As a spokesman confirmed, "There'll always be a Parton performing at Dollywood." Other initial ideas for the park included a dude ranch, a recording studio and even a "Dollywood University" to teach public relations to tourism staff.

Dolly had been looking for a suitable site for several years. Though some advised against it, she opted to stay close to her roots by giving something back to Sevier County. "They say charity begins at home, and I believe that." After several years of searching, a location came to the attention of Dolly's people which had some obvious advantages. Silver Dollar City was a historical frontier-themed park near Pigeon Forge, in the foothills of the Smoky Mountains, which extended to around 120 acres. Not only that, it was about 10 miles from the area Dolly had grown up in. "Many people who are raised in near poverty try to distance themselves from their upbringing," wrote one journalist, "but not Parton, whose ticket out turned into a round trip."

There had been a tourist attraction on the site, originally owned by the Robbins brothers, since about 1960, the principal attraction being the Rebel Railroad with a coal-fired steam engine dubbed Klondike Katie. In 1970 the site was purchased by Art Modell and renamed Goldrush Junction with new attractions added, such as the Lady Gay saloon. The Herschend Brothers bought the park in 1977 and more attractions such as a blacksmith's workshop, a woodcarving facility and fair rides were gradually brought in. One of the owners of Silver Dollar City, Jack Herschend was aware of Dolly's interest in creating a theme park in East Tennessee, and thought his operation might provide a suitable location. Rather than get into a costly competitive situation with both parties aiming for the same market, Herschend saw the sense in brokering a deal with Dolly.

What emerged was an arrangement whereby the park would continue to be managed and operated by Silver Dollar City with "creative input and direction" from Dolly. An extra nine acres of attractions would be inputted and all existing areas refurbished.

Most of Dolly's creative vision lay in steering Dollywood towards an accurate depiction of mountain people as skilled survivalists rather than ignorant rubes. "I've always been aggravated about how they portray mountain people in Hollywood and in the movies, like we are all these dumb, barefoot hillbillies . . . personally, I think that country people are the smartest people in the world, and I've been everywhere."

In July 1985 Dolly went to Pigeon Forge to seek financial support from the city commission. The venue for the meeting was changed from the modestly sized City Hall to a local theatre accommodating 2,000, which attracted a tremendous crowd of onlookers. Dolly won over officials with her grandiose plans for Dollywood and the economic benefits she believed it would bring to the area. They took little persuading since unemployment levels were high, despite the area's reputation as an attractive holiday destination, and many people, including some Dolly grew up with and their descendants, still lived in relative poverty. In return for her own sizeable contribution to the venture – ensuring, amongst other conditions, that she and certain star names would appear there – Dolly sought assistance from the council with the upgrading of streets and sewers, increased parking provision and general scenic improvements such as the removal of the many unsightly billboards at the side of the roads.* The state contributed around $1.5 million with the city adding around $500,000. Reports of the overall costs of creating Dollywood ranged between $40 million and $50 million.

The Dolly effect quickly affected land values with the cost of prime property jumping to around $1,000 per frontage foot virtually overnight. There were rumours that some owners were asking well in excess of that figure. While nobody doubted that Dollywood would be good for East Tennessee's economy the magazine *Southern Exposure* argued that skyrocketing land values would cause property taxes to jump and make land unaffordable for long time residents. Moreover, the article pointed out that historically, jobs created by the tourist industry tended to be low paid

---

* The nearby town of Pigeon Forge, home to the oldest commercial water-powered mill still operating in Tennessee, has acquired an unenviable reputation as one of the ugliest small cities in America. When the matter became an issue some years later, Dolly said she would be the last to take down her sign.

and menial (though a spokesman for Dollywood said they would pay above the minimum wage). There was also concern that debates over education and other important local issues would play second fiddle to important tourist concerns. Local officials denied this prognosis; they did concede that property values had risen dramatically, especially along Highway 441, leading to Pigeon Forge, Gatlinburg and Dollywood, but property taxes were not expected to follow. Though there clearly were some legitimate concerns, the view of the overwhelming majority was that making Dolly's fantasy real would be beneficial to the community. Amidst a voluminous amount of local publicity, Dolly attended the civic ceremony marking the start of work on Dollywood in the presence of dignitaries and local people. After waving to Sevierville's Mayor Wade, she told the crowd, "I used to make out with him in the back of a Chevrolet at the Midway Drive-in." Wade later said, "Everybody loved [Dolly's comment] but my wife."

Before Dollywood opened for its first season in 1986, Dolly conducted a comprehensive media campaign. Interviews were set up on all the major television talk shows including Johnny Carson, and Phil Donahue, *Entertainment Tonight*, the *Nashville Network,* and the three major network morning shows. Dolly's fame gave her access to virtually any show she wanted to appear on and for each appearance she spoke in glowing terms about what a fantastic time visitors would have, urging "Y'all come." Another favourite advertising line was, "We play lots of music and guarantee a cure for feet that don't stomp and faces that don't smile!" Articles advertising the wonders of Dollywood, all in virtually identical terms, appeared in numerous newspapers all over the Southern regions of America. It all added up to a well co-ordinated media blitz.

Dolly continually emphasised how her new venture would help the local economy, alluding to a significant philanthropic element to Dollywood's activities, particularly in the areas of education and literacy, which true to her word, developed over the years. Despite the fact that she disliked much of her school career, she was wise enough to know that better education was the key to improving people's chances in life.

Dollywood reinforced Dolly Parton's status as one of America's most iconic figures. A colourful and noisy parade of floats, marchers, trucks, cars and clowns paraded along Pigeon Forge's main street, lined by about 15,000, to mark the grand opening in spring 1986. Apparently a number of celebrities had expressed an interest in attending the launch but Dolly herself was not sold on the idea. "I hope I didn't hurt their feelings by not wanting them here, but I wanted it to be just for me." Governor Lamar

Alexander was invited, later recalling that while being shown around the museum dedicated to Dolly's life he arrived at the large photograph taken during Dolly's school trip to Washington in 1963. Scanning the faces in the picture Lamar said, "Where are you?" to which she replied, "There, in the front row, in the centre. What did you expect?"

The Governor was another who found that his own status counted for little when next to Dolly. As they trundled through the crowds in a 1909 Lewis Roadster, people asked him to move aside so that they could get a better view of her. Dolly consoled him by saying she was sure a lot of people had come to see him too but as he admitted, "I didn't mind. I was looking at Dolly too." Despite her commitments at the park over the opening weekend, including a promotional television spot on ABC's *Good Morning America* and a brunch attended by state legislators and members of the media, Dolly also found time to help promote healthcare in East Tennessee when she met the director of the Dr Robert F. Thomas Foundation – named after the doctor who delivered her – for a tour of the Sevier Medical Center. To assist fundraising efforts Dolly offered a week's holiday in her home in Hawaii as first prize in a raffle. She also undertook a spell as National Chairman of the Foundation. The doctor's mailbox with his name on the side was given to Dolly by members of Dr Thomas' family and remains a treasured possession.

By noon on opening day at Dollywood there were 12,000 visitors to the park. A thousand balloons (a present from Neil Diamond) drifted skyward as Dolly cut the ribbon to officially declare Dollywood open. The park – open to the public from April through to the end of October – was a hit from day one. The $14 entry cost for adults and $10.95 per child covered everything except food, drink and souvenirs.* Such was the demand that by May 1986 there were days when traffic queued for six miles on US 441 and according to one report tourism in the entire state of Tennessee was up 19%. While such a rise could not be attributable to Dollywood alone there is little doubt that it made a substantial contribution. The nearby towns of Gatlinburg and Pigeon Forge experienced substantial augmentations as well, around 20% and 35% respectively. Dollywood got its one millionth visitor just five months after opening at 10.14 a.m. on Wednesday, August 20, 1986. Teresa Wray of Dexter, Missouri, received keys to the towns of Gatlinburg, Pigeon Forge and Sevierville and also the keys to Dollywood's gates. Dolly, who was on tour at the time, spoke to her by phone. Ms Wray also received an engraved

---

* The equivalent prices in 2006 were $45.70 and $34.55.

crystal place setting, two $100 gift certificates and a free vacation in the Smokies.

In its first season, Dollywood attracted 1.34 million people, roughly twice Silver Dollar City's previous attendance record and could justifiably claim to be the fastest-growing theme park in America. The increase in visitor numbers was good news for local businesses. Farmers sold more food to the shops around Dollywood, hotels attracted more guests, and factories manufactured souvenirs for which there was an increased demand. For the majority of local people the economic upturn was welcome. However, as had been predicted, property prices rose significantly and the towns of Pigeon Forge and Gatlinburg became hugely commercialised and their main streets were soon overflowing with countless tourist-oriented shops, many tacky and tasteless. Dolly might well have felt comfortably at home within such surroundings which, she would have been the first to admit, chimed with the image she had contrived over the years.

By the time of Dollywood's first anniversary Dolly was pleased with what she had achieved, referring to herself in a press interview as "a female Walt Disney". She claimed that in the first year gross receipts for businesses in Pigeon Forge had, on average, gone up by nearly 50% resulting in the creation of a significant number of jobs. In May 1987 Pigeon Forge declared "Terrific Trio Day" – a public recognition of the phenomenal economic growth that had taken place as a result of all parties concerned working together.

The Smoky Mountains, a "rubber tire" destination, attracted large numbers of weekend visitors seeking a change of scenery and Dollywood made the area all the more appealing. Visitors were reminded that they were in bear country and pamphlets were printed which included the following advice: "If a bear persistently follows or approaches you without vocalizing or paw swatting, try changing your direction. If the bear continues to follow you, stand your ground . . . act aggressively and try to intimidate the bear." Dollywood was heavily advertised in Baptist churches and as part of an apparent policy not to offend parishioners Dolly's famous cleavage was not prominently displayed, only being seen on the mannequins in the museum displaying Dolly's dresses.

By hiring those close to her, it's likely that certain familial ties which had been damaged when Dolly made changes in her organisation in the early Eighties were restored. A good number of her relatives were involved. Brother Bobby, for instance, helped to build a replica of the family's mountain homestead but there were those who said Dolly was too generous in taking on kinfolk who were not sufficiently experienced. Dolly's father was said to be exasperated by the number of family members (there were nearly 100 Partons in the local phone book) who approached him in the hope of getting work. Carl was reluctant to allow images of himself to be displayed, though as a joke he consented to being photographed with a paper bag over his head with two holes for the eyes which he suggested should be called "the unknown husband". It was rumoured that when Carl first visited Dollywood after it was completed he joined the queues and paid his entrance money like everybody else. One piece of advice he gave that has been strictly adhered to over the years is that the park should be kept litter free, in keeping with the wholesome image Dollywood has always endeavoured to present.

Music and other forms of live entertainment performed by a variety of artists was an essential element of Dollywood's attraction. A large number of performers were required each year and advertisements were placed in the Tennessee press and beyond. One newspaper reported that a team of scouts was looking to audition new talent in various towns and cities including Dallas, Memphis, Knoxville and Chattanooga. They had a clear idea of the type of musicians they were looking for: country, bluegrass, "new grass" and nostalgia musical groups, singer/dancers comfortable performing country music, variety artists, novelty and speciality acts, actors with improvisational skills, comic flare and stage or street experience. Auditions lasted five minutes and people were told, "Please prepare upbeat material that best displays your individual performance skills."

An appearance at Dollywood provided musicians with a platform to greater things. One of the first artists who appeared in the early days was Suzy Bogguss whose Dollywood stint was a useful learning experience for her. As well as it leading to her first recording contract Suzy also gained valuable insights into Dolly's personality. "I had just moved to Nashville about maybe nine months before they came and did these audition kind of things for, I guess, a festival they had at the park, this is before it was Dollywood, it was called Silver Dollar City, and so I had three days that I'd been booked for and Dolly just happened to have been at the park when I was doing one of my little shows and so I actually got offered the gig . . . when the folks at Dollywood said, 'You know you're going to be opening concerts for Dolly,' I was, like, 'OK I'll do that.' It could have been a difficult decision . . . I was finally opening some doors in Nashville and here I am gonna go and move to this little town outside of Gatlinburg and when I got there it was the best experience in the world because I really got a concentrated education in country music . . . here I was in the middle of all these people . . . if I said that a song was written by the wrong person, these country fans would just correct me so it ended up being a great education for me other than the fact that I got to be around Dolly."

Suzy initially played four daily solo shows at the railway station and was also the female lead in the day's final two-hour-long Jamboree show. This meant working for anything up to 10 hours per day but it gave her and many other budding young artists a concentrated induction into the reality of working in the music business. Suzy was introduced to Dolly early on. "We had to have some pictures taken for promotion and I had my picture taken with Dolly. The first thing I remember about her was that when she talked to me she looked at me and she listened to me and I was a little bit shocked at that because having been in Nashville for a few months I'd met quite a few artists, people who were in the limelight, and I'd never got the kind of connection I got from her. It was like, when she'd ask me a question she'd ask me about my home town and where I was from and what kind of background, and why I liked music. She was totally listening to me and she really cared . . . I can tell when somebody looks at me and they have that little deer-in-the-headlight look, or they're looking over their shoulder to see if there's somebody better to talk to, and that was the thing with her, she absolutely connected, just for a few minutes, but it was enough."

The experience was all the more powerful since Suzy had regarded Dolly as a kind of imaginary mentor while travelling around from town to town playing small venues. In this way Dolly served, albeit unwittingly, as a guiding light for many aspiring artists seeking out their artistic direction (top country singer Patty Loveless being another example). "Whenever I would see [Dolly] on the big TV shows I always thought she was so savvy," says Suzy, "she always knew how to take the interview every direction she needed it to get, and in the same way be so charming and funny. You know she would make jokes at her own expense, not because she doesn't believe in herself or had low self-esteem . . . it was obvious that it was just part of how she pulls people together and says, 'By the time I'm done with you, you're going to like me' and that's the thing about her. Who could ever watch and go, 'I just don't like her.' You can't because she has the charisma that not many in this business have."

After six months at Dollywood, Suzy was offered a recording contract with Capitol. She was naturally excited but apprehensive because although this was what she had been working towards for years, she felt out of her depth. It just so happened that Dolly was going to be at the park over the next couple of days so Suzy asked to see her. Dolly had a lavishly fitted-out apartment within a yellow clapboard house in Dollywood where she met Suzy in between shows at the Celebrity Theater. "She was so beautiful and so gracious I almost melted . . ." Suzy recalls, "it was like Eva Gabor from the *Green Acres* show, she had on the long lingerie with the pretty little feathery stuff on it and I remember my breath just getting caught. I had talked to her before but I hadn't seen her in her abode with all this beautiful crystal and things around her . . . I could hardly speak. It was like being in front of royalty or something, it was an amazing thing, but I just sat down and talked to her about the fact that I'd been offered this record deal and I didn't really think I was in a position to be doing a lot of bargaining but I just wanted to know if she knew the head of the label and she just couldn't say enough nice things about him, 'a gentleman . . . he will not lead you some place you don't want to go.'

"She said, 'You know it is a crazy lifestyle and when you get travelling and stuff you can get in some trouble if you don't stay true to yourself 'cause you get really tired and you get tired of people around you, and you just don't want to get into any drugs or any kind of crutches.' This was the advice she gave me and it was only years later that it dawned on me what a precious titbit that was."

Suzy's career took off soon afterwards when she won the CMA Horizon award. The pressures were intense and as she said, "It was [Dolly's] words that came into my head, 'Don't get a crutch, don't get into anything that you can't get out of . . . you need to be awake and remember all of this 'cause it's only going to happen once,' so that really has always rung for me and the fact that she was there and she was present and she talked to me like I was an adult and not some kid . . . it was that thing of be yourself and hang in there." Suzy got married five days after her Dollywood season ended and as a pleasant parting gesture she was allowed to borrow numerous items – flowers, park benches, etc. for her wedding. Suzy has subsequently encountered Dolly fleetingly but still feels Dolly would be happy to meet if her schedule allowed it. Suzy says, "That's always one of the beautiful sides of her, she remains accessible, particularly to her peers."

Opening Dollywood was the fulfilment of another dream which helped raise Dolly's profile to new heights in America. However, she was still intent on pursuing other goals in the entertainment field – one which had been unfulfilled for some time.

# Chapter 20

BY the late Eighties it seemed Dolly had received more honours than she could keep track of. Some of these verged on the bizarre. A man named Barry Gibson travelled around America digging dirt from homes owned by the rich and famous, packaging them in small plastic vials which were then encased in wood blocks. Gibson sold each one, along with a certificate of authenticity, for $3.95, with Dolly's dirt selling better than all others. In London, a Dolly mannequin went on display at the Virgin Records store on Oxford Street. More conventional recognition came when Dolly was inducted into the Nashville Songwriters Association International Hall Of Fame along with Otis Blackwell, writer of 'Great Balls Of Fire' which Dolly had covered some years previously. Unfortunately she was unable to attend the ceremony; a result of her seemingly endless commitments. In 1986 the Grand Ole Opry celebrated its 50th anniversary with a special show for which Dolly was invited to sing with other legendary country figures such as Loretta Lynn and Willie Nelson.

Nashville journalist and writer Robert K. Oermann paid gushing tribute in *The Tennessean*. "The breadth of her appeal is awesome: she occupies the unique position of being deeply admired by her songwriting peers, adored by children, respected by the entertainment business, looked up to by women, worshipped by men, cheered by music fans, loved by the press and cherished by almost everyone who has ever met her. She is a world-class celebrity whose every move is chronicled by tabloids, whose health, career escapades and public appearances are scrutinised from every angle. And through it all she remains breathtakingly candid, charmingly humorous and immensely earthy." A rather more superficial accolade came when the America's Cup Crew, sailing the yacht Stars and Stripes, named their revolutionary new sail 'Dolly' because it filled with air and ballooned out. Never one to miss a chance to reinforce her public image Dolly sent a telegram. "Please accept thanks from a girl who, before you guys, used to think America's Cup was a 44-D."

Andrei Gromyko, the USSR Foreign Minister, was a fan of Dolly's and it was said that he entertained hopes of meeting her on one of his trips to New York, even though she was regarded as a symbol of Western decadence back home. Because of this her records were not available in Moscow and according to one newspaper report Gromyko dispatched his chauffeur to a Manhattan record shop to buy two copies of every Parton album in stock.

In 1987, the town fathers of Sevierville decided that the achievements of their most famous daughter should be marked by a permanent public reminder. For a fee of $60,000, a local sculptor, Jim Gray, was commissioned to fashion a statue of Dolly in bronze, which was placed in a prominent position in the garden in front of the local courthouse, an area reserved for honouring local heroes such as fallen servicemen. The sculpture showed a barefoot Dolly, with a moderate amount of cleavage showing, holding a guitar with a trademark butterfly on the neck. An inscription read, "This statue of Dolly Parton was erected through the generosity of the people of Sevier County."

There was a formal dedication ceremony on May 3 attended by various local dignitaries and guests and after the festivities were over Dolly went back to look at the statue with Carl. She later called it one of the highlights of her life to date and a great source of pride because, "Even after we're all dead and gone, it will still be sitting in the courthouse lawn." Along with the courthouse building (built in 1896) the statue is on the national register of historical sites.*

In early 1986 Dolly had commenced a project first mooted back in the mid Seventies. Originally nicknamed The Queenston Trio, a punning reference to the legendary folk revival group The Kingston Trio, Dolly, Emmylou Harris and Linda Ronstadt finally managed to find time in their schedules to record an album together. Apart from their busy performing schedules and the need for negotiations among managements and record companies, Dolly had been trying to get Dollywood off the ground, Emmylou Harris had been involved in a custody battle and Linda Ronstadt had suffered back problems. The first attempt had, in Dolly's words, involved "too many chiefs and not enough Indians. So we had a pow-wow between the three of us and said why don't we wait until we can do it properly. Let's weed these people out and get rid of some of the aggravations."

---

* Sadly, Dolly's statue was vandalised not long after the dedication ceremony with the boulder supporting the sculpture spray-painted with the letters BOXX (significance unknown) and the hands, face and guitar painted black. It was cleaned up soon afterwards and remains one of Sevierville's main tourist attractions.

In total contrast to Dolly's commercially oriented output, the album simply called *Trio* represented a heartfelt attempt to reconnect with her roots, featuring the type of singing and songwriting that she appeared to have shunned for some years. As writer Ken Tucker said, "It was significant that at precisely the moment when Parton had probably transcended the country artist label, she chose to remind her public of it." The sleeve showed the three kitted out in country kitsch glad rags which would not have looked out of place in Sixties Nashville. The producer for the album was studio designer and general technical whizz-kid George Massenburg who had produced some of Little Feat's Seventies albums. "The women ruled the sessions," he said. "It was the girls' record. These are three women who have taken great control of their lives and their careers and will not accept the old ideas about their place in music and in the world."

In Dolly's view the sessions went smoothly. "We didn't fight, we didn't argue, and our egos didn't get in the way. The project was the boss . . . could'na been better timin', because there's a lull in our careers right now." In a subsequent interview Linda Ronstadt put a different slant on the sessions. "Dolly's taste often didn't jive with ours; she had different ideas of what's pretty and fancy and impressive. It was uncomfortable to get around her taste without hurting her feelings or making her feel that we thought we were better than she was. I thought we did a masterful job with it. There were never any fights."

The production was sparse and an array of top musicians played on the album, including Ry Cooder, Mark O'Connor, Herb Pederson and Albert Lee. Lee had good reason to remember the sessions because his daughter was born in the middle of them and the girls joked that he should call the new arrival, EmmyDollyLou or some other amalgamation of their names. "[Dolly] was really sweet and bubbly from the first moment I met her," says Lee. "I remember sitting down at the piano and she said to me, 'Hi Albert sing me a song, sing me a song' . . . I was really embarrassed about singing in front of her so I never did. Dolly had her 40th birthday during the sessions and we had a cake. She was really sweet and easy-going . . . exactly in real life as you see her on TV, just so natural and friendly and giving . . . not putting on any airs." He was also impressed by her vocal ability – "It's hard to imagine her not doing anything perfectly the first time because she's got such a fantastic ear. She'd be able to find a note just out of the air, the perfect note" – and recalled the sessions being democratic, "very much give and take". Lee was aware of the presence of Judy Ogle who, "seemed to be taking care of things for Dolly" and acted as "a buffer". He also noted Ogle's predilection for keeping a record of the people Dolly met. "She usually had a camera with her to document whoever happened to be with Dolly and then she'd send a copy of the photograph to whoever she had a picture taken with."

The *Trio* album was laid down in a little over a week with two or three songs being recorded each day and was previewed at the CMA awards ceremony in October when Dolly, Linda and Emmylou performed 'My Dear Companion'. A few invited guests, including Linda's then beau, *Star Wars* producer George Lucas, and Emmylou's partner, English musician Paul Kennerley, were allowed to sit in on some sessions, but it seems Carl did not. Despite the inclusion of the old Phil Spector pop hit 'To Know Him Is To Love Him', the predominant feel was roots, country and traditional folk though the occasional addition of cello and viola lent a classical tinge to some songs. The idea of women singing songs together was in itself a case of carrying on an old country tradition though Dolly was the only member to have come from a rural background; Linda and Emmylou had comfortable upbringings and only latched on to country and folk music when hearing it on the radio in their teens.

The song 'Wildflowers' Dolly had written some 15 years before, keeping it back to provide the basis of a Southern musical based on her early life story. Apparently Emmylou and Linda asked for it to be recorded, pointing out that the musical Dolly had talked about for quite some time had still to materialise. The trio also covered Jimmie Rodgers' 'Hobo's Meditation' and the traditional songs 'Farther Along' and 'Rosewood Casket', the latter arranged by Avie Lee Parton. Emmylou claimed 'My Dear Companion' as being closest to the album's heart. "It's not old, but it sounds timeless and has real mountain roots." Clearly the vocal interaction between the three principals was the record's outstanding feature.

Both Emmylou and Linda paid tribute to their singing partner. "Dolly represents the finest of women's traditional music," said Emmylou. "Linda and I are in mutual admiration of Dolly as our favourite singer. Dolly's voice is almost the focal point of this record, in a way." "No one can copy Dolly," Linda declared, "but you try to go into her consciousness and sing the way she does from the heart. You get to ride along and feel the way she does." Writers Mary A. Bufwack and Robert K. Oermann called Dolly "the pulse of the trio".

*Trio* was generally well received by the critics. One described some of the music as sounding "quasi religious . . . three ladies keeping their eyes on heaven, plagued by treacherous men". Another raved, "Earth, wind and fire are no more elemental than these marvellous singers." John Rockwell, writing in the *New York Times* said, "The prevailing mood is gentle, romantic pain, suffused with religious devotion and emotional tenderness." However, not all the reviews were entirely favourable. Jerry Spangler wrote, "The collaboration should have been a dream come true. Unfortunately *Trio* turned out to be one of those kind of dreams you just can't remember when you wake up. It is undeniably good, at times very, very good. But it's not memorable." He went on to say that the album's magic lay in the harmonies but there weren't enough of them, "But when they do come together there are moments that make the soul cry out in sheer joy, but just as a glimpse of what might have been."

Journalist Pam Parrish spoke for many when saying, "This is how these voices were meant to be heard, with a minimum of instrumentation, the supple touches of qualified musicians who have been playing this stuff as long as Ronstadt, Parton and Harris have been singing it."

*Trio* was a hit with the public – staying at number one in the country charts for five weeks and making the *Billboard* Top 10, quite an achievement for a record of stripped-down traditional country and folk. Four singles were extracted, all of which made the Top 10 with 'To Know Him Is To Love Him' reaching number one. By late 1987 the album had gone platinum, receiving two Grammy nominations, winning in the category, Best Country Performance By A Duo Or Group, Album. Looking back two years later, Dolly said that *Trio* had been one of the highlights of her career so far along with *9 To 5*. As she said half jokingly, "I seem to have my best luck working with other women."

*Trio* was released on Warner Brothers at a time when Dolly was changing labels. She had been with RCA for approximately 20 years but the relationship had grown cold. By the mid Eighties many older country stars had fallen from favour with their record companies who were more interested in promoting more marketable younger acts. Some found themselves without contracts because their financial expectations, from when sales were good, went beyond what their labels were prepared to pay. It seemed particularly hard on Dolly who had given RCA a double platinum Christmas album as recently as 1984 although a third best of compilation, released in 1987, failed to sell. By the late Eighties Dolly could claim to be the most successful female country singer in terms of chart positions: 52 Top 10 records, including 20 chart toppers. However, many young country fans were turning to a new generation such as George Strait, Reba McEntire and Ricky Skaggs, dubbed the "New Traditionalists", whose brand of country music gave prominence to fiddles and steel guitars. In addition, the overall number of people buying country was dwindling.

Some younger music fans saw Nashville and many of its stable as some kind of reactionary throwback and were more in favour of the likes of Bruce Springsteen who though essentially rock singers, nonetheless featured country-tinged material in their repertoire.

There had been a surge of interest in country music in the late Seventies thanks to the short-lived *Urban Cowboy* phenomenon (named after the movie starring John Travolta) which glorified the lifestyle of the late-20th-century honky tonk cowboy. The craze extended beyond country music, taking in cowboy dress, pickup trucks, mechanical bulls in night clubs and a slew of other symbols of country living. The boom produced talk show appearances for established stars (including Dolly) and country music benefited from the exposure, rising to around 15% of total record sales as compared to the previous figure of less than 10%. However, the figures soon fell back, which meant yet more pressure on some of the genre's established stars.

Dolly was one of a number of major country artists, including fellow RCA stablemates Charley Pride and Waylon Jennings, who found themselves without a contract. She displayed no outward bitterness, although most of the friends she had made at the label had come and gone. "In fact, I was the only person I knew that was still at RCA that had been there when I started." Of the relationship with her record company, she said, "I often thought it was kinda like we loved each other a lot and we were comfortable in that situation, not particularly happy, sort of like an old marriage where you take each other for granted." Dolly claimed that they did not part as enemies. "Sometimes I like to make changes just for the sake of change, because it gives me new incentives." In reality the impetus came from RCA – the decision was taken for purely business reasons; there being little room for sentiment in the modern record industry.

Dolly's management entered negotiations with a number of record companies, eventually agreeing a deal with Columbia. As part of the arrangement Dolly would record one contemporary album and one country album per year on the basis that country fans did not like her pop material and vice versa so Dolly would not have to strike a balance within albums. In the wake of this successful outcome a party was held in a down-town Manhattan eatery, in the company of leading celebrities such as Andy Warhol, Grace Jones and Calvin Klein. Dolly wore the same silver-trimmed black outfit and mountainous platinum wig that late-night viewers saw when she made a surprise appearance on the *David Letterman Show* later that evening.

There was a breakthrough of a more personal nature when, after years of trying, Dolly finally managed to find a diet that worked for her, regarding it as one of her greatest achievements. Dolly could eat whatever she liked but instead of gorging herself on set meals she would instead consume a greater number of smaller meals throughout the day. On Oprah Winfrey's talk show she detailed her tactics. "I eat what's mine and I leave the rest for the angels and I always pretend that God's havin' supper with me, or the angels. And I don't want to eat their part, so I eat mine and I feel guilty if I steal the angels' food – but I do it sometimes."

She was now prepared to leave half a meal uneaten and started to properly chew her food, sometimes being instructed to chew for a time before spitting the food out, although she found this self-discipline to be irritating. She would try to include healthy meals but would not deprive herself of her beloved junk food from time to time. As part of her exercise regime she installed a gym at her Los Angeles home and tried to get into the habit of working out on a regular basis. She had found this hard in the past, joking that she used to sit back and eat cookies while watching Jane Fonda's fitness video.

Stories about Dolly's weight loss were plastered all over the tabloid press, and it was widely reported that she had dropped from 150 to 100 pounds, which she called her fighting weight. It's likely that at one stage her weight went as low as 90 pounds and her mother was so concerned that she insisted on feeding Dolly some of her home cooking – ham hocks, grits, country gravy and biscuits – to get it back up.

Dolly explained the impact losing weight had on her. "When I was fat, I ate all the time. I ate everything I wanted, and I had more personality. But I've noticed that since I've been skinny, I don't have the same tolerance as I used to have . . . I eat everything I want, I just don't eat a lot of it. So, in three hours I'm hungry again. My blood sugar gets low. And if you get in my face about something you ain't got no business being in my face for, if I'm hungry, watch out! Sometimes I will snap and bite somebody's head off. Then after I've done it, I won't believe it . . . a load of people think that I'm more short-tempered than I used to be because I'm arrogant and vain. They think that I act like that now because I look so much better – at least I do to me – but they totally misunderstand me. I may not have the exact tolerance level that I used to have, but other than that, I am not changed at all."

An early opportunity to show off her new look came with *Rainbow*, Dolly's second release of 1987 (and her first for Columbia). The sleeve shot, taken by famed portrait photographer Annie Leibovitz, showed a seductive Dolly, wearing a massive curly wig and dressed to the nines in black and silver evening wear with long black gloves, lying on her side, looking devoid of rural innocence. Unfortunately the album was the musical and lyrical antithesis of *Trio*, awash with synthetic pop-rock and low level soul music, making it hard to believe it was the same artist. As with much of her output over the previous decade Dolly's unique vocal qualities were lost amid a big upfront drum sound, frenetic, electronically generated rhythms and competing contributions from a posse of expert session musicians including Buck Trent, one of the Wagonmasters.* *Rainbow* was not so much bad as wholly undistinguished and despite heavy advertising it failed to sell in large quantities. The message seemed to be registering that out-and-out pop was not the best medium for Dolly to show off her musical attributes. The general view was that her heart belonged in country and the sooner she got back to it the better.

A generally poor response from the critics didn't help. Commenting on the song 'I Know You By Heart', a duet with soul giant Smokey Robinson, Norman Rowe said, "It would be difficult to say which performer is more miscast in this unfortunate musical encounter." Dolly considered their voices to be similar with "all the curves and twists". On the Motown kick, the album also featured Mary Wells' classic, 'Two Lovers', which prompted another reviewer's comment, "Dolly Parton doing soul makes about as much sense as Pavarotti doing country." *USA Today*'s record critic said of the album, "Imagine Porter Wagoner singing 'Whole Lotta Love'." In 1988, David Quantick, of *New Musical Express*, was blunt in his assessment. "Given that Dolly Parton is probably the greatest of her kind, it seems improbable that someone could put together a record which would forbid her from doing anything even remotely gripping or individual, yet some BASTARD at CBS has set out with this purpose in mind . . . Parton's voice is made to fight over AOR backing tracks and stale melodies that should have been left in the Tina Turner songwriter's demo reject pile."

Another reviewer talked of the album's "ugly disco gloop" while, writing in *Country Music People*, journalist Steve Derby perceived a wider malaise. "Ask yourself what Dolly is best at and see if you don't find yourself prefixing your answer with, 'she used to . . .'"

Dolly was presented with a glorious opportunity to publicise *Rainbow* and much else when in 1987 she was offered a high profile television show by ABC, again simply called *Dolly*. Although her previous television exploits had ended less than successfully and she had indicated that she

---

* Then again Trent was apparently the brains behind the electric banjo!

wanted to avoid the commitment of a weekly show, Dolly realised that with some changes, more creative control and her higher profile there was no reason why the idea should not come off a second time around. ABC came up with a vehicle which attempted to revive the variety show format.

As the show was in development Dolly gave a general idea of what was envisaged. "We're definitely going to do some comedy, and we'll certainly have music, and we'll be workin' with the people, talkin' with them, the regular American people, coverin' every story like a roving reporter kind of situation.* Probably we'll be doing some skits, and I'll probably have some characters on the show. We have not narrowed it down exactly." She said also that every week was to feature a down-home "Tennessee Mountain Home" section, during which Dolly would sing country songs. High profile celebrity guests (in the run-up to the show, Dolly dropped names such as Dustin Hoffman and Elizabeth Taylor) would pop up regularly. ABC clearly believed in the project, signing a two-year contract with Dolly, negotiated by Sandy Gallin, which involved an enormous investment on their part of $44 million, one of the most expensive television deals ever. The president of ABC entertainment, Brandon Stoddard, said, "There are few stars in the world who have the instant recognition and immense likeability of Dolly Parton . . . Dolly and television are made for each other." The show was described as "pivotal" in ABC's Sunday night line-up; their hopes and a lot of their money were riding on Dolly. The producer, Don Mischer, had major credits to his name such as the Kennedy Center Honors and the Tony Awards as well as many other television productions. For her part Dolly said, "I'm good at television. I come across real well in people's living rooms."

A *Nashville Banner* report of Dolly's news conference captured both her eye-catching appearance and the level of security she employed. "Dressed in urban chic with a touch of lacy innocence thrown in; her black, stonewashed jeans hug her spidery thin legs, topped off by black boots highlighted at the top with little squares of mirrored glass all around them. Parton adjusts the zipper on her black leather jacket, allowing a little more of her low-cut lace blouse to be revealed. Outside the room is Parton's entourage, a lady with a lipstick holder and a brush, and two men who watch Parton like a couple of school kids keeping an eye on the classroom

---

* One of these was to include a segment in which Dolly would talk with dieters and doctors about issues related to being overweight. This particular idea – under the working title This Little Piggy – never made it past the drawing board.

clock. Earphones are stuck in their ears and the bulges under their coats certainly aren't autograph books." Apart from her own past experiences of death threats Dolly was doubtless aware of the increasing phenomenon of stalking.*

The debut show attracted a substantial audience and was the fifth most popular TV show that week. However, the level of interest was short-lived and many who had tuned in out of curiosity failed to return over subsequent weeks. One visual problem was that Dolly had now lost so much weight that she looked unhealthily skinny and there was speculation that she might have an eating disorder, which she denied. For many fans a thin Dolly was not the image they had come to know. The prospect of putting weight back on filled her with dread. "I'd rather be dead than be that miserable again."

Despite slick production, flamboyant costumes and some top name guests the programme appeared dated and unsophisticated. On the very first show Dolly and Oprah Winfrey appeared together in a sketch featuring Dolly as an actress in a garish green dress, hoping to audition for *Porgy And Bess*. Winfrey tells her there is a "colour problem". Dolly returns wearing a red dress. Apart from the antiquated jokes Dolly simply looked uncomfortable as a quick-fire comedienne. Various different ideas were tried – including "Dolly's Date" where the likes of Tom Selleck were invited onto the show to flirt with the star – but none seemed to fit. Other sequences included Dolly and Rich Little dressing up as famous film duos such as Bogart and Bergman in *Casablanca*, a group of women chatting in a beauty shop and a teenager's wall posters coming to life. Sprinkled throughout were such Dolly aphorisms as "You know you can change the face of the world, but you gotta start with the one in the mirror." Like the original Dolly series in the Seventies, shows were rounded off with 'I Will Always Love You'.

Dolly complained that some of the tunes she was asked to sing, such as 'Someone To Watch Over Me', were just not her style; as she pointed out, she was not a Barbra Streisand or Judy Garland. In an interview Dolly gave after the first two shows there was already a hint that all was not well. "I know it's going to be a lot more fun when we get sure of ourselves and get the show worked out the way we want it." She characterised part of the problem as, "Hollywood trying to deal with a country girl's dream without having any idea of who I am." Though she and Sandy Gallin had creative control of the show's content Dolly felt that her wishes were

---

* In 1988 the FBI estimated that there might be as many as 100,000 stalkers in America.

sometimes ignored. On one occasion she accidentally omitted a line of dialogue she particularly liked but against her wishes, the producers pushed on without re-taping it.

Popular celebrities like Dudley Moore who should have been sure-fire winners came over as stilted and ill at ease as a result of the weak scripts and Dolly's awkwardness as a comedienne. The start of each show featured Dolly in a bubble bath, promising, "I'm really gonna burst my bubbles for you." Also featured were slow-moving camera shots which travelled all the way up Dolly's body from feet to head. There appeared to be no rationale behind this except titillation and it merely confirmed Dolly's oft repeated assertion that when she lost weight she lost it everywhere including her much vaunted chest line (though strenuous efforts had clearly been made to push her breasts up to make them as prominent as possible).

Glamour was the order of the day, particularly in the early shows, much of it courtesy of Dolly's most trusted designer Tony Chase. One of his more striking visual creations was a black evening dress, diamonds around the bodice, drawn in tight down to the knees and then dramatically flared out to the ground. Copious quantities of dry ice complemented the overwhelming effect. There were suggestions that the producers asked Chase to tone down some of the more revealing outfits but he baulked at this because he admired, "that glamour from the old school . . . Dolly is one of the last 'stars' . . . she's glamorous and a lot of women cannot carry glamour."*

At one stage in the show's run there was a carefully scripted section where Dolly supposedly had a question-and-answer as well as a good news session with the studio audience, which came over as forced and artificial. One woman stood up and said, "My good news is 10 years ago I was stopped for speeding and then three years ago I got married to the guy who stopped me for speeding." When a man asked Dolly, "Do you sing in the shower?" she replied, "No, but I don't wash myself onstage either."

In one particularly stiff, self-conscious comedy routine Dolly and children's entertainer Pee-Wee Herman stumbled through their lines as they moved around a multi-coloured set with strange, unearthly animals popping out from all over the place. The whole sketch was utterly banal

---

* Chase later created a white stage outfit for Dolly and, as an indication of his attention to detail, used between 12 and 15 women for the beading alone. "I have 'fill' beaders and 'star' beaders – the best. Only they work on the stuff for Dolly . . . she has incredible colouring. I am really not limited with her, it's like a blank canvas. Any colour can work. For a designer, that's a dream – somebody who has limitless possibilities."

and Dolly's glamorous outfit and sexy demeanour were totally out of place. Gallin later conceded the whole exercise was "overproduced and hysterical". There was the occasional one-liner which rose above the generally mediocrity. Describing her work ethic Dolly said, "I never stopped trying and I never tried stopping." Asked if she thought it was acceptable for a couple to live together before marriage she quipped that in her case the problem was living together after marriage. The new-look *Dolly* very much fell into the family entertainment category, so when Dolly had difficulty saying "chateau" in a sketch and let slip, "What is this cheap shat anyway?" the staff censor decreed that the scene would have to be redone.

The show was usually taped in Los Angeles but occasionally went on location. Dolly felt these shows worked best because they connected her with real people. The ingredients of one such show, from New Orleans, provided an idea of the quantity of set pieces required each week. After a brief clichéd introduction referring to "life down yonder in the Big Easy, the city that care forgot . . . sweet, unhurried and filled with music", Dolly was seen strutting in the street alongside a jazz funeral. After offering a smattering of the city's history she was then seen in the French quarter, taking a buggy ride, after which the action moved to the Storyville Jazz Hall where George Kirby, as Louis Armstrong, sang 'What A Wonderful World'. As the place filled up, the camera panned to a doorway where Dolly, brazenly wearing a beaded red dress, sang 'The House Of The Rising Sun'. Songs from Dr John, Allen Toussaint and Irma Thomas followed before the whole ensemble got together on Lee Dorsey's 'Working In The Coal Mine'. A guest chef then gave a cooking lesson – how to prepare blackened tuna – before Dolly, clad in lacy white, sang 'Shall We Gather By The River', and then, joined by a black gospel choir, rounded off proceedings with a gentle 'Blue Bayou'.

Dolly took a close interest in technical aspects of the show's musical content and production. Surprisingly the music budget for each show was only around 6% of the entire outlay even though the musical content constituted half the programme (though this fluctuated as producers chopped and changed the format). Musical director, Ray Bunch, helmed a small but effective band comprising seven or eight musicians with a strong rhythm section and an elaborate electronic set-up to reflect how current records were made. Bunch said that each show was akin to cutting an album, particularly when it came to appearances from rock bands like Tom Petty & the Heartbreakers. Petty and the band came to the studios to record and mix their track and the following day they recorded their live vocals at ABC. Bunch was impressed that Dolly genuinely cared about the quality. "If there's a question about quality and spending money . . . I never have to be concerned with what she'll say. It's carte blanche. She wants it done right, she takes the time, and she's here when we record, which I have found in previous TV specials doesn't happen much. She's here all the time, and she puts as much work into it as I do . . . she's just wonderful, and she is my primary consideration for doing this show, as well as, of course, the financial aspect."

Great physical demands were placed on Dolly and all others involved with the show. As with her previous television excursion there was a pressing need for new material each week which had to be rehearsed. Production took up two full days and nights, three weeks out of every four. There were constant delays as minor glitches were sorted out and each taping usually ran past midnight. If members of the audience started to dwindle they were instantly replaced from among the hordes waiting outside as standbys. Roger Miller was among the warm-up artists who performed routines to keep the audiences entertained. Yet for all the effort involved the show rapidly plummeted down the ratings and regular show post mortems and hurried changes became the order of the day.

A number of theories were advanced for the show's poor performance. Its Sunday night slot between programmes featuring a private eye and a doctor was deemed not to be conducive to producing the right kind of "audience flow". Both CBS and NBC were planning celebrity-filled mini series and some said this drew interest away from Dolly's show. Some pointed out that it was unusual to have a variety show in a prime time slot, usually reserved for sitcoms and crime dramas. Brandon Stoddard felt there was a difficulty with Dolly herself. "The problem with Dolly has been getting it into the right groove . . . when she is comfortable on screen, she is magic. When she is a little uneasy, it's . . . groaning . . . we're working to make sure she's comfortable."

A more general point was that the show was trying to revive a traditional variety format whose day had come and gone; the last successful programme of its like was *The Carol Burnett Show*, which had finished a decade before. "I think it's true what people said, that variety is dead," Dolly later commented. In recent years extensive concert tours, cable television, music videos and major talk shows had led to extensive exposure (some said overexposure) of certain artists. There was no exclusivity about the guest appearances on Dolly's show from Tom Petty, Bruce Willis, Merle Haggard, Lee Majors, Tammy Wynette and others.

In December 1987 Dolly was moved from Sunday to Saturday evening, a move which Gallin had been pressing executives to make for some time. Dolly was instrumental in jettisoning many of the lavish, glamorous sequences (and the cringe-worthy opening sequence in the bubble bath) in favour of items with a more down-home feel. The show's opening number 'Baby I'm Burning' was dropped in favour of country material and a Southern twang was more in evidence even though the network had stressed at the outset that they did not want the show to be "too country". On one of the later episodes Dolly and Willie Nelson sang 'Family Bible'. She confided to the audience that her grandmother asked if she would sing the song at her funeral but in the event Dolly was too upset to carry it off.

Though the show attracted millions of viewers (and Dolly won the 1988 People's Choice Award For Female Performer In A New TV Show) the numbers were unacceptably low for ABC and its advertisers. The series was axed and Dolly reportedly had the remainder of her contract bought out for around $11 million. While attracting favourable press comment in the early days, one common observation was that *Dolly* was too "town" initially but then became too "country". One TV critic carped, "Poorly based attempts at humour wedged between over-produced Parton songs. Sure, the costumes are gorgeous and yes, Parton is now incredibly skinny, but even the least discerning viewer needs just a wee bit more."

Others, including Dolly herself, criticised ABC for having revealed the amount of money invested in the show and how the future of traditional variety on television seemed to rest on her shoulders. Dolly's second attempt at a major television series would be her last. She had tried as well as she knew how to make a success of the opportunity but there were apparent limits to her popularity. The last *Dolly* was recorded in Nashville with members of the Grand Ole Opry as guests. During her visit Dolly was inducted into the Star Walk – an honour bestowed upon Grammy winning country stars – which required an impression of her hands in wet cement at the Fountain Square Mall in downtown Nashville. Apart from her hands, Dolly drew a cartoon of herself and embedded a rhinestone butterfly in the wet cement. "Several people asked me if I was going to leave the prints of something else, but I told them, 'Heavens no, I'm afraid some little kid might fall in and get killed.'"

Dolly was naturally disappointed at her failure in the television medium but after initially apologising for the show's lack of success, she was soon making light of the experience. When the subject of the fierce competition for ratings among television companies came up in an interview she quipped, "I did my best to keep ABC in third place." She later admitted that the programme might have soured her standing in Hollywood if it had run much longer, summing *Dolly* up as "a misguided TV variety show that died an agonisingly public death . . . I had hoped I could just trust all the people who kept saying 'Trust me.' I was just one little country hillbilly and nobody would listen to me much."

In 1989 Dolly returned to the small screen as a guest host on *Saturday Night Live*. She was happy to take parts in skits lampooning her measurements and TV flops, but drew the line at politics, religion and family. As a more lasting legacy of their involvement in the visual arts Dolly and Sandy Gallin had become partners in Sandollar – a television and movie production company based in LA. At first glance the name appeared to be a neat amalgam of their first names and money but in fact a sand dollar was a sea creature related to the starfish and sea urchin. Sandollar's initial venture was *A Smoky Mountain Christmas* (mostly filmed in LA for reasons of economy) which, when aired in December 1986, turned out to be the highest-rated ABC television movie of the previous two years. Though popular it added nothing to Dolly's reputation as an actor. The plot (loosely based around *Snow White And The Seven Dwarfs* not to mention aspects of Dolly's early life) concerns a lonely singer who, overwhelmed by the demands of her career, goes to stay in a log cabin in the mountains. The place has been taken over by seven orphans who become Dolly's adopted family. Conflict with the local sheriff and a jealous witch over her desire to keep the children, and the involvement of a reclusive mountain man played by Lee Majors, added drama to the tale. The film, which featured traditional songs as well as six new tunes written by Dolly, was high on schmaltz and its feel-good factor provided safe seasonal family viewing.

However, for Dolly, writing and performing music was the most important aspect of her professional life. Critics had panned her last effort *Rainbow* but in 1989, she was to confound expectation with an album which returned to a more familiar musical setting.

# Chapter 21

"JUST spell it the way it sounds." This was apparently Mac Davis's advice to Dolly when the pair wrote the title track to *White Limozeen*, released in 1989. The song was the product of an evening at Davis' Beverly Hills mansion after she suggested they get together to write "like we're hungry again". Despite Dolly's glamorous film-star appearance on the sleeve, the album represented a decisive step away from the pop music Dolly had recorded as part of her initially successful bid for broader recognition. She was well aware that of her recent albums, it was the traditional sounds of *Trio* which attracted critical plaudits as well as large sales. Eschewing the services of a slick pop producer Dolly instead went for Ricky Skaggs, who had been a prodigious country star from boyhood. The choice probably had its origins in Skagg's recent TV guest appearance on *Dolly* but she had already recorded several songs with him and recognised his recent commercial success in the 'new country' field.

The title of one track, 'Take Me Back To The Country' seemed to sum up the album's intent and there was a general sense of relief among many reviewers including journalist Robert K. Oermann who celebrated the record in a *Tennessean* article entitled, "Dolly Rides Back Into Country In 'Limozeen'." Dolly sounded revitalised, with her voice expressing delicate emotional nuances and subtle inflections of mood in a way that the overbearing pop production values had constrained. The backing on the album complemented and enhanced her voice, rather than trying to compete with it and the sound was enriched courtesy of excellent session players like Bela Fleck (banjo) and Stuart Duncan (fiddle). Also noticeable by their presence were Lloyd Green and Paul Franklin, leading exponents of country music's signature instrument, the steel guitar.

The Top Five album produced two number one hit singles, the feisty 'Why'd You Come In Here Looking Like That?' – accompanied by a memorable video in which bit-part actors, each worse than the one before, audition for a film part, until a handsome janitor who comes on to clean the stage takes Dolly's eye – and 'Yellow Roses', a straightforward girl meets boy, girl loses boy song featuring an instantly catchy chorus.

Other standouts were the raunchily autobiographical title track, ("walking the streets from the breadlines to the headlines") and 'What Is It My Love?' a profile of a harsh, macho and insistently domineering lover. Apparently the idea came about after Avie Lee told Dolly about one of her brothers' undesirable traits.

The album's one overtly religious song, 'He's Alive', built up to an earth-shattering crescendo amid gospel singers, violins and Dolly giving her all. Though powerful and affecting for some,* it struck others as bombastic and out of place when placed against the country-oriented material. Dolly had first heard the song years before. "One time I was driving back from Los Angeles with Carl in his pickup and we had the radio on. They started to play this song. We both got quiet as a mouse. We both got chill bumps. We agreed it was a great song. We stopped at the closest phone booth and called the radio station. We got the name of the artist and the publisher." (The DJ read the details off the back of the album sleeve.) Dolly had wanted to record 'He's Alive' ever since first hearing it. "Ricky [Skaggs], he's very into his religion. We dug it out and he was familiar with it. It turned out to be the perfect time."

Wearing an impressive silver and white gown Dolly earned a standing ovation when performing the song at the 23rd Country Music Association Awards backed by the 90-strong Nashville Christchurch Pentecostal Choir. Dolly also sang it at the 21st Annual Dove Awards (Christian and gospel music) and doubtless aiming at a target audience, she stated, "I think gospel music is going to become a greater music than it has ever been, and I hope to be part of it."

By 1991 *White Limozeen* had gone gold marking the end of Dolly's prolonged dalliance with crossover pop. "After I crossed over and made million sellers like 'Here You Come Again', I lost my way," she admitted. Dolly later confessed that one of her career regrets was not being a consistently successful artist with regular platinum sales *à la* Elton John or Kenny Rogers. Perhaps the film projects resulted in her being unable to put in the necessary effort to maintain her music career. Then again it was her wish to be successful in other media.

Having a luxurious home on Hawaii, Dolly talked about opening a venue there where she could perform and support local talent. In the event she decided to invest in a Honolulu restaurant called the Dockside Plantation (DP also stood for Dolly Parton as she reminded reporters). For the opening ceremony a masquerade ball was thrown to which a host of

---

* When released as a single, 'He's Alive' made number 39.

celebrities were invited, including Tom Selleck who arrived in full *Magnum* gear with shorts, aloha shirt and Detroit Tigers baseball cap. The doors to the toilets were labelled Buoys and Gulls. In keeping with the punning theme, one journalist described it as "nautical, but nice".

Unfortunately the restaurant, like the television show, was doomed. According to one, possibly apocryphal story, Dolly turned up one night to find that it was fully booked, meaning she had to eat elsewhere. After she sold the Dockside Plantation Dolly claimed she had become involved with people who knew little more about running a restaurant than she did.

In 1989 Sandollar was responsible for *Common Threads: Stories From The Quilt*, which sought to raise awareness about the burgeoning AIDS pandemic. The film, which told the story of the disease using five different stories, woven together via the NAMES Project/AIDS Memorial Quilt, won an Oscar for Best Documentary. Though not directly involved in the project Dolly knew many gay people, some of whom, like Sandy Gallin, became close friends. She related to the sense of alarm which the disease caused among heterosexuals as well as homosexuals, admitting that she had been naive and ignorant on the subject up to that point. Though generally avoiding public controversy, when people known to her started dying of the disease, Dolly was prepared to use her name for AIDS awareness campaigns, despite the risk of alienating her more conservative religious fans who equated it with the "sin" of homosexuality.

In 1988 Dolly hosted the 22nd Country Music Association's Awards from Nashville. Given her long and distinguished career and TV friendly persona it was surprising she had not been asked before. As a writer observed, for the second half of the show, "Dolly changed into a light-pink gown with the traditional style that has accented her figure for several years . . . the neckline was cut to show the usual amount of cleavage and the hem was slashed to show the usual amount of leg."

"Parton carried virtually the entire Country Music Association telecast on her shoulders . . ." gushed Robert K. Oermann, "she was simply a marvel of wit, enthusiasm and spontaneity . . . from out of camera range, throughout the telecast, you could hear Parton shouting encouragement to her fellow performers, cheering them for their victories and congratulating them for their work." Dolly caused much amusement among the assembled throng of country notables when she sat upon Randy Travis' lap. Soon afterwards, when going up to accept the award for Male Vocalist Of The Year, Travis quipped, "After all that, I found myself trying to remember what award it was I was coming up to receive!" The event marked the show's first two-hour broadcast over the CBS network, while another first was the inauguration of the Vocal Event Of The Year Award to recognise an outstanding collaboration by two or more individual acts. The prize went to Dolly, Emmylou Harris and Linda Ronstadt for *Trio*.

While Dolly attracted good viewing figures from British television audiences, in contrast to American television personalities like Johnny Carson who were used to her full-on personality, less ebullient English talk show hosts and bemused fellow guests were sometimes reduced to silent compliance. On Michael Aspel's show in 1988 Dolly appeared as star guest alongside comedians Harry Enfield and Victoria Wood. After a badly mimed video of 'I Know You By Heart' was shown Dolly chattered non-stop about the topics most interviewers with only a superficial interest in her career raised: the years of struggle and weight problems – her waistline was about 19 inches and current weight about 107 pounds (yes, some of it had come off her chest); the female health worries that had plagued her but were now resolved (no, she would be unable to have children); her travails in the early Eighties (yes, she had thought about suicide and was not ashamed to say so but no, she would not have gone through with it but understood how people might resort to drugs and alcohol).

As she got into her stride Dolly virtually took over the show. The normally verbose Enfield and Wood were sidelined – partly by Dolly and partly by their English reserve. Dolly cut across their contributions, observing that she and Wood had big breasts, and started to address the audience directly, asking if they knew that Aspel, by now a guest on his own show, was the new host of the long-running *This Is Your Life*. As the credits rolled, when host and guests are usually seen exchanging relaxed banter after the microphones had been switched off, it was noticeable that Enfield and Wood were silent, looking slightly ill at ease.

Of more significance, 1988 saw the onstage reunion of Dolly with Porter Wagoner for the first time since their acrimonious parting in 1979. The occasion was a visit to Nashville of the *Dolly* show and the public reconciliation was all the more surprising since communication between the pair had taken place through lawyers (and Porter had never been invited onto any of the shows recorded in Los Angeles). There had been press speculation for months and a confirmatory announcement eventually appeared in *The Tennessean* in January, though what role Porter would be offered was not clear at that stage. Wagoner could not have failed to see the irony of the situation; 21 years after he agreed to have Dolly on his show, thus launching a career which soon surpassed his own, he was uncertainly awaiting the chance to appear with Dolly on her terms. It soon emerged that he would sing several duets with his erstwhile protégée. George Hamilton IV recalls the occasion. "All the Opry stars and old-timers like me and the new kids, everybody was there at the invitation of Dolly. She was most gracious to Porter. She gave him a featured spot and treated him like her mentor, the man that really started her career rolling. She had reserved VIP seats for all the Opry members' wives . . . she treated everybody as fellow stars. It was very noticeable that she hadn't forgotten her roots . . . Dolly never got above her raisin'."

For their first professional encounter in years Dolly arrived late after getting stuck in traffic. Legend has it that her first words to Porter were, "I know how punctual you are and how cranky you are when someone don't show up on time." This "funny fight" helped to break the ice and as soon as rehearsals started the pair found that the original chemistry was still there. Their segment, recorded at the Ryman Auditorium, was intercut with a clip of Dolly's first appearance on Porter's show, performing 'Dumb Blonde'. As well as singing a selection of their hits backed by the Wagonmasters, Dolly paid a glowing tribute to Wagoner's contribution to her career and the pair joked about their time on Porter's show, in particular the advertisements for laxatives and products for the relief of period pain. However, there was no prospect of either Dolly or Porter resurrecting their professional relationship other than for old time's sake even though many traditionalists would have wanted for nothing better. A week later Dolly again appeared with Porter at the Ryman, at a concert to celebrate Roy Acuff's 50th anniversary as a member of the cast of the Grand Ole Opry. Many other stars, including Minnie Pearl and Chet Atkins, were on hand to honour "Mr Roy" the revered elder statesman of country music and the Grand Ole Opry.

Around this time Dolly sought to acquire one of her former family homes – the log cabin in Locust Ridge – roughly ten miles from Dollywood, back up in the hills. As well as offering a chance to reconnect with her roots, the house would act as a retreat from the pressures of her hectic professional life. The current owners agreed to sell but for a premium price rumoured to be a massive $300,000 (though other reports quoted considerably lower figures). The property had been owned by Dolly's great-grandfather at the beginning of the 20th century, for which he apparently paid $150. Dolly set about renovating the cabin, which came with a large tract of land, but soon found that, despite being well off the beaten track, word of her acquisition had spread and sightseers started appearing in droves. A round-the-clock guard ensured that over enthusiastic snoopers were kept away and Don Warden complained that more was spent on security than on originally buying the property. At one stage there was even talk of ditching the project altogether if people continued to show up in big numbers.

Plans for the site included a guesthouse, a barn, a village store and a private church. Renovation work cost around half a million dollars – a long way from the days when Avie Lee had her "wish book". Carl and Dolly's brother Bobby were closely involved in the redesign, which doubled the size of the original cabin. Though the kitchen was fully modernised the original wood burning stove was retained. Dolly's description, "It's like I've gathered everything from my past and my childhood and made it into a village," gave the impression of a family theme park. When the work was completed, Dolly described her new investment in 1990 as "my own hillbilly heaven . . . my own little place, my refuge". She also said it brought back "a time of dreams and innocence and fantasy". The article contained exterior and interior photographs of the cabin in all its remodelled glory with Dolly posing in a variety of outfits. The picture of rustic charm was somewhat displaced by details of suppliers and prices for many of the household items on display, such as rugs and quilts, being provided at the end of the article.

Amid the never-ending industry awards bestowed on Dolly there were more idiosyncratic accolades. The world's chauffeurs, doormen, bellhops and maids voted Dolly one of the 10 Best Known People Of 1988 and there were also reports that a specially bred rose, with huge Day-Glo pink blooms, had been named after Dolly. More conventionally she was invited to appear on Bob Hope's 1988 Christmas special and sang 'Hard Candy Christmas'. That Dolly was regarded as an appropriate choice of guest by one of the most famous living Americans was yet another indication of just how far her appeal had travelled. According to some press reports Dolly's earnings that year (including song royalties and touring) reached $13 million. However, no matter how much money she earned, Dolly's tastes remained fairly basic. Though she might have been capable of earning more than Frank Sinatra at Las Vegas she was still happy to shop at K-Mart.

Despite the ups and downs of her first three Hollywood outings, Dolly appeared in *Steel Magnolias*, co-starring with Olympia Dukakis, Sally Field, Shirley MacLaine, Daryl Hannah and a young Julia Roberts. It seems one of the film's producers had seen Dolly's performance as a bubbly waitress in a *Dolly* skit and offered her the part of Truvy, the proprietor of a homely beauty salon in a small Southern town – the kind of one-woman operation which would not have been out of place in Sevierville. "You'll see the Dolly I would have been had I stayed at home. She has a good attitude, full of jokes, full of heart, and tries to keep the peace with everybody." As part of background preparation for the film Dolly learned how to cut hair and got to meet Lis Landrum (who knew Dolly from the Porter days) on whom her part was based. Once more Dolly postponed live concerts, planned for the summer, in order to fulfil her filming commitments.

Writer Robert Harling had a sister who suffered from a serious form of diabetes. After he mentioned how hard it was to become a successful writer in New York, his sister said she wished she could help him in some way. Not long after this conversation she died. Harling's loss inspired him to write the Broadway play that *Steel Magnolias* was based on, which led to him becoming a successful writer. Harling explained the film's title was a reference to strong women who sustain others through the hardest of times.

The story takes place in a prosperous, well-manicured American town where the type of horrors which blight cities – street crime, drugs, vandalism – are conspicuous by their absence. The film was shot in Natchitoches, Louisiana (renamed Chinquapin for the movie) a town with a population of around 20,000, which Harling described as "reassuringly resistant to what the rest of the world calls progress". The inhabitants are white, church-going and evidently well-to-do, the only black faces are those of servants. A group of women meet regularly at Truvy's beauty salon.* The film's mood is initially light-hearted as the characters are introduced to the audience – Dolly's screen husband, played by Sam Shepard, is a man of few words who takes little interest in his wife's business, preferring to work on cars (the resemblance to Carl was striking) – but changes dramatically when Julia Roberts' character (Shelby) has a hypoglycaemic fit. Medical intervention brings about temporary relief and Shelby goes on to have a baby (against medical advice) but following a relapse she falls into a coma and is maintained on life support for a time but the decision is eventually taken to switch it off.

The scenes without dialogue in the intensive care unit were particularly harrowing. In the interests of realism director Herbert Ross hired some of the doctors and nurses who tended Harling's sister to play themselves.

* The sign outside Truvy's soon became a target for Dolly souvenir hunters.

Though Dolly enlivened the film's early stages by offering another high-spirited version of herself, her lightweight role diminished as the more proven actors took over. Ross was quite hard on Dolly, making it clear that he did not think much of her ability. "Well hell, I know I can't act," she fired back. "It's your job to teach me how. You hired me to make money for you." In a later *Daily Mirror* interview Dolly said her lack of acting ability did not impact on the character of Truvy because "she's a pretty flamboyant lady and so am I. She has a great sense of humour, a big heart and a big mouth . . . and how different is that from me, specially the big mouth?" Dolly was again able to show off her new hourglass figure and her waistline seemed to have diminished even further. Her one-liner, "There's no such thing as natural beauty," seemed particularly apposite. Recalling a time when her sullen teenage son brought a girlfriend home, Dolly quipped, "The nicest thing I can say is that all her tattoos were spelt correctly."

Once more Dolly was reminded about the drearier aspects of film-making. "You come to work at eight and then sit around and you might get around to doin' somethin' at three in the afternoon. I'm not used to waitin' around." *Steel Magnolias* was made on a budget of $25 million during a scorching hot Louisiana summer but the stars each had an air-conditioned mobile home on location as a dressing room; the producer made sure that all were the same size and colour in order to avoid any flaring egos. Dolly made use of her spare time by writing songs, though unlike her previous films she had no musical input into the soundtrack. To make her stay more pleasurable Carl stayed with Dolly for about five weeks and other members of the family also visited the set. The original accommodation provided for her was next to a lake where she was disturbed at all hours by a flotilla of boats with friendly neighbours shouting, "Hello Dolly." She eventually moved to a secluded property in some woods, accompanied by Judy Ogle, a bodyguard and her wig stylist David Blair.* Though she wanted privacy Dolly endeavoured to ingratiate herself with locals, shaking hands and posing for photographs now and again. When the other stars left the set, people would clap and wave, but when Dolly left they went wild. To show her appreciation, she sang *9 To 5* at the opening game of the local football season.

Frank Woodward, who was in charge of catering on the set, complained about the stars' idiosyncratic food requests with some items having to be

* In a sure case of exaggeration, Blair was later quoted that he had designed nearly 10,000 wigs for Dolly in 13 years.

specially ordered and flown in at considerable expense. Dolly, who liked plain Southern fare, and Sally Field were the only actors who ate what he regarded as normal food. Olympia Dukakis favoured macrobiotic grains, and Herbert Ross had a penchant for sushi and asparagus wrapped with fresh prosciutto. Food was not the only source of extravagance. In one scene involving an Easter egg hunt the levee behind the Chamber of Commerce was adorned with hundreds of silk crocuses, tulips, irises and daisies, which were stuck into the ground over the riverbank. Ross demanded hydrangeas, azaleas and begonias in bloom at the same time, seemingly oblivious to the fact that nature made this impossible. For the Christmas scenes, shot in 104-degree heat, 250 silk poinsettias were bought in.

The economy in Natchitoches received a major boost with the sudden influx of manpower required to make a film; one local businessman was quoted as saying that everyone in the town was earning one way or another from the film. Dolly and Darryl Hannah attended a premiere of *Steel Magnolias* at the movie theatre in Natchitoches. Two showings on four separate screens were needed to accommodate all those who wanted to be part of the festivities. At a press conference Dolly was asked what she thought of the film. "Well, I loved it. It's like asking a parent if they think their kids are pretty."

Reviews were mixed; widespread opinion considered the film to be a clever piece of populist cinema with a strong enough cast to render the whole enterprise likeable. *The Tennessean's* film critic described it as "a rare combination of high comedy and emotional romp". Writing in the *Daily Express*, Ian Christie felt the film lacked gravitas. "It adds up to a calculated assault on the emotions, expertly planned by director Herbert Ross and efficiently carried out by the cast, who bring all the shallowness to their roles that the script demands." One reviewer saw *Steel Magnolias* as a film for women, describing it as "an entertaining tribute to the oft-underestimated power of female friendships."

Dolly's performance was neither highly praised nor heavily criticised – both cinemagoers and movie reviewers found it hard to dislike her. The female cast seemed to gel remarkably well as Sally Field said, "We became a unit." Shirley MacLaine described their on-set relationship as "emotional democracy". To help Dolly laugh convincingly in one scene it was rumoured the other women did things which Field said could make them vulnerable to blackmail, namely simulating sex acts with inanimate objects. Field also sat next to Prince Charles and Princess Diana when the film was chosen as 1990's Royal Film Premiere and noticed that Diana cried during the film and that Charles was visibly moved.

*Steel Magnolias* was quite possibly the best film Dolly starred in but it marked the end of her involvement with major Hollywood films. Although having proved herself able to hold her own in the company of exalted company, it was clear Dolly was never going to be a great actress and the mechanics of film making she did not care for. Subsequent screen appearances would be restricted to all manner of television appearances and made-for-TV movies.

Meanwhile Dollywood was going from strength to strength. In 1989 it was reported that appearances by 35 stars and 200 special events were fitted into 123 days during the previous season. New attractions were being added each year and the park was now established as one of the main visitor attractions in Tennessee, much to the delight of local officials and tourism executives who were grateful for the continued boost it provided to the local economy (some called Dolly the Queen of East Tennessee). During opening weekend of the 1989 season an accident involving a new ride called the Thunder Express resulted in minor injuries to around 20 passengers. Dolly and Porter continued their series of sporadic reunions with a sold-out Dollywood appearance. In complete contrast to the old days it was Porter who left the stage after a few numbers. In one reporter's view, "It was easy to tell why Parton and Wagoner had to part ways. Wagoner seemed to want to slow the tempos, bouncing his hands like Lawrence Welk; Parton looked as if she was trying to hold back her boundless energy."

Although Dollywood was first and foremost a commercial operation, a philanthropic element was also being cultivated which aimed to improve the chances in life for local teenagers. Though Dolly herself had openly admitted to disliking her schooldays, she wanted to do her bit in persuading youngsters to gain maximum benefit from the education system. She recalled that her father was hindered by his lack of schooling, being unable to fill out forms, decipher labels or read stories to his children. It was a loss for Dolly and her siblings and a source of shame for Lee. In 1988 the Dollywood Foundation, a non-profit public organisation, was formed with the aim of encouraging and enabling more students from Sevier County to stay at school. Its motto: "Education, the key to a better life." Apart from donations and grants, funding came in the form of the high profile concerts given by Dolly and others at Dollywood each year. In 1988 and 1989 guests included Tammy Wynette, the Bellamy Brothers, Bill Monroe and Ricky Skaggs.

The Foundation's first major initiative, the Buddy Program, which ran from 1988 until 1993, was launched at the start of Dollywood's third season when around 1,500 Sevier County Seventh and Eighth grade pupils were invited to attend a seminar at the Celebrity Theater. The proposal put to them was that by forming a "buddy" relationship with a friend, the pair should encourage each other to stay at school until graduating. A contract (featuring Dolly's photograph and a facsimile of her signature) setting out the agreement would be signed and if the 'buddies' managed to stay the course then each would receive $1,000 from Dolly herself. Dolly rejected criticisms that the scheme legitimised bribery. "Every child needs an incentive and money is something they understand." She was also criticised by Sevier County residents who felt her efforts made them sound poor. "Well, I realise there are a lot of wealthy people in this area, and it's people like them that need to put their money where their mouth is and help these kids."

The blueprint was similar to the buddy system used in certain rehabilitation schemes where a recovering alcoholic or addict turns to a fellow member when he or she was tempted to lapse. The Buddy Program was credited with contributing to a reduction in Sevier County's dropout rate from over 30% to less than 15% by 1993.*

Dolly spoke in support of the Buddy Program at the opening of the East Tennessee Education Association's Convention in Knoxville which was attended by over 1,000 teachers. She particularly encouraged them to pay attention to pupils who might be embarrassed because their family lacked the things other families had. She quoted a recent example to illustrate her point: a boy who was in constant fights because of a body odour problem making him a magnet for ridicule. School personnel discovered that he had no mother, no indoor plumbing and therefore, no way to wash himself or his clothes properly. The problem was solved by the boy being given a locker next to the showers so that he could wash.

Dolly pointed out that one of her problems as a child was the considerable number of chores she had on top of her homework which remained a problem for children from poor backgrounds. Dolly later expressed the more intangible ways in which she hoped schools could contribute to the holistic development of children. "I'd like to see all of our schools begin in

---

* Other curricula in the Dollywood Foundation have included a pilot first-grade teacher assistant programme, adding a teacher and assistant for the county's Alternative Learning programme, computer labs for a Principles of Alphabet Literacy programme and emergency support for children in need of school clothes and supplies. In addition, a series of scholarships were instituted giving high school graduates who met the requirements of their chosen colleges, financial assistance of up to $1,000 or more with their further education.

the early grades to teach children to feel good about themselves; to have self-esteem, to set goals and dreams, to make each student feel special, and to somehow let them know that dreams can come true."

The Dollywood Foundation initiatives were by no means the first or last occasions on which Dolly provided support for good causes. Major donations had their potential publicity benefits but regardless of the extent to which this may have been a motivation, a considerable number of worthy causes benefited from her munificence. In May 1987 Dolly opened the Dolly Parton Wellness and Rehabilitation Center in the Sevier County Medical Center and also made a grant of $100,000 to the Dr Robert F. Thomas Foundation which raises funds to support the Center. The church at Dollywood displays a letter from Dolly as National Chairperson of the Dr Robert F. Thomas Foundation. In it she says, "Dr Thomas was a man of varied talents, a man of infinite love and compassion, abundant energy, contagious enthusiasm, genuine humility and great vision, a friend, a neighbour, counsellor, minister and doctor to the people of Sevier County for over 50 years. His dream was to put an end to pain and suffering. The Foundation aims to ensure continued growth and improvement in medical care for the people of Sevier County, but also to visitors to the mountains."

In 1989, during a two-week stay at the Breakers, Florida, Dolly performed three shows for IBM employees at the Royal Poinciana Playhouse. She apparently seldom left her suite and relied on room-service for meals, though she did throw a party for her one-year-old niece, Hannah, daughter of Rachel Dennison. Early in 1990 Dolly appeared with Kenny Rogers at the Mirage Hotel in Las Vegas for a week-long engagement as part of an extensive tour (Dolly's first for some years) and media blitz to support *White Limozeen*. There were two shows per night at 7.30 and 11.30 p.m. and the price per ticket, including cocktails, was $50. The lavishly extravagant show opened with a multi-media presentation combining still and action footage of the pair's careers projected onto seven geometrically shaped screens. Dolly wore a tight rhinestone-studded Lycra outfit with the type of sporty mini skirt worn by ice skaters. After 'Islands In The Stream' the pair sang 'Something Inside So Strong', a song about human rights and the need for global peace, in which a large choir took part courtesy of the large video screens. Once more there was irony in Dolly singing 'Coat Of Many Colors' to 1,500 well-heeled tourists in a $640 million hotel. One critic felt the show turned both artists into artificial superheroes. Another felt that Dolly had the rare ability to be as Hollywood as she wanted to be without losing her roots. Michael

Paskevich felt the band, featuring four electric guitarists, was over the top, particularly since they didn't get a chance to stretch out and show off their skills.

Dolly invariably included some gospel material ("I never feel right if I don't do a song to praise Him before I finish a concert") but despite the inclusion of authentic country instruments in Dolly's 10-strong "Mighty Fine Band" as she dubbed it (her first full road group since Gypsy Fever), a reviewer compared the intrusion of Dolly's disco-type songs to a fast-food joint's styrofoam cup suddenly washing up on a bank of a pure country stream.

In 1990 only one new Dolly album was released, a Christmas song collection *Home For Christmas* including 'O Little Town Of Bethlehem', 'Rudolph The Red Nosed Reindeer' and 'Joy To The World'. Though it made little impact on the charts that year, it sold well enough over subsequent years to go gold in 1994. Despite Dolly's iconic status, her star at Columbia was waning. However, the entrance in the early Nineties of a talented musician and producer was destined to become a key element in most of her subsequent output.

# ACT IV

# Full Circle
# (1990–2006)

# Chapter 22

BY the start of the Nineties much of the ground established by female country artists such as Dolly, Barbara Mandrell, Crystal Gayle and the Judds had been lost to a new breed of young, glamorous male singers including Clint Black, Alan Jackson and, above all, Garth Brooks.* Reba McEntire was just about the only female artist able to go head to head with the boys when it came to record and concert ticket sales. Dolly was still a respected figure and her competitive streak remained undiminished, despite the fact that, in her mid forties, she was older than the opposition. In 1992 she told Terry Wogan that with her "youthful spirit and good attitude" she was always evolving and doing her best to keep up with the times. "As old as yesterday, as new as tomorrow," was how she put it.

Dolly was rarely played on modern country radio but was able to ensure at least some airplay for herself (and other artists of a certain vintage) by buying her own radio station, WSEV in Sevierville. It was a particularly pleasing acquisition since it was the first station she broadcast from when she was a child. She also owned radio WDLY, broadcasting from "Radio Square" in Dollywood, one of the main jingles being, "Hi! This is Dolly! Thanks for turning me on."†

In 1990 Dolly took part in the *Jerry Lewis Labor Day Telethon*, a non-stop variety show lasting almost 24 hours, to raise money for research into muscular dystrophy. She recorded a version of 'My Tennessee Mountain Home' at Dollywood with children afflicted by the condition and a video of the occasion was shown during the Telethon. Dolly also headed a list of country singers who signed giant Christmas cards sent to members of the Tennessee National Guard serving in the Persian Gulf. It was widely reported in the local press that Dolly had written to Corporal Mark Watson who had mentioned in a previous letter home that a note from

---

* By the end of the Eighties the women's share of chart figures amounted to around 30% (an increase on previous decades when it fell as low as 10%) but by 1990 this had fallen back to approximately 12%.
† Both stations were subsequently sold in 2000 when Dolly felt she had taken them as far as she could.

Dolly would cheer him up. Striking a tone which went down particularly well among the many patriots in her home region Dolly wrote, "While we are here in our homes being decorated for Christmas and enjoying our mountain scenery, you are in a completely different world protecting our right to decorate our homes, to worship as we want, and all our many other rights of freedom which we do often take for granted." In a well-reported meeting Dolly met at her office Melissa Ellison, a girl suffering from spina bifida. While the cameras clicked, Dolly gave her a Dolly doll and other gifts to take home.*

Dolly was alert to any opportunity to generate favourable publicity no matter how minor. While performing in Phoenix she dedicated 'Applejack' to "Doug and Rose", the names of two fans she had met for a matter of seconds during a flurry of photo flashes and handshakes earlier in the evening. One reviewer commented drily, "That, dear students of public relations, is known as being a total professional in the entertainment biz. Chalk up another album sale."

However, there were occasions when Dolly's public pronouncements demonstrated questionable taste which might have been attributable to her penchant for memorable one-liners over bland platitudes. When attending a charity bash in Los Angeles for LIFE (Love Is Feeding Everyone) co-founded by actor Dennis Weaver, Dolly's remark that, in her case, LIFE stood for "Lord I'm fat enough" somehow did not sit happily with the worthy image of an organisation fighting starvation. When handed singer Juice Newton's two-week-old baby, Dolly said, "Oh lord, I can see the cover of the *Enquirer* now: 'Dolly Parton adopts baby.'"

Even the most mundane activities in Dolly's life attracted attention. When attending the Southern Hills Medical Center for an eye examination a legion of doctors and members of staff flocked to catch a glimpse of her. As always in such situations, Dolly was cordial and bestowed smiles and autographs though, if it had suited her, she could have slipped into the hospital, with minimum fuss, as many celebrities prefer to do.

Not all of the publicity Dolly received was entirely welcome. Tabloids such as the ever-present *Enquirer* appeared to be fixated with (in no particular order) her figure, health and marriage with the same stories being recycled roughly every year or so. Sometimes there were new concoctions, such as a 1991 *News Of The World* report, claiming that Dolly had a half-sister called Laura. This was credible in view of Lee Parton's admitted indiscretions but how true the story – that Dolly was living a life of luxury

---

* By 1990, around 400,000 Dolly dolls had been sold.

in Brentwood while her relation languished nearby in poverty – remains unverified. At one point a relation of Dolly's went to the tabloids with stories of Dolly's health being jeopardised by leaking breast implants and also offered graphic allegations about Dolly's ill-treatment of Carl and her affairs with actors and singers. The stories had little or no credibility and it was assumed the relative in question was simply out to make money. Given the size of the extended Parton family it was perhaps surprising that there were not more examples of such behaviour. Dolly said she suspected her female relative was offended after not receiving an invitation to a party Dolly threw in Nashville around the time of *Rhinestone*. Another story claimed Dolly was furious because a cousin had appeared topless in a girly magazine – a report that got repeated in other papers before it emerged that Dolly had no knowledge of the cousin in question. The story was used by at least one tabloid as a pretext for informing its readers that Dolly had turned down highly lucrative offers to pose nude for soft porn magazines.

Dolly became philosophical about such muck raking, joking that when reading the tabloids she believed everything they printed except the stories about herself. She had issued letters of rebuttal in the past, particularly when family members were involved but her general rule was to maintain a dignified silence, though if a story happened to break when she was on tour she occasionally took the opportunity to deny it to her audience. "You never get used to being embarrassed. You never get used to being hurt . . . but you get more used to it." There was talk at one stage that she might join forces with Cher, Roseanne Barr and Elizabeth Taylor in taking out a court action against certain newspapers but Dolly did not see this as worthwhile. "I won't spend my time dealing with negative things." Dolly was aware that while she might not actively court it, bad publicity was better than no publicity. "It keeps me hot," she told Larry King. "I don't care what they say, because you don't ever know if it's the truth or a lie in the tabloids." In another interview she conceded, "Some of it gets distorted . . . but it's all based on some sort of truth."

Despite her aversion to supporting overtly political causes or making socially controversial statements, in 1990 Dolly attended a party, along with 14,000 other well-wishers, in support of the Democratic Governor-Elect Ann Richards of Austin, Texas, who aimed to return government to the people. Other celebrities in attendance included Willie Nelson, Kris Kristoffersen and Cybill Shepherd. Democrat politician Al Gore's wife Tipper was prominently involved in a campaign to have warning notices placed on CDs containing lyrics deemed unsuitable for children, a campaign which divided opinions along conservative and liberal lines. It was reported in the Sevierville *Mountain Press* that Dolly disapproved of certain lyrics in rap songs which she deemed to be obscene. "It's like talking dirty in front of your momma and daddy or your brothers and sisters," she said, ". . . I believe when something gets that vulgar that it has some influence on kids . . . it is an influence in a bad way . . . such music should be looked into and considered." Although some of her own lyrics had been regarded as controversial, they were not written "just to be dirty".

Dollywood continued to develop and each new season brought further attractions to pull in the crowds. In 1990 a refurbished Dentzel carousel, approximately 100 years old, was acquired. The staff were protective of the new acquisition to the extent that people wearing damp clothes from one of the water rides, were provided with specially installed dryers before being allowed on board. Dollywood opened at Christmas for the first time and the park was transformed into a winter wonderland with the impressive sight of Santa's workshop, 500,000 lights and a 50-foot Christmas tree. An ABC television special *Dolly Parton . . . Christmas At Home*, which Dolly described as "the most expensive home movie ever", turned out to be something of a family reunion with her mother, father, brothers and sisters, about a dozen aunts and uncles and 15 or so nieces and nephews all taking part. A notable absentee was Carl. Dolly said that he had paid a visit but ". . . then I guess he'd had enough and went on . . . he was supportive. He hung out for a day or two. But it was a little too much family for him." Dolly revealed that she would open her gifts in Sevierville on Christmas Eve and then spend Christmas Day back in Nashville with Carl's family.

At the time Dolly was preparing for the Christmas special it was reported that she would no longer wear real fur – being converted by recent protests on behalf of various animal welfare groups. A one-hour radio version of the show (which featured such ditties as 'Santa Claus Is Going On A Diet' and 'Grandma Got Run Over By A Reindeer') was also broadcast worldwide via the Voice of America, the Armed Forces Network and the BBC to a potential audience running into hundreds of millions in over 100 countries.

Dolly also released *Home For Christmas*, an album in fact recorded that July. Dolly had the "big idea" that the musicians and production team would not be able to get into the Yuletide spirit unless the studio was decorated and the air-conditioning was turned down low to feel more like Christmas. A dinner was also organised and participants brought each

other gifts. The album included 'We Three Kings', one of Dolly's favourite hymns, because it reminded her of the melodies from old Irish and
English folk songs which in turn resembled the Appalachian songs she sang
when growing up, "songs that my mama taught me with the harmonies
that came from the Old World . . ." and Christmas standards such as
'Rudolf The Red Nosed Reindeer', 'The First Noel' and 'Jingle Bells'.
The album eventually achieved gold status in 1994.

Plans for a Dollywood 2 in Japan were announced during this time. An
initial agreement was signed with a Tokyo company to negotiate the
development of a Dollywood Theme Park in Ibaraki Prefecture, about
40 miles north of the city. The idea was to build seven major theme parks,
to be connected by common transportation systems, serving a population
of some 40 million people, thus creating one of the largest holiday destinations in the world. A delegation from America travelled to Japan and a
spokesman for the Japanese company said, "This park will be a great move
towards US and Japanese friendship, as well as presenting an opportunity
for further adoration of Dolly by her fans in Japan." For all the preparation
the project did not proceed.

In the midst of this came a newspaper report that Dollywood had been
fined $10,000 for overworking young staff. Apparently investigators found
80 violations of child labour laws with a number of teenage employees,
some as young as 14, found to be working longer hours than was legally
permissible. Dolly was said to be very angry.* *The Tennessean* also reported
that Frieda Parton had filed a workers' compensation lawsuit against
Dollywood as a result of an injury to her back said to have been sustained
when closing a dressing room door in summer 1989. Dollywood paid her
the maximum statutory benefits and also covered medical expenses.

For the opening of Dollywood's sixth season in 1991, not long after the
conclusion of the Gulf War, the annual opening parade through the streets
of Pigeon Forge was patriotically themed as a "Salute to the American
Spirit" with red, white and blue much in evidence. Over 20,000 people
lined the streets of Pigeon Forge to view the parade which took over two
hours to pass through. As before, the opening weekend was a heavily publicised media event, involving Dolly wearing 30 outfits, changing into
different costumes up to 10 times each day. One of the new educational

* Although Dollywood's staff are not highly paid and have to work fairly long hours, the
park has an admirable policy of hiring older staff. This is not solely for altruistic reasons but
rather a recognition of the qualities of experience and skills brought to the job. Most
employees have other work to move on to when the Dollywood season comes to an end.

attractions was the Eagle Mountain Sanctuary, which aimed to provide a home for injured eagles and to hatch baby eagles for release into the wild. The sanctuary was not only seen as a logical extension of Dollywood's basic theme – the heritage and traditions of the Smoky Mountains but also, in a canny move, the bald eagle symbolised the most treasured of all American traditions, freedom. Headlining guests for the opening concert in 1991 included Bob Hope and Alabama with proceeds going, as usual, to the Dollywood Foundation.*

The following year there was some controversy when Jane Fonda and husband Ted Turner were invited to attend the opening of Show Street at Dollywood. Many people, particularly in the conservative rural south, had never forgiven Jane for visiting North Vietnam at the height of the war in 1972, a stunt which earned her the epithet, "Hanoi Jane". Vietnam veterans in particular were outraged and threatened protests. In the event Jane decided to bow out as she and Dolly both thought it was for the best. Dolly was philosophical, "Everybody doesn't share the same point of view . . . and the show goes on."

Dolly and Carl's silver wedding anniversary fell on May 30, 1991, but unsurprisingly, there was no big celebration to mark the event; as a friend reportedly said, "To Carl, three's a crowd and four's a mob." For previous anniversaries the couple had gone to the laundromat where they first met, sat in the car and eaten some of their favourite fast food, perhaps a burger and fries from Krystals, but the building had been torn down to make way for a car park. Reflecting on her marriage Dolly said, "The word divorce has never been mentioned. In all our time together we've never said it – not even once . . . We both know when we've had enough of each other. He'll start sayin' things like, 'Honey, when are you gonna visit so-and-so?' or 'When are you goin' to do this?' and I'll say to him, 'What you're really askin' is when I'm goin' to leave, not soon enough?' We both know the time to go, the time when we've gotten bored with each other. But instead of lying, we have the sort of relationship where we can say things to each other . . . We're together just enough to keep it excitin'.'"

Interviewer Gill Pringle raised the issue of infidelity and Dolly provided another of her evasive replies. "Variety makes the world go round . . . as long as you're not hurting other people and you're enhancing life, which in turn enhances the life of other people. Let's put it this way, if we cheat

---

* The three previous benefit concerts, where fans paid up to $500 for a ticket, had raised around $500,000 for various causes.

we don't know it. So if we do cheat, it's very healthy for both of us."
Similarly, when the issue of whether Carl was jealous of the famous men
Dolly associated with she did not give much away. "Everyone thinks I've
screwed Burt and Sly, but Carl and I love each other." Dolly claimed that
they had never experienced any major falling out in all their time together.
"I might say to him, 'Go on, Carl, get right outta here and go somewhere,'
and he'll do that. We just cool it. But through all our years we've never
had major troubles." Many commentators have inevitably described Dolly
and Carl's set up as an open marriage. "Well, no, I have an open heart and
an open mind and sometimes I talk too much and I'm joking and people
take it the way they want to hear it."

While Dolly appeared to flirt with men quite readily her glamorous
image must surely have acted as an insuperable barrier to matters developing much further; in addition Carl was in the background giving Dolly the
perfect excuse for backing off. This did not mean, however, that she could
not get close to other men. "If I see somebody I'm fascinated by, we will
share a kind of relationship through conversation, through whatever we
feel is necessary, but it's always plain there's Carl, the one man I want to
grow old with."

In between recording sessions and tours Dolly regularly got away from
it all when she and Carl would pack their camper van and tour the
country, eating at roadside diners and enjoying the simple thrill of being an
ordinary married couple. Dolly disguised herself by foregoing make-up
and fancy clothes. When staying at run-of-the-mill motels, she would wait
in the van with the dog while Carl went in to register.

By the start of the Nineties, Dolly's song catalogue was in a mess. Stella
Parton: "I took three years out of my career to make sure that her publishing catalogue, every one of her songs, was cleaned up and that all of her
lyric sheets and lead sheets and the publishing and copyrighting and everything was brought up to par, because 100 years from now people may not
remember me but they'll go back into the files and they'll find a Dolly
Parton song and say, 'This is what this woman did.' I felt it was important
that someone who knew her as well as I do and who was a musician as
well, did that for her. Dolly has been so busy with her career and she's not
a good organiser of paper and filing and stuff like that, and she had
depended on other people to run her publishing company all those years
and they had not done a good job. It had been very neglected. I wanted to
make sure the lyrics were right because a lot of secretaries would type up
stuff and use the wrong word; you know I could talk to you in East

Tennessee dialect and you would miss certain words and you would think I said this when in fact I said that. I went over every lyric sheet to make sure every word was right and then I recorded over 500 of her songs, some of what I thought were her best, and I expanded the catalogue and did as many male versions and female versions as I could to make it a better catalogue."

While her younger sister was making these efforts on her behalf, Dolly started recording *Eagle As She Flies* with producer Steve Buckingham. The two had met the year before at the Nashville studio complex where Buckingham (then vice president of A&R for Columbia) was co-producing Ricky Skaggs' album *Kentucky Thunder* at the same time as Skaggs was producing Dolly's *White Limozeen*. "Dolly called and asked me to come in and have a meeting one day," Buckingham recalled. "She wanted to produce her own album and wanted to use her musicians, her band that she was playing with on the road, but the big wheels at Sony told her she couldn't do it, they said she would have to have a co-producer and then some of these so called big wheels said that they would be the perfect person to co-produce it with her and they wanted x amount of dollars and x amount of points and you know they were just, in her mind, and as she described it to me, kind of horning in on her deal . . . she asked me if I would help her and I said 'Yeah I'll help in any way I can but I don't want points, I don't want money, I don't even want credit as a co-producer.'"

Buckingham was an able musician as well as producer and had worked in many fields of music from jazz to Americana, R&B to country. His breakthrough as a producer came with 'I Love The Nightlife', a huge disco hit in 1978 for Alicia Bridges. He was flexible and empathetic, able to understand Dolly's vision and facilitate the musical goals she was working towards. The fact that she might want to include a range of styles on one album presented no difficulty to him.

"So then came the time to go in the studio to start recording," Buckingham continues, "and I thought it would be one of those things where I'd just sort of show up as a cheerleader from time to time, 'Sounds great', that kind of thing and I got there the first day and I could tell that they really did need help getting things organised. She was depending on one of her musicians to kind of pull it together and I don't think he'd ever really produced something this big on his own so to make a long story short I did pitch in and was there every day and suggested a few things. We did a duet with Ricky Van Shelton, a very big name at the time who I was producing. We cut the song that her brother

Floyd wrote, 'Rockin' Years' and one thing led to another and the album came out great."

Buckingham got first-hand experience of how generous Dolly could be with her musical team. "Dolly had pretty much given all of her points away to her band. I had not asked for points or credit or anything and she called me and said she was sending me something in the mail, and also that I was listed as co-producer. She took that upon herself and then sent me a cheque out of her own pocket as if I had been paid the regular royalty points as producer; and it didn't come from Sony it came from her, I mean I know that for a fact."

It was the starting point for a working relationship which has prospered ever since. However, Buckingham soon discovered that the executives at Columbia did not share his enthusiasm for Dolly despite her iconic status and ongoing popularity. "It was from then on she trusted me. I certainly believed in her but it was at a time when there weren't a lot of people in the hierarchy at Sony, particularly in New York, that did believe in her any more. They in fact called me out of a studio as we were working on the album and questioned me. I was producing other acts for the label and they were saying why was I spending time on this project and I said I think she still sings great, I think she still writes great and I was kind of called on the carpet for doing this, and then *Eagle As She Flies* went platinum and then when we got ready to work on our second album, *Slow Dancing With The Moon*, even though the first went platinum, they called me on the carpet again and said why are you taking time up doing this stuff. So it was kinda like we felt it was us against them."

It seems the executives were more impressed by current darlings Clint Black and Garth Brooks who they saw as the future. "It certainly wasn't because of her talent," says Buckingham. "It never went away, she never lost the pipes, the talent to write." Their professional involvement came at a time when Buckingham was becoming disillusioned with his job. He recalls occasional visits from the president of Sony who would arrive along with other executives from New York. "They would call everyone into the boardroom and I remember some of the things that were said specifically and I walked back to the studio the first time and that was when, in my mind, I started letting go my attachment to the company. At that time I was on a roll. I had signed a number of artists and I was producing a lot of the platinum artists."

From some of their comments Steve realised that he was expendable. "I jokingly said, when I was being questioned about why I was putting so much time in on [Dolly]. 'Well if I'm wrong, when you're down here next time, you can tell me I was wrong.' The comment was made to me, 'If you're wrong you won't be here next time.' It was like the light bulb went off over my head . . . Dolly read me like a book. When I walked back to the studio she asked what was wrong. I said nothing was wrong but she said, 'I know you better than that,' and so I told her and she said, 'We'll do something on our own,' which kind of put the bug in my ear of 'There is another way to do this' and down the road, when they said they would let her start her own label, Blue Eye, she said she would do it if I could be her partner and that's what led me to start pulling away.

"I was ready to get out of the business when Dolly first met with me . . . I was burned out. I had done a lot of R&B, a lot of pop, I moved to Nashville not really to get into country but I just kind of fell into it. The first artist I produced was Tammy Wynette . . . I landed [at Columbia] on the run and never looked back but by the end of the Eighties it was that constant pressure of singles that made it on radio that wore me out every week. I was with some friends, saying I had to do something different or I was going to have a nervous breakdown or heart attack. I wasn't made for this assembly line way of making music so I was seriously considering moving home, don't know what I'd have done, didn't have a plan . . . [Dolly] walks in and says 'Let's do this together', that type of thing, and we got on a roll."

The first fruits of their collaboration *Eagle When She Flies* made number one in the country charts and by 1992 had attained platinum status. The album, for which Dolly wrote nine of the 11 songs, retained a predominantly country feel (aided by the cover shots of Dolly in a wheat field) but also included pop-oriented material such as the poignant ballad 'Wildest Dreams', written by Dolly and Mac Davis, and Bill Owens' 'Dreams Do Come True', a song notable for its steamy lyrics. 'Best Woman Wins' was a duet with Lorrie Morgan, whose praises Dolly had been singing since the mid Eighties, and she had encouraged Sandy Gallin to assist with Lorrie's career. On a champagne flight to Los Angles in 1990 Dolly hatched the unusual idea of writing a duet for two women. According to some reports the song was inspired by the triangular situation involving Donald and Ivana Trump and the woman who would become his new wife, Marla Maples. Dolly sang the album's title track at the 25th CMA Awards show in the presence of President George Bush, but despite approval from the nation's leader, even in 1991, some Southern radio stations were reluctant to play a song which was perceived by some to be directly supportive of women's lib. Dolly said, "I think women will relate to it, and I think men will appreciate it." 'Eagle When She Flies' was originally written as a theme for *Steel Magnolias* but was not used, probably because it would have given Dolly too much prominence over her fellow female co-stars.*

There had been reports prior to the album's release that Dolly had visited rock'n'roll legend Carl Perkins and written with him. Of the songs worked on, 'Family' (written by Dolly and Carl) was a powerful meditation on how people can choose friends and lovers but not members of their own family; both had extensive experience of the subject, while hit single 'Silver And Gold' was written by Carl, Greg and Stan Perkins. The original intention was for Dolly to record 'Rockin' Years' with George Jones but Columbia apparently decided against this when Jones moved to MCA so Ricky Van Shelton was chosen instead. The schmaltzy video accompanying 'Rockin' Years', illustrating how people should always stay together, featured idealised shots of children exchanging an innocent kiss and an older couple resting on a veranda.

Reviews of *Eagle When She Flies* were generally favourable with many expressing approval that Dolly had kept things country. Writing in *Country Music People* Craig Baguley commented, "When she does return from the synth-wrapped junk of the rock scene to her musical heritage she seems to do so without alienating her grass roots support." Dolly too recognised the steadfastness of country fans. "They're definitely more loyal, and that's 'cause they're good, stable people to begin with. They've got their work and their families and after that, if they're devoted to you, they are devoted forever. The public doesn't really get to know their rock heroes. Rock artists themselves just usually go onstage and then immediately leave because there is such screaming and hollering. It's a different kind of audience. Rock fans will tear you to shreds, they get so excited. They'll have a different poster hanging in their bedroom every six months, and while country fans may not love their artists any better, they love them a lot longer."

In 1991 Dolly starred in *Wild Texas Wind* playing a Texan swing singer Thiola – known as "Big T" – who is swept off her feet by an apparently charming club owner who turns out to be a man given to sudden violent rages.† Dolly empathised with victims of domestic violence and had written songs exploring why certain women are drawn to abusive men.

---

* The song was accompanied by a memorable video featuring numerous shots of people from different races and backgrounds.
† It was reported that the original title for the film was to be *Big T* but NBC made it clear they were not going to back a film starring Dolly Parton under that name!

"There's a silent epidemic of abused women . . . they tolerate violence for the wrong reasons. Some even think it shows men are jealous and love them."* In approaching her role Dolly was aided by the fact that the abusive relationship at the film's heart reminded her of the struggles faced by Patsy Cline and Loretta Lynn, as well as several women she knew while growing up in East Tennessee. Despite spending two hours in make-up each day, Dolly's injuries looked only superficially convincing (a critic commented, "The bruises look mostly like a variation on her usual shellacked make-up job"), not least because her platinum blonde wig was carefully coiffured as always.

*Wild Texas Wind* was closely followed in 1992 with *Straight Talk,* an unlikely story about main character Shirlee Kenyon arriving in the big city after splitting from her partner. Due to a series of improbable occurrences, she is mistaken for a clinical psychologist and finds herself hosting a radio phone-in programme where she summarily dispenses common sense to help resolve the woes of her callers. In this respect Dolly was once more playing herself. Even the film's bedroom scene fitted Dolly's public image; tantalising suggestiveness but with the real action firmly out of view. Dolly compared it to "knowing your sister is making love with somebody. You know she's getting married, but you don't want to hear about the honeymoon. I think my audiences . . . don't want to see me in an uncomfortable situation, because it makes them uncomfortable."

The screenplay's tortuous journey to fruition gave an insight into the machinations of the industry and how scripts can earn money simply by an option being taken out on them. Dolly had originally been offered the script about seven years before but was unable to immediately commit because Sandy Gallin was on holiday so it was then bought on behalf of Bette Midler, before it passed from Goldie Hawn to Julia Roberts, who then decided it wasn't for her, whereupon it found its way back to Dolly. Her co-star was the handsome James Woods – a rather surprising choice since his previous acting forte had been cops and criminals – who plays a local reporter suspicious about Shirlee's real background. (Needless to say there were rumours of an affair between the leads in the tabloids, one even suggesting Woods was the man Dolly would leave Carl for.)

The original idea was for Shirlee to sing duets with Woods, but, as Dolly wryly observed, in both *The Best Little Whorehouse In Texas* and

---

* Dolly remained interested in the issue and in 2003 contributed a song, 'Endless Stream Of Tears' to a fundraising album called *Respond II.*

*Rhinestone* she had found herself singing with actors who couldn't carry a tune, so she was in no hurry to repeat the experience. Dolly wrote the songs for the soundtrack, including 'Light Of A Clear Blue Morning', which featured as incidental music.

The film, which wasn't particularly successful at the box office, was described by one critic as, "An old-fashioned star vehicle, which inhabits that perilous hinterland between full-throttle emotion and pure unabashed kitsch." In another early Nineties screen outing, Dolly had an extended cameo singing at Jed Clampett's birthday party in the 1993 film *The Beverly Hillbillies*, which also featured two of her co-stars from *9 To 5*, Lily Tomlin and Dabney Coleman. Sandollar Productions Inc. reached an agreement with Walt Disney Television to co-operate on the development of television films and specials. For the film *Beethoven's 2nd* (1993) Dolly duetted on the theme song, 'The Day I Fall In Love', with soul singer James Ingram, who had also worked with Linda Ronstadt and Kenny Rogers.

Somewhat inevitably, while critics found Dolly's screen presence charming, they were, as usual, less enthusiastic about her thespian skills; her singing and songwriting being always destined to garner most praise.

In 1992 one of Nashville's downtown trolleys (small tram-like buses) was named the 'Dolly Trolley' – the first to be named after a country music star and part of an effort to persuade some of the seven million visitors to Music City to make use of the service. Of greater significance, that same year, Eighties soul pop sensation Whitney Houston recorded 'I Will Always Love You' for the movie *The Bodyguard* (in which she starred with Kevin Costner). It became a massive hit, staying at number in the *Billboard* charts for a record 14 weeks. Houston's awards included Grammys in the categories Record Of The Year and Best Female Pop Vocal Performance. As one of the presenters Dolly had the double pleasure of announcing that her own song had won and making the presentation to Houston who performed her elaborately soulful version of the song for millions of viewers worldwide. Dolly quipped how when she wrote the song 22 years before, she had a heartache but it was amazing how money could heal it.

Houston's version subsequently appeared in numerous Best Of lists, made number 40 in the *Rolling Stone* 100 Greatest Pop Songs and number one in VH1's 40 Greatest Love Songs.[*] The song earned Dolly millions of

---

[*] BMI has it listed as the 13th most played song of the 20th century with five million airplays.

dollars prompting writer Colin Escott to joke that her royalties exceeded the GDP of some smaller countries. On one talk show Dolly quipped that when she originally recorded the song, she was able to put some money in the bank but Whitney's version allowed her to buy the bank. Steve Buckingham: "I felt it was never evident enough that she wrote great songs but Whitney Houston's 'I Will Always Love You' helped to change that and provided more evidence to the common person that Dolly could write these amazing thoughts."

Numerous other cover versions of the song followed including LeAnn Rimes, John Tesh and James Galway. More recently the Welsh soprano Katherine Jenkins recorded a version in Italian, *L'Amore Sei Tu* and Rik Waller, one of the contestants in the British *Pop Idol*, made number six in the UK pop charts with his version. Dolly herself re-recorded a duet version with Vince Gill in 1995 which won the CMA's Vocal Event Of The Year award and made number 15 in the country charts, a welcome success at a time when Dolly Parton records were failing in the charts significantly. Most bizarrely, Iraqi dictator Saddam Hussein chose Houston's version as the theme song for his unopposed re-election campaign in 2001.

'I Will Always Love You' has become Dolly's most successful and, arguably, best-known song. However, it could have turned out differently. The original plan was for Houston to sing Jimmy Ruffin's 1966 hit, 'What Becomes Of The Broken Hearted' as the lead single from *The Bodyguard*. However, when the film's producer discovered the song was to be used in the movie *Fried Green Tomatoes* he asked Costner to come up with a replacement. After Houston's version became successful, the tabloid press reported a feud between the two performers, supposedly resulting from Dolly reneging on an agreement that she would not perform the song for a number of months while Houston's version remained in the charts. The rumour was repeated in a 1996 Houston biography though both women have gone out of their way to dispel such stories, choosing to lavish glowing praise on each other's interpretation of the song. For many purists, Houston's cover was a case of soul excess, whereas Dolly's gentle original brought out the sensitivity and tenderness in the song's message which struck a chord with so many, something which Dolly professed surprise at. "I never thought that one song would be so successful . . . I still cannot believe how much that song seems to mean to people." This is probably due to the message of the song being something that every one wants to hear at some stage in their life.

One other little-known story behind 'I Will Always Love You' is that

"I took a chance on this appearance interfering with my music because I knew that if I really had the talent I could overcome it all – the poverty, the mountain background, the bizarre artificial look. I just wanted to know myself that you can come from nothing and make something of your life."

*With two of country's most influential pioneers Les Paul (left) and Chet Atkins (right) in 1979. Atkins said he first received a tape of Dolly from Grand Ole Opry announcer Grant Turner but turned it down because of her age and voice. Chet later signed her to RCA in 1967 on Porter Wagoner's recommendation.* (FRANK EDWARDS/REX FEATURES)

*Surrounded by the Village People, Los Angeles, 1979. Dolly continues to have an especially loyal gay following. "Gay isn't something you do. It's something you are... how can it be wrong to be who you are? How can that be a sin? I don't care what people do in their bedrooms and people shouldn't care what I do in mine..."* (MPTV/LFI)

Scenes from some of Dolly's celluloid vehicles (above left): at the 9 To 5 premiere
with co-stars Lily Tomlin and Jane Fonda, 1980 (EMPICS)
(above right) as madame Miss Mona in The Best Little Whorehouse In Texas (1982) (REX FEATURES)
(below) with Sylvester Stallone in 1984's Rhinestone. (SNAP/REX FEATURES)

*Dolly with her rarely photographed PA, Judy Ogle. "She knows everything it's humanly possible to know about me," said Dolly. "We met when we were around seven… The day I walked into the schoolroom, our eyes just kinda interlocked. We were just ugly, poor little trashy kids. But that thing within me said, 'this will be your lifelong friend. This is the one.'"*
(RON GALELLA/WIREIMAGE)

*Dolly with Kenny Rogers, 1981. Their spur-of-the-moment duet, 'Islands In The Stream', written by the Bee Gees, became a massive worldwide hit in 1983.*
(EVERETT COLLECTION/REX FEATURES)

*Dolly's recurring weight problems were grist to the tabloids' mills. Throughout the early Eighties Dolly tried out various severe diets until stumbling upon the right one. In contrasting photos, taken 10 years apart, Dolly steps out accompanied by her long-serving manager Sandy Gallin.*
(THE SUN/NI SYNDICATION AND JIM SMEAL/WIREIMAGE)

*Keeping it in the family (above) in the studio with sisters Stella (left) and Frieda (centre) and with brother Randy (below).* (BETTY GALELLA/WIREIMAGE, RON GALELLA/WIREIMAGE AND EMPICS)

*At the* Steel Magnolias *premiere, November 1989, with co-stars L-R: Daryl Hannah, Shirley Maclaine and Sally Field. Dolly said her lack of acting ability did not affect her role of Truvy because "she's a pretty flamboyant lady and so am I. She has a great sense of humour, a big heart and a big mouth… and how different is that from me, specially the big mouth?"*

*With fellow female country legends Loretta Lynn (left) and Tammy Wynette. In 1993 the three collaborated on an album,* Honky Tonk Angels. *After many years of ill health, Tammy died in 1998. Dolly paid tribute to her as "my little girlfriend… she was like a little sister and I loved her dearly."*

Above: The entrance to Dollywood,
Dolly's theme park in the Smoky Mountains,
which opened in 1986 and continues to attract
large numbers of visitors each year;
(right) Dolly's bronze statue unveiled in 1987
outside Sevier County Courthouse; (below) Dolly
with Linda Ronstadt and Emmylou Harris.
The three recorded together again in 1994
but due to disagreements and schedule conflicts
the Trio II project was shelved until 1999.
Reports of tension and disagreements emerged
in the press; (below right) Dolly with
her musical confidante and producer Steve
Buckingham, December 2000.

*Dolly arrives at the* Vanity Fair *Oscar Party, March 5, 2006. "I don't want a tombstone. I want to live forever. They say a dreamer lives forever. I want to be more than just an ordinary star... I want to be somebody that left somethin' good behind for somebody else to enjoy... I'm not near what I want to do, with what I want to accomplish... I want to be somebody that extremely shines. A star shines, of course, but I want to be really radiant."* (LFI)

what might have been the greatest cover version of all never saw the light of day. Elvis Presley wanted to record it (he had also shown interest in 'Coat Of Many Colors') but his manager 'Colonel' Tom Parker insisted on Dolly giving up half the publishing rights to the song. Her non-negotiable principled stance meant Elvis did not record her songs at a time when her own fame was a long way off. Dolly was disappointed that she never met 'the King' – "there was something about him that I held sacred within my self" – even though her fame in the early Seventies meant that a suitable occasion could surely have been arranged. Despite his dubious business practices, Dolly professed herself to be a great admirer of what the Colonel had done with Elvis' career – "he built that mystery up about him" – which mirrored how she had engineered her own image.

After the considerable success of 'I Will Always Love You' Dolly could have afforded to retire or, at least, take it easy for a while. (With all her other sources of income she was rated among Hollywood's 10 richest women). But as one of her long-time backing singers Jennifer O' Brien described, "Dolly's real unusual. She is the most fascinating person I've ever known . . . her mind works very fast. Things that would interest anyone else for quite a while, she seems to grasp right away, and then she has to move onto something else. Dolly gets bored very easily."

# Chapter 23

SECURITY and the intrusion of the tabloid press into Dolly's private life had been a constant concern for some years. She also quickly discovered that her fame drew individuals into using her name and image to promote their own interests. This was usually harmless – Dolly look-alike contests for instance – but some went further in ways which caused problems. Ideas for business ventures involving Dolly flooded into the office and in most cases such overtures were ignored or brushed aside by Dolly's staff without creating any animosity. However, one Florida businessman, former restaurant owner Dennis Donoghue, was more persistent than most and Dolly and her advisers could have been forgiven for regretting they gave him any encouragement at all.

Donoghue claimed to have had a series of dreams (in 1990) about 'muffin-like' characters, in a town he christened 'Muffkinville', with Dolly Parton singing along with them. He reportedly spent $6,000 trying to create prototypes of the "Muffkins" and developed a portfolio of characters and stories. Apart from his own savings he claimed backers were prepared to invest about $200,000 in the venture. Dolly's advisers apparently saw some merit in the idea, a number of meetings and phone calls took place and Donoghue sent in prototype models of his Muffkin characters for evaluation. However, it was eventually decided that the idea was not one which Dolly's organisation could support, partly because Dolly was considering her own animation project, and a polite rejection letter was duly despatched. Donoghue was not one to take this lying down, spending more than $20,000 on newspaper advertisements in an effort to attract Dolly's attention to help him "make my dream come true". When Dolly failed to make contact, he complained, "When you see these great performers you get these great images . . . I by no means say that Dolly has to do the project. But it's uncharacteristic for a performer to treat me in the mean-spirited way that I've been treated."

Donoghue was particularly upset because he alleged his prototype figures were now unusable because of damage caused when Dolly's people returned them by mail. It emerged that he was seeking up to $6,000 in compensation. "Someone has to make amends . . ." read the advertisement which appeared in the *Hollywood Reporter* and *Daily Variety*, "don't just continue to sing about it, please do it: put a little love in your heart, spare me but a few minutes of your precious time." Dolly's lawyer, who claimed that the figures had been properly wrapped, responded, "What can one say about a nuisance . . . I consider it a non-issue. I consider it bad form and a form of publicity seeking and harassment. Dolly is too much of a lady to respond to any of this. We're not going to respond to silliness." Donoghue's campaign got as far as a conversation with Sandy Gallin before the matter disappeared.

Dolly's engagements in 1993 included a prestigious appearance at the Carnegie Hall on May 14, reviewed by Jon Parales of the *New York Times*: "All of Dolly Parton's contradictions showed up in the opening two-hour concert on Friday night at Carnegie Hall. As taped crickets chirped, a fiddler walked onstage to play what might have been a folk tune, backed by an electronic keyboard. A banjo player turned up, and the tune shifted to bluegrass tempo; then it mutated into the show tune, 'Hello Dolly' as the singer made her entrance down the aisle in a dress that was all sequins. Backward country gal turned glittering pro, Miss Parton gets away with some of the tackiest pop gambits by flaunting her down-home roots." The same newspaper had spotted her the year before at one of her favourite New York haunts, Wally's and Joseph's, where once more she made something of a splash. "Miss Parton did not exactly melt into the crowd . . . 50% blonde mane, 40% bust and 10% twiggy support system keeping it all on the move . . . she was wearing a black bodysuit, yellow and black stiletto heels, crystal paper weights as rings on each hand and a canary yellow waist length jacket embroidered with black western curlicues."

In 1993 the paparazzi scored a considerable coup when Dolly was photographed leaving a plastic surgery clinic. Though constant companion Judy Ogle and a nurse tried their best to shield her, part of Dolly's face and a few strands of hair were visible under bandages which extended around her head and under her chin. Dolly had of course contributed greatly to the untrammelled desire for such shots because she lived all of her public life behind a mask. *The Sun*, along with many other tabloids, had a field day, charmingly describing her as looking like "a car crash victim after 11 hours of agony under a plastic surgeon's knife". One report compared her to a mummy. It was reported that Dolly had been in the clinic for approximately 12 hours and in surgery for about five. Various quotes attributed to Dolly claimed she had splashed out around $20,000 on cosmetic surgery around her eyes, lips, chin and neck and also that "love handles" had been removed from her waist. It was also pointed out how Dolly was following a recent trend of having several operations done at once so that she would be out of public action for a shorter time and that after three weeks of recuperation she would be appearing at the US TV People's Choice Awards.

Understandably unhappy at being caught out by the paparazzi, Dolly sought to play down the more vivid tabloid accounts, saying she just had her "1,000-mile maintenance before my warranty ran out . . . I'd just had a little surgery, but they made it sound like I got caught up with the chain-saw murderer. You get embarrassed to see a picture like that, but when you become public property, you can't bitch about not only bein' seen at your best. We all have down times . . . what I won't volunteer will catch up with me soon enough and I won't lie about it." She later summed up her decision to have surgery as, "I'm not obsessed with being younger, I'm obsessed with looking better," and provided some details. "I had the pelican pouch under my chin removed, some liposuction, some under-eye work." She also told the surgeon that while she was under the anaes-thetic, he could do a "nip and tuck or suck and puck" anywhere that seemed to need it.

Years before, when an interviewer asked whether her breasts were real she replied that as a religious girl she regarded it as sinful to use technology to interfere with her body. How times had changed. She now described plastic surgery as, "the modern day fountain of youth . . . who in their right mind wants to come out a wrinkled old prune with a lumpy, flour sack figure? If God didn't want plastic surgeons, he wouldn't have given them the hands to do it." In general she was very defensive about the whole subject. While continuing to deny that she had breast implants (she later confessed she did resort to this – "in order for them to stand up like little soldiers, you put something in there to help them.") Dolly explained what she underwent was, "more of a reconstruction job because I went on a diet and lost a lot of weight, and they started to droop a bit . . . I just wanted to lift them off the street . . . they're not bigger than they were, if anything they're a little smaller."

For Dolly her physical being was merely one aspect of her general per-sonality. "The way I look is the way I like to look. I'm just an extremist and so I like to dress the part – if I have extreme parts of my body, then I might as well have extreme hair-dos or have extreme clothes to match the boobs and the hair-do. And my personality is really extreme. I do just as I please – I always have and always will. I try to live my own life, I don't try to live somebody else's life, and I don't like people tryin' to live my life. Now there, how do you like that, buddy? I mean that."

Dolly's fixation with her external appearance may have been extreme but it was merely an exaggeration of the show business maxim that artists had to be outlandish, regardless of their talent, in order to be successful. It was a fact that many people who only saw her on TV perceived her to be a fast-talking, engaging and amusing country girl who could sing a little. While acknowledging that this emphasis on image risked trivialising her craft Dolly had no regrets because she believed it was necessary in order to achieve recognition; a sad but realistic reflection on the entertainment industry. "It happens a lot of times and I wish it didn't, but there's no way to stop it, because, as you know, if you're not skinny and beautiful, you've either got to be a fat and jolly character or good-looking and that's sad, because there's a lot of talent without the looks, but looks with no talent gets more breaks. That's unfair."

However, it does not explain why she continued to maintain the façade once she had become established. Perhaps she feared the public's fickle nature and that she would only continue to be successful if she kept up the disguise people had come to expect.

That same year, *Slow Dancing With The Moon* was released, produced by Steve Buckingham, who was now firmly established as Dolly's pivotal studio figure; the days of Porter Wagoner seeking to impose his will in the studio were a distant memory. The range of styles made the album hard to categorise but as with *Eagle When She Flies* the pair didn't stray too far from a modern country sound. A stellar mix of young and old guests included: Alison Krauss, Mary-Chapin Carpenter, Rodney Crowell, Pam Tillis, Collin Raye, Tanya Tucker, Marty Stuart, Vince Gill, Emmylou Harris, Ricky Skaggs and Chet Atkins as well as a posse of top country pickers.

The number of young rising artists appearing on the record was a deliberate ploy reflecting the current bias against older stars which Buckingham sought to overcome. "You can't get on radio if you're over 30," said Dolly. "The greatest artists, active and good, get dropped by labels because of new country. That's why I brought young people into my record, those who idolise George Jones, me, the older artists. They patterned themselves after us and they were thrilled, excited to death to sing with me and me with them. But I also thought it was a good way of trying to get played on radio. If they won't play Dolly Parton, they'll play her with Billy Ray Cyrus, Kathy Mattea and Billy Dean. I thought about it in a business way, but I didn't sell out, I got people who sound good, and combined them to make sense to everybody. I also believe in keeping up with the times. I've been luckier than a lot of artists. I've done television, movies, and I hang in there better than people with more talent. I count my blessings every day." However, she did let slip, "Well, if I have to stoop and kiss ass, I will."

The unpalatable truth was that though many younger artists were paying homage to a legendary country artist, modern radio and television programmers were looking for the next big thing. At awards ceremonies they acknowledged the respect awarded to the likes of Dolly before turning their promotional sights onto the latest hat act with the right profile – young, handsome with a reasonable voice that could be manipulated in the studio. Billy Ray Cyrus was one of a number of artists who played at Dollywood's opening charity concert around the time when 'Achy Breaky Heart' was launching him to international prominence. As she had done with Suzy Bogguss, Dolly answered his questions and gave him advice on the potential pitfalls, describing Billy Ray as "a very kind and generous soul". In part she wanted to give the younger artists the benefit of her experience but also wanted to be seen as relevant.

The CD booklet for *Slow Dancing With The Moon* featured fulsome tributes to Dolly from the likes of Rodney Crowell: "Dolly Parton, part Mozart, part Aphrodite, part Mae West. Classically clever, completely captivating, electrifying and smart. A poet in a well-tailored suit. All glamour and substance. Beautiful legs and schoolgirl giggles with the voice of an angel and songs I wish I'd written . . . and man what an attention span. She even laughs at my jokes, I'm in love." Alison Krauss, who had sung on *Eagle When She Flies*, wrote: "Nothing will ever top getting to sing with Dolly Parton. Now I can die." Dolly was one of the first mainstream artists to nurture Alison's work after a recommendation from Carl who had seen her on a country music programme. Dolly revealed Alison started crying when they met. "I just claimed her. It was like she was my little soul mate; like if I'd have had a child, it would probably have been like Alison." The booklet also displayed Dolly's playful humour with a photograph of her and Steve smiling broadly in amusement at the tabloid headline – "Dolly Parton Will Never Sing Again" – Buckingham is holding up.

The sleeve showed Dolly looking coquettish in an old-fashioned evening dress and at least two songs continued the suggestive theme. '(You Got Me Over) A Heartache Tonight' (with Billy Dean) described a brief romantic encounter, while 'I'll Make Your Bed' concerned a woman who lacked certain housekeeping skills but promised to make up for it in the bedroom. The contrast between the light country melody and the song's carnal message was striking. 'Romeo', featuring Dolly, Kathy Mattea, Mary-Chapin Carpenter and Tanya Tucker playfully ogling Billy

Ray Cyrus, would not be on any feminist's playlist but must have been great fun to cut nonetheless.

Dolly wrote or co-wrote eight of the album's 12 songs; the light rock number 'Full Circle' which kicked off the album, and the title track, a poignant ballad of romance and loss, were written by Mac Davis. Dolly also covered the infectiously upbeat song 'Put A Little Love In Your Heart', originally a hit for its co-writer Jackie DeShannon. In 'High And Mighty', set to an uptempo gospel groove, Dolly, backed by the Christ Church Choir, joyfully celebrated the comfort religion can bring. 'High And Mighty' was also the name given to a television programme Dolly was said to be working on, about a woman in the ministry, although Dolly admitted she was having problems getting it accepted. "Anytime you do anything that has to do with God, it's touchy. But this isn't about shovin' anything down anybody's throat, and I would never allow it to become a mockery of the spiritual."*

Aided no doubt by the presence of so many current newcomers and a slickly amusing video to accompany 'Romeo', *Slow Dancing With The Moon*, eased into the country Top Five and the *Billboard* Top 20 and within six months it had gone platinum. The singles 'Romeo' and 'More Where That Came From' were also released as extended dance mixes to capitalise on the new line-dancing craze which saw clubs sprouting up all over America and beyond.

Dolly's penchant for working with other artists of stature continued throughout 1993. She duetted with Neil Diamond on 'You've Lost That Lovin' Feeling' for a European-only release and recorded *Honky Tonk Angels*, a collaborative album with fellow legends Tammy Wynette and Loretta Lynn, affectionately referred to as the "older embattled queens of country music" by one writer. Over the years the three had met on numerous occasions – backstage at the Grand Ole Opry, at awards ceremonies and on countless flights to and from Nashville – and often ended up singing together as well as raising the possibility of making an album together. Given the ages the women were at in their lives Dolly was minded to call the album *Hot Flushes* but was overruled. When the album eventually came together 22 tracks were cut out of an original list of over 50 and a final 12 selected. Each took turns at singing lead with Tammy singing most of the low parts as Dolly and Loretta were not able to sing any lower.

---

* There were also reports that Dolly was interested in making a musical drama, *Sister Sunshine*, in which she was to play an evangelist. Neither idea was realised.

There were logistical problems in getting all three in the studio at the same time as Loretta recalled. "We were together long enough to get our songs picked out, and we had a good time while we were doing that. But then it got right down to the nitty-gritty . . . I was heading for Branson. Dolly, she was in Hollywood doing something. Tammy was in the hospital. So that separated us. So I went in and sung 22 songs five times – didn't hear 'em back – and did the harmony on all the choruses. When I left, I said, 'Tell Dolly to take me off wherever she wants me off, and put her harmony on.' I just did the best I could do, and I left."

The album combined standards such as 'It Wasn't God Who Made Honky Tonk Angels', 'Please Help Me I'm Falling (In Love With You)' and 'Wings Of A Dove' with a composition from each woman. "We were just doing country music the way everybody remembered country music," said Steve Buckingham. Not content with having assembled three of the leading female country singers of modern times, Buckingham brought in Kitty Wells to sing on 'It Wasn't God Who Made Honky Tonk Angels', the song which launched her career in the early Fifties and with the assistance of modern technology, the trio sang along with Patsy Cline on the Hank Williams' classic 'Lovesick Blues'. Loretta was a little apprehensive about singing along to the original recording because Patsy had been a very close friend of hers. "I feel like Patsy's gonna come back and haunt us." All three became quite tearful when recording 'Let Her Fly', Dolly's composition about her late grandmother, because Tammy and Loretta had also lost grandmothers.

'Silver Threads And Golden Needles' was supported by a video which had the three women singing the song backstage as a procession of stars try to get in the stage door. Despite their status all are turned away until Chet Atkins, previously refused admission, is allowed in.* The novelty song, 'I Dreamed Of A Hillbilly Heaven', in which the singer dreams of meeting with all the deceased greats of country music allowed Dolly to have a gentle dig at Porter. Up in heaven Roy Acuff and Tex Ritter are holding a "tally book" with the names of the country music greats who will be arriving at St Peter's gates in years to come. Dolly reels off a list of names before saying, "Well, where's Porter Wagoner's name?" the inference being that he might not merit inclusion. After a short pause she exclaims, "Oh there it is." *Honky Tonk Angels* performed well commercially, even making the pop 50, no mean feat for an old-style country album and went

---

* In 1993 Dolly took great pleasure in presenting Chet Atkins with his NARAS (the National Academy of Recording Arts and Sciences) lifetime achievement award.

gold in 1994. Once more Dolly seemed to experience good fortune when working with other women.

Another of Dolly's projects was also closely connected with the fairer sex, when she teamed up with Revlon to launch a range of make-up under the title Dolly Parton's Beauty Confidence for which she was reportedly paid around $2 million. At first sight it was not a groundbreaking concept, yet the pitch employed to market the products tied in, to some extent, with a more modern and enlightened attitude to a woman's appearance. By the early Nineties women were being advised to eschew plastic surgery or liposuction and to enhance their natural appearance with beauty products. Journalists in America even talked about "beauty shrinks" and "emotional coaches" whose role was to foster the notion of self-acceptance in women who found it hard to be happy with their natural appearance. This approach was an important element of Dolly Parton's Beauty Confidence.

In a glossy brochure which mixed Dolly-style advice on how to apply make-up and ways to deal with unexpected skin problems with a few snippets about her life and experiences, Dolly told women readers that it was her hope to "make you look and feel better about yourself" and aimed to "bring out the real beauty and confidence inside every woman" – ironic considering that Dolly had gone to great lengths to alter her natural appearance by artificial means. The message was reinforced by the inclusion of lyrics headed 'Try', 'Be Somebody', 'Pretty Is As Pretty Does' and 'Confidence'. In the pamphlet's introduction Dolly said, "I've combined my personal experience with guidance from experts in the beauty field to develop super, goof-proof formulas everyone can use!" There were plenty of references to Dolly's primitive make-up techniques from her Smoky Mountains upbringing (products included 'Smoky eye pencils' and 'Tennessee Rose moisturific (*sic*) lip colors'). Dolly said that she now did her own make-up for television and photo-shoots because no one knew her face better than she did. She also revealed her own beauty secrets; if waking up with tired puffy eyes, place a slice of raw potato on each eyelid and lay down for 15 minutes, "During which time, you should try to energise yourself with positive thoughts." Naturally Dolly couldn't take things too seriously. "When people ask why I wear five-inch heels, I tell them it's 'cause I can't find six-inch ones." To top it all off was a list of "Dolly Dos" ("Be sure your skin is as clean as a mountain morning before applying make-up", "For the most natural effect, always apply blush while smiling!") and "Dolly Don'ts" ("Don't put blush too close to your eyes or you'll emphasise crow's feet, under-eye circles and bags").

As part of the Revlon deal, a 30-minute "infomercial" was produced to advertise the cosmetics range which was initially intended for sale via TV only. The price range for a kit containing a variety of make-ups and perfumes was $80–$100. Revlon saw the venture as an opportunity to exploit an untapped market of women who did not spend a lot on make-up because they were put off by sophisticated beauty advisers behind department store counters, baffled by wall displays featuring over 80 choices of lipstick or were simply tired of making mistakes with their selections. Market research had shown that Dolly boasted a strong following across all demographics and was associated with honesty and sincerity so Revlon decided she would be the perfect star for women who didn't trust their own judgement.

Revlon's President and Chief Executive, Jerry W. Levin, said that he saw about 25 celebrities a year who wanted to do a cosmetic's line, but while most were only really interested in money, Dolly was sincerely interested in the business and had been an active participant in the project. When promoting the range, she was asked if she was wearing the make-up herself to which she replied, "Yes, and plenty of it." Despite such high hopes, the campaign was a commercial flop and was pulled after only a few months with some observers suggesting that Dolly had the wrong image for the products being sold. Some of the excess stock found its way to the gift shop at Dollywood where it was sold for several years.*

The failure was surprising given Revlon's considerable experience in the field, Dolly's high profile and her obsessive interest in her own appearance. Despite the Revlon project's rapid demise Dolly was sought out for advice on various health issues and pronounced on such subjects as the merits and use of energy boosters in magazine features next to Goldie Hawn advocating the benefits of meditation or Liz Hurley praising the restorative qualities of a catnap.

In 1994 Dolly received both The Living Legend Award and the Minnie Pearl Humanitarian Award from the Music City News Awards – the first time an artist had received both honours in the same year. Her reputation as a humanitarian had recently extended to fellow musicians who had hit hard times. In 1992 the Nashville press reported that Dolly had loaned a house to Terry McMillan – a studio musician who had worked with her – and his family when their house in Antioch burnt down. The previous year, Dolly was one of many helping Reba McEntire after most of her

---

* Individual items turn up on eBay to the present day.

band was killed in a plane crash, a disaster which sent out shock waves as there were few in the music business that did not spend hours on aeroplanes. Reba decided to go back on the road shortly after the funerals but had to get a band together in one week, which was barely enough time to assemble much less rehearse six musicians and a vocalist.

Dolly called Reba when she heard of the tragedy. "She said if I need anything to tell her and that I could use her band and her whole organisation if necessary," Reba said in her autobiography *My Story*. "No wonder I have been a huge fan of hers from the beginning. I thanked her and asked if I could use the services of Gary Smith, her bandleader and record producer . . . he knew every good musician in Nashville. We asked him to form a band for us." Despite the magnitude of the challenge a suitable group of musicians was put together, the first show being at Columbus, Ohio. Although emotionally draining, as Reba put it, "those guys held up like troupers."

In 1995, it was reported that Dolly had written a song called 'Howard J DeCaussin', in memory of Dollywood's vice president for maintenance and construction, who recently died of a heart attack. Dolly presented an autographed copy of the lyrics and a recording of the song to his widow. During the first Gulf War, a newspaper in Rowan County, North Carolina published the "Ribbon Of Hope" featuring the names of locals serving in the Middle East. In a typically tabloidesque story, one of the men, Eddie Greene, had a friend, Airman, First Class, Gordon Mossman of Missouri who was suffering from recurrent headaches and Eddie wanted to do something to make him feel better. While stationed in Arkansas, the soldiers had seen Kenny Rogers and Dolly Parton and Gordon fell for Dolly. Eddie wrote to her asking if she might write a letter to his friend. The request reached Dolly who sent autographs to both men. The paper reported that Gordon hadn't had a headache since.

Clearly such stories were publicised and, in public relations terms, were invaluable but others never reached the public domain. For instance, it's understood that Dolly provided a degree of financial support for the late Carl and Pearl Butler who had been good to her back in those far-off early days in Nashville.

Dollywood continued to expand and prosper although it was operating in a competitive commercial market against a variety of other attractions and some years attendance figures were lower than projected. Attractions were regularly added in the hope of luring new visitors while at the same time satisfying those frequent visitors who bought season passes. A Country Fair section – a hark back to one of Dolly's favourite excitements from child-hood – was added, along with a 60-ft-high "Wonder Wheel", an exact replica of a turn-of-the-century Ferris wheel. A Fifties themed area was created covering six acres, which included a Cas Walker general store. Live radio station WDLY broadcast a range of country-oriented music to residents and tourists throughout the Smokies region from 10 a.m. to 7 p.m. Visitors to Dollywood were able to see into the studio and crowds swelled when celebrities were being interviewed. Another addition partic-ularly congruent with Dolly's image was the Butterfly Emporium which allowed visitors to walk through a spectacular atrium, with a capacity of 13,000 cubic feet, amid hundreds of live butterflies. A special hatching area offered the opportunity of witnessing the miracle of metamorphosis as new butterflies emerged from their chrysalises.

Dolly also planned to build theatres as part of a mission to make her part of East Tennessee one of the biggest visitor attractions in America. For the opening of Dollywood's 1994 season, concerts by Dolly and Kenny Rogers were staged to raise money for the Dollywood Foundation. Dolly surprised Kenny by presenting him with a wagon, custom made at Dollywood with the initials KR carved on the front, for his ranch.

Dolly had previously described aspects of her life in song form but in 1994 she pulled much of it together with the publication of her autobiog-raphy, *Dolly, My Life And Other Unfinished Business*. The dust jacket read: ". . . Dolly reveals with great humour and heartfelt honesty the real woman behind the superstar, who, after scaling the heights of success, still con-siders herself a simple girl from the country." Though strongly sanitised, the book was eminently readable with a mixture of serious historical content and wry observation snappily delivered with Dolly's usual mix of sentimentality, sauciness and down-to-earth pragmatism.

However, the recounting was entirely one sided with the general feeling that Dolly had simply selected and polished certain incidents in her life, presenting them in a way that reflected the image she wanted to project. Major conflicts were described with a light revisionist touch and little emerged of the true bitterness which must surely have accompanied key episodes such as the split from Porter. At times the prose was remi-niscent of her between-song concert patter and an audio tape featuring Dolly reading extracts followed on the book's heels. As always Dolly laid strong emphasis on the spiritual side and towards the end of the tape it sounded as though she was preaching from a pulpit as she relayed how her life, both good and bad, had been part of God's plan. Her encomium was rounded off with recitations of the Lord's Prayer and Psalm 23.

Inevitably the book raised more questions than it answered although Dolly threw some new light on important areas such as the prominent role Judy Ogle played in her life, how important musical director Gregg Perry had been and her unorthodox relationship with Carl. The reader could be forgiven for wondering what kept them together. Among Dolly's revelations: Carl enjoyed talking politics and religion which she avoided, he disliked the food she prepared and would usually rustle up plainer fare for himself, he was a man of routine, she a woman of spontaneity, he took little or no interest in her numerous business interests and if having problems in particular areas of her life Dolly tended to filter what Carl needed to know. One area which brought them together was a love of dogs. Dolly spent a remarkably part of the book describing one in particular, Popeye, and how Carl had "grieved uncontrollably" for a year after he died.*

The book appealed to a wide readership and, unlike the Revlon cosmetics venture, was a great success, spending over two months on the *New York Times* best-sellers list. However, some writers, such as Margo Mifflin, were less than charitable in their reviews. "This is less a life story than a tinny, freeze-dried acceptance speech . . . a shapeless curriculum vitae." Dolly later conceded that she had mixed feelings about writing the book. A number of advisers had spoken enthusiastically about the project for some time and she felt pressured into doing it, not least because of the financial potential. She also admitted the book contained a degree of deliberate titillation (for instance, she revealed that she and Judy Ogle sometimes shared a bed), and that a lot of information was omitted in order to avoid offending people. With regard to Carl's feelings she was characteristically cryptic. "I love him too much to put him through a lot of the stuff I brought on myself." On reflection Dolly felt that it might have been better to wait so that the "whole story" could be told† (though if past form is a reliable indicator Dolly will always edit material under her control to achieve her desired effect).

With her recent material being largely overlooked by country radio and television, for Dolly's next album, she intended to put commercial considerations to one side by indulging in something she had wanted to do for some time – an album of her favourite old country and folk songs in front of a live audience in East Tennessee.

---

* Despite such apparent dichotomies, four years after the book's publication, it was reported that the pair were to renew their wedding vows.
† At the time of writing a second autobiographical volume is currently under consideration.

# Chapter 24

IN 1994, with the support of Steve Buckingham, Dolly founded her own label, Blue Eye Records, in a bid to assert creative control as well as independence from Columbia, though initially the company managed the label. The traditional music on *Heartsongs,* the first Blue Eye/Columbia offering, was recorded live at Dollywood. "Welcome to my Smoky mountain home . . ." she chirped, "I thought that this would be a perfect time to do something that I have always wanted to do, make an album of songs that I love and grew up singing, heart songs." In a rather disingenuous dig at the musical path that had led Dolly through pop, disco, soul and rock'n'roll she said, "I spent many years trying to make a living doing this kind of music and I couldn't. Now that I don't need the money any more maybe I can."

The idea for *Heartsongs* was hers alone though Buckingham was in charge of production and assembling a group of top bluegrass and traditional country singers and pickers including Randy Scruggs, Alison Krauss, Ronnie McCoury, Jimmy Mattingly (who played for Garth Brooks until 1995), Adam Steffey and Ron Block. "It was practically an acoustic orchestra, and then I brought in Altan (an Irish Celtic vocal group), because I suggested the idea of finding a young version of the Chieftains.

"We rehearsed in Nashville for three or four days. I had books for everybody with the charts and the lyrics and we were very well organised, then we packed up and went to Dollywood, rehearsed for a couple of days there, it was a huge undertaking. I mean I was exhausted by the end of it and plus when we did the recordings we did two on a Saturday and two on a Sunday. I was onstage to try to cue Dolly and play guitar and lead the band. We had musicians coming in and out of the wings and it was like a circus but it was really magic and Alison [Krauss] to this day says that it was the greatest musical experience she's ever had . . . good gosh the logistics of putting that thing together, it was like Desert Storm."*

---

* After Sunday's first show, at Dolly's spontaneous suggestion, the band rehearsed an impromptu version of 'Tennessee Waltz', with Pig Robbins on piano, which was performed at the last show. However, Dolly elected not to include it on the album.

290

The album included Dolly-arranged traditional songs such as 'Mary Of The Wild Moor', 'I'm Thinking Tonight Of My Blue Eyes', 'Wayfaring Stranger' and 'What A Friend We Have In Jesus' as well as some of her own classics including 'To Daddy' and 'Coat Of Many Colors'. Dolly heaped glowing praise on her parents, present in the audience; Lee in particular, "the best daddy a bunch of kids could ever have". She played down his taste for alcohol claiming that though she had seen him drunk, she never saw him drinking, the not wholly credible inference being that he only indulged when on market visits to sell his tobacco crop. "He never would have anything round the house to drink. Mama wouldn't allow it first of all and he wouldn't have done that to us kids anyhow." Lee's extended benders were treated as a subject for merriment, implying he had been forgiven for his past slips as a parent. When talking about the time Lee went to Michigan to find work in a car plant, Dolly claimed that her father returned to the Smokies because he missed his wife and children attributing to him the following idealised lines, delivered in hushed, breathless tones. "With God's help and these two hard-working hands of mine I'll live and die right here in the mountains and I'll raise my kids the best way I know how."

Dolly's look back also included a surprise reworking of the theme to Cas Walker's programme and the Black Draught laxative advertisement she sang on Porter's show. She recalled her mortification at having to advertise Cardui, a remedy for problems associated with menstruation, for the Chattanooga Medicine Company, the show's sponsor. This segued neatly into the finale, an exuberant version of 'PMS Blues', Dolly's heart-felt complaint about that most feminine of maladies which was surely based on bitter personal experience. *Heartsongs* made the country Top 10 though it only made the lower reaches of the pop charts. The following year Dolly released another Columbia/Blue Eye album *Something Special*, containing a mixture of new and old songs including the version of 'I Will Always Love You' recorded with Vince Gill, which made number 15 in the country charts. What would be Dolly's last outing with Columbia came in 1996 with a collection of more recent songs, *I Will Always Love You and other Greatest Hits*. Reflecting a marked decline in Dolly's fortunes the album only just made the country Top 50 while missing the pop charts altogether.

Approaching her 50th birthday, Dolly had become the best-known female country music singer ever, as well as one of the most famous icons in popular culture. A decade earlier she had been rated the third most photographed person in the world behind the Pope and Madonna. In *Country Music People* Douglas McPherson wrote, "No other country singer, living or dead, has achieved such prominence in the world cultural awareness . . . her image is as universally recognisable as that of the billowing skirted Marilyn Monroe or the sequined Vegas-style Elvis. She's familiar like Coca Cola and McDonald's." Dolly's frequent appearances in men's magazines such as *Playboy* and *Penthouse* focused (unsurprisingly) on the sexual aspects of her life (although the 1978 *Playboy* interview delved intelligently into many other areas). At 50, Dolly said she would pose nude for *Penthouse* on her 100th birthday.

One particular aspect of Dolly's appearance brought a burst of worldwide publicity in 1996 that she could hardly have predicted. A team of scientists working in the Roslin Institute, near Edinburgh, made history when they successfully created the world's first adult cloned mammal, a sheep, with cells taken from a six-year-old ewe. The team realised that there would be a lot of media publicity surrounding their groundbreaking achievement and the question arose as to what they should call their new arrival. The cells had been taken from the mammary glands of the ewe, prompting one of the technicians to quickly suggest "Dolly" as the obvious choice. Within a short time Dolly the sheep became the most famous animal on the planet thus helping to activate more CD sales for the other Dolly. Dollywood officials sought permission for Dolly the sheep to go on display at the park; the potential for publicity and crowd pulling was enormous but the idea was a non starter. Dolly was an experimental animal created under Home Office Regulations and she could therefore only be moved to premises licensed under The Animals (Scientific Procedures) Act 1986.

Dolly articles in women's magazines such as *Ladies Home Journal* and *Woman's Own* tended to paint a picture of her as a modern woman with a difficult set of challenges, balancing an illustrious career, home commitments and health issues. Invariably, such publications sought to find out how she coped and to elicit useful advice for their less-exalted female readers. The feminist magazine *Ms* seemed to overlook Dolly's blatant exploitation of her body (she was dismissive of feminist complaints on this topic) preferring to see her as a woman who had succeeded in a man's world, a heroine figure who empowered other women, particularly from the blue collar sector.

Away from mass readerships, Dolly also became a subject of interest to the academic world. Even the more highbrow broadsheets saw Dolly as a unique phenomenon and a shrewd businesswoman whose achievements were by no means limited to her music. In a lengthy 1995 article, 'Star Image Of Dolly Parton', Pamela Wilson stated in her introduction, "As a fluent and savvy promoter of 'Dolly', Parton provides a fascinating case study in the construction of a star image, specifically one that mediates the often contradictory ideals of gender, region, and class." Referring to Dolly as "an icon of hyper-femininity", the essay examined a number of articles in the serious press with various quotes being used to illustrate how she manipulated her physique to gain attention and create the "Dolly" persona and the rather disquieting effect it had on males unused to such an exaggerated version of femininity.

As well as reiterating how Dolly's health and weight issues resonated with the ordinary working woman, Wilson made the point that Dolly "is keeping the upper hand and stage managing her own 'exploitation'". Wilson also detected a certain disdain for women in the higher echelons of society and Dolly herself revealed that some of her mountain habits followed her from Tennessee. "I still like to pee off the porch every now and then. There's nothing like peeing on those snobs in Beverly Hills." Wilson considered Dolly to be a feminist, one who was, "drawing upon a model of feminine action in which women subvert, and gain strength from within, the dominant patriarchal system". Dolly may have been considered some kind of feminist but she was careful not to associate herself with the public outpourings of mainstream feminists who were widely loathed by her more conservative fans.

The conclusion to Wilson's article acknowledged Dolly's power to inspire people though the verbiage used was on a different plane from that employed by the great majority of mainstream journalists. "As a popular feminist and advocate of the rural working class, Parton employs a counter-hegemonic rhetoric that seems sentimental, emotional, and nonthreatening to those in the power bloc, who often perceive it as comical and ineffectual. Yet her subversive strategies are powerful. Far from serving as a vehicle for the dominant ideology, Parton's star image provides a rich, multidimensional configuration of signifiers that exploit the contradictory meanings inherent to that image. 'Dolly' may well make Parton's fans aware of their own social positioning and thereby encourage alternative readings and practices."

Another academic article, also from 1995, 'Yes, It's True; Zimbabweans Love Dolly Parton' by Jonathan Zilberg, illustrated the considerable reach of Dolly's work and influence. As well as mirroring Wilson's observation that Dolly gave voice to working-class values, Zilberg claimed her openness regarding her underprivileged past allowed Zimbabweans (and others in similar situations) to identify strongly with her and her music. "So many Zimbabweans relate in the most basic ways to Dolly Parton, her music, and to the experiences she sings of. Her songs bring them pleasure, relaxation and even strength and hope. Furthermore, they seem to relate to the Christian values . . . with the potential to uplift one's spirits in difficult times, for example, with the song 'One Day At A Time' . . . Again, in addition to the bitter-sweet messages conveyed . . . it is the expressive way in which the songs are sung that makes them so popular. Deep sentiment is thus conveyed through the timbre of the voices and instruments and this is, to some extent, what makes this medium so appealing to Zimbabweans of all classes, ages and linguistic backgrounds . . . it moves them deeply, some people even cry."

In 1995 Dolly was selected for jury duty between January and June in Williamson County, Tennessee. Dolly was able to be excused from this particular civic duty on the basis of her busy schedule but undoubtedly, her attendance would almost certainly have disrupted court proceedings. One appearance she did honour that year was on the stage of the Grand Ole Opry, her first in seven years. Strictly speaking, under the Opry's requirement, members had to regularly appear in order to be able to play, but the powers that be were happy to make an exception in Dolly's case.

In January 1996, there were posters up all over Nashville wishing her a happy 50th birthday. Republican State representative Jim Boyer expressed a wish to establish an unofficial State Hero for Tennessee and Dolly was who he had in mind to be the first recipient of the honour. Sam Venable of *The Tennessean* even proposed that Sevierville be renamed "Dollyville". In the event, neither idea was taken up.

The Dollywood Foundation continued to look for ways to foster educational opportunities for youngsters and in 1996 the Imagination Library, an initiative encouraging the desire in young children to read, was launched. Under the scheme every newborn child in Sevier County was provided with a bookcase and one new book per month – starting with one of Dolly's own favourite books, *The Little Engine That Could* – until the age of five (60 in total). Books were chosen by a committee consisting of representatives from the fields of education, child development, academia and early childhood literacy. By getting young people reading, the initiative aimed to improve literacy skills which in turn would result in improved job prospects and enriched lives. Connections between crime and poor literacy skills were well documented and in the long term the project could help to reduce the risk of offending. The idea might have seemed obvious but the reality was that many five-year-olds in Sevier County had never held a book. Dolly's father was particularly proud of the initiative; Lee could have been forgiven for wishing there had been something similar when he was growing up and some of his children had failed to complete their schooling.

The beauty of the venture was its simplicity. In its first two years the library catered for nearly 5,000 children, distributing around 70,000 books. The scheme received complementary support with "imagineers" travelling to day centres and reading to children.* As part of its steady expansion, the Imagination Library entered a partnership arrangement with Tennessee governor Phil Bredesen's Books from Birth Foundation. The legislature voted through substantial financial support for the scheme as "seed money" to encourage private sponsors to contribute as well.† In view of the gravitas of the objective it was suggested that Dolly might consider toning down her appearance for public engagements in support of the project. "This is who I really am . . ." she fired back, "I'd rather look like a whore."

Dolly personally lent her support to other projects of educational benefit. In 1997, she went for a walk in the Smoky Mountains National Park with a group of children from a local elementary school. Each person was blindfolded and given the task of identifying a number of objects found in the park. Dolly guessed correctly on fur and bone, but failed to identify a walnut.

From a germ of an idea the Imagination Library grew into an efficient educational system, with an annual turnover running into millions of dollars, which continues to help many thousands of children improve their communication skills – some books are published in English and Spanish – as well as inspiring adults to organise events to raise funds for the scheme. In order to maintain and increase the flow of funds into the Dollywood Foundation an increasingly corporate approach was pursued. In 1998, an affiliate programme was introduced by the newly appointed executive

---

* By 2005, 93 of Tennessee's 95 counties had adopted the scheme, which is also being replicated in other states, and has now been greatly expanded and systematised with funding provided by a combination of local government grants, business sponsors, private donations and of course money raised at Dollywood.

† To become involved, a community must make the programme accessible to all pre-school children in their area. The community pays for the books and postage, promotes the programme, registers the children, and enters relevant information in a database. From there, The Dollywood Foundation takes over and arranges for delivery of the books to children's homes.

director, Madeline Rogero, who had over 20 years' experience working with non-profit groups. For a $5,000 tax-deductible donation corporations received high-visibility recognition in the form of VIP concert packages which included six box seats for concerts at Dollywood, six Dollywood admissions and tickets for one concert a month on a Sunday evening from June to September. The donor would also get the opportunity to meet Dolly and other artists at backstage receptions. One contribution of $5,000 provided 20 pre-school children with a personal, 60-volume Imagination Library and bookcase.

In 2002 Dolly received a major honour from the American Association of School Administrators in recognition of the beneficial effects of the various educational projects she and the Dollywood Foundation had nurtured since the late Eighties. She was also honoured by the Association of American Publishers, joking that people were starting to call her "the book lady", a title she felt put years on her. Though Dolly has assisted many good causes Stella Parton feels that those related to education are closest to Dolly's (and her own) heart. "We understand the lack of education and the drawback of that, the heartache of not having education. I think my dad was a brilliant man but he couldn't read or write and that always was hard for us, to see him be so smart and see him never be able to pick up a newspaper and read it . . . education is probably the most important thing that she contributes to."

In 2003, the Imagination Library handed out its millionth book and given the constant expansion of the scheme the numbers were expected to dramatically increase. A study published that year, 'Literacy Outcomes And The Household Literacy Environment: An Evaluation Of Dolly Parton's Imagination Library', by the non profit High/Scope Educational Research Foundation of Ypsilanti, Michigan found that participating adults became more comfortable reading with their children and more aware of children's literacy levels. Eight hundred families in three participating communities were interviewed; 70% of parents were reading more to their children after joining the programme, the greatest impact being in single-parent homes and households where parents had low education levels.

The Imagination Library became a substantial operation but for Dolly this was nothing unusual. It was estimated that if she retired she would put many people – musicians, dieticians, gardeners, restaurant and theme park staff, manicurists, domestics, wig designers, etc. – out of work.* "I feel like

---

* In one interview Dolly mentioned a figure of 2,500, though other reports have quoted 3,500.

a small nation, I'm responsible for so many people." "Dolly" had become a substantial conglomerate which apart from music took in theme parks, the catering industry, books, films, fashion and philanthropic activities. One journalist described her as CEO of her own brand.

Dolly released one album of new material in 1996, *Treasures*, a truly mixed bag of cover versions, as part of a new deal between Blue Eye and the Rising Tide label owned by MCA. Dolly and Steve Buckingham assembled musicians hailing from every part of the extended country music family. "I tried getting records played on new country radio, but without any success," Dolly said in 1997, "and I wondered what I should do. Country radio doesn't want a pop record but they don't want the type of country records I've been making either. The songs on *Treasures* are just wonderful songs and I hope that will be enough."

The result was a far more pleasing set than *The Great Pretender*. For Cat Stevens' 'Peace Train' the addition of South African vocal group Ladysmith Black Mambazo and a choir which included Kim Carnes and Matraca Berg, provided a dramatic world music sound. Ladysmith Black Mambazo sang in a Zulu style called 'Isicathamiya', developed by black workers in the mines and factories, which, to Dolly, sounded as though they were talking in tongues. It took her back to the sounds she heard in church when she was a child. Buckingham contacted the group after Dolly told him she wanted a vocal sound like the ones heard on a US commercial for LifeSavers Candy and Paul Simon's *Graceland* album. He discovered that Ladysmith Black Mambazo had sung on both.

A video was made to accompany the song, featuring clips from the Vietnam War interspersed with shots of people putting flower garlands on soldiers. Pictures of people of every race, creed and colour were flashed up; the message was resolutely liberal and anti war. In one piece of crude symbolism, a film of a house being blown up was reversed to show it restored to its original state. The final shot showed Dolly, wearing a white dress to go with her platinum hair, holding a white dove.

The album included pleasing if unremarkable readings of country standards such as Merle Haggard's 'Today I Started Loving You Again', with John Popper guesting on vocals and 'Behind Closed Doors', with blind piano player Pig Robbins, who had played on the Charlie Rich original in 1973. Dolly recalled that in the studio some of the guys said, "Hey Pig, I wish you could see what's going on. I went and took his hands and just let him feel all over me. I wanted him to 'see' what I had on. And of course they had a field day with that." John Sebastian, former frontman of the

Lovin' Spoonful, played autoharp on Dolly's exquisite reading of Randy Vanwarmer's 1979 hit 'Just When I Needed You Most' with Alison Krauss singing harmony vocals. Alison also sang on Dolly's take on Neil Young's 'After The Goldrush'. During a television special to promote *Treasures*, Dolly conceded that she had no idea what the song was about (she was not alone, apparently Neil Young didn't know either) but that to her it suggested the Second Coming or an alien invasion. The special featured interviews with some of the artists and writers of the songs. For 'Something's Burning', written by Mac Davis and made a US hit by Kenny Rogers & The First Edition, Dolly said, "I thought we could ask Mac what made him write it and how horny was he at the time, 'cause it's such a passionate sexy song . . . every time I sing that song I get so worked up. I tried to jump the engineer the day we's recording it."

One notable inclusion was 'Walking On Sunshine', a major feel-good pop hit for Katrina & the Waves in 1985 and a favourite of Carl's. It was given a bouncy uptempo treatment with electric guitars and country fiddle competing for the listener's attention during the instrumental breaks. The song was later issued as a 12-inch techno dance remix single (as was 'Peace Train') presaging yet another genre for the Dolly bandwagon to attach itself to. This was not an entirely new phenomenon as some of Dolly's earlier hits such as 'Two Doors Down' had been given dance and disco treatments back in the Seventies and Eighties. From the late Nineties onwards people who knew very little about Dolly Parton were dancing to rave and house mixes of some of her best-known songs in clubs around the world. These club versions appealed to all age groups and persuasions on the dance circuit, particularly the gay and lesbian community, for whom Dolly had become a major icon, as well as kids who were not even born when the likes of 'Jolene' or 'Two Doors Down' were hits first time around.

Several of the remixes were unofficial – a case of DJs responding to a perceived desire among their audiences – but in some cases, '9 To 5' for instance, the remixes were so popular that official releases followed. Many of these recordings were of the hardcore club variety and, beyond the presence of snippets of the melody line, bore no resemblance whatever to anything that could be called country or even mainstream pop. 'Walking On Sunshine', for which Dolly's vocals were stripped of their entire musical accompaniment and redressed in the studio with up-to-the-minute arrangements, made number one in the USA Dance Charts and the UK line-dancing charts (an impressive achievement since the original single was not released in the UK). Once more Dolly emphasised the

point that her talents and appeal went far beyond the humble country
music she started out on.

Dolly plugged *Treasures* at the 1996 CMA Awards show with all the
urgency of a fledgling singer trying to achieve her first breakthrough.
However, with little support from country (or any other) radio stations,
the album didn't sell and in view of the poor performance of the *I Will
Always Love You and other Greatest Hits* collection earlier in the year, it was
clear that the pattern of diminishing sales of recent years had become the
norm with record sales now in the lower hundreds of thousands. Dolly
said if she had to make a living out of her albums she'd "starve like some
of my old friends". While Dolly had built up outside interests, many of
her contemporaries found themselves in varying degrees of financial
insecurity, having become "hick rich" – get rich quick, spend it quick.
Both George Jones and Merle Haggard had complained about their plight
when interviewed on television. "Today you can't get a country record
programmed if you are over thirty . . ." Dolly sympathised. "There needs
to be more of a balance."

Fortunately Dolly was provided with sound professional advice when
making investment decisions and, over the years, she has demonstrated her
business acumen. Apart from lucrative music publishing and a theme park,
Dolly's numerous other ventures have included property development,
restaurants, farm equipment, hardware stores, garden centres and macadamia
trees.* It was no coincidence that another venture Dolly was said to be
working on was a series of books called "I Am" which reiterated her individual awareness method based on positive thinking.

Despite the recent success of her musical publishing business, by the mid
to late Nineties, interest in Dolly's catalogue had diminished. In the past
people had approached her for permission to record her songs but the idea
of actively marketing them did not arise, nor did it appeal to her. She
finally hired song pluggers to promote some of the thousands of compositions sitting in her basement as logically, this side of her business was the
most lucrative. Regardless of commercial considerations, she continued to
write. "Most people could be taught to sing or perform, but everybody
cannot express the voice of many . . . I can say some things some housewife
would love to say, and she don't know how to say it or wouldn't have the
nerve to say it, but she hears me say it and she'll say, 'Boy, if that ain't me

---

* More recently it was reported that Dolly has expressed interest in acquiring the Piggly
Wiggly chain of supermarkets and starting a line of frozen foods.

right down the line!' There ain't no way I could go through life and not write. Why, I'd go insane, I guess . . . it would be like goin' hungry. You know, you get hungry and you have to eat or you starve to death, and I would probably starve to death from lack of expression . . . what it gives you, is freedom of emotion."

"It's like I can kind of relieve my heart and relieve my mind," Dolly told the *Nashville Banner* in 1996. "It's my way of expressing life and relieving things. I write when I'm puttin' on my make-up. I write when I'm takin' a bath. I take a tape recorder or a notepad close by. I never go anywhere without a tape recorder or a pencil and paper." As an example of her prolific nature Dolly claims to have written 20 new songs within the space of one day, 17 of which were recorded by herself or other artists. In an interview with Larry King she claimed that she was unable to predict which of her songs would be hits, even obvious contenders like 'I Will Always Love You' and 'Jolene'. She felt the need to write them came from "somewhere deep down".

# Chapter 25

IN 1997 Dolly's official fan club, the Ambassador Club, was wound down. It had started out as a small amateur concern, later taken over and run by the Dollywood Foundation which authorised an independent magazine *Paper Dolly*. The magazine ceased publication in mysterious circumstances possibly suggestive of financial impropriety, something Dolly understandably found disheartening. She was also unhappy when members of her fan club expressed their dissatisfaction after she sang only four songs in the course of a three-hour benefit concert at Dollywood – tickets for which ranged from $35 to $500. The fans felt they had been misled by the promotion, "Parton in Concert". Dolly explained that she had a busy schedule and a large organisation to support so it was not always possible for her to perform a full show at the Dollywood benefit concerts. She also underlined the key goal of the concerts was to raise money for the Dollywood Foundation. (Since its inception, the benefit concerts had raised over $2 million.) Some fans were less than impressed – "I don't give a ★★★★ about education here. I live in Indiana. I just want to see Dolly in a show" – and a few asked for (and were given) a refund.

The incident made Dolly decide to close the operation down. As she said in a letter to members: "After lots of soul-searching . . . I believe the present arrangement is still unfair. Many of you are donating your hard-earned money, because you care for me . . . not because you believe in the programs of my Foundation." All fan club activities were discontinued, something which caused great disappointment; one of the high points for many members was an annual meeting at Dollywood between Dolly and several "Dolly Ambassadors". The club also created an opportunity for fans around the country to get together and share stories. A number of websites and newsletters sprang up as a result of individual initiatives by fans with a desire to provide information on Dolly but she made it clear that she would not endorse another fan club.

After many years of ill health, Tammy Wynette died in April 1998. Like Dolly, Tammy wore a lot of make-up and looked forward to Dolly visiting her in hospital. "She'd want me to come, see her and kind of paint her up a little bit." Tammy's televised memorial service was held in Nashville at the Ryman with many stars honouring her. Dolly remembered Tammy as "my little girlfriend . . . she was like a little sister and I loved her dearly." She reminisced about how she and Tammy used to talk about their wigs. "I think that's why God gave us talent, because he screwed up our hair so bad," she joked. She began singing 'Shine On', but was forced to cut it short after becoming overcome with emotion. "Thank you. That's all I can sing right now," she told the crowd.

In 1998, for the first time in over 10 years, Dolly attended Fan Fair, the annual week-long industry bash which enabled fans to see and meet various celebrities. When Dolly appeared onstage with Lee Ann Womack to sing 'Jolene' the crowd responded with fervent enthusiasm and mobbed Dolly at the autograph table. To mark the opening of Dollywood's 1998 season, the *Tennessee Star Journal* described Dolly as Sevier County's favourite daughter, proclaiming, "The staff of the *Tennessee Star Journal* welcomes home the Smoky Mountain Angel, Dolly Parton. Dolly, we loved you then, and we love you now!"

For her next album Dolly aimed to go back to the beginning of the Dolly Parton myth and sing as though she was eager for success, as she had been as a child, a theme neatly summed up in the album's title, *Hungry Again*. To get herself into a creative frame of mind, Dolly spent about three weeks between her Smoky Mountain retreat and a lakeside cottage she owned near Nashville. She spent a fair bit of the time alone because constant companion Judy Ogle was with her ailing mother. However, Dolly's brother, Bobby, lived nearby so she was not without company. "I never get lonely because I make it a point not to. I like to be alone some-times, as long as there is somebody in the next room or somebody close to a telephone." Dolly used the time on her own to reflect on what she had achieved and what she still wanted to accomplish. Rather than attempt to pander to the dictates of the modern scene (to her disgust the powers that be regarded her as a "heritage artist"), she resolved to "write from the heart" and hoped a reasonable number liked the results.

Dolly drank only juice for the first week, water for the second and fruits and juices in week three. Fasting was not unusual for her. In the Pentecos-tal Church of God, people sometimes fasted one day a week and over the years Dolly had sometimes fasted for spiritual reasons and, more prosai-cally, to lose weight. Fasting sharpened her senses and focused her self-discipline; the lack of food gave her headaches followed by hallucinations and by about the end of the first week, in her light-headed state, the songs started to pour out.

The result of Dolly's sojourn was an astonishing 37 songs – 12 of which were chosen for *Hungry Again*. Many of the songs were autobiographical, though as always embellished with a judicious use of poetic licence. Dolly decided to forego the production services of Steve Buckingham and instead hired her cousin Richie Owens who she used to babysit for and whose father Louis Owens once ran Dolly's publishing company. Pursuing a back to basics approach, the album was recorded in Owens' basement studio; his children could be heard upstairs at times. Dolly appreciated the fact that with Richie, she "didn't need to go through a bunch of people" to get things done. What eventually emerged was a highly personal album. Staying with the country feel which had permeated much of her recent output the album contained a mix of country, rock and gospel all delivered with a refreshing rough-hewn feel. Owens made sure the instrumental and vocal backings provided the right backdrop to Dolly's vocals. 'Honky Tonk Songs' combined a loose Rolling Stones sound with lyrics ("Why don't more women sing honky tonk songs?") faintly echoing the sentiment of 'Just Because I'm A Woman'. The poignant story song 'Blue Valley Songbird',\* about childhood abuse and hopes for a better future which are ultimately dashed, showed that Dolly had lost none of her gift for tugging the listener's heartstrings. The album featured two overtly religious and spiritual songs. 'When Jesus Comes Calling For Me' described the comfort a confidence in the afterlife brought through childhood memories of an old man called Zeke, while 'Shine On', the song Dolly sang at Tammy Wynette's funeral, celebrated the unique value of each human being. It had something of the feel of 'Amazing Grace' and was performed virtually as a cappella with the lightest of instrumental backings on bouzouki and autoharp. A team of background vocalists including Rhonda and Darrin Vincent was augmented by Jimmy Boling and the House of Prayer Congregation and, to generate the right atmosphere, was recorded live at the House of Prayer, Dolly's grandfather's old church.

*Hungry Again* was well received by the critics but fared poorly sales-wise. Rising Tide had closed down so Dolly was switched to another MCA label, Decca Nashville. Such manoeuvrings were hardly conducive to effective promotional support for the album. Steve Buckingham was dismissive about each new set of arrangements. "We had just exchanged one set of problems for another, same kind of people with different names, with the same kind of stress and pressure." Dolly was disappointed but

---

\* In 1999 Dolly starred in a television film loosely based on and named after the song. However, whereas the song was powerfully evocative, the film was low-grade fodder. Dolly (unusually wearing an auburn wig) looked too old for the part she was playing.

undaunted. "I'm easy to spot and that's the way I like it . . . I always try to fit in to the present." She promoted *Hungry Again* through a series of personal appearances and a short trip to England for a series of exuberant appearances on high profile television shows including the *National Lottery Draw* (where she managed to squeeze three songs into the short programme as well as plugging Dollywood) and the *Richard And Judy* chat show. Thanks partly to her presence the album made a respectable showing in the British charts, her first for some time.

Ever since the phenomenal success of the original *Trio* album in 1987, there had been speculation and rumours about a follow-up; however, getting Dolly, Emmylou Harris and Linda Ronstadt together to discuss song ideas and rehearse was far from easy. Emmylou said in an interview that getting hold of Dolly was a particular problem. She had talked to Linda about it, and they rehearsed songs but, "it's very difficult to get in touch with Dolly . . . she has more people around her." One proposal was to cut an album by Linda and Emmylou with Dolly appearing as a special guest but Dolly wanted it to be a full *Trio* album or nothing. Songs had eventually been recorded in 1994 with George Massenburg once more in charge of production but due to disagreements and schedule conflicts the *Trio II* project was shelved until 1999. Reports of tension and disagreements emerged in the press. There were complaints about Dolly's lack of commitment after she missed the first 10 days of recording due to other engagements. Amid claims and counterclaims that she failed to honour an agreement to take part in appearances to promote the album and that her vocals were removed from some of the songs, Dolly tried to defuse the situation with humour by telling Linda, "I've got so many irons in the fire, that sometimes I burn my own ass."

Dolly claimed she had been willing to do promotional work if the release date could have been put back from autumn to spring when she promised she would be available to promote it. Linda's irritation at Dolly spilled out in a subsequent interview. "I had booked all these triple scale players and it was going to be very expensive to put them up. Emmy stayed at my house so that we could save money." Dolly was quick to respond. "They bitched a fit and dumped the greatest project ever . . . I was made to feel hurt, insulted, burdened with guilt . . . I would have lived up to my word but my word wasn't good enough for them. Finally I just said the hell with it, sue me . . . never came to that. Apologies all round and the thing moved forward . . . I realise now that we're just a bunch of crotchy, cranky women, set in our ways and getting up there around 50 and going through change-of-life mood swings."

Dolly told *Ladies Home Journal* that *Trio II* could have been entitled, "The Three Tempers . . . Ronstadt loves to work in the studio and works so slow, it drives me nuts. I wanted to say, 'Wake up, bitch, I got stuff to do.'" When asked elsewhere if friendships were affected, Dolly offered a "pouty shrug" and said, "We were never all that close, just girl friends in the business." In her 1994 autobiography Dolly owned up to being the main problem for "getting it all together" and issued a public apology to Emmylou, Linda and their fans, expressing the hope that the project would all work out, though at one stage Dolly thought it might "die on the vine". Interviewed subsequently by Alan Cackett in 1999 Linda was diplomatic. "I think we are good colleagues . . . our relationship has always been based on a common love for traditional music . . . The sum is greater than the parts . . . it's like standing in a room full of mirrors, our voices reflect off one another and take on the characteristics of each other. When it's really good I can't figure who is singing which part. That's when it's magical." She described Dolly as a natural talent but said that any suggestions for doing things differently, "would just roll off her . . . she does it her way and that's it."

As a result of the logistical difficulties of getting all three stars together for a photo shoot it was decided to feature childhood photographs of the three women on the CD booklet. During the period when the project was shelved, five of the 10 tracks, including 'After The Goldrush' (a different version of which appeared on Dolly's *Treasures* album) were featured on Ronstadt's 1995 album, *Feels Like Home*. Despite the presence of three such venerable stars, radio stations, consistent in their ageist approach to compiling playlists, largely ignored the album. However, the public once more went for the pure vocal sounds and the delicate, stripped down production which made the likes of 'High Sierra' and the old Carter Family song 'Lover's Return' memorable if somewhat earnest. Other stand-out tracks were Randy Newman's 'Feels Like Home' and Dolly's 'Do I Ever Cross Your Mind?'

*Trio II* sold more copies than any of the individual women's recent solo releases had managed and was nominated for a Grammy. In 2001 the album achieved gold status. *After The Goldrush* won a Grammy for Best Country Vocal Collaboration.*

In 1998 the news emerged that Dolly had amicably terminated her managerial relationship with Sandy Gallin. He had stepped down as

---

* It was Dolly's fifth Grammy, Linda's tenth and Emmylou's ninth.

chairman of Gallin-Morey Associates to take up a new job as Chairman and CEO of Mirage Entertainment & Sports Inc., in Las Vegas. Sandollar was to be dissolved with current projects being assigned to the producers who had worked on them, though it was understood that the company would continue work on a number of ongoing projects including *Buffy The Vampire Slayer*. Dolly's touring schedule was less hectic, she no longer had a regular band and commercially she was functioning substantially below the level Gallin had helped to bring about. With Dolly's days of Hollywood wheeling and dealing behind her and with a loyal group of people around her who had been there from the start, it was felt that between them they could take care of business. The pair remained friends and it's likely that Gallin continued to provide advice from time to time.

Dollywood celebrated its 14th season in 1999 and to coincide with the opening by Dolly of the Southern Gospel Hall of Fame in the park, the theme was gospel music. During the initial festivities there were performances by Dolly and members of her family and an album of Southern gospel standards *Precious Memories* was released on Blue Eye that year. Songs on the record, which was available only at Dollywood with proceeds going to the Dollywood Foundation, included 'Amazing Grace', 'In The Sweet By And By' and 'When The Roll Is Called Up Yonder'. A television special featuring songs from the album was also broadcast.

The end of the millennium brought the usual pile of awards and accolades. Among the most impressive was a Reuters survey which found that Dolly was the fifth most popular female singer of the 20th century. (Barbra Streisand was first). *Modern Maturity Magazine* named Dolly one of the 50 sexiest people over 50 and at the more unusual end of the spectrum, Dolly was doubtless honoured to be named the 1999 Celebrity Catfish Lover. When the Gatlinburg Hard Rock Café opened for business a few miles from Dollywood, the centrepiece of the banqueting room was a display containing the dress Dolly wore for the cover of *Something Special* plus one of her guitars.

In the wake of the good sales of *Hungry Again* and *Trio II* in Britain, Dolly crossed the Atlantic again for another momentum-sustaining round of interviews and TV appearances which boosted sales of *Hungry Again* by around 70,000. As a clear indication that her talents were being recognised in more intellectual circles she appeared on the serious arts programme, *The South Bank Show*, presented by Melvyn Bragg. As she wandered over to her chair she was heard to ask her interrogator disarmingly, "Have you got a bunch of haaard questions for me?" before telling Bragg how nice his hair looked. "So does yours" he politely replied. The conversation was interspersed with film clips from various stages of her career with Dolly delivering her usual answers with typical aplomb. She acknowledged that she was commercially eclipsed in the Nineties but was determined to keep going even if she had to "make records myself and sell them out of the trunk of my car". Four million viewers tuned in to watch even though the show went out on a Bank Holiday weekend when a number of big films were being shown on competing channels.

On a rather less rarefied level Dolly appeared on the *National Lottery Programme* and, as on her previous appearance, viewing figures shot up to over eight million. She and fellow guest Boy George performed a duet, 'Your Kisses Are Charity', which they had specially recorded. "She was the greatest icon I have ever met," George gushed. "She's better than Madonna. She wanted no fancy demands or limos." Though Dolly was dressed to impress she felt that George, with a long rhinestone necklace and earrings, outdid her. Apparently she leaned over to him at one point and remarked, "I wish I'd known, I could have gone a lot further than this." Earlier in the year, Dolly and Elton John got together to write songs for the film *Women Talking Dirty*, which Elton was producing, and included in the final version was a new dance mix of 'Jolene'. The film's premiere took place at the Toronto Film Festival later in the year.

Dolly's spectacular contribution to country music received full recognition when she joined the elite band of people inducted into the Country Music Hall of Fame, being the second youngest living artist to receive the honour behind Chet Atkins. When first hearing the news she reportedly said, "I thought you had to be ugly or dead to get in." The ceremony took place at the 1999 CMA Awards ceremony in Nashville and her fellow inductees were Johnny Bond and Conway Twitty. Kenny Rogers, chosen to present Dolly with her Hall of Fame plaque, introduced a montage of childhood photographs and clips from her career taking in the *Porter Wagoner Show* and various performances of Dolly classics such as 'Dumb Blonde', 'Coat Of Many Colors', 'Jolene' and 'I Will Always Love You'. There were also brief clips from her Hollywood films as well as some of the colourful interviews she had given over the years. Before receiving her award she performed 'Train Train', from her forthcoming album, to rapturous applause. Despite being a seasoned professional, Dolly was overcome by the emotion of the occasion and her acceptance speech was a tearful affair, regularly interrupted by bursts of applause. She gave thanks to the people who had played a part in her career: her parents, her family, Porter, Don and Ann Warden and Judy Ogle. The latter three had, "kinda kept me sane while all this was going on". Also mentioned were Bill

Owens, "who saw something in me way back early on when I was a kid and thought that we could do something with it", Cas Walker,* Dorothy Gable, Eddie Shuler, Fred Foster, Buddy Killen, Sandy Gallin and Jim Morey. As was doubtless his preference, Carl was not mentioned.

Dolly was presented with her Hall of Fame medallion at a private reception the following January with various luminaries as well as members of her family present. There was further recognition for Dolly at the CMA Awards ceremony when Shania Twain won the award for Entertainer Of The Year (only the fifth woman to do so). Like Dolly, Shania had known hard times when she was struggling to get a break, singing 'Coat Of Many Colors' to entertain drunken miners and loggers in her native Canada, and had caused resentment in certain circles by including pop and rock in her repertoire. When receiving her award Shania confirmed that Dolly was her idol and had been a major influence on her musical development. Dolly (along with Emmylou Harris and Linda Ronstadt) had been nominated in the Vocal Event Of The Year category for *Trio II* but lost out to Vince Gill and Patty Loveless. However, since Loveless was unable to attend, Dolly once more found herself centre stage when she joined Vince Gill to sing the winning song, 'My Kind Of Woman, My Kind Of Man'. Afterwards she quipped to Gill, "I'm no Patty Loveless, but you're no Porter Wagoner!"

Induction into the Hall of Fame might have signified to some the twilight of a career. However, in Dolly's case, the honour came at a time when she had just completed quite possibly the best album she had ever made, which once more took her in a different direction. *The Grass Is Blue* made the point that regardless of all the other things going on in Dolly's life it was the music that was paramount. Steve Buckingham had been approached by Lawrence Welk, the boss of the Welk Music Group, just as it was about to acquire Sugar Hill Records. The label served a niche audience with its small roster of prestige artists and produced around 25 albums of contemporary traditional roots music annually.† Buckingham had accepted Welk's job offer because it offered him an opportunity to get away from the pressures of turning out an endless stream of formulaic songs for country radio. It also meant leaving the organisation Dolly worked for, but she was entirely supportive. Soon after Steve made his move, Decca Nashville closed down leaving Dolly without a major label

---

* In 1999 Cas Walker died at the age of 96.
† Over the years the label's artists have collected around 40 Grammy nominations, winning on 10 occasions.

recording contract. Steve stayed in touch with events through friends and press reports and then by chance, in June 1999, the pair found themselves on a flight to Los Angeles.

Steve Buckingham: "We moved seats so we could talk. Dolly is not the type who would ever go, 'Man I'm really down because I got dropped,' you never hear those kinds of words from her. It's like, onto the next thing, don't look back, no big deal, so we went to dinner that night in LA and I told her that we'd just bought Sugar Hill, predominantly a bluegrass label. A lot of people in the company had done these informal polls – who's out there, who's never done bluegrass that you think would do it great and we'd love to hear it, and Dolly, well her name just kept popping up. It was June 30, 1999, the night we had dinner, and I said would you ever consider doing a bluegrass record and she said she had to do a movie but she said she had the month of August open." The idea of doing a bluegrass album appealed to Dolly. She loved the purity, the non-electrified country instruments, the mournfulness, the distinctive harmonies and the "mountain depth". According to bluegrass musician Marty Raybon, Dolly "was bluegrass to start with . . . she's kinda come back to her roots . . . she came out of a rural area . . . and that was the sound, vocally and lyric-wise."

Raybon dismisses any suggestion that Dolly was attracted to bluegrass because of a lack of success with country. "Dolly Parton's got more money than she can burn . . . that allows you to think about what you really want to do and what you really love." Dolly echoes Raybon's view that bluegrass was part of her personal heritage. "This music is just a part of me. I just had to get rich so I could sing poor again . . . it's my roots, my Smoky Mountain DNA." Things moved quickly as Steve Buckingham explains. "Sure enough, August 1, we were in the studio cutting *The Grass Is Blue* – that's how fast we put that together, a month; did the deal in a month, put the band together picked the songs and were in the studio 30 days later." The deal, which established a pattern for subsequent releases, was that Dolly would record the album at her own expense and then lease it to Sugar Hill who would be responsible for marketing; once more Dolly's Blue Eye logo would appear on the CD alongside that of Sugar Hill.

Talking about the origins of the albums he has done with Dolly, Steve says, "Dolly would come in with a concept, *Eagle When She Flies* or *Slow Dancing*, and would almost always have most of the songs written or, if they were outside tunes, picked . . . she would have done that herself, that's the way she works. It's not like, let's get together and Dolly looks at you and says I have no idea what to do for the next album, those are not words you hear out of her mouth. She'll then trust me to help her go through the songs, she may have 25 songs, and she would sit there and play things for me and over a period of a few days, nights a week whatever, let me narrow it down to 12 or 14. She would get my input for that, then she would trust me to work out the arrangements. Quite often we'd go into the studio ourselves with just me playing guitar and put things down, so that by the time we would get into the studio I would do the charts for the musicians. She would leave it up to me to put the musicians right. By the time we got into the studio the guys would have a pretty good road map to go by, but we're always very open with those kinds of players, 'throw your ideas into the pot,' and everybody contributes, but I will do the charts and usually in the studio I'll play guitar with Dolly singing it in the control while everybody follows along and kind of gets an idea of the song.

"Basically that's what we did with *The Grass Is Blue*. Once we decided to do the album, I gave Dolly a couple of CDs worth of old material to listen to, she came back with things she'd written as well as some things that she liked, old songs that she knew, it was a mixture. 'Travellin' Prayer', the Billy Joel tune, was totally her idea. 'Cash On The Barrel Head' was her idea. It was a favourite song of Carl's who thought it a pity that Dolly couldn't sing it because it was written for a man. However, Dolly simply changed 'son' to 'hun' ['And that'll be cash . . . on the barrel head hun'] and it all made sense. 'A Few Old Memories' and 'Sleep With One Eye Open' were both things on a CD I gave her then she wrote 'Steady As The Rain'. I think she picked out 'I Still Miss Someone'. 'Endless Stream Of Tears' and 'Silver Dagger' – she took some of the old mountain tunes and rewrote a story around them."

Steve was not sure where Dolly's idea for 'Train Train' came from but commented that Dolly and Carl liked to drive around listening to the radio, which is how she was often inspired. Buckingham recalled how he first heard the title track, which neatly encapsulated the musical style of the album. "Well she was doing a movie in Nashville called *Blue Valley Songbird* and she called me from the bus and said, 'I think I've written the title cut for the album,' and she was playing guitar and singing it over the phone." Dolly claimed the writing process for 'The Grass Is Blue' benefited from some divine intervention while 'I Wonder Where You Are Tonight' was, unbeknown to Dolly, written by her fellow Hall of Fame inductee Johnny Bond. For 'A Few Old Memories' Patty Loveless changed her travel arrangements in order to provide backing vocals. Loveless had good reason to go out of her way to make a contribution as she

310

was another artist Dolly had helped in the early stages of her career. As a teenager Patty had pitched a song to Porter, who in turn introduced her to Dolly, who offered advice on subjects ranging from the dangers of the Nashville scene for a young singer to the best kind of make-up.

'Silver Dagger' was a public domain song Dolly's mother was very fond of. Dolly's arrangement included words she had collected from various relatives, including her mother, and it was among her favourite songs on the album. Recording proceeded smoothly and quickly with seven tracks laid down on the first day. Dolly was "in awe" of the musicians Buckingham assembled, referring to them as "God's Bluegrass Band". "They moved my soul . . . just listening to that kind of music, it's like feeling your mamma and your daddy. It's like feeling the ground that you grew up on and walked on as a child, so I think it just took me back so far in my life and my time, and it hit a chord in me that just rang real spiritual and real true." Dobro player Jerry Douglas made it clear he would not be interested in a "tongue in cheek" bluegrass album and insisted there be a real banjo part on every song.

Because Dolly was backed by some of the best bluegrass artists in the business, there was no need for multiple takes. Steve Buckingham: "The music was live, Dolly did the vocals live and did a great job, and she always wants me to 'get everything on there' as she says. About the only thing I had to overdub were background vocals. I picked different pairs of harmony singers for different songs – Alison [Krauss] and Dan [Tyminski] on some, and Rhonda and Darrin Vincent sang on some, and then Dolly would come in there again and re-sing everything so fast, people can't believe it . . . You run it, she sings it, you back it up, you run it again, she sings it, you put it all down, maybe get three or four vocal passes then you just go straight on to the next song.

"After three or four hours she's sung the entire album again and then you just pick what's the best performance, so some of those songs were the original live performance with the band when we cut the tracks. Some of them might have been a re-sing after she heard the harmony vocal but that was it . . . I mean we were done, mixed, everything before the end of August and had the album out in October." Steve describes Dolly as "old school" when it came to her approach in the studio. "She leaves it up to Gary [Paczosa, responsible for recording and mixing] and me, never nit-picks about, you know, there's too much highs on the vocal, never, she's just that old school professional, comes in prepared, always on time, expects everybody else to be on time, expects everybody else to have their act together and totally leaves everybody's job up to them. During a song she'll say if something is not feeling right to her or if it's too fast or if the key might not be exactly right but the technical stuff, she never gets involved in that."

"I knew on the first track on the first day [that *The Grass Is Blue* was going to be a great album] . . . there was a lot of scepticism, a lot of people didn't take her seriously. Dolly has created such an outrageous persona that I think sometimes people are blinded by, as she calls it herself, a cartoon, but she's one of the greatest singers, and a great musician." Buckingham's comments contrast with a narrower view of Dolly expressed in a 1998 article in the *Nashville Banner* which pondered what Jackson Taylor – 'Applejack' in the song of the same name – would have made of her. "Would he wonder when it was Dolly Parton ceased being that precocious mountain girl with a holler full of talent and became this creature of show business . . . has she become a victim of her image, forever married to the wigs and the breast jokes and the tight gowns."

For Buckingham, this entirely missed the point. "There are a lot of people who'd love to see Dolly turn up in a denim shirt and blue jeans and do nothing but bluegrass for the rest of her life, but she can't just be a one-dimensional artist, there's too much inside her. She's that earthy, deep thinking introspective songwriter from the mountains but she's also this glitzy showgirl and she can't just be just one segment of Dolly Parton. She's all Dolly; if you like Dolly you have to take the deep thinking Dolly, the great musician Dolly, the incredible songwriting Dolly, along with the glitzy Dolly, the corny Dolly, the showgirl; I mean it's all her."

The response among critics to *The Grass Is Blue* was universally positive and contributed to a sense of Dolly's lengthy musical career being regenerated. Stella Parton: "She's had 30 years of musical experience and development of doing film stuff . . . she's taken all that and now she's back full circle doing what she originally was doing and I think it's brilliant work and I don't think she's encumbered by management or influence from LA or a label or the public as a matter of fact . . . she's actually free to create this music."

As a pure, some would say reactionary, musical form, the bluegrass scene had gained popularity in the Nineties with the rise of artists such as Alison Krauss who helped raise its profile. Yet there were some purists who found it hard to accept Dolly's sudden emergence on the scene given that she had dabbled in so many wholly different styles. According to bluegrass musician Wayne Bledsoe, Ricky Skaggs' return to the genre had been accepted because he had started out with the Stanley Brothers, highly influential early bluegrass exponents, so that he was still seen as "part of that first generation of hard core traditional bluegrass . . . Dolly and Marty (Raybon) and Patty (Loveless) can't call on that, and while the audience they're attracting is a new audience, a lot of the older audience is not accepting them the way the new people are. But they're a plus for bluegrass because they're bringing in a whole new youth spectrum into bluegrass which is going to make its future even brighter."

Bass player Byron House (who has played with Dolly in recent years) described Dolly as the "real deal. [Her] technical quality is amazing but the heart that you feel being delivered . . . it makes it a joy and a real pleasure to deliver your best performance to support that. You know she's gonna knock it out so you know you gotta step up there, when the light goes on, don't mess around it's time to deliver the goods. She's gonna do it and you don't want to be holding that up." Of the awards Dolly received for *The Grass Is Blue* he said, "She has every right to lay claim to them."

As well as winning the Grammy for Best Bluegrass Album, Dolly had one of the biggest thrills of her life when she subsequently won Album Of The Year at the International Bluegrass Music Awards in Louisville, Kentucky. Steve Buckingham accompanied her. "I have never seen her that excited . . . she was shocked, absolute surprise, she thought there were still some hardcore people who felt she's just trying to horn in on bluegrass. She absolutely did not expect to win anything, because she kind of felt like she was an outsider . . . I've been around her when she's won Grammies and everything else and this really overwhelmed her and I think we carried all that energy into the next album when we did *Little Sparrow*."

Dolly rounded off the millennium with an appearance at Nashville's Opryland Hotel's Delta ballroom in front of a crowd of over 2,000. Dolly declined to work on New Year's Eve appearing instead the following day in a short, glittering silver skirt which lit up the venue like a ballroom globe. Her set included a mixture of material from all sections of her career, so there was room for 'Jolene', the party enlivening 'Two Doors Down', 'Here You Come Again', 'Islands In The Stream' (with Richard Dennison taking Kenny Rogers' part), the inevitable 'Coat Of Many Colors' and 'I Will Always Love You'. Reflecting her recent recorded output there was a bluegrass segment featuring harmonies from Alison Krauss and the show closed with gospel songs, culminating with 'He's Alive', for which Dolly was backed by members of the Christ Church Choir. Picking up on widespread concerns about computer failures on the first day of 'Y2K' Dolly delivered a string of double entendres. "Well, if I had a glitch, I'd scratch it . . . all I know about hard drives is what I learned in my '63 Chevy" and had a hard time explaining away the "megabytes" on her neck. "I guess I was the original laptop." She was pleased that she had never had any problems with a "floppy disk". When talking about the fact that she came from a family of 12, Dolly said her parents were not Catholics, "Just horny Baptists and holy rollers."

The Opryland concert encapsulated all the key aspects of the dazzling career Dolly had created for herself for more than 30 years and was also a clear statement of intent that the show would go on into the new century.

# Chapter 26

FOR Steve Buckingham, the wave of critical approbation that greeted *The Grass Is Blue* and the momentum it generated carried over to the next project. However, Dolly's musical curiosity made her less content to repeat a successful formula. As she put it, "I don't chew my tobacco but once." While retaining a similar bluegrass sound courtesy of virtually the same posse of top pickers and singers, *Little Sparrow* shifted musical focus in subtle ways. The album was a delicate blend of mountain-country and bluegrass, with threads of Celtic music also evident – a mix Dolly described as blue mountain music, a broader canvas than pure bluegrass. The ideas for most of the songs came to her in a three-day burst of creativity in Los Angeles.

Making the album was a daunting prospect for Buckingham. "I was more nervous . . . *The Grass Is Blue* got the best reviews of her career and won a Grammy. I told my engineer Gary, 'Good gosh, talk about nowhere to go but down.' The first time we had nothing to really live up to other than to show people she can really do this." He felt the universally favourable response to the previous album spurred Dolly on. "We got into the *Little Sparrow* album and I knew that was even, if anything, more special. She was more confident, not that she's ever not confident, but she knew she was on a roll, coming off of the Grammy, coming off of those reviews."

Over the decades, Dolly had embraced many styles of music from traditional country and folk music to disco and soul. Though some worked better than others, she had rarely sounded more assured and comfortable than with her blue mountain music. "I believe this album has more depth, breadth, and soul than all of the other albums I have done . . . hopefully it captures the best of everything I have ever lived or felt, written or sung." She conceded that artists tended to claim the album they had just finished was the best they had ever done, but Byron House, who played bass on some tracks, thinks the album genuinely got close to Dolly's essence. "She'll tell you that . . . this is music she kind of grew up with . . . it's real dear to her heart and she says that's the kind of music she will always want to do . . . The way she writes a song, with her guitar or a banjo, that's really what I strive for as a player, to get inside that kernel of inspiration from which springs the song itself. It's a living part of her so that's the spring, anything we can draw from that, that'll help bring it into life. Her great songs spring out of that sort of mountain bluegrass well source, that instrumentation . . . it's almost lifestyle but it's a way of being, it's acoustic, it was round before all the big changes in technology. It's wonderful the way current technology allows us to share it, but that's really what it was about, sitting on the porch. The sound that's captured on those albums could have well been heard in bygone days."

Songs such as the light-hearted 'Marry Me' or a revamp of the gloomy 'Down From Dover' sounded like the kind of numbers Dolly's parents might have listened to when growing up. Thirty years previously, 'Down From Dover' was not played on radio because the subject of an abandoned pregnant woman was regarded as too controversial. Even in its original form a verse was omitted due to Porter Wagoner considering it too graphic. Social mores had changed enough for it to be reinstated.

Dolly was enjoying something of a creative rebirth. Freed from the product dictates of major record labels and with her modern material rarely gaining radio play, she could now include a song six or seven minutes long if she so desired. On *Little Sparrow* she even included a bouncy bluegrass version of the Cole Porter Classic, 'I Get A Kick Out Of You'. Once more the critics fawned. *Billboard*'s headline: 'Dolly Rules. An Instant Classic', summed up the general view. Dolly dedicated the album to her father Lee who had died in November 2000, aged 79. She remembered him fondly as a man who was widely trusted, who could borrow money on the strength of his name. Dolly was touched that so many relatives flocked to the funeral home to pay their last respects and share stories, which inspired her to write the lines, "They say that you're dead, but to me you've never been more alive."

Dolly was greatly amused by one review of *Little Sparrow* which said, "Dolly sings her guts out." She said, "I thought that was the funniest thing I'd ever seen. I just roared. I've heard, 'Dolly sings her head off' and 'Dolly sings her butt off' and 'Dolly sings her face off.' So now I've sung everything off and my guts out."

*Little Sparrow* received two Grammy nominations, Best Bluegrass Album and Best Female Country Vocal Performance for 'Shine'. Dolly won her seventh Grammy in the latter category while Alison Krauss won the former. As part of the promotion for the album in America, Dolly embraced new technology by engaging in an internet chat. Sales of Dolly's recent albums had been particularly strong in Britain and *Little Sparrow* continued the trend, soon topping 100,000, remarkably only about 50,000 less than in America. Dolly acknowledged her fans in Great Britain. "I have always had a great rapport with the British audiences. They have accepted my whole person, my looks, my personality . . . sometimes it seems as if I'm more loved and appreciated over there than I am over here." Dolly once more crossed the Atlantic to do the rounds of prime time television shows such as *Parkinson, So Graham Norton* and *Richard And Judy*, boosting their ratings in the process. Dolly and her entourage took over two floors of the Churchill Hotel in London. Her visit to Britain was rich in irony. She was promoting her most outstanding and authentic musical work in years, yet much of her airtime was spent fielding the usual questions about bosoms and plastic surgery. It was, as she well knew, a paradox of her own making.

The combination of plastic surgery and stage make-up made for a striking change in Dolly's appearance on the predominantly black and white sleeve for *Little Sparrow*. "I'm like a show dog or a prize horse," she told one interviewer. "You got to keep them clipped as long as they're going to be in the show." Rather than resembling a woman in her thirties, which seemed to be the aim, Dolly looked more like her true age, employing artificial techniques in an attempt to look younger. Skin and flesh had been removed from under her jaw thus startlingly emphasising its line. There was also a sharper definition to her nose and cheekbones.

Given her high profile use of cosmetic surgery Dolly was asked to take part in an infomercial on the subject. While advocating the practice she was also admonitory. "I would advise people if they're going to do it to find the best doctors . . . so many people get maimed and screwed up . . . I've had a bad tendency to scar, so I've had to be very careful any time I get anything done." Over the years Dolly had "done" her eyes, teeth, lips (the "bee-stung" look as a journalist described it), liposuction, excess skin removal and used botox and collagen, though she claimed she did not want to get to the stage of looking "tighter than a banjo head". Quite a lot of the work was in response to her dramatic weight loss in the Eighties, such as the lifting and augmentation of her breasts ("shock and awe" as Dolly recently described them; at times it seemed she was referring to something else rather than a part of her body). Dolly, who once joked that Carl wouldn't have to cheat on her because he gets a new wife every three or four months, refuted any idea that because she was recording more homespun music, she should tone down her appearance to match. "You ain't never going to see no down-home looking Dolly. Never! . . . that's half the magic, besides I don't think I could sing a lick if I didn't have on rhinestones." It's almost as if her gaudy appearance acts as a form of compensation. As she told *Cosmopolitan*, "I choose to look that way because my personality is so open and I'm so full of energy that I don't feel I'm *enough* when I don't wear a ton of make-up, or when I wear my hair flat. I want my looks to match what I feel like inside, and I want it to be overwhelming whether it looks appealing or not."

Dolly's continuing popularity was amply demonstrated in 2000 when she hosted the Academy of Country Music Awards, attracting an estimated viewing audience of around 30 million.* When Dolly headlined MerleFest, the famous bluegrass event in Wilkesboro, North Carolina, the festival attracted a record crowd of nearly 80,000.

In her 1994 autobiography, Dolly talked of out-of-body experiences and from time to time, tabloid papers suggested that Dolly was a believer in the supernatural, for instance, having premonitions of dying in a car crash on her birthday. Lawrence Grobel, the journalist who interviewed her for *Playboy* in 1978, recalled staying up talking with Dolly into the early hours, "mostly about ghosts and spirits and things that go bump in the night". Grobel concluded she was "kind of interested in that stuff", and believed it probably related to her upbringing in the rural South.

Years later Grobel was offered the opportunity of interviewing Charles Manson. Because Grobel lived in the Hollywood Hills, not far from where Manson still had followers, he was concerned that they might try to get to the convicted murderer through him. After soliciting advice from various people he was inclined to accept the assignment when late one night, Dolly called him. When he told her about the proposed assignment, her language became curt. "I don't know what this is worth to you, but I want to tell you what I think about it. The man is pure evil. He's the Devil. His kind rubs off on anybody who meets him. If you see him, if you even talk to him, if . . . have you talked to him yet?" Grobel assured her he hadn't. Dolly continued, "Well, consider this then, if you so much as talk to him – even on the phone – then I will never see you or talk with you again. I feel that strongly about it. I've kept my life as pure as I can make it. I've kept away from evil and the bad vibrations that come from being around evil, and I truly believe that man is the Devil. If you ever had anything to do with Charles Manson, I wouldn't want the vibes you would pick up to get around me. Now I know that it may not be fair to tell you this, but I'm telling you from my heart. That's the way I am. It's your decision to make, but if you value my friendship at all, you'd better steer clear of that one."

* The following year, when LeAnn Rimes hosted the awards, the figures fell by about half.

Suitably warned, Grobel elected not to interview Manson but it seems the damage was done. After receiving Dolly's annual Christmas basket of jellies, candies, polished glass and herb-scented balls, Grobel sent a letter thanking her and suggested lunch. He merely received a pro forma letter in response containing photographs and brochures about Dollywood with details of gifts he might want to purchase. There could have been an innocent reason – chiefly Dolly's hectic schedule – why his request was ignored but the impression remained that her upbringing gave her an unearthly fear of perceived evil forces.

After the dreadful events of September 11 she cancelled all public events that week. "It's hard," she said in an interview with the *Knoxville News-Sentinel*. "That's when you really need to stay upbeat if you can . . . it's always good to help the other people that can't get up from this. I think everybody is dealing with this tragedy in their own kind of way . . . I'm a very patriotic person, but I also know that when things are at their worst, I need to be at my best . . . Everybody deals with this differently. I deal with it internally . . . I see how everybody else deals with it and I am able to write about their emotions. It allows me a way to express sorrow, not just for myself but for the people who can't put their emotions into words. It's very strange and deep places where I am going."

For *Halos And Horns* – the follow-up to *Little Sparrow* – Dolly took on the role of producer, backed by a group she called the Blueniques, a play on "unique bluegrass", her favoured description of the kind of music she now played. As Dolly told *Maverick*, "I called on some of the musicians who had been staples at Dollywood." She used the auditions to make demo recordings of her songs in Knoxville and "the album just seemed to come to life", the spontaneity making *Halos And Horns* turn out "fairly live". The Blueniques included Jimmy Mattingly and Terry Eldredge. Mattingly had played in Dolly's band during the Nineties before joining Garth Brooks in 1995, playing on three multi-million selling albums, until Brooks' retirement from the road.

Eldredge was in awe of Dolly when they first met. "When she walks in a room, it's like, 'Oh my God, it's Dolly Parton,' but within a minute or two she'll make you feel comfortable . . . there's no ego, there's no attitude . . . she's there to do a thing and she knows you're there to do a thing with her, she wants to make you feel comfortable, but she wants to feel as comfortable as she can too."

Dolly was assisted in her production duties by banjo supremo Gary Davis and the rest of the band also contributed. As with the previous two albums the album was traditional in feel, with acoustic guitars, country fiddle, mandolin and dobro much in evidence. Jimmy Mattingly's fiddle playing was particularly valuable, sensitively reflecting and enhancing the varied palette of emotions which Dolly's vocals brought to the songs and tugging at the heartstrings. The song selection was very personal to her. In 'Hello God', inspired by the events of 9/11, Dolly appeared to doubt God though as the song progresses her despair was aimed more at mankind.

Another song inspired by the attacks on the World Trade Center was 'Color Me America', which Dolly premiered that year at the second annual Smoky Mountain Christmas benefit concerts for the Dollywood Foundation. (The song also appeared on Dolly's album *For God And Country* in 2003.) An unsubstantiated rumour at the time claimed that some radio stations were not playing Dolly's music as a result of her alleged refusal to support events aimed at raising money in the wake of 9/11. However, in 2002, Dolly performed at a benefit in Minneapolis for the Families of Freedom Fund to provide scholarships for the children of the victims. The concert replaced an earlier event called off as a result of a bomb threat.

Also dusted off for inclusion were two songs from Dolly's past. The choice of a particularly heartfelt and emotional 'What A Heartache', suggested the wounds regarding Gregg Perry had not yet healed. 'Shattered Image' also got another outing. Written in 1967, the song was inspired by Dolly's feelings about unwanted intrusion into her life, including gossip about her sexual mores, an issue that never went away.

'Dagger Through The Heart' was another old song that spoke of rejection and betrayal in the most painful terms. 'Raven Dove' was a semi-religious meditation on life and death and a yearning for a better world, which may well have had its origins in Dolly's daily prayer habit. "I pray every day, throughout the day. I ask God to be my business partner, my photographer, my accountant, my lawyer, my producer . . . I always talk to God, and I *always* believe He will answer me. And He does . . . But He answers me with a feeling inside . . . all of a sudden I feel like I know what to do about a particular situation." She told *The Times* the following year that the lack of a spiritual dimension contributed to the troubles afflicting the world. "If we were God-loving, God-like, Christ-like people, we wouldn't be having the problems we do but we're having them because nobody will forgive, nobody will love, we're all so selfish and just get into our own little place of what is right and what is wrong and so we're all just screwing up big time."

Dolly wrote all the songs on *Halos And Horns* except for two Seventies pop/rock numbers: 'If', written by David Gates and recorded by his band Bread and most surprising of all, Led Zeppelin's rock anthem 'Stairway To Heaven'. Dolly revealed that Carl had been a "Led head" for years and that it was "kinda like our song", one the pair enjoyed listening to while out driving together. It demonstrated how virtually any song could be played in a country style depending upon the quality of the song and the arrangement. Though inevitably not as memorable as the original, Dolly and the Blueniques cleverly highlighted the delicate melodic progressions in the song and Robert Plant, who had always thought of it as a spiritual song, was said to have approved of Dolly's version, particularly the use of a choir.

Another unusual song was 'These Old Bones' about an old woman clairvoyant who was regarded as not "right in the mind" by the authorities, and had a bag of bones which she tossed and rolled. What was remarkable was Dolly's impersonation of the old woman for the choruses. Stella Parton: "I think that is just the wildest thing, it's like that was just channelled through my mother or something, she sounds like my mother, just exactly like her. She used my mother's voice just for fun but the story is just such a good story."

With *Halos And Horns,* critics were once again impressed. One said it contained, "Timeless music delivered with the power of an uncorked hydro-electric dam and mellowed ever so slightly by age and experience." At a charity event reuniting the stars of *9 To 5* (held in 2003), Jane Fonda remarked of the album, "It's got all the joys and complexities of life and is what she is as a human being." Dolly gave her own view. "What this album turned out to be and, what I had hoped, is some of everything that I have ever been and what I am . . . because not only did I take some songs of old and rework them, I did some new songs that sounded like they were old. I love that solid hard country sound, it took me all the way back to my early days in Nashville. The gospel influence has always been a part of me, and I wanted to bring that in."

Dolly continued the arrangement of leasing the album to Sugar Hill, having put it together at her own expense. Thanks no doubt to her strong financial position she was able to commission top photographer Annie Leibovitz to shoot the sleeve pictures. Dolly's manipulation of her physical appearance through surgery and make-up meant that her appearance looked noticeably different for each album. For *Halos And Horns* her face was pale and smooth, like a Venetian mask, and appeared almost to be separate from her body. However, her blue denim shirt and frayed sleeves were in keeping with the music's rustic flavour. This image was in sharp contrast to Dolly's Nashville office where interviewer Barbara Toner noted the pink walls, pink blinds, and pink butterfly soap in the bathroom. "Even the office manager is wearing fuchsia lipstick to match her fuchsia trouser suit."

The album made the country Top 10 in America* with sales hovering around the 150,000 to 200,000 mark. Buoyed by the excellent reviews Dolly professed not to be troubled by such sales figures and was happy to see newer and younger talents making their mark. The critically acclaimed trio of albums – *The Grass Is Blue*, *Little Sparrow* and *Halos And Horns* – had the broader effect of reintroducing country audiences to East Tennessee mountain music and folk tales. By continuing to make music in this fashion, Dolly was carrying on in the tradition of such legendary country names as the Carter Family, Roy Acuff and the Louvin Brothers.

In 2001 Dollywood saw its 30 millionth visitor and Splash Country, a $20 million water park adjacent to the area, was opened. Dolly was on hand for the opening jamboree. With her considerable experience, she was invited to be the keynote speaker at the International Association of Amusement Parks and Attractions convention in Atlanta. The Imagination Library continued to catch the attention of school authorities across America, with more signing up to the programme each year.† Also during this time it was announced that Dolly would expand her commercial empire with a new Dixie Stampede theatre restaurant planned for Australia. The project failed to materialise but Dolly received permission to open a restaurant in Orlando, Florida.‡

Dolly found time to appear on albums by other artists, contributing 'Cry, Cry Darling' for the Bill Monroe tribute album *Big Mon*, produced by Ricky Skaggs. She also provided vocal backing on 'Once Upon A Christmas' with Christian group Selah on their *Rose Of Bethlehem* CD. In 2001 Dolly, along with Charley Pride, Porter Wagoner and Mark Knopfler, was an honorary pallbearer at the funeral of guitar legend and

---

* Thus making Dolly the artist with the largest number of Top 10 entries in the country charts, just ahead of Loretta Lynn and Merle Haggard.

† It is anticipated that around four million free books will have been distributed to children in nearly 600 communities across 42 states by 2006. As a result of a partnership arrangement with the Bureau of Indian Affairs, around 100 Native American communities, mostly on reservations, have also participated.

‡ The restaurant opened in 2003. At the present time, there are a total of four Dolly-owned Dixie Stampede restaurants. The first, which opened in 1988, located in Pigeon Forge, the others in Myrtle Beach, South Carolina and Branson, Missouri.

record company executive Chet Atkins who had been an important figure in Dolly's early career as well as the butt of her risqué humour. While Chet was rehearsing for a television show at Opryland, "Dolly came walking across the stage with a pair of real tight pants on and she walked right up to me and said, 'I saw you lookin' at my crotch.'" An embarrassed Chet snapped back, "Well you do that too once in a while, don't you?" to which she replied, "Oh, sometimes," giggling as she ambled off. Writer Nicholas Dawidoff recounted another encounter involving Atkins. "She grabbed me by the ass three times last year. I was gonna sue her for sexual harassment, but only for $50 'cos I kind of enjoyed it you know." On occasion Dolly used this kind of earthy approach to break the ice. Ronny Light recalls the time musician Darrin Vincent was introduced to Dolly; for many people the occasion can be overwhelming. "She said, 'Darrin come over here.' She had some low-cut dress on and she pulled his head and buried it in her bosom. She does things like that."

Dolly maintained her interest in movies and there were reports in 2001 that she would star in a film version of the novel *Miss Julia Speaks Her Mind* with one of her *Steel Magnolias* co-stars, Shirley MacLaine although this has yet to come to fruition. Dolly went into the studio with Steve Buckingham to record songs for the soundtrack of the film *Frank McKlusky, C.I.* in which she played the lead character's wife. The film received generally poor reviews, though there was (as always) praise for Dolly's screen presence.*

A family matter that surfaced in the local press was a court action arising out of problems surrounding the administration of the financial affairs of Dolly's 77-year-old widowed mother, Avie Lee. Nine of the children, including Dolly, were of the view that she was not competent to look after her finances and sought a legal order in Sevier County to this effect in order to give them legal control over Avie Lee's estate, estimated to be worth around $1 million. The twins, Floyd and Frieda Parton, were not parties to the lawsuit and instructed a lawyer to represent their mother's interests, in opposition to their siblings. The twins' lawyer was instructed to reach a compromise that would allow Avie Lee to live as independently as possible by remaining at home. Matters were unresolved until Avie Lee died in December 2003. As Stella put it, "The beautiful thing is, when my mother finally passed away, each one of us agreed to exactly the same thing." She was buried at Caton's Chapel Cemetery alongside her husband Lee.

---

* Disney executives decided that the film was not good enough for general release and it went straight to video.

Accolades for Dolly continued to mount up. In Country Music Television's survey of the 40 Greatest Women Of Country Music Dolly came in at number four.* VH1's 100 Greatest Love Songs Of All Time featured 'Islands In The Stream' at number 80 while Whitney Houston's cover of 'I Will Always Love You' took the top spot. In 2002, *Rolling Stone* assembled a list of the 50 essential albums by female artists and 1975's *Best Of Dolly Parton* came in at 34. The accompanying critique read, "Dolly sings Dolly's own complex psychological epics, crisply deep-fried and put over with an insouciance that takes your breath away." Less appealing was her nomination for a Golden Voice Award, which recognised legendary artists still active but receiving little airplay or chart appearances.

Dolly had even been nominated for an Orville H Gibson Guitar Award in the Best Female Country Guitarist category, a reminder that in addition to her better-known musical talents Dolly was an accomplished guitarist. In the event she lost out to Kim Richey. Doubtless she would have been a great deal more proficient had she been prepared to remove her artificial fingernails. The fact that she is able to play the guitar with long fingernails is in part due to her practice of playing in open tuning.

In 2002 Dolly was named Tennessee's official ambassador for film and music and her popularity was such that a petition was started to persuade Dolly to run for the office of governor of Tennessee. Some 5,000 signatures were obtained but though she was flattered it was hardly surprising that Dolly turned it down. She had spent much of her career doing her level best in maintaining the loyalty of a diverse audience by steering clear of politics. The idea of being a prominent figurehead making controversial and unpopular decisions went against the grain.

That year Porter was inducted into the Country Music Hall of Fame, belatedly in the view of some, not least himself. As part of the celebrations famed Nashville producer Jack "Cowboy" Clement was asked to host a show honouring Porter and fellow inductee Bill Carlisle in the theatre at the Hall of Fame in downtown Nashville. As Clement explained, his brief included "getting artists to sing some Porter Wagoner songs . . . turned out that Dolly agreed to do one. They'd been on kind of the outs for a while . . . but they got back together . . . they wound up singing my song 'Someone I Used To Know'. It had to be songs that related to Porter in some fashion, so she sang 'I Will Always Love You' which is really probably her swansong, and she sang the living shit out of it." Clement's

---

* Emmylou Harris was number five and the top three, in ascending order, were Loretta Lynn, Tammy Wynette and Patsy Cline.

remark about Dolly and Porter having fallen out was not strictly true, certainly in recent times. Indeed, two years before, when Porter cut his first new album for nearly 20 years he sought Dolly's reaction. "We know each other probably as well as two people can know each other," he said at the time. "I thought she'd give me an honest answer." Dolly responded with a lengthy and positive letter praising the album as, "by far the best thing you've ever done". As a result Porter called the album *The Best I've Ever Been.*

Dolly undertook her first concert tour in a decade – a much-scaled-down affair from when she would do over 200 shows in a year. The main purpose of the tour, which featured country, bluegrass and folk, as well as some of her pop hits, was to promote *Halos And Horns.*\* In 2002, there were 13 American concerts and, towards the end of the year, a European leg taking in seven venues with capacities ranging from 1,000 to around 2,500. Virtually all tickets for the concerts sold out and in Glasgow the demand was so great that a second show was arranged. Dolly had not given a live concert in Britain for nearly two decades and reviewer Janet Aspley, who took in the Hammersmith Apollo show in London, was pleasantly surprised. "I was quite prepared to discover that technology had enhanced her voice as much as it has her body over recent years, but there it was, clear and pure as a mountain stream, rippling across all the glitz and glamour to cut a path straight to the heart." Another writer said, "And there was that voice again – that voice that can break hearts at a hundred yards . . ." *Halos And Horns* topped the British country charts and had a knock on effect of stimulating further sales and chart re-entries for the previous albums.

The experience of being on the road reminded Dolly of how much she enjoyed appearing in front of live audiences. She even said she didn't really care whether her music was played on the radio any more, although she immediately qualified these remarks. "Well, I mean, of course you care and wish you could be accepted everywhere, but I'm not catering to that any more. And I'm happier than I've ever been."

\* Dolly had considered touring to promote *The Grass Is Blue* and *Little Sparrow* but there were difficulties putting together a suitable road band.

# Chapter 27

BACK home after the 2002 UK tour, an American journalist discovered that Dolly's lifestyle remained unchanged. "Even now when she's on a plane, she often orders things from the in-flight catalogues." Dolly said she would always remain "white trash" and offered to show the writer her apartment. The pantry revealed cans of corned beef hash, tins of spam, loads of white bread and a giant chunk of Velveeta. There was also a pig-shaped ceramic with a bag of bacon grease inside, neatly labelled with the date. As Dolly explained, "The people who come to clean the house on a Thursday have to fry up some bacon so I have bacon grease to cook with."

In 2003 a compilation album, *Ultimate Dolly Parton*, appeared gathering the best of Dolly's Seventies and Eighties output – from 'Joshua' to 'Why'd You Come In Here Lookin' Like That?' Of the 20 songs, 19 had been number one hits but the album only made number 20 in the American country charts, although it reached the top in Britain. Ironically, *Just Because I'm A Woman*, a tribute to Dolly released later that year, performed far better.

The album, described by one reviewer as a "golden handshake from her peers", though in reality almost all were from younger generations, came out 35 years after Dolly had released her album of the same name. The women artists, brought together by Steve Buckingham, were mainly associated with alternative country and Americana, with the notable exception of Shania Twain. All came up with original readings of Dolly's songs, which highlighted her songwriting gift across a wide range of styles. Alison Krauss slowed '9 To 5' right down imbuing it with a bluesy feel appropriate to the subject matter, while Me'Shell NdegeOcello deconstructed 'Two Doors Down', transforming it into a different song altogether.

Norah Jones delivered a typically soulful interpretation of 'The Grass Is Blue'* and Emmylou Harris offered a heartfelt 'To Daddy'. Although

---

* Norah and Dolly performed a duet version of the song at the 37th Annual CMA Awards. The contrast between Norah's understated, tasteful clothes and Dolly's usual grotesquerie was striking.

Linda Ronstadt did not contribute, other artists included Shelby Lynne, Melissa Etheridge, Kasey Chambers, Mindy Smith and Sinead O'Connor (singing 'Dagger Through The Heart') who announced it would be her last recording before retiring. Dolly contributed a new version of the title track.

*Mojo*'s review was fulsome in its praise. "In storytelling and melody, the elegance, economy and heartfelt clarity of Parton's writing deserves comparison with not only Hank Williams or Johnny Cash but George Gershwin or Irving Berlin." As part of the album's promotion, Dolly appeared on old friend Oprah Winfrey's television show, duetting with, Shania Twain, Alison Krauss and Melissa Etheridge. Dolly congratulated Melissa on her recent legal union with another woman. In an interview with gay lifestyle magazine *EXP*, she joked, "Why shouldn't they have to suffer just like us straight couples do?" adding on a more serious note, "If you're going to live as a family and be a family you should have the same rights as everybody else." Dolly had avoided taking a public stance on such a controversial issue in the past. Not everybody brought up in the boondocks of East Tennessee took such a liberal view of homosexuality but Dolly's years in Los Angeles and the movie industry had helped to form her opinion.

"Gay isn't something you do. It's something you are . . . how can it be wrong to be who you are? How can that be a sin? I don't care what people do in their bedrooms and people shouldn't care what I do in mine . . ."

Dolly was the first to admit that when AIDS hit the headlines in the Eighties, she was naive about the subject, as were many people from a similar background. "When I went to Los Angeles," Dolly told *A&U*, "I became best friends with my manager Sandy Gallin, who is gay. Many of Sandy's associates, friends and creative teams were gay people. They are some of the finest, most creative folks there are . . . I became friends with many of them, like Steve Rubell of Studio 54 in New York. It wasn't long before I learned first hand of the devastating impact of AIDS . . . I have lost many dear friends to it . . . both gay and heterosexual. That's when I really began to understand and get involved in the fight."

Tony Chase, who designed hundreds of Dolly's favourite outfits, and who did much to glamourise her image, died of the disease in 1994. Although never officially confirmed, many Dolly fans believe the song 'Crippled Bird' from her 1995 album *Something Special* was inspired by Chase's death. "I helped him with medicine and financially . . . I kept Tony close to me until the end. I've lost some family members and in-laws, also . . . some were gay and some were not. Just recently, we lost

Herb Ritts . . . another dear, dear friend."* Sandollar financed *Common Threads: Stories From The Quilt* which examined the first decade of AIDS through five personal accounts. One Sandollar executive, Howard Rosenman, was a co-founder (as was Sandy Gallin) of Project Angel Food in Los Angeles which provided meals for people with AIDS. "At Dollywood, at least twice each year, when I am there, we have a special Make-A-Wish get-together," said Dolly. "Many times, there have been kids, moms and men that have the AIDS virus." Dolly also contributed a track to the 1994 AIDS fund-raising album, *Red Hot And Country.*

Dolly's connection to the gay scene likely started around the late Seventies after her shows in New York when drag artists started impersonating her. Danny La Rue famously sang a version of 'Baby I'm Burning' in full Parton gaud. In the wake of the popularity of *9 To 5* the participants in Dolly look-alike contests were often male. Michael Creed, who runs a Dolly fan newsletter in Britain and who is himself gay, recalls, "In one interview she did around the time of *9 To 5*, Dolly was asked about her gay fans, but she didn't call them gay, she said she had a lot of friends who were sissy . . . she wouldn't use that language now." Gay men in particular (though Dolly has many lesbian fans also) were attracted to her over-the-top glamorous image – big hair, stilettos, and rhinestone outfits. Dolly was flattered. "I've had a big gay following for years because I'm so outrageous in the way that I see life, not just in my appearance. Drag queens fascinate me. I'm really complimented that they think so much about me that they want to dress up like me."

Other female stars, with exaggerated glitzy images, who also appealed to gay men, were Marilyn Monroe and Mae West, both of whom it was suggested Dolly might portray in films at various times in her career. However, Michael Creed feels that Dolly's appeal runs deeper. "I think it's that image they were attracted to originally and then they got into her personality, the wit and the self-deprecating humour . . . and then they get to know her life story, being poor and then making it big." Michael sees parallels between Dolly's journey to stardom and the course of many gay people's lives. "You could say they have a struggle initially in coming out and then realise when they do there was probably nothing to worry about and often when a lot of gay men do come out, after years of frustration, they become very extravagant and over the top." And then there was the music. "The songs have an appeal as well, the heartbreaking songs, but

---

* Herb Ritts was an outstanding photographer who took the stills for *The Best Little Whorehouse In Texas.*

they are also songs of hope. Gay men are attracted to the story songs of someone who struggles and then says, 'What the heck, this is how it should be and what life's like anyway there's no need to worry' . . . [Dolly] is seen as being on the side of the underdog . . . she can relate to people who have had a tough time and she wouldn't pull anyone down because of their sexuality or disability or whatever. You don't ever hear her say anything negative about anyone. She's also not afraid to mention the word 'gay' in songs, for instance 'Single Women' and 'Family'. She is on record as saying that she has gay people in her own family and that may have helped her to be more understanding."

In 2005, Dolly contributed a song, 'Sugar Hill', to the album *Love Rocks* issued by the Human Rights Campaign, a major gay rights group. Other participating artists included Christina Aguilera, Emmylou Harris, Carole King and Yoko Ono – all of whom were alarmed by moves to make same sex marriage illegal. "The constitution of this country is based on human rights, justice and freedom," said Ono, ". . . for politicians to say they're going to change the Constitution so that gays can't get married, I think it is outrageous . . . anybody can fall in love regardless of the difference of religion, or race, or sex, or age. Love is love. It's beautiful." Representing the conservative viewpoint, Melissa Fryrear of Focus on the Family said of the CD, "This is another example of celebrities using their platforms to promote a liberal ideological agenda that equates homosexuality with heterosexuality."

More recently, 'Travelin' Thru', written specifically for the film *Transamerica*, was another instance of Dolly expressing her support for controversial gender issues.\* The plot followed the travails of Bree, a woman who has undergone a sex change operation (or "gender reassignment"). The use of the word "pilgrim" in the lyrics illustrates Dolly's sympathetic, religious-tinged views, conjuring up images of pioneering 17th-century settlers seeking religious freedom. For Dolly such a struggle chimed with Bree's quest for her own form of freedom in the face of prejudice and lack of understanding.

Dolly's high profile support brought into sharp relief the contrasting beliefs of her fan base. In *EXP* the interviewer cheekily put to her: "If I may use a breast analogy, on one teat you have the gays suckling, and on

---

\* The song received an Oscar nomination in the category Achievement In Music, Original Song, but lost out to 'It's Hard Out Here For A Pimp' (from *Hustle And Flow*) when the results were announced in 2006. 'Travelin' Thru' did go on to win a number of other awards.

the other teat, the right-wing rednecks." Dolly replied, "Yes, and don't think I don't pay for that. In fact, sometimes because I love all people I do get a lot of flack from the Bible belt. At my park I have people protesting – 'I'm never coming back because you're endorsing gays and you support this and that and know that's not right!' I have many, many gay and lesbian friends . . . so I'm certainly not going to sit in a seat of judgment." Dolly had to do battle with some of the business organisations associated with Dollywood over the issue but she made it clear that she would rather close the park than turn anybody away.

Dolly welcomed those with diverse and divergent views. As an example Dollywood hosted Annual Young Christian Days featuring "a brand new line-up of sensational Christian music and dynamic seminars . . . the exclusive Saturday activities are sure to generate excitement and anticipation for the most popular Christian Youth event in the South East." One of those taking part was Phil Driscoll, a Grammy and Dove award winning artist who delivered a robustly anti-drugs message. In 2001, as part of an initiative to support cultures from around the world, an international Festival of Nations was held at Dollywood which featured approximately 400 entertainers from around 15 countries and a wide range of authentic foods were available for visitors to sample. The first unofficial 'Gay Day', was held at Dollywood in 2004; a focus for gay people to come together and share their common appreciation of Dolly and her works, something which had been happening at Dollywood on an ad hoc basis for some years.

Dollywood officials had taken exception the previous year when one gay group, whose website featured a cartoon likeness of Dolly and a butterfly logo, announced their intention of holding a 'Gay Day at Dollywood'. A letter advising the group that they were welcome to visit the park but had no right to use the name as part of their promotional material was duly despatched. Dollywood spokesman Pete Owens was careful to point out that there was no question of discrimination, merely a case of preventing the use of the Dollywood name and logo without permission. Homosexuality was a sensitive subject among gay people in the South, many of whom feel they are the object of persecution.[*] When Dolly's 2002 tour had ended in Kansas City there was a small protest

---

[*] In 2004, the commission in Dayton, Rhea County, Tennessee (famous for the "Monkey Trial" of 1925 when science teacher John Scopes was prosecuted for teaching evolution in the classroom) passed a law banning gays and lesbians from living in the county. The law was quickly rescinded but nonetheless the incident attracted considerable and largely incredulous publicity.

organised by evangelical Christian the Reverend Fred Phelps who, amongst other things, was unhappy that Dolly had a gay manager even though Sandy Gallin had not been overseeing her affairs for some years.

Gay Day 2004 attracted protests outside the park by the Ku Klux Klan but for Dolly this was not a new experience. In the late Seventies she appeared on a CMA Awards show to collect another trophy and was kissed by country star Charley Pride. She was touring in the south at the time and several people came up to her and shouted "nigger lover", while crosses were burned near her house. In the late Nineties, Michael Creed discovered an anti-gay undercurrent when he and two friends, Joe and Mark visited Dollywood, where they met up with a female friend of Joe's. When she heard they were planning to drive from Pigeon Forge to Nashville and then on to Elvis Presley's mansion, Graceland, in Memphis, Michael was taken aback at her warning. "She said, 'Whatever you do, stay on the main route, do not deviate and do not talk to anyone.' When Joe asked why, she said, 'With your accents and the fact that you are gay I wouldn't want you to come to any harm.' I thought it rather strange. You think of the Southern people as very hospitable and friendly, but she said if you go off the main route you don't know who you're going to come across."

Michael believes the gay issue causes some difficulties for Dolly on a personal level as well as in her business dealings. "Dolly has strongly founded spiritual and religious beliefs, reasonably traditional Christian views, so it's a kind of battle between that side and the liberal accepting side."

Given the number of interviews she has conducted over the years Dolly sometimes made remarks she later regretted. She was thus able to empathise with the Dixie Chicks when they found themselves embroiled in controversy following remarks made by lead singer Natalie Maines at a concert in London. On the eve of the invasion of Iraq, she told the audience she was ashamed that President Bush came from her home state of Texas. Dolly said, "It's kind of like me, she opens her mouth sometimes before her brain kicks in . . . but it's time for Americans to forgive them and move on." In 2004 controversial remarks Dolly had made a decade before were once more raised publicly. During a *Vogue* interview, in response to being asked about any failures she had experienced, Dolly quoted the example of a mini-series she had tried and failed to get off the ground about a country singer who switches to gospel after a near-death experience. She said it was rejected because, "most people out here [Hollywood] are Jewish, and it's a frightening thing for them to promote

Christianity." Dolly was accused of anti-Semitic stereotyping and of unfairly conjuring up a picture of Jewish control of Hollywood.

Recognising the sensitivity of the subject Dolly quickly issued an apology though she claimed her words had been misinterpreted. In 2004, the incident was included in a book *Never Again? The Threat Of The New Anti-Semitism* by Abraham Foxman, National Director of the Anti-Defamation League. Although Foxman did not label Dolly anti-Semitic or racist he accused her of casually peddling old stereotypes. Dolly's original comments were probably careless and ill-advised but the re-raising of the issue 10 years after the fact seemed harsh and inappropriate. Being included in a learned book as an example of religious prejudice alongside those who were genuinely anti-Semitic was surely unmerited. The incident perhaps served to justify the wisdom of Dolly's own adage, "Choose what you say rather than say what you choose."*

While expressing genuine regret about the incident, in her 1994 autobiography she managed to inject a little humour. "There I was trying to explain to some of the Jewish writers about Pentecostalists, the whole holy-roller talking-in-tongues thing. I said something like, 'I can imagine how hard it would be for a Jew to write this. It would be like a hillbilly trying to write the story of Judaism.'" Dolly said Christian beliefs were important to her but that she was not "one of those who believes that a person has to embrace them to be a decent and worthwhile human being. Spirituality is the most intimate part of a person's make-up, and it's strictly up to the individual to choose how to express it."

Dolly had been interested in making an album of patriotic and religious songs for some time and in 2003 she released *For God And Country*. Like many Americans Dolly saw no contradiction between being highly patriotic and socially liberal. However, as with the gay issue, the album exposed a fault line between people broadly on the left or right, politically and socially. For the sleeve Dolly lived up to her recent statement, "I will get more outrageous as I get older, just for the fun of the whole thing." She stood on one leg, the other suggestively bent forward, on a huge billowing American flag, wearing a matching mini skirt and jacket with vertical red and white lines and blue collar and cuffs. Facially Dolly bears more than a passing resemblance to Jack Nicholson's character of The

---

* One irony of the whole incident was that in 1999 Dolly purchased the film rights to *The Jew Store*, Stella Suberman's memoir of a Jewish family growing up in a small town in Tennessee in the Twenties and the trials and tribulations of their life in the face of hostility and prejudice.

Joker in *Batman*. The album included 'Color Me America' and 'Welcome Home', referring to both a soldier being reunited with his family and a soldier killed on the battlefield travelling into the next world. A video was shot featuring several hundred men and women of the American Navy at Port Hueneme, California.

Also included was the moment-of-inspiration song 'Light Of A Clear Blue Morning', originally released in 1977, an emotional recitation of the 23rd psalm 'The Lord Is My Shepherd', the military standard 'Ballad Of The Green Beret' (a US hit for Sgt Barry Sadler in 1966), 'There Will Be Peace In the Valley For Me' and inevitably, 'The Star Spangled Banner'. The album was clearly aimed at Dolly's conservative loyalists, perhaps as a sop to placate them in view of her involvement with more controversial issues. One reviewer said, "You are more likely to enjoy this album if (a) you are an American and (b) you agree with the basic sentiments that America is the best country in the world and that God is on our side." The album reached 23 in the country chart but made no significant impact elsewhere. In another gesture of support and solidarity for the war effort (but without necessarily implying support for the decision to invade Iraq), in 2005 Dolly appeared at a special concert at the Grand Ole Opry, performing 'Viva Las Vegas', 'Coat Of Many Colors' and 'Rocky Top' as well as introducing guests, including Secretary of Defense Donald Rumsfeld, during a worldwide telecast which included a satellite link to US troops in Iraq.

Despite fast approaching her 60th birthday, Dolly maintained a high work rate, collaborating with rising and recent stars. The arrangement suited both sides. Dolly achieved publicity by associating with some of the current big sellers and thus circumvented the general embargo placed on older artists by television and radio. The songs she recorded often achieved a degree of commercial success she had not attained in years. By paying homage to one of the all-time great figures of country music, the younger artists were seen to be showing deference to country music's heritage, imbuing their work with a degree of borrowed gravitas. Dolly professed herself particularly fond of those who were "real heartfelt singers". While she had reservations about the clean-cut images of some of the younger stars ("Might be nice if one or two of them got drunk once in a while"), she was also proud that "they don't abuse drugs and alcohol like the older ones," a reference to stars such as George Jones and Johnny Cash – though it was an inescapable fact that such bygone abusers had produced more memorable music.

An illustration of Dolly's tie-ups with various artists gives a flavour of the eclectic nature of her collaborations. In 2002 Dolly achieved success in a number of gospel and Christian charts with 'Stand By The River', a duet with gospel star Dottie Rambo. She also teamed up with veteran British rocker Rod Stewart for 'Baby It's Cold Outside'. When the Bellamy Brothers decided to do an album of re-recordings of their hits with guest artists, Dolly was the obvious choice for the tongue-in-cheek 'If I Said You Had A Beautiful Body (Would You Hold It Against Me?)'. Dolly found herself at the top of the country album charts (with a strong showing in the pop charts) when the duet she sang with Brad Paisley, 'When I Get Where I'm Going', was included on his big-selling *Time Well Wasted* album. Another high profile pairing saw Dolly and Elton John perform his latest single 'Turn The Lights Out When You Leave' and her cover of 'Imagine' at the Country Music Association Awards show in New York. Dolly wore blue jeans with highly decorated flares below the knee. Though inevitably garnering much publicity, this particular appearance was not well received because their musical styles simply did not gel.

In 2005 Dolly recorded 'Creepin' In' with Norah Jones, which won a Grammy nomination. Detroit based rock duo The White Stripes, renowned for their dynamic live performances, paid Dolly the compliment of covering 'Jolene'. No doubt she was pleased with the publicity provided by a band with such youth appeal even though the raucous vocals removed all the subtlety and charm of the original.

Though Dolly's television appearances had tailed off by the early years of the new millennium Dolly faxed Reba McEntire to say that she had a clear week free and effectively invited herself onto Reba's socially aware sitcom, *Reba*. Her appearance, as larger-than-life real estate agent Dolly Majors, went down well and further appearances were discussed. There was even talk of a spin-off show based on the Dolly Majors character.

Dolly's support of good causes continued with a charity auction in aid of the Dr Robert F. Thomas Foundation when a bidder paid $10,000 for the honour of dining with her. Dollywood became the number one man-made attraction in Tennessee. By the close of the 20th Dollywood season in 2005, during which Leroy Van Dyke appeared as a special guest artist, visitor numbers had increased on the previous year by reaching nearly two and a half million. The park continues to flourish with many new attractions being added to enhance the customer experience and maintain visitor numbers in what is a highly competitive market place.

In 2003 one of Andy Warhol's paintings of Dolly went on display in an exhibition at the Bellagio Casino in Las Vegas. That same year she was one of the five nominees for the CMA Female Vocalist Of The Year award, an honour she had first been nominated for in 1968. It was remarkable that at this stage in her career she was still up there, competing with much younger stars for some of the major honours in the business. (In the event she lost out to Martina McBride.) Dolly also won the 2003 BMI Icon award and in 2004 she was given the honour of being made the official representative of tourism for the state of Tennessee. Her face could be seen on the side of London taxis in an attempt to promote the delights of the Volunteer State. *Rolling Stone* placed 'Coat Of Many Colors' at number 299 in its 500 Greatest Albums Of All Time, one of only 12 country albums to be chosen. Dolly ranked at number 189 on VH1's list of the 200 Greatest Pop Culture Icons. The only other country artists who made the list were Johnny Cash, Shania Twain and Garth Brooks. In 2004, in its Top 50 Women To Watch list, *The Wall Street Journal* named Dolly as one of the most important women in the world for the future of business and industry. The only other entertainer included was her friend Oprah Winfrey.

In 2004, Dolly was awarded the Living Legend medal by the US Library of Congress for her contributions to the cultural heritage of the United States. The following year it was announced that Dolly was to be one of 10 recipients of the National Medal of Arts, the highest governmental honour for excellence in this area. Among others honoured were actor Robert Duvall and jazz musician Wynton Marsalis. Dolly did not attend the ceremony to receive her medal from President George W. Bush because she had previously been invited to the opening of a restaurant owned by her brother. She was quoted as saying that no disrespect was intended but family came first. Perhaps so, but her decision was in stark contrast to many occasions in the past when engagements and commitments that might assist her career took precedence over all else.

*Live And Well*, a double CD which had been recorded live in 2002 at Dollywood as part of the *Halos And Horns* tour, was released in 2004. As it said on the sleeve, the album "reveals to all . . . the absolute sheer joy, fun and energy of her legendary live act". The songs came from all stages of Dolly's career and encompassed folk, pop, country and rock, all delivered by the Blueniques with her trade mark "unique bluegrass". The pop element was kept to a minimum. Three of Dolly's biggest hits, 'Islands In The Stream', 'Here You Come Again' and 'Two Doors Down', were briefly performed as part of an a cappella medley. In the past such songs would have been among the high points of her concerts. The sleeve photographs revealed more effort by Dolly to hold back advancing years but despite her efforts with make-up and plastic surgery her appearance was unsettling. Dolly's artificial look, posed against a black backdrop, was more redolent of an exhibit at Madame Tussauds than a vibrant artist in concert. Plastic surgery was unable to make her hands look any younger and surprisingly a close-up shot was included on the sleeve which perhaps signified an acceptance of reality at some level even though all evidence suggested the opposite.

A DVD of the concert was also released which clearly demonstrated that Dolly had lost none of her sparkle or extraordinary vocal range from half whispers to full-throated hollers. Kitted out in uniforms of blue shirts and black waistcoats, The Blueniques simply dazzled with their instrumental virtuosity; Jimmy Mattingly's haunting country violin seemed to telepathically match Dolly's vocals. As with the CD sleeve, the DVD failed to mask the ill effects of her plastic surgery. Attempts to keep Dolly's skin looking smooth had succeeded up to a point but as she talked and sang her facial musculature lacked natural flexibility; at times her eyes produced an unintended, slightly startled look. One British journalist wrote, "Seeing her up close, her lips are ridiculously swollen, the top one looks like she's taken a punch from someone and when she smiles, the right side of her face seems to go looking for the left." Dolly's carefully rehearsed between-song patter was corny, just the way her audience liked it.

When Dolly undertook a 'Hello I'm Dolly' tour in 2004, taking in 39 shows in 36 cities, some naively expected it to be her farewell tour. Ticket sales were generally strong though not every show was a sell-out. Dolly reached an agreement with the Grascals (a new bluegrass group comprising top musicians such as Jimmy Mattingly) whereby they undertook to back her on the dates but they would be free agents to do their own shows and recordings. Some disapproval was expressed about the fact that some pre-recorded vocals were used in Dolly's concerts. Another aspect, on this and other recent tours, which drew criticism, was the use of prompt screens.

Bluegrass artist and promoter Tom Travis had seen Dolly's 2002 show in Manchester. "There were monitor screens hanging from the balconies, on the stage and in other strategic positions around the auditorium giving her instructions and prompts for every word and gesture, 'slap thigh' for instance. It was so planned that it lacked excitement and spontaneity. Adrenalin and a few raw edges would have been far better. She had some of the most exciting young pickers onstage with her but they seemed controlled and repressed. She should go out there and enjoy the opportunity for some great picking and singing, let her hair down and have a ball." Many of her diehard fans would doubtless disagree with Travis' assessment. However, despite the self-evident professionalism and skill of her performances, it was undeniable how choreographed her appearances became, right down to the one-liners ("Mama had one in her and one on her . . .") Dolly had been delivering for almost three decades. When an audience member shouted out extravagant praise, she would invariably snap back with, "I thought I told you to wait in the truck." The wonder is that after all this time she appeared to chuckle with genuine amusement when saying the lines.

While working on Dolly's 2004 tour, front-of-house engineer Matt Naylor said, "I basically set the mix making sure that Dolly is always on top so that it's the same, but she makes it easy because she is very consistent every night . . . she has great vocal and mike technique. All you can say is, 'Wow, what a pro,' no attitude, always gives 100% onstage and is just fun to be around."

Dolly went on the road again in 2005 for The Vintage Tour which took her to around 40 cities. The tour was memorable for one rare omission on Dolly's part. At Birmingham she somehow omitted 'Coat Of Many Colors', the first time in 36 years that the song had not been included in one of her concerts. She later apologised for the oversight, assuring fans that the song was and always would be a fixture in her live set list. A concert in Myrtle Beach, South Carolina was cancelled as a result of Hurricane Ophelia and inevitably New Orleans was called off because of Hurricane Katrina. Perhaps as an example of the dangers of not sticking to a script, in September, during the last of four shows at Dollywood as part of a National Music and Harvest Celebration, Dolly remarked she was glad her name wasn't Katrina. In view of the extreme suffering inflicted on the Crescent City, it was a remark which seemed in dubious taste.* After the concert, Dolly came down with laryngitis and was barely able to speak above a whisper resulting in a number of television appearances, including *The Tonight Show with Jay Leno*, having to be cancelled. She phoned Steve Buckingham who was concerned because he'd never heard her so hoarse. "She went to the doctors at UCLA that week and there was some problem related to acid reflux." Even though the ailment was quickly dealt with, Buckingham uses it as an example of how a short-lived problem was distorted by the press. "She's been fine ever since even though there's tabloids over here saying 'Medical Crisis: Risk To Dolly's career', and all that."

It was also around this time that a story emerged of Dolly's consideration for her old friend and mentor Porter Wagoner when he found

---

* She might have had in mind that one of the tropical storms which struck America in 2002 was called 'Dolly'.

himself in trouble with the Internal Revenue Service. When needing to raise money one of his most readily realisable assets was his song publishing. After outlining his predicament to Dolly, she bought the copyrights for a figure reckoned to be several hundred thousand dollars thus helping Porter out of his difficulty. When his situation improved he wanted to recover the copyrights and approached Dolly. As a mark of how much water had passed under the bridge, she transferred them back to him without asking any payment. Ronny Light felt it was a case of repaying an old debt. "I think she recognised that she wouldn't be where she is if it hadn't been for Porter's help." Porter appeared on a television show holding up the letter from Dolly agreeing to reassign his copyrights. According to Ronny, "He was proud of what she'd done and he wanted everybody to know that's the kind of person she is."

The Vintage Tour promoted Dolly's 2005 album of Sixties and Seventies called, appropriately enough, *Those Were The Days*. The idea was to record as many of the songs as possible with the artists who wrote or originally recorded them. Though not credited as a producer, Steve Buckingham was closely involved in making arrangements for the large number of people involved. "It's not just a matter of getting the artists, it's getting to the artists. It's a matter of then working out the deals with the artists' labels and their representatives and yeah it's a whole different set of problems . . . 50% of the time was doing the music and 50% of the time was getting the legal part of it done [what Dolly referred to in her sleevenotes as "star wrangling"].

For the title track a cast of Grand Ole Opry notables including Porter, Billy Walker, George Hamilton IV and Jimmy C. Newman (who had given up part of his slot to give the teenage Dolly a first shot on the Opry stage) were assembled to provide background atmosphere. Buckingham "tracked down" Mary Hopkin to her native Wales and sent over a file containing details of her background vocals which she recorded there. Steve detailed some of the other artists who were approached for the project. " 'Blowin' In The Wind' we tried to get Dylan, he wouldn't do it [Dylan's son Jacob also declined] . . . 'Where Have All The Flowers Gone', we went to New York, put Norah Jones on doing harmony and back here Lee Ann Womack put another harmony on. 'Where Do The Children Play' . . . a year and a half ago I started contacting Yusuf Islam [formerly Cat Stevens] about possibly getting back into recording and we went back and forth with e-mails. I went over to London and visited with him and then there was this whole deal when he was stopped coming into the US by homeland security and that whole international incident. He was coming here to record with me. He was flying with one of his daughters from London to DC, DC to Nashville and I had everything set up here, the musicians . . . he had six new songs and I was literally on my way to the airport. His office called me from London and said something's wrong and that started that whole thing.* I sent it over to Yusuf, he put a wonderful vocal on it and a great acoustic guitar part. In the end he didn't let us use the vocal which broke our hearts but we respected his feelings. He wasn't happy with his performance [he thought it was in the wrong key for his voice] even though we all thought it was magic . . .

"For 'Both Sides Now', we were within 24 hours of having Joni Mitchell on it but one of her parents became very ill so I went to New York and cut Judy Collins on it." Other artists included Kris Kristofferson ('Me And Bobby McGee'), Roger McGuinn ('Turn, Turn, Turn') and Keith Urban, the handsome blond Australian heart-throb who had made it big in America and was engaged to film star Nicole Kidman, duetting with Dolly on an easy-listening bluegrass version of 'Twelfth Of Never'. As the last note faded, Urban can be heard to say, "You give me chills Dolly," eliciting one of her trademark chuckles, somewhere between a giggle and a guffaw. Neither Sean nor Julian Lennon were willing to participate in 'Imagine', the first single release from the album and surely a strange choice for Dolly since it was seen by many as a manifesto for socialism, pacifism, atheism and radical leftist dogma. In advocating a world without religion or possessions it went against two major crutches in her life. One journalist was moved to query just what exactly Dolly did stand for. The video accompanying the song featured several of John and Yoko's home movies, Yoko apparently agreed to their use because she liked Dolly's interpretation of the song. Record executive Tony Brown thought that Dolly was "as deep as John Lennon ever tried to be . . . she can write 'Coat Of Many Colors'."

Dolly expressed some concern that because so many artists who agreed to take part in the project had been involved with the anti-war movement in the Sixties people might, bearing in mind America's current involvement in the Middle East, "get the wrong idea . . . I'm certainly not into any kind of political thing or protest. People who know me will know I have chosen these songs to really kind of uplift and to give hope, like they

---

* Yusuf Islam was apparently on a "no-fly list" because the US authorities had it that his activities might in some way be linked to terrorism. It transpired the authorities had mistaken him for somebody else.

were written for at the time . . . we don't want to be at war, but of course we have to fight if we have to. We don't want to lose our children in war, but of course we do. So we write about it and sing about it, and it kind of helps us relieve our grief and express ourselves." She referred to herself as a peace-loving patriot but said the troops had to be supported because, "They're out there fighting for what they believe in."

Though many of the songs had been the by-products of passion and rebellion associated with particular eras, her new interpretations mainly came across as pleasant listening. The exception was the old Civil War ballad 'The Cruel War' in which a woman offers to disguise herself as a man in order to accompany her lover to the battle zone. Dolly's wobbly, emotion-filled vocals brought to mind her most powerful performances.

The distinguished guest list was a remarkable tribute to Dolly's position in the music business. Steve Buckingham acknowledges how Dolly's cartoon image can deflect attention from her status. "She knows that and it's like she's in on the joke . . . she's been very successful at creating that image, to the point that some people only see that and they don't realise she's a great writer or singer . . . but people in the music business, they know, they totally get it, they know the talent. Alison Krauss to Norah Jones, all age groups all genres, I've seen them crowd around her at the Grammies or some place and not just the country world; the pop world, the hip hop world, they get it, they know how good she is . . ."

# Chapter 28

AFTER almost 40 years in the limelight Dolly's private life is seemingly still up for grabs by the tabloid press. In her autobiography she complained that serial killers on death row had more right to privacy. Steve Buckingham believes that while Dolly is usually able to shrug the stories aside, the ones about family members do get to her. "Luckily she's got a good sense of humour. She talked about the tabloids recently and said, 'Well every few months they need to sell some papers so they drag out one of the old stories.' Sure enough just recently I saw one at La Guardia airport, 'Dolly medical crisis'." Buckingham does not subscribe to the public view that Dolly regards all publicity as welcome. "She's not a woman who craves publicity, she has all she needs. She never complains about it but it's not like, 'Oh my God they're not putting me on the cover of the tabloids' . . . I mean sometimes it bugs her, like when her parents died and somebody dragged up some story about her being furious because her husband didn't come to the funeral, which is not true I'm pretty sure . . . those things that are more personal. Then again she's not the kind to sit around and mope about it all day. It may cross her mind for a minute and then it's on to work. She doesn't subscribe to the old saying the only bad publicity is no publicity . . . she knows where she is in the world. People recognise her all over the world . . . people never say I wonder if that's Dolly Parton . . . there's no doubt."

While Dolly continues to maintain properties across America, her principal home remains in Brentwood, Tennessee – an affluent, predominantly white, area with enormous churches whose car parks are filled to overflowing on Sundays. At the time it was built, Dolly and Carl's house was surrounded by fields but nowadays much high-quality development has taken place extending up to the Parton's boundaries though they have sufficient land to ensure they are not overlooked. Willow Lake Plantation is surrounded by well-tended, sloping lawns and nearby is a chapel and a pets' cemetery where Dolly and Carl's dogs are buried. To the front of the house is a large flagpole from which the Stars and Stripes are regularly flown. The mansion is voluminous enough to house Dolly's enormous collection of clothes and shoes as well as the countless awards she has received over the years. She also hoards many of the massive number of mementoes and gifts, including handmade butterflies, sent to her by fans.

Naturally the house has become a favourite stop on tours of the stars' homes. Tourists might be able to view the exterior but the interior has always been territory reserved for family and close friends. Dolly very rarely gives parties for people in the music business and music journalists are not generally invited in her home either. "I'm not really close to anybody in the business other than during show business. I love all the people and we see each other when we are performing or at the conventions or the banquets, but I've never had a person to my house from the music business and I never intend to. That's only because when I'm home, my time is so limited. I want to be with my family, I don't want to socialise. We can always be show business somewhere else. I just don't get time at home to be bored with the things I do; usually all of mine and my husband's friends are people outside the business."

Even on rare occasions when music people were invited over it was unlikely they would see much of Carl. Ralph Emery recalled the occasion when Barbara Mandrell and her husband Kenny Dudney were to lunch at Dolly's house. Kenny was pleased because he would get a chance to meet Carl, about whom he knew there was an aura of mystery, but Dolly was quick to point out that though he might see Carl, he would not be dining with them. In the event the engagement was cancelled. Dolly described Carl as the kind of person who "don't like to dress to go out to dinner", not caring for fine wines or sophisticated food. Writer Alanna Nash met him in the mid Seventies when granted a rare interview with Dolly at a house the couple were renting in Woodmont Boulevard, Nashville (they had temporarily decamped there because of unspecified fears that Dolly's health was being adversely affected by the water supply at Willow Lake Plantation). Nash described him as, "Tall and thin, bordering on gaunt. He was dressed in blue jeans, a flannel shirt, an old army jacket, work boots, gloves and a blue wool cap. But he was still ruggedly handsome."

He did not sit with his wife and her guest but appeared every now and again. "Y'all growing roots?" was his way of hinting the meeting might have been going on too long. Barbara Walters, the well-known American talk-show host, was once granted the rare privilege of an interview with Dolly at the Brentwood mansion. She asked Carl to take part and various suggestions were made to put as little pressure on him as possible. He was adamant that he would not co-operate allegedly saying, "Hell, no, I told you 10 years ago not to ask me to do that stuff. I just don't want to go to the hardware, I don't want to go to the co-op, I don't want to go to all the places I go to and people say, 'I know you, I saw you on the Barbara Walters show.'" Dolly apparently suggested the pair of them could do a tractor photo shoot without him having to speak, all to no avail. If people appeared at the front gate while he was working in the garden, asking to speak to Carl Dean, assuming they were journalists trying to snare that most elusive of interview subjects, Carl was likely to say he was the gardener.

Another striking aspect of Dolly and Carl's unconventional relationship is that they hardly ever refer to each other by their real names; reportedly only doing so on rare occasions as a sign of anger or extreme irritation during a row. It is said that Carl does not liking calling his wife Dolly because everybody else does, preferring to use "angel cakes" and "princess". The couple commonly call each other "mama" and "daddy". It has been suggested that Dolly got the idea of calling Carl "daddy" from the scene in *Bonnie And Clyde* where, after Estelle Parsons' husband is shot, she leans over and cries, "Oh daddy . . . daddy."

The mere fact that Dolly and Carl are still together after 40 years of Dolly's remarkable career suggests their marriage formula is successful, providing a degree of stability and continuity that other high profile celebrity couplings almost certainly would not have done. It is doubtful whether Dolly would have wanted to share the limelight with a high profile husband and the fact that she has been publicly linked with other men in her professional life is part of the arrangement, not a threat to it. As she told *Newsweek* "I need my husband for the love, and other men for my work. But I don't depend on any man for my strength." One commentator neatly described what is probably the key element contributing to the success of their relationship. "If the assumption is that their marriage works well, then they seem a happy example of the adage that the tightest hold on someone is with an open hand."

Willow Lake Plantation remains Dolly's sanctuary, one of the few places she can slough off the wigs, make-up and fancy fashions and just lounge about in casual "baby clothes" as she calls them; a place where she can "restore" herself, ready for the next round of professional engagements.

Judy Ogle continues to be involved in all aspects of Dolly's life, a personal assistant in the broadest possible sense. "Judy is the only person in this world I could be with 24 hours a day, 365 days a year," Dolly said in appreciation. Tabloids such as the *National Enquirer* and the *Sun* have speculated whether the two were ever lovers, greatly fuelled by comments Dolly made in her 1994 autobiography. Dolly retorted that it would be no big deal if she and Judy did have a gay relationship, "It just doesn't happen to be true. Why is it that they have to dirty every beautiful thing?"

Stella Parton feels that she escaped some of the tabloids unwelcome attention by following her sister to Nashville. "I'm fortunate that I've lived in this town because at least it's a big enough city . . . I don't get treated too badly because I'm like a mole, I know when to pop my head up and when to pop it down. I've learned the hard way . . . the other thing is people make the assumption that we do have it easy when in fact it's made it very difficult." One minor irritation Stella often experiences is when people ask her, "How's your sister?" to which her stock response is "Which one?"

Being the centre of attention was something Dolly had craved since she was a young girl growing up in the Smoky Mountains and much of her adult life had been spent achieving and sustaining her fame. However, though she expects a certain amount of star treatment she remains remarkably down to earth and thoughtful in her dealings with people. Bass player Byron House says that as a boss, "She's the best . . . the first thing that comes to mind is she's a hard worker, nobody's gonna work harder than Dolly . . . she projects that attitude, totally professional but you can have fun while you're doing it and she's so appreciative of the talent that individuals bring. I've got two or three letters from her after various engagements we've had, expressing genuine thanks. I remember leaving her a message that something we had appeared together in was showing on TV. I said I had heard it was really good but we didn't get it on our satellite where we lived. Two days later there was a VHS tape at my house with a recording of the programme. She hadn't physically taped it herself but she had taken the trouble to make sure somebody else did."

George Hamilton IV takes a similar view. "Everybody loves Dolly. She's a trip, she's a hoot and a holler." On one occasion when George was appearing at Dollywood he pointed out his wife and Dolly went right over to her. His wife was astounded and thrilled. As George puts it, "She makes you feel like you are somebody even if you ain't."

Steve Buckingham recalls an occasion when Dolly expressed a wish to see his mother who was "getting up in years . . . she had her driver get the bus to take us to Richmond to meet my mother, which is a 10 or 12 hour drive . . . she spent the morning with my mother talking, took pictures together, she just could not have been nicer. Then she went back to Nashville and wrote a song about my mom and my dad, who had died decades ago, got back on the bus two months later for her to play this song for my mother and give her a CD just for her. To the day my mother died a couple of years later it never left her mind about Dolly coming to visit her . . . and this is not exactly a woman sitting around with nothing to do."

Dolly's role as "Aunt Granny" reflects the part she plays in her extended family's lives. Willadeene points out that though Dolly has always been very generous to her young relations she has a tendency to spoil them, recalling a time when Dolly took a group of nephews and nieces to Disney World. "She let all of them eat what they wanted – candy, pizza, spaghetti – and they drank Cokes, if they wanted them, for breakfast . . . she even let the older ones smoke, drink wine and tell her dirty jokes. She even let a couple of them steal!" Dolly also showers presents and treats on the children of musical colleagues, including Gary Paczosa's daughter and Alison Krauss' son; to such children she cuts an unforgettable fairy godmother figure. Dolly has said that she regards Alison as part of her family and that they are so close they must have been together in a previous life.

Legendary country producer Jack Clement is a man with a mischievous sense of humour and he enjoys the same quality in Dolly. She visited his studio in recent years to add her vocal to a song one of Clement's friends had made with Arlo Guthrie. Jack hadn't seen Dolly for some years. "We're up there and I'm showing her my studio and she said, 'I probably slept with everybody in town since I saw you last,' and I said, 'Well I was thinking about taking a nap.' She's a hoot. One time, we were at the board. I had somebody taking pictures of it and we're sitting at the console and he's getting a side shot and Dolly's got this kind of low-slung bra that day and I'm doing my best not to look like I'm looking down into it. I'm looking over the board and pointing here and there and trying to avoid looking to the right and then somebody points at her and says, 'Cowboy, look!' and then Dolly said, 'Well why do you think I got these things?' So then I got up on top of the console and looked right down in there . . . that's the kind of gal she is, nothing sexual about it really, she's a fun-loving country girl, she's a trouper, she's an epitome of something . . . like Johnny Cash in a way, they both love attention."

However, for Jack, first and foremost a record producer, Dolly's singing is what he admires most. "Dolly can sing with anybody 'cos she's incredibly talented for one thing, an astute musician. She ain't just some hillbilly singer. She can get phrasing and she can work her voice. She started out singing harmony when she stole the show . . . back in the Sixties girls tended to be back-up singers or girl singers but with Dolly that's where the musicianship came in. She could blend her voice in there like a horn or something, she combines it with whatever she's hearing, she's unique, ain't nobody like Dolly. She's the best in a number of categories . . . I would put Tammy right in there with Dolly except Dolly can sing rock'n'roll, there's a Jerry Lee Lewis in there somewhere. Thing about Dolly, she just likes to sing, she's the epitome of that word natural . . . she likes to entertain people, she was born with it, she can't shake it and I hope she never does. She's got it man, that girl has got it. Dolly understood singing – she didn't have to but she did – some people have great voices but they don't understand exactly what they have to do. She's born with it, leave it alone, let it go where it wants to go."

Interviewed in 2005 Dolly revealed how she liked to relax with a book from the *New York Times* bestseller list. "To me a great book is like a new lover: you can't wait to get back to it." Steve Buckingham, who has been a pivotal figure in her life for more than 15 years, believes that Dolly's restless creative energy means that even if she does slow down, she could never countenance retirement. "I won't say she's a workaholic because that can be taken as a negative, but her life is centred around her work, her work being songwriting and creating . . . she's the most creative person I've ever known and I've been around a lot of creative people. She constantly has ideas, not just song ideas . . . we've taken long drives together. I remember one time we were driving from Nashville to Washington DC for her to do an interview on National Public Radio and she keeps notebooks everywhere, legal pads and pens to write with and she's constantly writing ideas down. She'll be talking and she'll say a phrase and go, 'Mmm, that's good,' and she jots it down.

"She'll think of everything from a song title to a really, in her mind, cool name for a restaurant, or something that would be a catchy name for a clothing line or, 'Wouldn't that be a great idea for a movie, wouldn't this be a great idea for a TV show.' It's never ending . . . it's like a fountain of ideas . . . my job as a producer is like, Dolly's the pitcher and I'm the catcher in a baseball game and she throws a thousand balls at me and I just have to figure which 10 to really catch, because it comes at you constantly, the wheels are almost always turning. She does get laid back from time to time and just takes it easy but she's restless, a gypsy, likes to be on the move, even if it's in town, just going for a ride for a few hours, just to be out and about. If she ever said, 'I'm gonna take a two-week vacation, just go to some resort and just sit and read,' I'd probably be calling for help because something would be wrong, those words never come from her mouth. She may go off for two weeks to her cabin in the mountains and write but that's a case of writing and creating and getting deep into that part of her mind."

"She can have an idea that she might have had two or three years ago, doesn't have to come to fruition right away, she'll even write songs and then come back two years later and say, 'If I could go back to that song, rework it here and there, it could fit this movie.' She does that kind of stuff all the time, it never goes to waste. Things don't fail; they'll come up some other way." Though she works hard, Steve does not believe Dolly sees this as really pushing herself. "I think that's just her natural flow . . . there'll be schedules, like when she's been doing TV and radio interviews all day and she's exhausted but she says, 'This is what I do,' and that's why she's always Dolly when you see her. She doesn't come to the studio in sweat pants . . . she's from that school of thought that says, 'If somebody sees me only one time I want to look the way they think Dolly Parton should look,' and she always looks that way." Even at home her restless energy never lets up. "She's up two or three in the morning cooking, thinking, writing, praying . . . that's just what she does. It's not that she's an insomniac, she just doesn't sleep much. [Dolly claims that if she has any more than five hours sleep it makes her feel sluggish.] She's got a different metabolism, a different inner drive, that's why she is what she is, I think. She may sleep for two hours, get up and write, go back and sleep an hour and get up and then cook; she'll take naps during the day. If she has to be up till late in the night then she'll get up later in the morning."

Buckingham believes that Dolly's drive to create is the most vital single element in her life. "It's no secret she's devoted to her family, all the sisters and brothers and nephews and all that, but from my standpoint, looking in, everything centres around her creativity, her work, especially her songwriting. She says if it wasn't for that, none of the other would be there and not just for her but for the rest of the family and all the people that depend on her for a living . . . you'll never hear her complain about the price of fame, that's what she does, she came from such a poor background and had such big dreams . . . to be able to achieve that she's never gonna complain . . . she says her dream is to die onstage."

Though Dolly is a woman of many passions, Steve is in no doubt that "for her, songwriting is the basis for everything. When she was inducted into the Songwriters Hall of Fame in New York I was with her. She's already in country music's Hall of Fame and the country songwriter's Hall of Fame but when she was inducted into the Songwriters Hall of Fame in New York a few years ago and we were talking I said, 'This is George Gershwin, Hoagy Carmichael, Irving Berlin,' and that was a very meaningful honour to her . . . she says songwriting is the centre of it all."

So far as future plans are concerned Dolly intends easing back on touring and recording in order to concentrate on the score for a Broadway production of *9 To 5* which will probably open sometime in 2007. She has already written more than 15 songs and will be involved with various aspects of production to be set in the late Seventies period of the original film, though she will not play a part – a run of three months or more of doing the same show night after night would not be her thing. She now gets fewer film offers and the ones that do make it to her she regards as "junk". The offer of voiceover work for the cinema is an avenue Dolly might well pursue. It has also been reported that Dolly is working on a children's book with the working title, *I Am A Rainbow*, relating the moods of children to colours – yellow for fear, red for angry, blue for sad, and so on. She will inevitably continue to make guest appearances on high profile television shows as well as other people's albums. As Buckingham says, "It's hard to predict what she will be doing in the next few years because she's a fountain of ideas."

Another rumoured project, one which has been talked about for years and which must surely come to fruition at some point, is a musical based on Dolly's life story. The problem facing whoever is assigned the task will be what to leave out. Actor Kristin Chenoweth is said to be a candidate for the part of Dolly.

In considering Dolly's future, Stella Parton's views are coloured by a degree of sisterly concern. "I think if her health holds up, physically and mentally, she'll just continue to write beautiful stuff and record really thought-provoking things." Stella does, however, feel that her sister should consider adopting a less prominent place in the public eye. "In life I think we have seasons of popularity and I don't think Dolly's very popular right now and I think it would be a good time for her to step back out of the spotlight and out of the tabloids and out of the press and out of TV and even off radio and just go be quiet for a while and get out of everybody's face for a while so that they want to see you again. It's like a relative that just shows up too often, you like them but you don't want them to be there for every Sunday dinner."

Stella admits that such a course of action would be highly unlikely. "It might not be in her nature and that might be to her detriment physically and emotionally . . . I hope that's not the case. I hope that she's sensitive enough to her own artistry to do that. I would like to think she is . . . I say that with all the love and compassion I have in my heart for her . . . I'm her sister and I probably know her as well as anyone and that's why I make her uncomfortable sometimes . . . but I would like for her to rest and not be out there trying to get to the public all the time. I think you only owe the public a certain amount and I can't see that she owes that to the public at this point. I think it's time for her to rest after 50 years, rest awhile and then if you wanna come back and do something at 65 or 70 then do that, but don't just keep trying to be 25, don't keep trying to be 35, be 60, rest a minute, give yourself a break, give us all a break.

"I wish she wouldn't push herself that hard, it's not like she has to, not like anybody's making her do it, that's why I'm saying I just think she needs to know she can. It's like, 'If I leave they might forget me, might not love me,' well who cares? In my mind I think that's what it is. It's like she's afraid if she doesn't keep their attention they'll stop loving her . . . I wouldn't care if it was me . . . I wish she could give herself a break . . . there's so much she loves to do, she loves to cook, she loves to play with children, she loves to walk in the woods, she loves to walk in the meadows and play in the flowers . . . why not just do that for a while?"

Despite the well-intentioned wishes of her younger sister, it seems unlikely Dolly could contemplate the idea of the show going on without her. "I'll be flying until I fall dead. I just won't give up, I won't be a'dyin' on the ground." Indeed the pace might even increase. "The older I get, the earlier I get up. I'm like, hurry, I just love life and I want to make the most of it. I'll be this way when I'm 80, like Mae West . . . I may be on crutches, in a wheelchair, or propped up on some old slant board but I'll have my high heels, my nails and make-up on, my hair'll be all poufed up and my boobs will still be hanging out. It's not a big job being Dolly, it's just my life." On another occasion, Dolly joked, "I want to be an 80-year-old lady whose sex life they're still wondering about." Even if she were to fade from the public eye it seems Dolly would still be able to find plenty to interest her. "Nobody could ever know all of me. I don't. I'm even fascinatin' to myself. I'm mysterious to myself because I often do things that I wouldn't have thought the day before I would do. But that's good – I don't get bored with myself."

According to Suzy Bogguss, "[Dolly] always looks forward, thinks about what is going to be interesting next. I think she's always thinking, 'How can I reinvent myself to keep myself fresh and to keep people wanting to hear my music and stay with me?' Very few artists have been able to do that . . . continue to grow yourself and keep people interested in what you're doing." Suzy recognises Dolly's determination but says, "It's not an ugly thing, it's a beautiful thing. It's a vitality it's not that drive like,

'I have to be on top so I can be powerful', it's a vitality thing that comes from within her like a light and it just to me is so inspiring because I think I want to keep that light alive within me too, I want to continue to love music, I don't want to let the machine part take over so that it's no fun any more; that's why we want it so much."

Suzy also reiterates the point made by Stella about the importance of the fans. "If you really stripped it down, all of the people who make the music, it's like we all just want to be liked, we all want to be loved. Sometimes people will come to an autograph line and they'll say, 'Aw you must be so tired, bless your heart for sitting out here,' and I'm like, 'Oh yeah, this is really hard for me having to come to listen to you guys telling me how great I was tonight, this is tough.'"

Dolly herself has said, "I just love people. I want everybody to love me and I just love everybody. It would really hurt me if something bad happened and people didn't love me or accept me. I think it would really put my pilot light out . . . I try to make it a lovefest when I go out there . . . Sometimes I get so excited over a certain moment onstage, I could just swear that it's the same thing as sex . . . music is the closest thing to it for me."

While it's to be hoped that Dolly will be around for years to come, she has expressed some typically positive thoughts on the afterlife. Dolly believes it will be a time of resolution, of answers to the great questions, and the old gospel hymn 'Farther Along', one of her favourites, captures the spirit. "I get excited about death. Death is the ultimate angel who sets us free. It's the door into eternal life. I'm curious about death because I believe there is still something greater to come. We prepare all our lives to die and go back to that great divine energy."

---

A journalist once referred to Dolly as an endangered species, a one-off who came up the hard way, creating a sound and a style uniquely her own; who was prepared to take risks in order to achieve her overarching goal of superstardom. As the years go by, and her body of work is scrutinised and reassessed, the films, the talk shows, the business deals, the awards ceremonies, even her theme park, all evidence of a fulfilled life, will fade, along with the forgettable pop material, but what will remain in the long term will be a remarkable and substantial body of work, including some timeless classics. As Stella says of her compositions, "Dolly makes the original and other people are doing prints." They are there to be appreciated by future generations who will also discover her boundless energy and outlandish appearance as captured on old videotapes and DVDs. In the words of

Allison Moorer, who sang on Dolly's tribute album, *Just Because I'm A Woman*, "When it's all said and done, Dolly Parton is one of the few people who will have said and done it all her way. She's an American original."

When asked by Terry Wogan what she would like people to say of her on her 100th birthday, Dolly shot back, "That she looks good for her age."

# SELECTED DISCOGRAPHY

## (ALBUMS ONLY)

### HELLO, I'M DOLLY
February 1967 (Monument)
Dumb Blonde/ Your Ole Handy Man/ I Don't Wanna Throw Rice/ Put It Off Until Tomorrow/ I Wasted My Tears/ Something Fishy/ Fuel To The Flame/ The Giving And The Taking/ I'm In No Condition/ The Company You Keep/ I've Lived My Life/ The Little Things

### JUST BETWEEN YOU AND ME (with Porter Wagoner)
January 1968 (RCA)
Because One Of Us Was Wrong/ The Last Thing On My Mind/ Love Is Worth Living/ Just Between You And Me/ Mommie, Ain't That Daddy/ Four O Thirty-Three/ Sorrow's Tearing Down The House (That Happiness Once Built)/ This Time Has Gotta Be Our Last Time/ Before I Met You/ Home Is Where The Hurt Is/ Two Sides To Every Story/ Put It Off Until Tomorrow

### JUST BECAUSE I'M A WOMAN
April 1968 (RCA)
You're Gonna Be Sorry/ I Wish I Felt This Way At Home/ False Eyelashes/ I'll Oil Wells Love You/ The Only Way Out (Is To Walk Over Me)/ Little Bit Slow To Catch On/ The Bridge/ Love And Learn/ I'm Running Out Of Love/ Just Because I'm A Woman/ Baby Sister/ Try Being Lonely

### JUST THE TWO OF US (with Porter Wagoner)
September 1968 (RCA)
Closer By The Hour/ I Washed My Face In The Morning/ Jeannie's Afraid Of The Dark/ Holding On To Nothin'/ Slip Away Today/ Dark End Of The Street/ Just The Two Of Us/ Afraid To Love Again/ We'll Get Ahead Someday/ Somewhere Between/ Party/ I Can

### IN THE GOOD OLD DAYS
February 1969 (RCA)
Don't Let It Trouble Your Mind/ He's A Go Getter/ In The Good Old Days/ It's My Time/ Harper Valley P.T.A./ Little Bird/ Mine/ Carroll

County Accident/ Fresh Out Of Forgiveness/ Mama Say A Prayer/ Always
The First Time/ D-I-V-O-R-C-E

## ALWAYS, ALWAYS (with Porter Wagoner)

July 1969 (RCA)

Milwaukee Here I Come/ Yours Love/ I Don't Believe You've Met My
Baby/ Malena/ The House Where Love Lives/ Why Don't You Haul Off
And Love Me/ Always, Always/ There Never Was A Time/ Good As
Gold/ My Hands Are Tied/ No Reason To Hurry Home/ Anything's
Better Than Nothing

## MY BLUE RIDGE MOUNTAIN BOY

September 1969 (RCA)

In The Ghetto/ Games People Play/ 'Til Death Do Us Part/ Big Wind/
Evening Shade/ I'm Fed Up With You/ My Blue Ridge Mountain Boy/
Daddy/ We Had All The Good Things Going/ The Monkey's Tale/
Gypsy Joe and Me/ Home For Pete's Sake

## THE FAIREST OF THEM ALL

February 1970 (RCA)

Daddy Come And Get Me/ Chas/ When Possession Gets Too Strong/
Before You Make Up Your Mind/ I'm Doing This For Your Sake/ But
You Loved Me Then/ Just The Way I Am/ More Than Their Share/
Mammie/ Down From Dover/ Robert

## PORTER WAYNE AND DOLLY REBECCA (with Porter Wagoner)

March 1970 (RCA)

Forty Miles From Poplar Bluff/ Tomorrow Is Forever/ Just Someone I Used
To Know/ Each Season Changes You/ We Can't Let This Happen To Us/
Mendy Never Sleeps/ Silver Sandals/ No Love Left/ It Might As Well Be
Me/ Run That By Me One More Time/ I'm Wasting Your Time And
You're Wasting Mine

## AS LONG AS I LOVE

April 1970 (RCA)

Why, Why, Why/ I Wound Easy/ I Don't Want You Around Me
Anymore/ Hillbilly Willy/ This Boy Has Been Hurt/ Daddy Won't Be
Home Anymore As Long As I Love/ A Habit I Can't Break/ I'm Not
Worth The Tears/ I Don't Trust Me Around You/ I Couldn't Wait Forever/
Too Lonely Too Long

## A REAL LIVE DOLLY

July 1970 (RCA)

Introduction By Cas Walker/ Wabash Cannon Ball/ You Gotta Be My Baby/ Tall Man/ Medley: Dumb Blonde-Something Fishy-Put It Off Until Tomorrow/ My Blue Ridge Mountain Boy/ Y'All Come/ Bloody Bones (A Story For Kids)/ Don Howser Makes Presentation/ Comedy By Speck Rhodes/ Run That By Me One More Time/ Jeannie's Afraid Of The Dark/ Tomorrow Is Forever/ Two Sides To Every Story/ How Great Thou Art

## ONCE MORE (with Porter Wagoner)

August 1970 (RCA)

Daddy Was An Ole Time Preacher Man/ I Know You're Married But I Love You Still/ Thoughtfulness/ Fight And Scratch/ Before Our Weakness Gets Too Strong/ Once More/ One Day At A Time/ Ragged Angel/ A Good Understanding/ Let's Live For Tonight

## THE BEST OF DOLLY PARTON

November 1970 (RCA)

Mule Skinner Blues/ Down From Dover/ My Blue Ridge Mountain Boy/ In The Good Old Days/ Gypsy Joe And Me/ In The Ghetto/ Just Because I'm A Woman/ Daddy Come And Get Me/ How Great Thou Art/ Just The Way I Am

## GOLDEN STREETS OF GLORY

February 1971 (RCA)

I Believe/ Yes I See God/ Master's Hand/ Heaven's Just a Prayer Away/ Golden Streets of Glory/ How Great Thou Art/ I'll Keep Climbing/ Book Of Life/ Wings Of A Dove/ Lord, Hold My Hand

## TWO OF A KIND (with Porter Wagoner)

February 1971 (RCA)

The Pain Of Loving You/ Possum Holler/ Is It Real/ Flame/ Fighting Kind/ Two Of A Kind/ All I Need Is You/ Curse Of The Wild Weed Flower/ Today, Tomorrow And Forever/ There'll Be Love

## JOSHUA

April 1971 (RCA)

Joshua/ Last One To Touch Me/ Walls Of My Mind/ It Ain't Fair That It Ain't/ J J Sneed/ You Can't Reach Me Anymore/ Daddy's Moonshine Still/ Chicken Every Sunday/ Fire's Still Burning/ Letter To Heaven

## THE BEST OF PORTER WAGONER & DOLLY PARTON

July 1971 (RCA)

Just Someone I Used To Know/ Daddy Was An Old Time Preacher Man/ Tomorrow Is Forever/ Jeannie's Afraid Of The Dark/ Last Thing On My Mind/ The Pain Of Loving You/ Better Move It On Home/ Holding On To Nothin'/ Run That By Me One More Time/ We'll Get Ahead Someday

## COAT OF MANY COLORS

October 1971 (RCA)

Coat Of Many Colors/ Traveling Man/ My Blue Tears/ If I Lose My Mind/ The Mystery Of The Mystery/ She Never Met A Man (She Didn't Like)/ Early Morning Breeze/ The Way I See You/ Here I Am/ A Better Place To Live

## THE WORLD OF DOLLY PARTON

1972 (Monument)

Volume One: Dumb Blonde/ Your Ole Handy Man/ I Don't Want To Throw Rice/ Put It Off Until Tomorrow/ I Wasted My Tears/ Something Fishy/ Fuel To The Flame/ The Giving And The Taking/ I'm In No Condition/ The Company You Keep/ I've Lived My Life/ The Little Things

Volume Two: Why, Why, Why/ I Would Easy/ I Don't Want You Around Me Anymore/ Hillbilly Willy/ This Boy Has Been Hurt/ Daddy Won't Be Home Anymore/ As Long As I Love/ A Habit I Can't Break/ I'm Not Worth The Tears/ I Don't Trust Me Around You/ I Couldn't Wait Forever/ Too Lonely Too Long

## THE RIGHT COMBINATION: BURNING THE MIDNIGHT OIL (with Porter Wagoner)

January 1972 (RCA)

More Than Words Can Tell/ The Right Combination/ I've Been This Way Too Long/ In Each Love Pain Must Fall/ Her And The Car And The Mobile Home/ Burning The Midnight Oil/ Somewhere Along The Way/ On And On/ Through Thick And Thin/ Fog Has Lifted

## TOUCH YOUR WOMAN

March 1972 (RCA)

Will He Be Waiting/ The Greatest Days Of All/ Touch Your Woman/ A Lot Of You Left In Me/ Second Best/ A Little At A Time/ Love Is Only As Strong (As Your Weakest Moment)/ Love Isn't Free/ Mission Chapel Memories/ Loneliness Found Me

## TOGETHER ALWAYS (with Porter Wagoner)

September 1972 (RCA)

Together Always/ Love's All Over/ Christina/ Poor Folks Town/ Take Away/ Ten Four Over And Out/ Lost Forever In Your Kiss/ Anyplace You Want To Go/ Looking Down/ You And Me, Her And Him

## DOLLY PARTON SINGS, "MY FAVOURITE SONGWRITER, PORTER WAGONER"

October 1972 (RCA)

Lonely Comin' Down/ Do You Hear The Robins Sing?/ What Ain't To Be, Just Might Happen/ The Bird That Never Flew/ Comes And Goes/ Washday Blues/ When I Sing For Him/ He Left Me Love/ Oh, He's Everywhere/ Still On Your Mind

## WE FOUND IT (with Porter Wagoner)

February 1973 (RCA)

Love City/ Between Us/ We Found It/ Satan's River/ I've Been Married Just As Long As You Have/ I Am Always Waiting/ Sweet Rachel Ann/ That's When Love Will Mean The Most/ Love Have Mercy On Us/ How Close They Must Be

## MY TENNESSEE MOUNTAIN HOME

March 1973 (RCA)

The Letter/ I Remember/ Old Black Kettle/ Daddy's Working Boots/ Dr Robert F. Thomas/ In The Good Old Days (When Times Were Bad)/ My Tennessee Mountain Home/ Wrong Direction Home/ Back Home/ Better Part Of Life/ Down On Music Row

## LOVE AND MUSIC (with Porter Wagoner)

July 1973 (RCA)

If Teardrops Were Pennies/ Sounds Of Night/ Laugh The Years Away/ You/ Wasting Love/ Come To Me/ Love Is Out Tonight/ In The Presence Of You/ I Get Lonesome By Myself/ There'll Always Be Music

## BUBBLING OVER

September 1973 (RCA)

Bubbling Over/ Traveling Man/ Alabama Sundown/ Afraid To Live And Afraid Of Dying/ Love With Me/ My Kind Of Man/ Sometimes An Old Memory Gets In My Eye/ Pleasant As May/ In The Beginning/ Love, You're So Beautiful Tonight

## JOLENE

February 1974 (RCA)

Jolene/ When Someone Wants To Leave/ River Of Happiness/ Early Morning Breeze/ Highlight Of My Life/ I Will Always Love You/ Randy/ Living On Memories Of You/ Lonely Comin' Down/ It Must Be You

## PORTER 'N' DOLLY (with Porter Wagoner)

May 1974 (RCA)

Please Don't Stop Loving Me/ The Fire That Keeps You Warm/ Too Far Gone/ We'd Have To Be Crazy/ The Power Of Love/ Sixteen Years/ Together You And I/ Without You/ Two/ Sounds Of Nature

## LOVE IS LIKE A BUTTERFLY

September 1974 (RCA)

Love Is Like A Butterfly/ If I Cross Your Mind/ My Eyes Can Only See You/ Take Me Back/ Blackie Kentucky/ Gettin' Happy/ You're The One That Taught Me/ Highway Headin' South/ Once Upon A Memory/ Sacred Memories

## BARGAIN STORE

February 1975 (RCA)

Bargain Store/ Kentucky Gambler/ When I'm Gone/ Only Hand You'll Need To Hold/ On My Mind Again/ I Want To Be What You Need/ Love To Remember/ You'll Always Be Special To Me/ He Would Know/ I'll Never Forget

## BEST OF DOLLY PARTON

July 1975 (RCA)

Jolene/ Lonely Comin' Down/ The Bargain Store/ Touch Your Woman/ When I Sing For Him/ I Will Always Love You/ Love Is Like A Butterfly/ Coat Of Many Colors/ My Tennessee Mountain Home/ Traveling Man

## SAY FOREVER YOU'LL BE MINE (with Porter Wagoner)

August 1975 (RCA)

Say Forever You'll Be Mine/ Something To Reach For Again/ Our Love/ Beginning/ I Have No Right To Care/ If You Were Mine/ Love To See Us Through/ How Can I/ Life Rides The Train

## DOLLY – THE SEEKER: WE USED TO

September 1975 (RCA)

We Used To/ The Love I Used To Call Mine/ Hold Me/ Most Of All Why/ Bobby's Arms/ The Seeker/ My Heart Started Breaking/ Because I Love You/ Only The Memory Remains/ I'll Remember You As Mine

## ALL I CAN DO
August 1976 (RCA)
All I Can Do/ Fire That Keeps You Warm/ When The Sun Goes Down
Tomorrow/ I'm A Drifter/ Falling Out Of Love With Me/ Shattered
Image/ Boulder To Birmingham/ Preacher Tom/ Life's Like Poetry/ Hey,
Lucky Lady

## NEW HARVEST . . . FIRST GATHERING
February 1977 (RCA)
Light Of A Clear Blue Morning/ Applejack/ My Girl (My Love)/ Holdin'
On To You/ You Are/ How Does It Feel/ Where Beauty Lives In
Memory/ Higher And Higher/ Getting In My Way/ There

## HERE YOU COME AGAIN
October 1977 (RCA)
Here You Come Again/ Baby Come Out Tonight/ It's All Wrong, But It's
All Right/ Me And Little Andy/ Lovin' You/ Cowgirl And The Dandy/
Two Doors Down/ God's Coloring Book/ As Soon As I Touched Him/
Sweet Music Man

## HEARTBREAKER
July 1978 (RCA)
I Really Got The Feeling/ It's Too Late (To Love Me Now)/ We're
Through Forever ('Til Tomorrow)/ Sure Thing/ With You Gone/ Baby
I'm Burning/ Nickels And Dimes/ The Man/ Heartbreaker/ I Wanna Fall
In Love

## GREAT BALLS OF FIRE
May 1979 (RCA)
Star Of The Show/ Down/ You're The Only One/ Help/ Do You Think
That Time Stands Still/ Sweet Summer Lovin'/ Great Balls Of Fire/ Almost
In Love/ It's Not My Affair Anymore/ Sandy's Song

## PORTER & DOLLY (with Porter Wagoner)
June 1980 (RCA)
Making Plans/ If You Go, I'll Follow You/ Hide Me Away/ Someone Just
Like You/ Little David's Harp/ Beneath The Sweet Magnolia Tree/
Touching Memories/ Daddy Did His Best/ If You Say I Can/ Singing On
The Mountain

## 9 TO 5 AND ODD JOBS
November 1980 (RCA)
9 To 5/ Hush-A-Bye Hard Times/ The House Of The Rising Sun/

Deportee (Plane Wreck At Los Gatos)/ Sing For The Common Man/ Working Girl/ Detroit City/ But You Know I Love You/ Dark As A Dungeon/ Poor Folks Town

## HEARTBREAK EXPRESS
April 1982 (RCA)
Heartbreak Express/ Single Women/ My Blue Ridge Mountain Boy/ As Much As Always/ Do I Ever Cross Your Mind?/ Release Me/ Barbara On Your Mind/ Act Like A Fool/ Prime Of Our Love/ Hollywood Potters

## THE BEST LITTLE WHOREHOUSE IN TEXAS (Soundtrack)
July 1982 (RCA)
20 Fans/ A Lil' Ole Bitty Pissant Country Place/ Sneakin' Around/ Watchdog Report-Texas Has A Whorehouse In It/ Courtyard Shag/ The Aggie Song/ The Sidestep/ Hard Candy Christmas/ I Will Always Love You

## GREATEST HITS
October 1982 (RCA)
9 To 5/ But You Know I Love You/ Here You Come Again/ Two Doors Down/ It's All Wrong, But It's All Right/ Islands In The Stream (duet with Kenny Rogers)/ Old Flames Can't Hold A Candle To You/ Do I Ever Cross Your Mind/ I Will Always Love You

## THE WINNING HAND (with Willie Nelson, Kris Kristofferson and Brenda Lee)*
December 1982 (Monument)
You're Gonna Love Yourself (In The Morning)/ Ping Pong/ You'll Always Have Someone/ Here Comes That Rainbow Again/ Bigger The Fool, The Harder The Fall/ Help Me Make It Through The Night/ Happy, Happy Birthday Baby/ You Left Me A Long, Long Time Ago/ To Make A Long Story Short (She's Gone)/ Someone Loves You Honey/ Everything's Beautiful (In It's Own Way)/ Bring On The Sunshine/ Put It Off Until Tomorrow/ I Never Cared For You/ Casey's Last Ride/ King Of A Lonely Castle/ Little Things/ Bandits Of Beverly Hills/ What Do You Think About Lovin'/ Born To Love Me

## BURLAP AND SATIN
May 1983 (RCA)
Ooo-Eee/ Send Me The Pillow That You Dream On/ Jealous Heart/ Gamble Either Way/ Appalachian Memories/ I Really Don't Want To

---

* Dolly's contributions date from 1965–1967.

Know/ Potential New Boyfriend/ A Cowboy's Ways/ One Of Those Days/ Calm On The Water

## THE GREAT PRETENDER

January 1984 (RCA)
Save The Last Dance For Me/ I Walk The Line/ Turn, Turn, Turn/ Downtown/ We Had It All/ She Don't Love You (Like I Love You)/ We'll Sing In The Sunshine/ I Can't Help Myself (Sugar Pie, Honey Bunch)/ Elusive Butterfly/ The Great Pretender

## RHINESTONE

May 1984 (RCA)
Tennesssee Homesick Blues/ Too Much Water/ The Day My Baby Died/ One Emotion After Another/ Goin' Back To Heaven/ What A Heartache/ Stay Out Of My Bedroom/ Woke Up In Love/ God Won't Get You/ Drinkinstein/ Sweet Lovin' Friends/ Waltz Me To Heaven/ Butterflies/ Be There

## ONCE UPON A CHRISTMAS (with Kenny Rogers)

December 1984 (RCA)
I Believe In Santa Claus/ Winter Wonderland-Sleigh Ride/ Christmas Without You/ The Christmas Song/ A Christmas To Remember/ With Bells On/ Silent Night/ The Greatest Gift Of All/ White Christmas/ Once Upon A Christmas

## REAL LOVE

February 1985 (RCA)
Think About Love/ Tie Our Love (In A Double Knot)/ We Got Too Much/ It's Such A Heartache/ Don't Call It Love/ Real Love (duet with Kenny Rogers)/ I Can't Be True/ Once In A Very Blue Moon/ Come Back To Me/ I Hope You're Never Happy

## THINK ABOUT LOVE

March 1986 (RCA)
Think About Love/ It's Such A Heartache/ Tie Our Love (In A Double Knot)/ She Don't Love You (Like I Love You)/ We Had It All/ Do I Ever Cross Your Mind?/ I Can't Help Myself (Sugar Pie, Honey Bunch)/ Even A Fool Would Let Go

## BEST OF DOLLY PARTON VOL. 3

1987 (RCA)
Don't Call It Love/ Save The Last Dance For Me/ Real Love (duet with Kenny Rogers)/ We Had It All/ Tie Our Love (In A Double Knot)/ Think

About Love/ Potential New Boyfriend/ Do I Ever Cross Your Mind?/ Tennessee Homesick Blues

## TRIO (with Emmylou Harris and Linda Ronstadt)
February 1987 (Warner Brothers)
The Pain Of Loving You/ Making Plans/ To Know Him Is To Love Him/ Hobo's Meditation/ Wildflowers/ Telling Me Lies/ My Dear Companion/ Those Memories Of You/ I've Had Enough/ Rosewood Casket/ Farther Along

## RAINBOW
November 1987 (Columbia)
The River Unbroken/ I Know You By Heart (duet with Smokey Robinson)/ Everyday Hero/ Red Hot Screaming Love/ Make Love Work/ Could I Have Your Autograph?/ Two Lovers/ Dump The Dude/ Savin' It For You/ More Than I Can Say

## WHITE LIMOZEEN
May 1989 (Columbia)
Time For Me To Fly/ Yellow Roses/ Why'd You Come In Here Lookin' Like That?/ Slow Healing Heart/ What Is It My Love?/ White Limozeen/ Wait 'Til I Get You Home/ Take Me Back To The Country/ The Moon, The Stars, And Me/ He's Alive

## HOME FOR CHRISTMAS
September 1990 (Columbia)
First Noel/ Santa Claus Is Coming To Town/ I'll Be Home For Christmas/ Rudolph The Red-Nosed Reindeer/ Go Tell It On The Mountain/ The Little Drummer Boy/ We Three Kings/ Jingle Bells/ O Little Town Of Bethlehem/ Joy To The World

## EAGLE WHEN SHE FLIES
March 1991 (Columbia)
Rockin' Years (duet with Ricky Van Shelton)/ Country Road/ Silver And Gold/ Eagle When She Flies/ Best Woman Wins (duet with Lorrie Morgan)/ What A Heartache/ Runaway Feelin'/ Dreams Do Come True/ Family/ Wildest Dreams

## STRAIGHT TALK (Soundtrack)
March 1992 (Hollywood Records)
Blue Grace/ Light Of A Clear Blue Morning/ Dirty Job/ Blue Me/ Straight Talk/ Fish Out Of Water/ Burning/ Livin' A Lie/ Thought I Couldn't Dance/ Burning To Burned/ Light Of A Clear Blue Morning (Reprise)

## SLOW DANCING WITH THE MOON
February 1993 (Columbia)
Full Circle/ Romeo/ (You Got Me Over) A Heartache Tonight/ What Will Baby Be/ More Where That Came From/ Put A Little Love In Your Heart/ Why Can't We?/ I'll Make Your Bed/ Whenever Forever Comes/ Cross My Heart/ Slow Dancing With The Moon/ High And Mighty

## HONKY TONK ANGELS (with Loretta Lynn and Tammy Wynette) November 1994 (Columbia)
It Wasn't God Who Made Honky Tonk Angels (with Kitty Wells)/ Put It Off Until Tomorrow/ Silver Threads And Golden Needles/ Please Help Me I'm Falling (In Love With You)/ Sittin' On The Front Porch Swing/ Wings Of A Dove/ I Forgot More Than You'll Ever Know/ Wouldn't It Be Great/ That's The Way It Could Have Been/ Let Her Fly/ Lovesick Blues (with Patsy Cline)/ I Dreamed Of A Hillbilly Heaven

## HEARTSONGS
September 1994 (Columbia/Blue Eye)
Heartsong/ I'm Thinking Tonight Of My Blue Eyes/ Mary Of The Wild Moor/ In The Pines/ My Blue Tears/ Applejack/ Coat Of Many Colors/ Smoky Mountain Memories/ Night Train To Memphis/ What A Friend We Have In Jesus/ Hold Fast To The Right/ Walter Henry Hagan/ Barbara Allen/ Brave Little Soldier/ To Daddy/ True Blue/ Longer Than Always/ Wayfaring Stranger/ My Tennessee Mountain Home/ Heartsong (Reprise)/ Cas Walker Theme/ Black Draught Theme/ PMS Blues

## SOMETHING SPECIAL
September 1995 (Columbia/Blue Eye)
Crippled Bird/ Something Special/ Change/ I Will Always Love You/ Green Eyed Boy/ Speakin' Of The Devil/ Jolene/ No Good Way Of Saying Goodbye/ The Seeker/ Teach Me To Trust

## TREASURES
September 1996 (Rising Tide/Blue Eye)
Peace Train/ Today I Started Loving You Again/ Just When I Needed You Most/ Something's Burning/ Before The Next Teardrop Falls/ After The Goldrush/ Walking On Sunshine/ Behind Closed Doors/ Don't Let Me Cross Over/ Satin Sheets/ For The Good Times

## HUNGRY AGAIN
August 1998 (Decca/Blue Eye)
Hungry Again/ The Salt In My Tears/ Honky Tonk Songs/ Blue Valley Songbird/ I Wanna Go Back There/ When Jesus Comes Calling For Me/

Time And Tears/ I'll Never Say Goodbye/ The Camel's Heart/ I Still Lost You/ Paradise Road/ Shine On

## TRIO II (with Emmylou Harris and Linda Ronstadt)

February 1999 (Asylum/Elektra)

Lover's Return/ High Sierra/ Do I Ever Cross Your Mind?/ After The Goldrush/ The Blue Train/ I Feel The Blues Movin' In/ You'll Never Be The Sun/ He Rode All The Way To Texas/ Feel's Like Home/ When We're Gone, Long Gone

## PRECIOUS MEMORIES

April 1999 (Blue Eye)

Precious Memories/ Power In The Blood/ In The Sweet Bye And Bye/ Church In The Wildwood/ Keep On The Firing Line/ Amazing Grace/ Old Time Religion/ Softly And Tenderly/ Farther Along/ What A Friend We Have In Jesus/ In The Garden/ When The Roll Is Called Up Yonder

## THE GRASS IS BLUE

November 1999 (Sugar Hill/Blue Eye)

Travelin' Prayer/ Cash On The Barrelhead/ A Few Old Memories/ I'm Gonna Sleep With One Eye Open/ Steady As The Rain/ I Still Miss Someone/ Endless Stream Of Tears/ Silver Dagger/ Train, Train/ I Wonder Where You Are Tonight/ Will He Be Waiting For Me?/ The Grass Is Blue/ I Am Ready

## LITTLE SPARROW

January 2001 (Sugar Hill/Blue Eye)

Little Sparrow/ Shine/ I Don't Believe You've Met My Baby/ My Blue Tears/ Seven Bridges Road/ Bluer Pastures/ Tender Lie/ I Get A Kick Out Of You/ Mountain Angel/ Marry Me/ Down From Dover/ Beautiful Lie/ In The Sweet By And By/ Reprise: Little Sparrow

## HALOS AND HORNS

July 2002 (Sugar Hill/Blue Eye)

Halos And Horns/ Sugar Hill/ Not For Me/ Hello God/ If/ Shattered Image/ These Old Bones/ What A Heartache/ I'm Gone/ Raven Dove/ Dagger Through The Heart/ If Only/ John Daniel/ Stairway To Heaven

## ULTIMATE DOLLY PARTON

June 1993 (BMG)

Joshua/ Coat Of Many Colors/ Jolene/ I Will Always Love You/ Please Don't Stop Loving Me (with Porter Wagoner)/ Love Is Like A Butterfly/ The Bargain Store/ Here You Come Again/ It's All Wrong But It's All

Right/ Heartbreaker/ I Really Got The Feeling/ You're The Only One/ Starting Over Again/ Old Flames Can't Hold A Candle To You/ 9 To 5/ But You Know I Love You/ Tennessee Homesick Blues/ Islands In The Stream (with Kenny Rogers)/ To Know Him Is To Love Him (with Linda Ronstadt and Emmylou Harris)/ Why'd You Come In Here Lookin' Like That?

## JUST BECAUSE I'M A WOMAN: SONGS OF DOLLY PARTON
November 2003 (Sugar Hill)
9 To 5 (Alison Krauss)/ I Will Always Love You (Melissa Etheridge)/ The Grass Is Blue (Norah Jones)/ Do I Ever Cross Your Mind? (Joan Osborne)/ The Seeker (Shelby Lynne)/ Jolene (Mindy Smith)/ To Daddy (Emmylou Harris)/ Coat Of Many Colors (Shania Twain with Alison Krauss and Union Station)/ Little Sparrow (Kasey Chambers)/ Dagger Through The Heart (Sinéad O'Connor)/ Light Of A Clear Blue Morning (Allison Moorer)/ Two Doors Down (Me'Shell N'dedgéOcello)/ Just Because I'm A Woman (Dolly Parton)

## FOR GOD AND COUNTRY
November 2003 (Blue Eye/Welk Music)
The Lord Is My Shepherd/ The Star Spangled Banner/ God Bless The USA/ Light Of A Clear Blue Morning/ When Johnny Comes Marching Home/ Welcome Home/ Gee, Ma, I Wanna Go Home/ Whispering Hope/ There Will Be Peace In The Valley For Me/ Red, White And Bluegrass/ My Country 'Tis/ I'm Gonna Miss You/ Go To Hell/ Ballad Of The Green Beret/ Brave Little Soldier/ Tie A Yellow Ribbon/ Color Me America/ The Glory Forever

## LIVE AND WELL
September 2004 (Blue Eye/Welk Music)
Disc One: Orange Blossom Special/ Train, Train/ The Grass Is Blue/ Mountain Angel/ Shine/ Little Sparrow/ Rocky Top/ My Tennessee Mountain Home/ Coat Of Many Colors/ Appalachian Memories/ Applejack/ Marry Me
Disc Two: Halos And Horns/ I'm Gone/ Dagger Through The Heart/ If/ After The Goldrush/ 9 To 5/ Jolene/ A Cappella Medley: Islands In The Stream-Here You Come Again-Why'd You Come In Here Lookin' Like That?-Two Doors Down/ We Irish/ Stairway To Heaven/ I Will Always Love You

## THOSE WERE THE DAYS
October 2005 (Blue Eye/Sugar Hill)
Those Were The Days (with Mary Hopkin and The Opry Gang)/ Blowin'

In The Wind (with Nickel Creek)/ Where Have All The Flowers Gone? (with Norah Jones and Lee Ann Womack)/ Twelfth Of Never (with Keith Urban)/ Where Do The Children Play (with Cat Stevens)/ Me And Bobby McGee (with Kris Kristofferson)/ Crimson And Clover (with Tommy James)/ The Cruel War (with Alison Krauss, Dan Tyminski and Mindy Smith)/ Turn, Turn, Turn (with Roger McGuinn)/ If I Were A Carpenter (duet with Joe Nichols)/ Both Sides Now (with Judy Collins and Rhonda Vincent)/ Imagine

# SOURCE NOTES

Dolly Parton has fascinated people from every walk of life for most of her professional career, an interest that extends far beyond the confines of her music. Over the last 40 years or so, countless thousands of reviews, interviews and features ranging from the superficial and inaccurate to the highly perceptive and in-depth have appeared in newspapers and magazines all over the world catering to reader interest in Dolly's private, professional and business life. She has also been the subject of learned articles by academics interested in sociological phenomena associated with her fame and achievements. Such widespread media interest, sometimes highly intrusive, has not always been to her liking yet she has acknowledged that being in the public eye helps to maintain interest in her as an artist and in her business ventures, such as Dollywood.

Dolly has largely courted publicity and has succeeded in retaining a high media profile long after most of her country contemporaries have largely faded from view. Whilst I endeavoured to read as many articles as possible, the fact is that I could only guarantee of seeing a small percentage of the total print devoted to her. Hopefully the vast amount I read as part of my research constitutes a representative sample. I am particularly indebted to the Country Music Foundation and the Nashville Public Library for making available large quantities of press cuttings going back to the Sixties. Special thanks to Michael Creed who, along with a partner, runs the newsletter *Dolly Part'ners UK*.

The internet is now a research tool of infinite scale with large quantities of new material being added each day. Key in "Dolly Parton" to Google and you are presented with over 600,000 sites. Facts and figures, pictures, film and album reviews, song lyrics, opinions, are all available at the click of a mouse. As with the massive number of articles written about Dolly over the years it is only possible to assess a small percentage of the total. Dolly does not have an official website but a number of particularly dedicated fans have set up websites in her honour, some of which are very informative, well organised and user friendly. Particularly helpful were www.raredolly.com, www.dollyon-line and www.dollymania.net.

Video material, mainly featuring Dolly's two television series, was provided by the Country Music Foundation in Nashville. Again, Michael Creed provided a large quantity of miscellaneous video material including films, interviews, guest appearances and even clips from home movies showing Dolly as a young girl. Michael also lent me *The Journal Of Country Music* Volume X, Number 1 (1985) which contains an informative article "excerpted from an autobiography of Porter Wagoner" that was said to be "still in progress". It apparently still is.

Dolly's four cassette readings from her 1994 autobiography were illuminating – not simply for the content which was of course available in the book but for the passion she put into the task, delivering the words like a stage performance. It serves to demonstrate Dolly's powerful ability to conjure emotions for her audience even in the sterile environment of a recording studio and illustrates why Dolly is the star she is.

Of the books in the following Bibliography, I particularly drew on Willadeene Parton's works on the Parton and Owens' family's life and Steve Eng's biography of Porter Wagoner which contained a lot of information not readily available elsewhere.

# BIBLIOGRAPHY

Anderson, Bill. (1993). *I Hope You're Living As High On The Hog As The Pig You Turned Out To Be*. New York: Simon and Schuster.

Bane, Michael. (1984). *Willie*. New York: Dell Publishing.

Bufwack, Mary A and Oermann, Robert K. (1993). *Finding Her Voice, The Illustrated History Of Women In Country Music*. New York: Henry Holt and Co.

Byworth, Tony. (1984). *Giants Of Country Music*. London: Hamlyn.

Campbell, Glen with Carter, Tom. (1994). *Rhinestone Cowboy*. New York: Villard Books.

Carlisle, Dolly. (1984). *Ragged But Right: The Life And Times Of George Jones*. Chicago: Contemporary Books Inc.

*Country Music Who's Who*. (1972). Nashville: Record World.

Cusic, Don. (1991). *Reba: Country Music's Queen*. New York: St Martin's Press.

Dawidoff, Nicholas. (1997). *In The Country Of Country*. London: Faber & Faber.

Dew, Joan. (1977). *The Women Of Country Music – Singers And Sweethearts*. New York: Doubleday/Dolphin.

Doggett, Peter. (2001). *Are You Ready For The Country*. London: Penguin Books.

Eggar, Robin. (2001). *Shania Twain: The Biography*. London: Headline.

Emery, Ralph with Carter, Tom. (1991). *The Autobiography Of Ralph Emery*. New York: Macmillan.

Emery, Ralph with Carter, Tom. (1993). *More Memories*. New York: GP Putnam's Sons.

Eng, Steve. (1992). *A Satisfied Mind: The Country Music Life Of Porter Wagoner*. Nashville: Rutledge Hill Press.

Escott, Colin. (2003). *The Story Of Country Music*. London: BBC Worldwide Ltd.

Fleischer, Leonore. (1988). *Dolly: Here I Come Again*. London: W H Allen and Co.

Gobernick, Lisa Rebecca. (1993). *Get Hot Or Go Home: Trisha Yearwood, The Making Of A Nashville Star*. New York: William Morrow and Company, Inc.

Gray, Andy. (1975). *Great Country Music Stars*. London: Hamlyn.

Horstman, Dorothy. (1995). *Sing Your Heart Out, Country Boy*. Nashville: Country Music Foundation Press.

James, Otis. (1978). *Dolly Parton: A Photo-Bio*. New York: Jove Publications, Inc.

James, Otis. (1978). *Dolly Parton: A Personal Portrait*. New York: Quick Fox.

Jones, George with Carter, Tom. (1996). *I Lived To Tell It All*. New York: Villard Books.

Kingsbury, Paul and Axelrod, Alan (Editors). (1988). *Country: The Music And The Musicians*. New York: Abbeville Press (in association with the Country Music Foundation Press).

Kosser, Michael. (1979). *Those Bold And Beautiful Country Girls*. Leicester: Windward.

Krishef, Robert K. (1980). *Dolly Parton*. Minneapolis: Lerner Publications Company.

Laundon, Stan. (2004). *Chasing Fireflies*. Crewe: Trafford Publishing (UK) Ltd.

Leamer, Laurence. (1997). *Three Chords And The Truth: Behind The Scenes With Those Who Make And Shape Country Music*. New York: Harper Collins.

Lomax III, John. (1985). *Nashville: Music City USA*. New York: Harry N. Abrams, Inc.

Lynn, Loretta with Vecsey, George. (1976). *Loretta Lynn: Coalminer's Daughter*. New York: Warner Books.

Malone, Bill C and McCulloh, Judith (Editors). (1975). *Stars Of Country Music 1975*. Chicago: University of Illinois Press.

Malone, Bill C. (1987). *Country Music, USA*. University of Texas Press.

Malone, Bill C. (2002). *Don't Get Above Your Raisin': Country Music And The Southern Working Class*. Chicago: University of Illinois Press.

Miller, Stephen. (2003). *Johnny Cash: The Life Of An American Icon*. London: Omnibus Press.

Mitchell, Rick. (1994). *Garth Brooks: One Of A Kind, Working On A Full House*. London: Sidgwick & Jackson.

McCloud, Barry and contributing writers. (1995). *Definitive Country: The Ultimate Encyclopedia Of Country Music And Its Performers*. New York: The Berkley Publishing Group.

McEntire, Reba with Carter, Tom. (1994). *Reba: My Story*. New York: Bantam Books.

Nash, Alanna. (1979). *Dolly: The Intimate Biography Of Dolly Parton*. London: Granada Publishing Ltd.

Nash, Alanna. (1998). *Behind Closed Doors: Talking With The Legends Of Country Music*. New York: Alfred A. Knopf, Inc.

Nash, Alanna. (2002). *Dolly: The Biography* (Updated Edition). New York: Cooper Square Press.

Nassour, Ellis. (1981). *Patsy Cline: An Intimate Biography*. New York: Tower Books.

Nelson, Willie with Shrake, Bud. (1988). *I Didn't Come Here And I Ain't Leaving*. London: MacMillan.

Obstfeld, Raymond and Burgener, Sheila. (1997). *Twang! The Ultimate Book Of Country Music Quotations*. New York: Henry Holt & Co, Inc.

Oermann, Robert K. (1996). *America's Music: The Roots Of Country*. Atlanta: Turner Publishing Inc.

Parton, Dolly. (1979). *Just The Way I Am*. Boulder, Colorado: Blue Mountain Press.

Parton, Dolly. (1994). *My Life And Other Unfinished Business*. New York: Harper Collins.

Parton, Willadeene. (1985). *In The Shadow Of A Song: The Story Of The Parton Family*. New York: Bantam.

Parton, Willadeene. (1996). *Smoky Mountain Memories: Stories From The Heart Of The Parton Family*. Nashville: Rutledge Hill Press.

Parton, Willadeene. (1997). *All-Day Singing And Dinner On The Ground: Recipes From The Parton Family Kitchen*. Nashville: Rutledge Hill Press.

Saunders, Susan. (1986). *Dolly Parton: Country Goin' To Town*. New York: Puffin Books.

Reise, Randall. (1989). *Nashville Babylon*. London: Guild Publishing.

Rovin, Jeff. (1993). *Country Music Babylon*. New York: St Martin's Paperbacks.

Rubenstein, Raeanne and McCabe, Peter. (1975). *Honky Tonk Heroes: A Photo Album Of Country Music*. New York: Harper & Row.

Scobey, Lola. (1977). *Dolly: Daughter Of The South*. New York: Kensington Publishing Corp.

Starr, Victoria. (1994). *KD Lang: All You Get Is Me*. London: Harper Collins.

Wootton, Richard. (1982). *The Illustrated Country Almanac: A Day By Day History Of Country Music*. London: Virgin Books Ltd.

Wynette, Tammy with Dew, Joan. (1981). *Stand By Your Man*. London: Arrow Books Limited.

# Index

05/07 (62200)